Holistic Business Model Transformation

Hartmut F. Binner

Holistic Business Model Transformation

Systematic Process Digitization with the Support of the MITO Method Tool

Springer

Hartmut F. Binner
Prof. Binner Akademie
Hannover, Germany

ISBN 978-3-658-37366-5 ISBN 978-3-658-37367-2 (eBook)
https://doi.org/10.1007/978-3-658-37367-2

The translation was done with the help of artificial intelligence (machine translation by the service DeepL.com). A subsequent human revision was done primarily in terms of content.

This Springer imprint is published by the registered company Springer Fachmedien Wiesbaden GmbH, part of Springer Nature.
The registered company address is: Abraham-Lincoln-Str. 46, 65189 Wiesbaden, Germany

Preface

The question of whether another MITO Organization 4.0 book on holistic business model development and design should be published in addition to the 5 MITO books already mentioned in the bibliography is relatively easy to answer. The increasingly comprehensive and sophisticated cloud services from various providers with integration into the company-specific digital business platform enable unprecedented networking of customers, suppliers, employees, products, services, fellow competitors and all other stakeholders in real time. According to these cloud service providers, their cloud solutions always relate to improvements in customer value in the horizontal value chain without, however, questioning the function-oriented organizational barriers in the companies to which they offer their cloud services.

There is still no consistent process orientation in companies despite this digitization-driven development. Although the need for change is invoked in ever new leadership concepts and change management strategies, as is currently the case with the topic of "agility", the existing function-oriented organizational structures are not even mentioned in the process. How can a cross-company horizontal value chain be designed optimally, i.e., with flat hierarchies and few interfaces as the basis for process digitization, if there are hierarchical and vertical organizational structures based on the division of labor and deep hierarchies that prevent employee-oriented participative involvement based on the principle of command and obedience? Even if the currently intensively discussed democratic leadership concepts and agility methods focus precisely on self-determined team organization, sustainability is missing because of the lack of organizational structure changes due to the non-existent or non-possible transfer of responsibility within a process-oriented value culture. Likewise, the methodological competence for the practical implementation of these change management activities, which is the focus here, is lacking.

Furthermore, the knowledge gained from the application of the MITO Organization 4.0 configuration approach and the questions of the users repeatedly result in suggestions for detailed descriptions and extensions of the MITO model to a holistic business model in German "Geschäftsmodell". This includes the following explanations of the MITO model scalability and integrability of many well-known design concepts to complete the holistic Organization 4.0 business model development and purpose design approach.

In addition, there are more and more new use cases of the MITO method-tool approach with the end-to-end analysis, diagnosis, therapy and evaluation, which are mapped in the form of standard reference solutions, for example for the implementation of the CSR prequalification, the occupational health and safety regulation or currently the new risk governance, compliance and anti-corruption standards.

The MITO tool-supported holistic business model transformation, which is the focus here, with its organizational, cultural, and product- or customer-specific design topics, taking into account the digitization trends described at the outset, also supplements the existing MITO model and method knowledge and bundles it into a holistic Organization 4.0 design approach as the basis for a successful change management process. In the MITO model, Deming's PDCA improvement cycle, Kaplan/Norton's Balance Score Card concept or the EFQM Excellence Model can also be mapped together with the DGQ's TQM approach. In this book, the basic statements already available are largely dispensed with.

I would like to thank my office manager, Mrs. Carola Groth, for coordinating the preparation of this book, Mrs. Anna Scheckter for creating the pictures, Mr. Roland Meiswinkel for the corrections, and especially Hernn Philipp Schmidt for the critical revision of the texts.

Hannover, Germany Hartmut F. Binner

Contents

List of Figures

Introduction

1

Abstract

This book explains a closed-loop change management process for the implementation of a digital business model. The benefits of the holistic Organization 4.0 MITO configuration management approach that readers can derive from the description are most quickly and easily illustrated via the following management summary.

1.1 Management Summary

The content chapter structure of this MITO book with the description of the different transformation design views is based on the superordinate operational control loop principle within the MITO model segments shown in Fig. 1.1. Whereby the management segment (M) is still subdivided into the leadership segment on the default side and the management segment on the feedback side. The MITO business model based on this supplements the 5 model segments with the downstream customer and upstream supplier segments and integrates the process level model into the MITO model representation for the conception of the process-oriented management and control system. With the support of these model structures, a goal-oriented change management process for digital business model transformation is achieved in conjunction with systematic process digitization. This starts from the existing traditional business model and, with the shown interlinked key topics under the name Organization 4.0, is to ensure a sustainable and successful implementation of the future company-specific digital business model.

H. F. Binner, *Holistic Business Model Transformation*,
https://doi.org/10.1007/978-3-658-37367-2_1

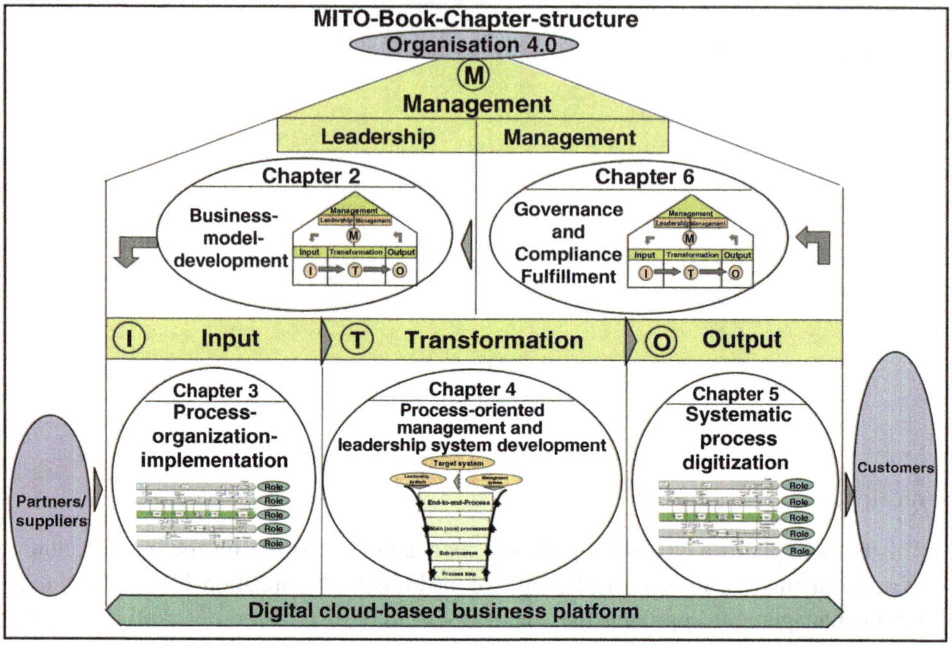

Fig. 1.1 MITO book chapter structure

In accordance with the logical sequence of a goal-oriented change management process, the following task-related chapter contents are involved:

- *in* Chap. 2:
  Within the MITO leadership segment, the holistic business model development with the requirements analyses and the strategy and target specifications derived from them for the current actual situation is described in a method-based manner as the starting point for the change management process for the development of a digital business model.
- *in* Chap. 3:
  In the MITO input segment it is about the organizational transformation with the method-supported development of a process-oriented order structure according to the BPMN 2.0 process visualization standard in the swimlane representation.
- *in* Chap. 4:
  As a prerequisite for the cultural transformation, the indicator-supported development of an integrated process-oriented leadership and management system across all process hierarchy levels in the balanced scorecard structure with the associated employee-oriented value culture claim is explained for the order control on the specification side and the result measurement on the feedback side in the transformation segment.

- *in* Chap. 5:
  After the creation of the organizational and cultural prerequisites, the digital transformation takes place in the output segment with process digitization in line with requirements on the basis of a large number of digital business model innovations with the help of a digitization master plan.
- *In* Chap. 6:
  Finally, in the MITO management segment, the evaluation as corporate, risk governance and compliance proof of a successful holistic business model transformation is also carried out in an exemplary manner based on methods. Due to identified deviations, the MITO control cycle starts again from the beginning.

As Fig. 1.2 shows, the design and implementation of the operational control loop tasks is explained in a separate model in each chapter in addition to the reference to the higher-level MITO business model segment. In the implementation of the development, design and transformation tasks, the MITO method tool is applied in all business model segments. Here, the focus in all 5 chapters is on conveying system and method competence for the reader using practical examples.

The models used in Chap. 2 are the MITO business model itself, which is explained in detail below. In Chap. 2, the role-based swimlane representation as an essential

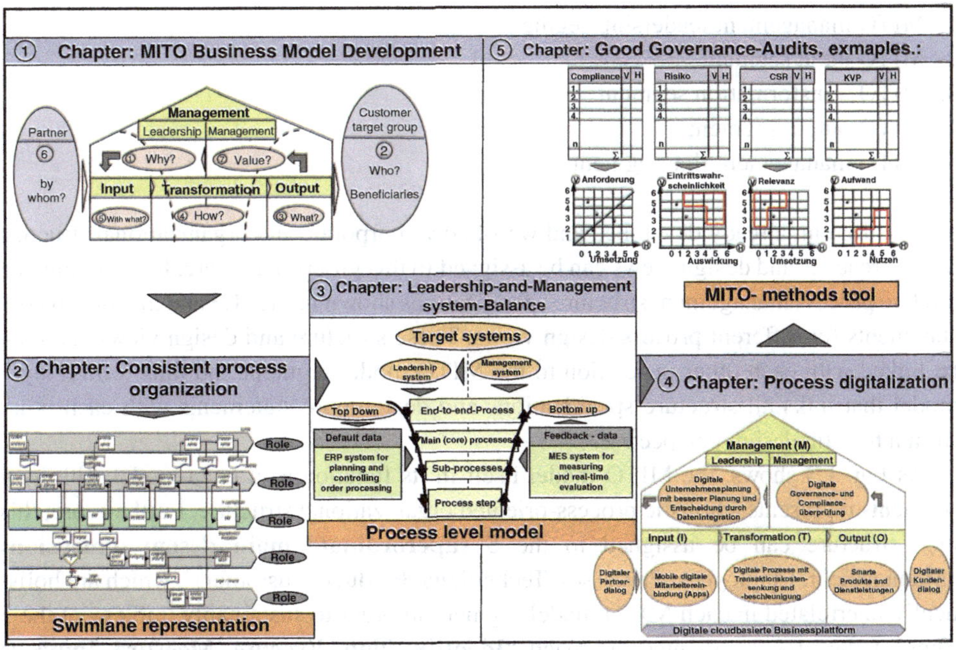

Fig. 1.2 Method-based Organization 4.0 business model implementation

component of the globally valid BPMN 2.0 process visualization standard is used in the implementation of the end-to-end process organization. In Chap. 4, the continuous process level model is the basis for the conception of an integrated value-based management and fact-based control system that is intended to implement the corporate and process goals specified by the corporate target system in a governance- and compliance-oriented manner with the employee at the center. Chapter 5 also uses the MITO model structure to determine the digitalization action areas with the digital business model innovations, which are implemented via the digital master plan by means of use case descriptions. Chapter 6 describes the practical use of the MITO method tool for the various governance audits. All models described are originally developed by the author and are subject to copyright.

1.2 MITO Model Links Process Management Top-Five Structure and Top-Ten Design Core Statements

The MITO model, as the overarching reference and regulatory framework of the Organization 4.0 approach for the implementation of the process-oriented organization with subsequent process digitization, offers the possibility to work within the 5 MITO model segments already shown in the introduction in Figs. 1.1 and 1.2:

1. MITO management leadership segment
2. MITO input segment
3. MITO transformation segment
4. MITO output segment
5. MITO management line segment

Many different, already developed and well-known corporate and organizational structuring approaches and design views can be assigned to this group. These are, for example, the top five process management structure specifications shown in Fig. 1.3 and the top ten core statements for different process design views. These structure and design views can then be linked with each other in relation to the MITO model segment and thus form a layer model that links all structure specifications and design core statements with each other from a holistic design perspective.

As Fig. 1.3 shows, the MITO model itself in its function as a meta-model with its 5 segments represents a holistic process-oriented organizational structure. Furthermore, this meta-structure can be assigned to the **5 superordinate main design dimensions** "Management, Employees, Processes, Technology, Product (Customer)", which are holistically interrelated in each MITO model segment in order to sustainably implement the 5 steps of the process-oriented approach **"Identify, Plan, Execute, Measure, Improve Processes"** in this way, also MITO model segment-related.

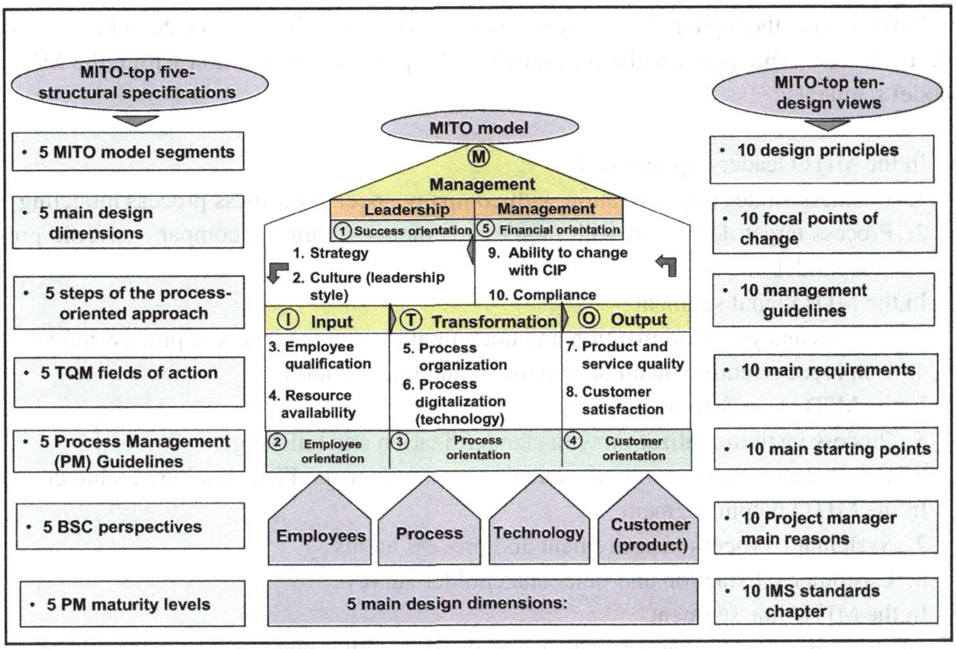

Fig. 1.3 MITO model-related top ten process management core statements, e.g.

The 5 superordinate **fields of action of the TQM strategy** with “success, employee, process, customer and financial orientation” together with the associated key figures from the Balance Scorecard key figure system can also be assigned to the MITO model framework. These are the success, employee, process, customer and financial action areas with the associated BSC metrics. The **5 process maturity levels are** also based on the MITO control loop model. They are:

Level 1: Processes known and defined (management segment)
Stage 2: Processes planned and structured (input segment)
Stage 3: Processes controlled and executed (transformation segment)
Stage 4: Processes monitored and measured (output segment)
Level 5: Processes continuously improved. (management segment)

Within this top five MITO reference framework, different design views can now also be assigned to the MITO model segments, each with top ten main criteria. The **10 main success factors** for sustainable competition are shown in the MITO model itself in Fig. 1.3. Two of these are named in each of the MITO segments shown.

Furthermore, the top ten design viewpoints shown on the right-hand side in Fig. 1.3 are the **10 design principles for** the introduction of a process organization within the MITO model segments:

- In the MITO leadership segment:
  1. Business strategy specification with company-specific business process modeling
  2. Process target derivation with target agreements within the company-specific process model
- In the MITO input segment
  3. Process analysis, optimization and documentation in the business process model
  4. Employee retention, team development and qualification
- In the MITO transformation segment
  5. Process institutionalization with standardization and tailoring
  6. Process automation within the existing application and IT technology architecture
- In the MITO output segment
  7. Systematic process measurement and process audits
  8. Customer satisfaction and other stakeholder surveys
- In the MITO line segment
  9. Continuous management reviews, evaluation with process maturity assessment
  10. Learning company with knowledge storage for CIP

Furthermore, the **10 focal points of change** can be clearly assigned:

In the MITO management segment	Customer/market changes
	Organizational changes
In the MITO input segment	Social changes
	Personnel changes
In the MITO transformation segment	Economic changes
	Technological changes
In the MITO output segment	Ecological changes
	Product changes
In the MITO line segment	Social changes
	Rule changes

Likewise, the **10 Organization 4.0 leadership guidelines**:

- In the MITO leadership segment:
  1. Lead on site
  2. Set the goals
- In the MITO input segment
  3. Develop yourself and your employees
  4. Inform yourself and others

- In the MITO transformation segment
  5. Live as a role model
  6. Create enthusiasm and motivation
- In the MITO output segment
  7. Show attention and respect
  8. Represent the voice of the customer
- In the MITO line segment
  9. Create trust, security and continuity
  10. Make CIP part of everyday life

Together with the **10 main business-related requirements**:

- In the MITO leadership segment:
  1. Leadership requirements
  2. Strategy requirements
- In the MITO input segment
  3. Employee requirements
  4. Resource requirements
- In the MITO transformation segment
  5. Process organization requirements
  6. Technical requirements
- In the MITO output segment
  7. Product requirements
  8. Service requirements
- In the MITO line segment
  9. Governance requirements
  10. CIP requirements

This is followed by the **10 main starting points for** meeting the requirements.

- In the MITO leadership segment:
  1. Trust Organization
  2. Business model innovations
- In the MITO input segment
  3. Participation
  4. Methodological competence
- In the MITO transformation segment
  5. Process optimization
  6. Digitization

- In the MITO output segment
  7. Smart products
  8. Agility
- In the MITO line segment
  9. Sustainability
  10. Learning organization

Following are the **top 10 reasons change** management **projects fail:**

- In the MITO leadership segment:
  1. Unclear requirements and goals
  2. Lack of BPM implementation experience at management level
- In the MITO input segment
  3. Lack of resources at project start
  4. Lack of qualified employees
- In the MITO transformation segment
  5. Lack of support from top management
  6. Lack of project management methodology
- In the MITO output segment
  7. Ignoring undesirable developments
  8. Lack of power measurement
- In the MITO line segment
  9. Missing feedback
  10. Departmental egoism prevents joint success

The implementation of Integrated Management Systems (IMS) as independent management systems, as described in point 2.10, is oriented towards the new **High-Level-Structure in terms** of chapters:

In the MITO leadership segment with	Chapter 5: Leadership and Chapter 6: Planning
In the MITO input segment with	Chapter 7: Support (Resources)
In the MITO transformation segment with	Chapter 8: Operation
In the MITO output segment	Chapter 9: Evaluation of performance
In the MITO line segment	Chapter 10: Improvement

On the MITO Model Structure.

The contents of current design concepts such as lean and CIP management, 6-sigma or holistic production systems (GPS) can also be mapped in these control loop-oriented MITO meta-model structures and linked with each other within the MITO segments. In this way, a comprehensive and holistic business model, process organization, integrated management system (IMS) and knowledge management design is possible via a uniform structural specification, which credibly describes the purpose of the company as a result.

1.3 MITO Model Scaling and Integration

From a systems engineering organisational development perspective, the MITO model forms the reference and regulatory framework within the above-mentioned five MITO model segments for the consistent introduction of a process organisation with the associated three organisational subsystems shown in Fig. 1.4:

- MITO target system
- MITO guidance system
- MITO line system

Together, these act as a corporate or operational control loop that can be scaled up to any desired organisational level. From a macro perspective, the MITO model can be applied to a national economy, further related to the entire company, to specific company divisions and from a micro perspective in relation to all main and sub-processes down to the individual process functions.

For the effective and efficient execution of tasks within an organization, an entrepreneurial **target system** must be specified that is implemented by the employees via the management-related leadership system. Via the hierarchical process level model, **resources are provided** in the MITO input segment at each process level, controlled implementation

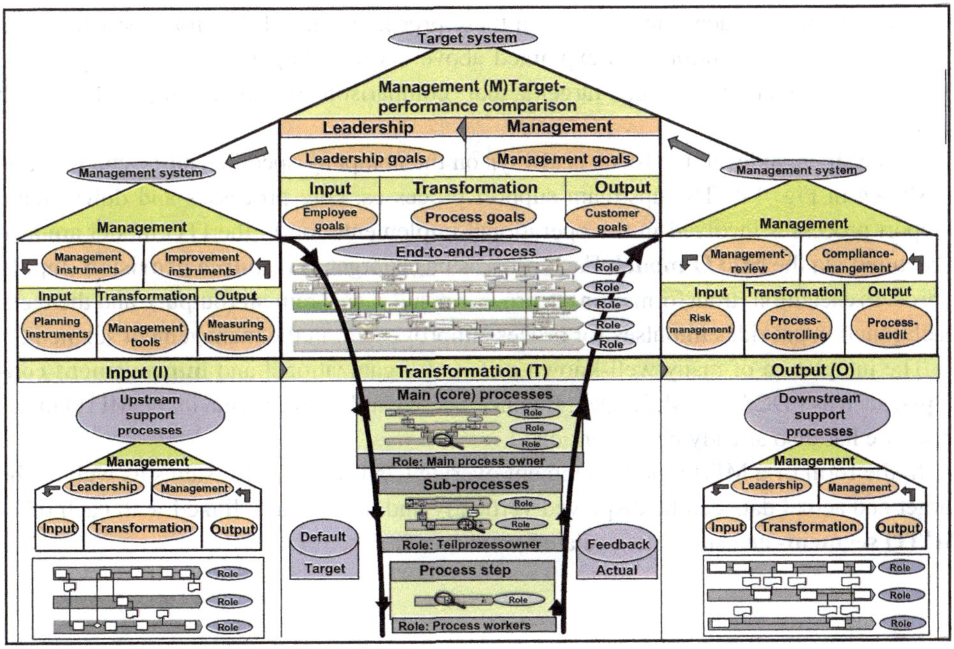

Fig. 1.4 Consistent strategic and operational MITO model scaling and integration

takes place in the MITO transformation segment, results are measured in the MITO output segment on the feedback side, and **feedback is provided** to the MITO management segment to check the achievement of objectives. In addition, a **target-achievement-actual comparison** is carried out at each process level. In the event of deviations, this also provides the impetus for continuous process improvement (CIP). This principle applies to any goal-oriented organization regardless of size, industry and purpose.

In addition to the scalability explained above, i.e. adaptation to any object size, the MITO model structure also enables the integration of the different organizational development views and systems into a holistic design view.

As further shown in Fig. 1.4, the organizational goal, **leadership and management system** explained below in Chap. 4 is also structured uniformly according to the MITO model and thus covers all tasks within the strategic management level. These 3 organizational subsystems are in turn inserted into the higher-level MITO business model structure in order to ensure in this way, from a strategic point of view, the integrative linkage for the enforcement of the operational control loop. The integration of the MITO target, process model, leadership and management system is achieved by simply superimposing the respective individual models, referred to here collectively as the MITO business layer model.

The operational implementation is carried out via the upstream **support processes** in the input segment, the core process execution in the transformation segment and the product and service handover to the customer with feedback to the management segment in the output segment For each role involved in these processes, the MITO model structure can be used for the description – as explained above – with: "target setting (management), input, transformation, output, target/actual comparison (management) during task execution".

At the strategic level, the focus is always on the company-specific end-to-end process, as shown in Fig. 1.4. The upstream support processes, core processes and downstream support processes involved in the operational implementation in the ITO model are also structured via the **MITO model**. Each process has a target, a **resource provision** (input), a process execution (transformation), a process result measurement (output), and the feedback function provides impulses for process improvement in the management segment.

The integration of many well-known different organizational and **improvement concepts**, such as PDCA, TQM, EFQM, Balance Score Card or Six Sigma in the MITO metastructure has also already been mentioned.

In the form of a MITO model segment overview, all MITO subsystems as well as the target and actual data can be displayed vertically and horizontally linked with each other **MITO segment**- and subsystem-related, as shown in Fig. 1.5.

MITO-Modell-Segmente / Part-systems	Sucess factors, e.g.	Process model	Target system	Management system	Management system	Controlling loop	IMS Requirements, e.g.
MITO management segment	• Strategic value culture guideline • Mission statement	Management processes, e.g.	Strategy and Management goals	Strategy and target agreement target key figures	Strategy and target agreement actual key figures	Strategy and management-Target-actual-Comparison	
MITO-Input-segment	• Employee qualification • Employee satisfaction	Upstream support processes, e.g.:	• Employee goals • Infrastructure goals	• Target employee key figures Target infrastructure key figures	• Employee actual key figures • Infrastructure actual key figures	Employee goals-Target-actual-Comparison	• QM • UM
MITO-Transformationssegment	• Process organisation • Process digitalization	Core processes,e.g.:	Process level goals	Process level target key figures	Process level actual key figures	Process levels-Target-actual-Comparison	• CSR • KVP • usw.
MITO-Output-segment	• Product and service quality • Customer satisfaction	Downstream support process, e.g.:	Process level goals	Process result target key figures	Process level actual key figures	Process result Target-actual-Comparison	in every process integrable
MITO management segment	• Ablity to change • Compliance	Management processes, e.g.:	• Governance goals • Compliance goals	• Governance target key figures • Compliance target key figures	• Governance actual key figures • Compliance actual key figures	Governance and Compliance-Target-actual-Comparison	

Fig. 1.5 MITO organization development integration matrix

The integration of the **organizational design parameters**, such as requirements, success factors, potentials, goals, strategic approaches, risks, weak points, measures, competencies, key figures, etc., is also carried out in the same way by superimposing the associated **MITO design models** and the MITO segment-related links that are possible with them, i.e. the assignment of the parameters that apply there, such as requirements, goals, strategies, weak points, etc., for each MITO segment. Each MITO segment, i.e., the management, input, transformation, output, and control segments, represents a subsystem of the holistic control-loop-related MITO business model, which can be described in great detail and transparently in its interactions.

Whereby the practical design implementation of the MITO model statements always takes place at the role-based swimlane representation of the respective considered management, leadership or **support process** and core process within each process level with the **potential variables** assigned there such as costs, times, qualities. The respective requirements, goals, key figures, etc. are factually-temporally-logically assigned to the swimlane role under consideration. Scalability, integrability and horizontal as well as vertical **interconnectivity** of the organizational design and structural elements or parameters are therefore the outstanding differentiation features when using the MITO model or the **MITO business model** based on it.

1.4 Cloud-Based Business Model Platform Development

The **change management** process for digital **business model transformation** is therefore the focus of this book because no organization can afford to ignore this development. The constant improvement of **cloud computing** offerings is putting established companies under increasing pressure to drive **process digitization** in their own companies in order not to lose out to competitors. At the beginning, it was the serious cost advantages of cloud computing, i.e. the replacement of internal data centers with considerable cost savings and a previously unknown IT cost transparency in the use of scalable computing power and IT infrastructures and resources, which resulted in the further development of cloud-based services into business model platforms with the networking capabilities contained therein in real time, which now result in further considerable advantages over traditional IT concepts.

By providing mobile development platforms with **open source software**, apps and applications can be developed much faster than usual with the support of these cloud services, i.e. with a high degree of agility and flexibility. Cloud computing offers automatic backups and software updates, as well as built-in redundancies and disaster recovery in case of emergency.

With the large cloud computing service provider, services run securely on a worldwide network in data centers that offer higher security than individual data centers in a company. Even micro businesses can access virtually unlimited computing power in the cloud at a low cost. With a **digital business model platform**, management in the company must decide which **stakeholders** (employees, customers, consumers, vendors, products, suppliers, etc.) are allowed access and with what rights and permissions. This is always in connection with the introductory cost consideration, which refers, for example, to the reduction of acquisition and operating costs for hardware and software, IT, management and personnel costs, energy costs for operation and cooling, as well as for the maintenance costs that are usually eliminated.

In order to exploit these advantages, especially for medium-sized companies, it is very important to develop the right digitization strategy now. To do this, however, it is first necessary from an organizational perspective – as described in the following Chap. 3 – to replace the existing vertical function-oriented organizational structures based on the division of labor with a horizontal organizational **process structuring**. Here, the primacy of the organization in systematic process digitization takes precedence over technological considerations. Based on this, Chap. 5 explains a systematic path to horizontal and vertical process digitization and networking in several steps.

Systematic Business Model Development and Design

2

Abstract

The permanent challenge for management is to recognize the change necessary to achieve the company's goals, to actively promote it and to systematically shape it, i.e. to transform it and to permanently secure the changes implemented. From a business perspective, the term "**transformation**" refers to the process of change from a current "as-is" state to a targeted "to-be" state in the near future. This is a fundamental and permanent change that results, for example, from new competitive models, technologies, ecological constraints, demographic developments and other serious changes and forces companies to act if they want to operate successfully in the long term.

2.1 Holistic Business Model Change Management

For most companies, the classic starting point is to develop a company-specific business model for a particular product or service and the customer target group addressed by it, and to align the structural and process organization accordingly for sustainable competitive success. This is often triggered by strategic turning points, i.e. when the competition changes significantly due to new technologies, products, processes or new rules of the game on the market. This is currently the case. An organizational turning point is currently, for example, the move away from function-oriented vertical organizational structures in favor of horizontal value chains that are focused on the customer.

H. F. Binner, *Holistic Business Model Transformation*,
https://doi.org/10.1007/978-3-658-37367-2_2

A technological turning point is the **digital transformation**, i.e. the digital networking of customers, employees, machines, processes, orders, materials, suppliers, storage locations, transport equipment and other objects via the cloud. In this context, new digital business models with previously unknown product and service offerings are emerging in the digitalized value chain. This is combined with greater adaptability, i.e. agility to new customer requirements, higher delivery capacity, short development times for smart products and services with mobile access via customer portals and customer apps, as well as other specific measures to improve customer benefits over the product lifetime.

Another turning point is the holistic business model approach as opposed to the classic product and process strategy approach, because in the future digital business models will be competing with each other on the basis of customer benefits, rather than individual products or processes.

However, this change management process will only be successful if the management is able to integrate these changes into the corporate and **value culture**. This means that it must present the goals, strategies, and organizational structures transparently and involve those affected, i.e. above all the employees, in the decision-making processes. Only by linking organizational, cultural and digital transformation can the desired holistic digital business model transformation be achieved as a result.

In the following, a method-supported change management approach is explained that aims to successfully implement this holistic company-specific business model transformation digitally. Process models, methods and tools are provided for this purpose.

The necessary internal changes due to external pressure for change or transformation often do not find implementation. The reasons for this are manifold. **Types of resistance** can be distinguished, for example, according to:

- Rational resistance
- Emotional resistance
- Economic resistance
- Psychological resistance
- Open or hidden resistors
- Passive resistors
- Active resistors
- Constructive resistances
- Destructive resistances
- Individual organizational resistance

These **resistances** must be overcome by communicatively involving all stakeholders in the change management process.

A holistic business model transformation based on the following systematic answers to the **7 basic business model questions**

1. Why? (Positioning)
2. Who? (Marketing logic)
3. What?
4. How? (Value creation logic)
5. With what? (Ability logic)
6. By whom? (Cooperation logic)
7. Value? (Earnings logic)

Within the **MITO control loop model** can therefore only succeed – as shown in Fig. 2.1 in 4 steps – by combining it with an organizational transformation, a cultural transformation and a digital transformation. The change management process required for this is implemented via the MITO Organization 4.0 concept described here.

The point of reference for the implementation of the individual four **transformation fields** is a process-oriented **organizational structure** according to the BPMN 2.0 standard, in which the process participants are graphically depicted in a role-based **swimlane**

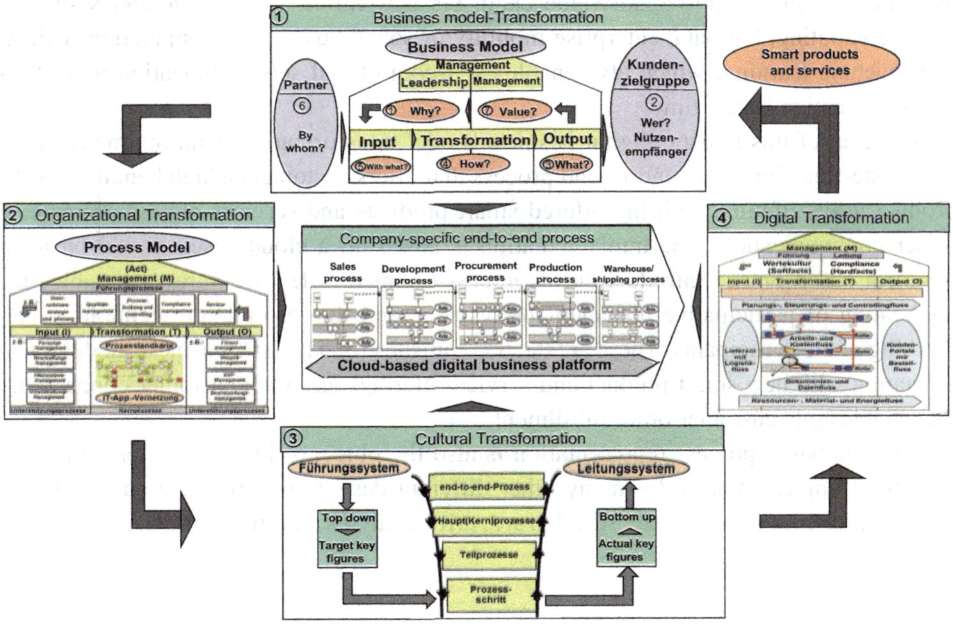

Fig. 2.1 Holistic digital business model transformation

representation in the factually logical temporal sequence of task completion with the associated information and communication flow.

The holistic process-related business model transformation takes place according to a uniform implementation scheme that is specified by the MITO model. The goal of this holistic **digital business model transformation** – starting in step 1 from the existing, i.e. not yet digitized, business model – is an optimally error- and waste-free digitized **end-to-end process** that offers customers a high level of benefit with the smart products and services offered and online customer and partner communication. The implementation is based on a cloud-based digital business platform.

With regard to **organizational transformation**, in step 2 it is necessary to develop a company-specific process model in which the management processes, upstream support processes, core processes, downstream support processes and leadership processes are defined. In a further step, these processes must then be analyzed, modeled and documented. This is also the basis for the introduction of a wide variety of integrated management systems in accordance with a uniform high-level IMS structure, as explained in Sect. 4.10.

The **cultural transformation** based on a previously implemented process organization in step 3 then enables managers to provide transformational leadership, i.e. employees are managed on an equal footing with personal responsibility and the necessary room for maneuver within the horizontal value chain in a participative manner.

The digital transformation in step 4 enables informational networking in agile order execution within the horizontal value chain via new information technologies such as cloud computing, big data, enterprise mobility or social business in conjunction with AI and machine learning, which also enables self-control and self-optimization as well as predictive action in real time.

The goal of this holistic digital business model transformation is an optimally error- and waste-free digitalized end-to-end process that offers customers a high benefit over the product usage lifetime with the offered smart products and services and an online customer communication. The implementation is based on a cloud-based digital business platform based on the introduction of process-oriented order structures. It enables the application of participative management systems, and the information technology networking of the participants. These are the prerequisites for a holistic business model transformation with new smart product and service offerings and with customer connectivity that enable agile customer order fulfillment.

The role-based process representation is also the object of knowledge for a method-supported implementation for many other different design and optimization views. For example, for competence, load, risk, hazard, error analyses, and much more.

In summary, the digital business model transformation described here under the name MITO Organization 4.0 concept is a holistic process-oriented organization, IT configuration design and learning concept that digitally implements the change management process from a function-oriented to a process-oriented organization using the MITO configuration management approach with the **MITO model** and the role-based swimlane representation.

2.2 MITO Business Model Description

A business model enables a visualization and structuring of all design elements or organizational components that are necessary to enable a successful implementation of the company-specific vision and mission. The focus here is no longer only on the selection of strategic product or business fields in the market (portfolio strategy approach) as a means of positioning one's own company activities against competitors, as is the case with classic market behavior and competitive strategy considerations, but on the concentration of a comprehensive customer benefit consideration with realization through cross-company digitalized value chains.

By answering the 7 W-questions described in detail below, the MITO business model describes in the order mentioned how a company achieves its business goals in its business processes by keeping its customer value proposition. A well-known business model is the **canvas model** by Pigneur and Osterwalder, which contains a total of 9 design elements, all of which can also be found in the MITO business model – but here structured as a control loop. Another well-known business model is the St. Gallen **navigation concept** with the four dimensions "What?, Who?, How?, Value?". These are also now included in the MITO business model, but with additional dimensions.

The visualization of the contents of a current or future digital business model is carried out here via the **MITO model** with its five model segments "Leadership, Input, Transformation, Output, Management" with the inclusion of customers and suppliers, which depict the necessary business activities within the hierarchical process level model in the form of a company control loop, each defining a central aspect or building block. The sum of these aspects or activities describes very precisely the company's purpose, which must be implemented successfully, i.e. competitively. This visualization has the great advantage of capturing all building blocks and thus the company-specific business DNA at a glance and thus achieving a common understanding of the management team. The methodological competence of the management to carry out the right analyses to answer the 7 basic questions is also very beneficial in the implementation. The MITO method tool described in Sect. 2.6 is available for this purpose.

In the **MITO business model**, all three organizational subsystems, i.e. the target, management and leadership system as well as the company-specific hierarchical process level model with the design elements contained therein are linked with each other in the form of an operational control loop within the five model segments "Leadership, Input, Transformation, Output, Management" supplemented by the two customer and supplier elements. Figure 2.2 shows this MITO business model with the associated 7 W basic questions to be answered.

The necessary analyses, diagnoses, therapies and evaluations to answer these 7 W-questions as a prerequisite for a successful **business model implementation** are carried out with the support of the MITO method tool via MITO portfolio checklists provided for this purpose. The practical implementation of this business model then takes place in relation to the analyzed and documented **value chain**, which is mapped as an **end-to-end process** based on roles and can be further broken down to the work system or process step level via the process level model.

The direct link between the MITO model segments and the end-to-end process mapping is that the management in the leadership segment convincingly communicates the mission and the process targets to the employees in the form of target agreements and with a role model function. In the input segment, the resources for process execution are to be provided via upstream support processes. This is followed by the actual product or service creation with the existing core competence of the company in the transformation segment.

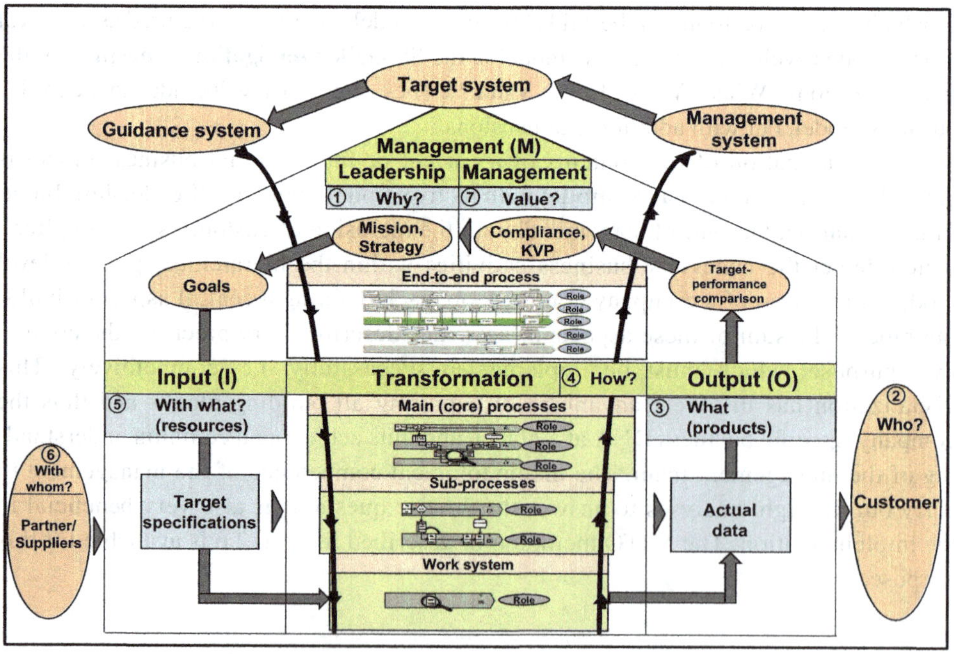

Fig. 2.2 Holistic MITO business model

The result in the **output segment** is the execution of the product or service in accordance with specifications and quality. In the **management segment**, strategic controlling and risk management take place with a review of whether the company's objectives have been achieved in compliance and in line with the value. This provides the impetus for continuous improvement.

2.3 Business Model-7 W Basic Question Description

The starting point in stage 1 for the later **process organization implementation** with the value culture change and process digitization to be considered is the answering of the strategic 7 W basic questions, which are depicted as a control loop within the MITO business model shown.

As already explained above, this business model describes the logical functioning of how a company develops successfully in society and implements its business idea in public or on the market. Logic is the study of the principles of correct, i.e. conclusive, thinking and reasoning.

Via the MITO business model shown in Fig. 2.3, the seven basic questions or principles to be answered logically within the five MITO model segments "Management Leadership, Transformation, Output, Management Leadership" are also mapped in the given sequence

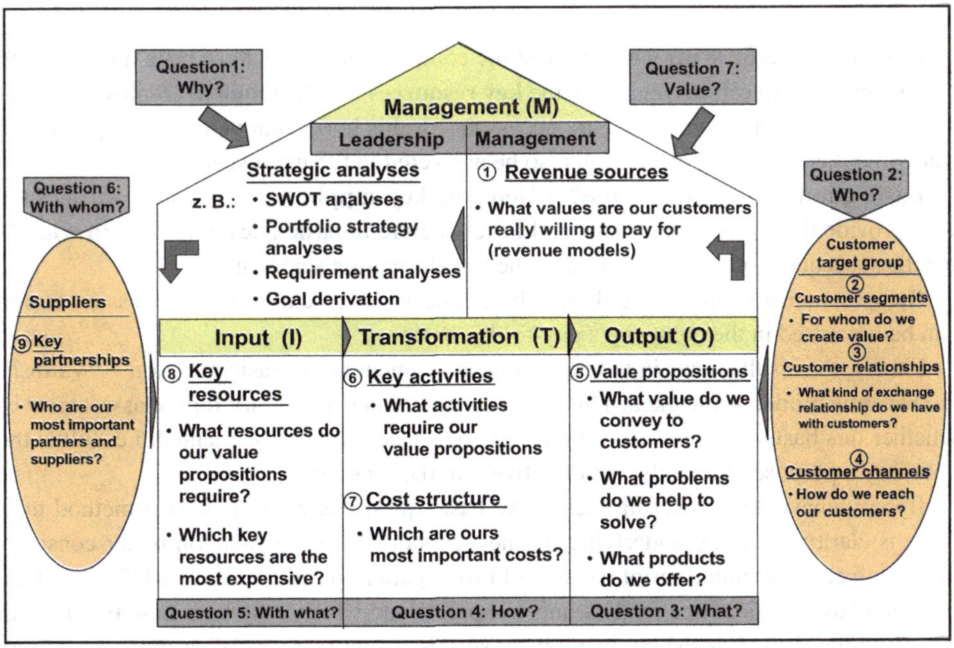

Fig. 2.3 7 MITO business model questions with assignment of the 9 business model canvas elements

in the form of a cybernetic control loop. Complementary to this, 9 design elements of the canvas model are assigned. Systematically, with the support of prepared MITO portfolio checklists, these seven basic questions are answered by those responsible.

Basic question 1. Why?/why?: Here the business idea and the resulting purpose of the company organisation under consideration and the overriding objective are described in the management segment, which is then subsequently used as the basis for deriving the strategy to fulfil the company-specific organisational objectives.

The purpose of the entrepreneurial action in answering W basic question 1 "Why?" results in its entirety from the answers to the following W basic questions according to the MITO business model structure. The purpose and definition of the company are thereby clearly and unambiguously, but in particular credibly, elaborated.

Basic question 2. Who?: This is about the stakeholders, i.e. essentially the **key customers** and other institutions that make use of the organizational service. It is essential that the specific stakeholder requirements and the customer benefits of the target group are precisely analysed for the customer value proposition provided.

Basic question 3: In order to generate the required stakeholder benefit, the appropriate **key products** and services must be provided as a problem solution for the customer in an output-related manner.

Basic question 4: If the products and services for the selected customer target group are known, the **key processes** that are necessary within the horizontal value chain for the production of products and services can then also be designed in the transformation segment.

Basic question 5: With what?: Once the company processes have been analysed and documented, the questions regarding the **key resources**, i.e. the required employees, infrastructure and information, which are necessary for this horizontal value-added process to run without errors and wastage, can also be answered in the input segment.

Basic question 6 "With whom?": Here, the **key suppliers** and partners are selected who provide the required resources and infrastructure in basic question 5 **"With what?"** for the subsequent process execution in the transformation segment.

By systematically answering these 6 basic questions, an end-to-end process execution can be organized in the company's day-to-day business.

Finally, the result shows in the management segment at the basic question 7 **"Value?"** the **revenue model** has worked. This value contribution is necessary for the assessment of whether this business or business model can be successfully implemented, i.e. fulfils the company's purpose efficiently and effectively in the long term.

By systematically answering these 7 W basic questions with the MITO method tool, there is clarity about the underlying business model of the organization under consideration with clear delimitations of the area of investigation. It must be clarified, for example, in which business field one really wants to operate and which **customer benefits** one can actually offer. Why has the company been successful up to now? What must be done in terms of value, organization, products, processes and resources in order to continue to be successful in the future? Which decisions are necessary for this and how quickly do they have to be implemented? Is it possible to follow the market dynamics? These questions and many more can be worked through systematically using the MITO business transformation model, always with a focus on the business processes, using the MITO method tool in a holistic manner.

2.4 7 W Basic Question Answering with the MITO Method Tool

In the MITO method tool, a whole number of classical management, CIP, creativity and QM methods are combined in an overarching problem-solving cycle consisting of

1: Analysis, 2: Diagnosis, 3: Therapy, 4: Evaluation.

Are linked with each other. These methods, which are also shown in Fig. 2.4, can be applied systematically to many tasks according to a uniform process model – referred to here as the **MITO King's Path**. The focus of analysis is, for example, on processes, customers, employees, markets, products, **stakeholders**, requirements, goals, weak points, and many more. Two-dimensional analyses can then be performed using the prepared portfolio checklists for the respective task topics, which are also shown in Fig. 1.1, whereby the user can use a wide variety of assessment variants (BV).

As an example, the **evaluation variants BV1**: V = requirement and H = degree of fulfillment and BV2 with "V = target and H = actual" are shown. In this way, the user receives a clear statement graphically during the diagnosis in which segment there is a need for action. Furthermore, an ABC analysis is always integrated into the method application, so that the evaluation criteria are automatically prioritized during the evaluation within the portfolio diagram, e.g. A = difficult, B = medium, C = easy or A = high, B = medium, C = low.

The results from the diagnosis phase are then automatically transferred to the therapy phase in order to derive a goal/measure tree, which is also graphically displayed in the result. A to-do list with responsibility and deadline is also automatically generated for each measure. The structured procedure of **cascading** in this phase, which is stored in the MITO tool, is also referred to as the MITO royal road, because it makes it easier for the tool user to **select the method** for implementation, or it specifies it.

After the measures have been implemented, an **evaluation** or maturity assessment can be carried out in phase 4, again in two dimensions – for example, an evaluation with V = efficiency and H = effectiveness. Furthermore, maturity models are also stored in order to determine the process maturity level in a process analysis, for example.

Figure 2.4 lists a large number of MITO tool applications as examples. Each of these applications has its own reference portfolio checklists that allow the user to immediately and systematically carry out the MITO problem-solving cycle "analysis, diagnosis, therapy, evaluation". Since the results are always also documented in digital form, the MITO method tool can also be used excellently for simple and fast

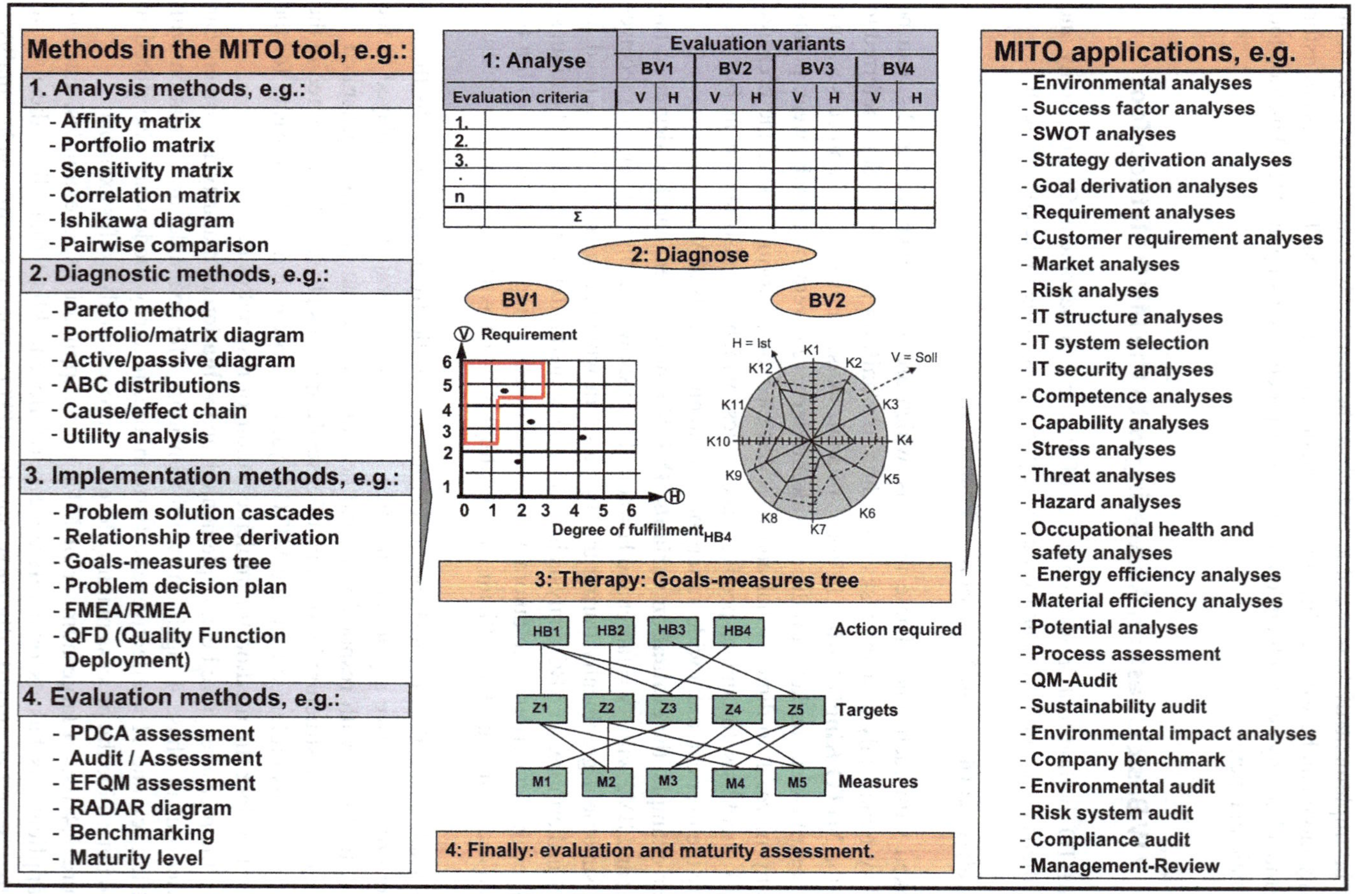

Fig. 2.4 MITO method tool application

verification of compliance with the requirements of a wide variety of Integrated Management Systems (IMS).

There are also a large number of **MITO reference checklists** for systematically answering the seven basic questions for successful business model implementation, as they are interlinked in the MITO model as a cybernetic control loop, which support the user in systematically solving a large number of different problems with the MITO method tool. In the following, some analysis examples are always given in relation to the respective 7 W basic question, for example for

Basic question 1 (Why?/Why?):
- Environment analyses
- Strengths/weaknesses analyses
- Opportunity/risk analyses
- Market potential analyses
- Market volume analyses

Basic question 2: Who? (Customer benefit)
- Customer benefit analysis
- Customer requirements analysis
- Customer satisfaction analysis
- Customer service analysis
- Complaint analyses

Basic question 3: What? (Products and services)
- Product analyses
- Service analyses
- Functional analyses

Basic question 4: How? (Processes and procedures)
- Process organization
  - Analyses of potential
  - Vulnerability analyses
  - Interface analyses
  - CIP analyses
  - Error analyses
- Technology insert
  - Project analyses
  - IT structure analyses
  - IT system selection analyses
  - IT architecture analyses
  - IT implementation analyses
  - IT network analyses

Basic question 5: With what? (Employees and infrastructure)

- Competence analyses
- Qualification analyses
- Load analyses
- Capability Analysis
- Resource efficiency analyses
- Infrastructure analyses
- Facility Analysis
- Supervisor evaluation
- Employee evaluation

Basic question 6: With whom? (Suppliers and partners)

- Supplier evaluations
- Logistics analyses
- MOB analyses
- Supply chain analyses
- Outsourcing analysis
- ABC analyses

Basic question 7: Value? (Revenue model)

- Governance analyses
- Compliance analyses
- Management reviews/evaluations
- Balance sheet/P+L account
- Process cost analyses
- Maturity analyses

In the following, the tool-supported answering of the 7 W basic questions will be dealt with in detail and reference portfolio analyses with the MITO method tool will be explained by way of example.

2.4.1 Answers to the Basic Question 1 "Why? (Meaningfulness/Purpose)

The central aspect of basic question 1 "Why?" is the answer to the company's purpose with the associated goals, visions, mission and strategies for achieving the goals with which the company wants to strategically position itself in the competition. SWOT analyses can be used to derive the MITO model segment-related company-specific success potentials and success factors that are required or need to be activated for the competition.

The strategy approaches described in Sects. 2.9 and 2.10 are derived from this. Furthermore, stakeholder analyses must be carried out in order to determine the interests and also the power structures of the stakeholders who can influence the development of the business model.

Environmental analyses are used to analyze economic, ecological, political, sociocultural, technological and other trends that represent opportunities or risks for the implementation of the business model. Market and target group analyses are used to identify relevant market segments and carry out benchmarks with the most important competitors.

Every organization must have clarity about the purpose of the company. Therefore, basic question 1 refers to answering the core business and which customer is willing to pay a bill for the created product or service. The structured answer to this basic question also provides essential support for company founders (startups) when creating a **business plan**.

In order to evaluate a business plan in terms of its prospects of success, but also to analyse it in terms of the necessary planning activities, the MITO business plan portfolio matrix shown in Fig. 2.5 is an essential aid. The starting point is the criteria specified in seven individual clusters for a business plan assessment:

1. Business idea
2. Personal requirements
3. Market assessment
4. Competitive situation
5. Product/service generation
6. Financial situation
7. Future developments

If required, the user can add further clusters with the corresponding individual criteria or delete other criteria that are not relevant from his point of view.

The individual criteria named in the portfolio matrix can now be evaluated two-dimensionally according to different freely selectable **valuation variants** (BV). A total of four valuation variants are shown here.

- Evaluation variant 1 with V = foundation relevance, H = implementation
- Evaluation variant 2 with V = requirement, H = implementation
- Evaluation variant 3 with V = significance/value, H = feasibility
- Evaluation variant 4 with V = barriers/problem relevance, H = degree of overcoming

Each of these four assessment variants (BV) represents its own particular analysis view and must each be assessed separately. The results of the assessment with scores from 1 to 6 are graphically represented in the portfolio diagrams. A percentage evaluation is also possible. The fields of action for each individual **evaluation variant** in these portfolio

lfd Nr.	Business plan evaluation, e.g.:		BV1 (V)	BV1 (H)
1.	**Business ideas, e.g.:**			
1.1	Customer benefits elaborated		4	3
1.2	Differentiating features		3	2
1.3	Chancen-Risiken benannt?		4	2
		Σ C	11	7
		Σ C / n	3.7	2. 3
2.	**Personal requirements, e.g.:**			
2.1	Education?		3	2
2.2	Special skills?		4	3
2.3	Qualification?		3	4
		Σ C	10	9
		Σ C / n	3.3	3
3.	**Market assessment, e.g.:**			
3.1	Customer target group clarified?		5	4
3.2	Market development positive?		4	4
3.3	Customer contacts available?		4	3
		Σ C	13	11
		Σ C / n	4.3	3.7
4.	**Competitive situation, e.g.:**			
4.1	Competitor comparison available?		3	4
4.2	Strengths/weaknesses known?		2	5
4.3	Environment analysis carried out?		3	3
		Σ C	8	12
		Σ C / n	2.7	4
5.	**Production/service generation, e.g.:**			
5.1	Process transparency established?		4	4
5.2	Resource requirements determined?		4	3
5.3	Site selection carried out?		4	2
		Σ C	12	9
		Σ C / n	4	3
6.	**Financial situation, e.g.:**			
6.1	Security for loan in place?		6	4
6.2	Cost transparency verifiable?		4	4
6.3	Liquidity clarified?		5	2
		Σ C	15	10
		Σ C / n	5	3.3
7.	**Future developments, e.g.:**			
7.1	Resource availability available?		3	5
7.2	Market development correctly assessed		4	4
7.3	Laws fulfilled?		5	5
	Scale: 1 = low 6 = high	Σ C	12	14
		Σ C / n	4	4.7
		Total	81	72
		Tota / nl	3.9	3.4

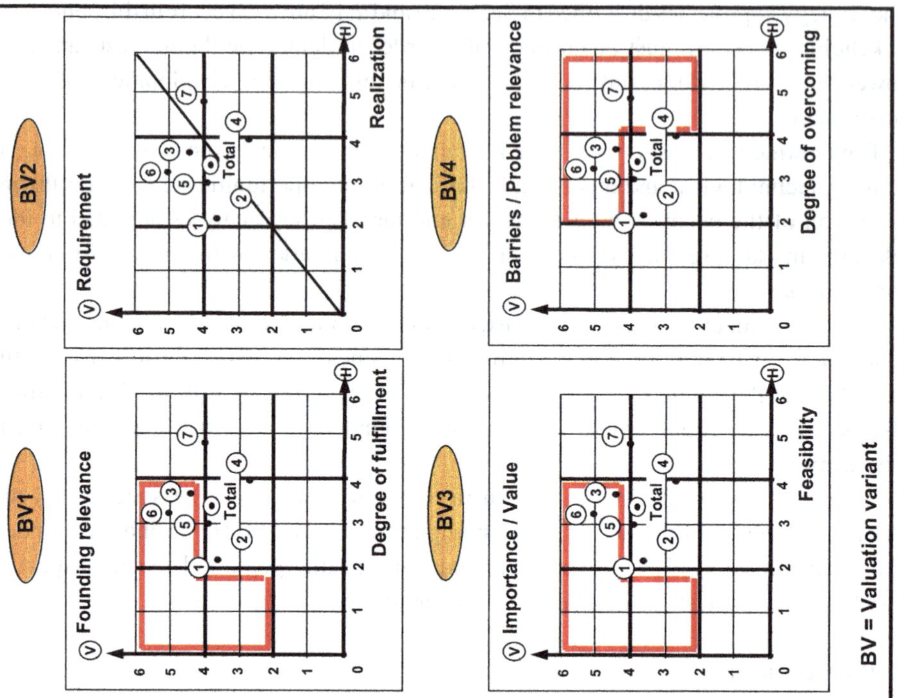

Fig. 2.5 MITO tool-supported business concept/business plan assessment portfolio

diagrams are drawn in. The user can immediately see which individual criteria within his business plan analysis still require **action**.

In evaluation variant 1, the first step is to locate the relevant start-up activities for which the degree of fulfilment is still too low. Through suitable measures, the user – in this case the company founder – must try to land in the upper right portfolio segment for the relevant criteria to be developed in order to increase the degree of fulfilment. In evaluation variant 2, it is determined whether the existing business model requirements are also fulfilled or implemented. The ideal solution is on the diagonal, because here the requirements are implemented exactly via the corresponding degree of implementation. All criteria or requirements that lie above the diagonal are not fulfilled. The implementation must be improved by suitable measures. Below the diagnosis there is an overfulfilment. Assessment variant 3 checks whether the localised criteria can be implemented at all. If it turns out that feasibility is not possible at all for certain relevant criteria, the user must consider other options and should not waste so much energy looking for a solution that is not feasible. Assessment variant 4 locates possible barriers in the respective foundation activities and shows the necessary degree of overcoming in order not to fail due to these barriers.

However, there are quite a number of other valuation variants (BV) not considered in detail here that can also be used for business concept and business plan evaluation, for example:

BV5: V = effort, H = benefit
BV6: V = frequency, H = importance
BV7: V = **degree of target achievement**, H = effort

These evaluations serve, for example, to prioritise the individual start-up activities during implementation. With the so-called royal road in the use of the MITO method tool, various objectives and measures can now be derived in a cascade for the individual needs for action in order to arrive at a tree of objectives/measures with a to-do list that allows users to systematically work through the identified need for action for a successful business model implementation.

Another exemplary MITO reference checklist for answering basic question 1 "Why?" is the **corporate culture analysis** portfolio matrix shown in Fig. 2.6. In the comparison, 4 companies U1 to U4 are evaluated according to 2 evaluation variants (BV1: V = importance, H = degree of fulfilment and BV2: V = external image and H = self-image). The need for action for each individual value culture criterion, arranged in rows, becomes clear from the graphical presentation of results for each evaluation criterion. The localized **culture deficits** are eliminated via a cascade of goals and measures.

In the case of the company target, for example, a value culture target could be specified with a score of >4. In the result diagram, the value culture scores from 1 to 6 assigned to the 9 portfolio diagram sub-segments can be graphically displayed via the column totals of V and H per company, but also for each individual criterion, to show whether this target value has been achieved.

	Value culture, e.g.	*U1		U2		U3		U4	
		V	H	V	H	V	H	V	H
1	Power	5	3	3	2	4	2	3	5
2	Recognition	3	2	4	4	5	2	4	4
3	Democracy	3	4	4	2	6	3	2	5
4	Goal orientation	2	3	5	3	4	3	2	4
5	Authority	4	3	4	3	3	3	4	4
6	Self-assertion	5	3	4	3	4	2	3	4
7	Orientation towards some goals	3	3	3	2	5	3	2	9
8	Creativity	3	2	4	3	4	4	3	5
9	Optimism	3	4	5	2	4	4	3	4
10	Openness	5	3	4	3	5	4	3	4
11	Team orientation	3	3	2	2	5	4	2	4
12	Compliance with rules	3	3	3	2	5	4	3	4
13	Perfection	5	3	3	2	5	5	3	4
14	Distance	2	3	5	3	4	4	2	5
15	Nonconformism	3	2	4	3	2	2	2	4
16	Emotionality	3	2	3	5	4	4	3	4
17	Helpfulness	3	2	4	3	5	4	3	3
18	Tolerance	4	3	4	3	6	4	3	4
19	Reliability	3	3	5	3	4	3	3	4
20	Discipline	3	3	3	2	4	4	5	4
21	Sacrifice	4	3	4	3	4	5	4	3
22	Modesty	4	5	2	3	4	2	4	3
23	Self-criticism	5	4	3	2	3	2	5	4
24	Comfort	2	4	4	3	3	2	4	4
25	Harmony	3	4	3	2	4	5	4	4
26	Restraint	2	6	2	2	2	4	5	4
1 = low 6 = high	Σ C	88	77	94	71	108	88	84	104
	Σ C / n	3.4	3	3.6	2.7	4.2	3.4	3.2	4

*U = company

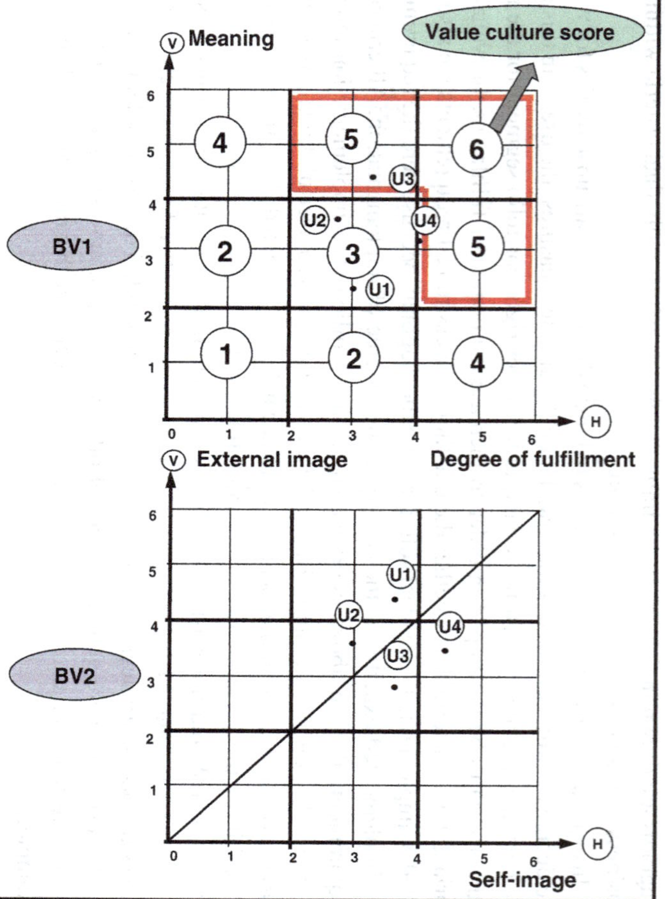

Fig. 2.6 MITO-supported corporate culture analysis

This is followed in Fig. 2.7 by the business area-oriented **organizational guideline evaluation**. Here, the 3 evaluation variants BV1: V = requirement, H = implementation, BV2: V = importance, H = urgency, BV3: V = effectiveness, H = efficiency per business area within the graphically marked fields of action in the **portfolio diagram** are used to determine which line-by-line guideline criteria still require improvement during implementation. The managers could also be evaluated according to these criteria column by column.

In Sect. 2.8, the development of the mission statement once again goes into great detail under the heading "**Code of Conduct**" on a large number of rules of conduct that are intended to serve as an orientation aid for employees and at the same time as digital proof of a required CSR pre-qualification.

In order to identify the need for action, in which core competences within the business areas arranged in columns there is still a need for qualification, different core competence assessment criteria are used and evaluated.

The portfolio diagram shown in Fig. 2.8 with the presentation of the assessment results shows the need for action of the business field-related core competencies with regard to V = market strength and H = **competence strength** within the fields of action "Build, Develop, Hold, Retreat" shown in the portfolio diagram. The corresponding measures must be taken for this.

The **competence evaluations** can also be carried out in the same way, column by column, in relation to the required employee-related competences in process execution or product manufacture, instead of the business area-related analysis view.

In order to make a statement about the fulfilment of the requirements in the implementations of the vision and mission statements, these are evaluated on the basis of the evaluation criteria shown in Fig. 2.9 within the 5 clusters:

- Mission statement
- Corporate philosophy guidelines
- Self-representation guidelines
- Corporate image guidelines
- Company policy guidelines

And, in the case of assessment variant (BV)1*, the results of the assessment are shown graphically in the portfolio diagram in two dimensions according to "V = requirement and H = implementation". All criteria above the diagonal still require **action** and must be improved during implementation by means of suitable measures.

In evaluation variant (BV)2 with "V = importance and H = degree of fulfilment", a review of the company's objectives with regard to the implementation of the vision and mission statement can be carried out by specifying a grade within the 9 portfolio diagram sub-segments from grade 1: not fulfilled to grade 6: fully fulfilled. All assessment criteria that are not in the upper right **portfolio segment** must be improved through suitable measures, as they have not yet reached the targeted implementation level grade 6.

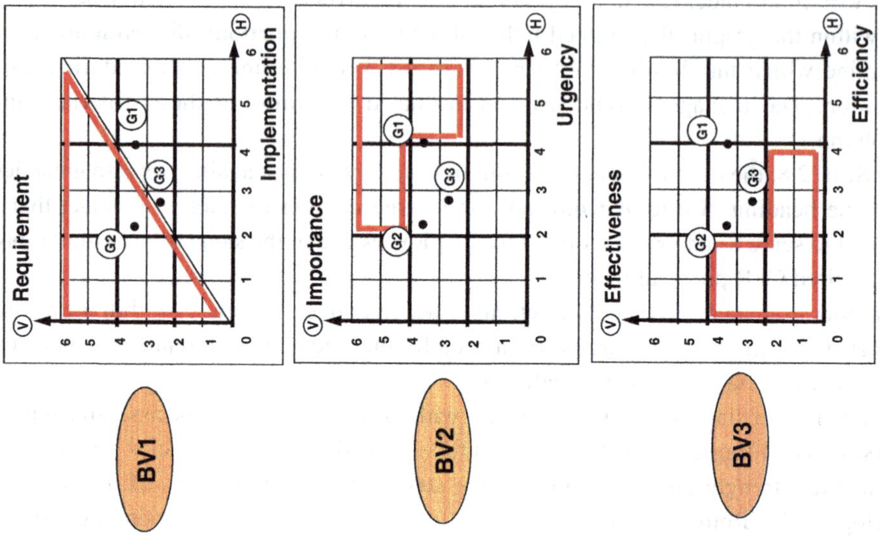

lfd Nr.	Criteria related to. e.g.:	G1		G2		G3	
		V	H	V	H	V	H
1	Holism	4	3	4	4	4	2
2	Transparency	3	3	5	3	4	2
3	Culture of trust	3	5	3	4	3	3
4	Participation	5	4	5	3	5	4
5	Efficiency and humanity	3	3	3	2	4	4
6	Leadership culture	4	4	4	4	4	5
7	Results orientation	4	5	4	3	4	2
8	Learning organization	5	4	5	2	3	2
9	Open conflict management	2	4	2	3	3	2
10	Customer proximity	3	4	3	2	4	5
11	Value system	2	6	5	2	2	4
12	Employee development	4	5	3	2	3	3
13	Quality	4	6	4	2	3	2
	Scale: 1 = low, 6 = high — ΣC	43	52	45	29	38	34
	$\frac{\Sigma C}{n}$	3.3	4	3.5	2.2	2.9	2.6

G = Business areas

Fig. 2.7 Business area-oriented **organisational guidelines** – portfolio assessment

lfd Nr.	Evaluation criteria. e.g.:		*G1		G2		G3		G4	
			V	H	V	H	V	H	V	H
1.	Customer-oriented, e.g.:									
1.1	Customer differentiation features		5	3	6	2	5	4	3	2
1.2	Service differentiation features		3	2	3	4	3	5	5	2
1.3	Quality differentiation features		3	4	3	4	2	3	6	1
		ΣC	11	9	12	10	10	12	14	5
		$\frac{\Sigma C}{n}$	3.7	3	4	3.3	3.3	4	4.7	1.7
2.	Employee-oriented, e.g.:									
2.1	Market differentiation features		5	3	4	3	3	4	5	2
2.2	Supplier differentiation features		3	3	4	2	4	3	4	2
2.3	Employee differentiation features		5	3	3	2	2	4	3	2
		ΣC	13	9	11	7	9	11	12	6
		$\frac{\Sigma C}{n}$	4.3	3	3.7	2.3	3	3.7	4	2
3.	Process-oriented, e.g.:									
3.1	Cost development		3	2	3	5	5	3	5	1
3.2	Improvement characteristics		3	2	5	3	4	4	6	3
3.3	Method differentiation characteristics		3	4	3	2	3	3	4	2
		ΣC	9	8	11	10	12	10	15	6
		$\frac{\Sigma C}{n}$	3	2.7	3.7	3.3	4	3.3	5	2
4.	Success-oriented, e.g.:									
4.1	Product differentiation characteristics		2	4	5	2	2	3	3	2
4.2	Management differentiation characteristics		3	3	4	2	2	4	5	3
4.3	Turnover/profit development		3	4	6	2	3	3	5	2
		ΣC	8	11	15	6	7	10	13	7
	Scale: 1 = low 6 = high	$\frac{\Sigma C}{n}$	2.7	3.7	5	2	2.3	3.3	4.1	2.3
		Together	41	37	49	33	38	43	54	24
		Together/n	3.4	3.1	4.1	2.8	3.2	3.6	4.5	2

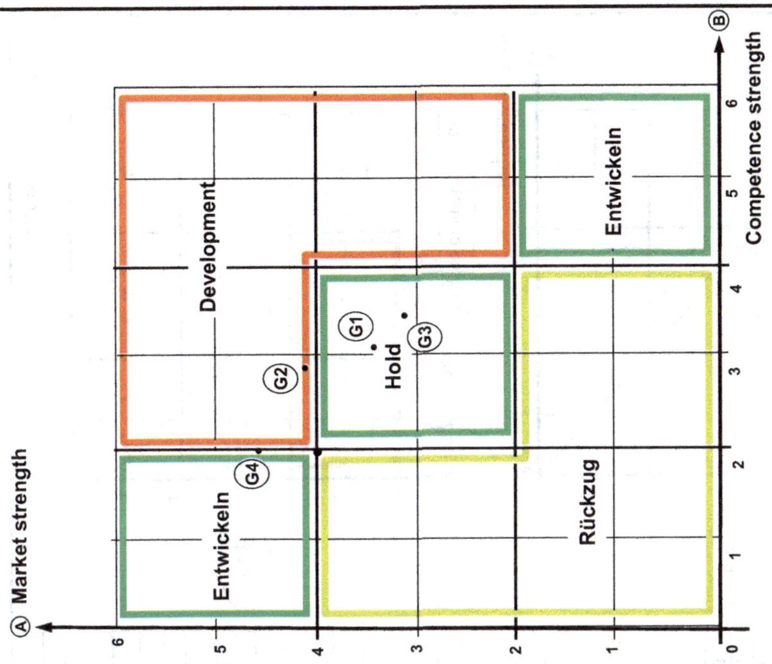

*G = Business segment

Fig. 2.8 Business area-related core competence portfolio for assessing the company's own competitive situation

lfd Nr.	Evaluation criteria, e.g.	V	H
1.	**Corporate mission statement**		
1.1	Standards and values	5	3
2.2	Attitude and style of the company	3	2
2.3	Corporate principles	4	3
2.4	Management structures	2	3
	Σ C	14	11
	Σ C / n	3.5	2.8
2.	**Corporate philosophy specifications**		
2.1	Willingness to innovate	2	3
2.2	Striving for growth	3	2
2.3	Willingness to take risks	4	2
2.4	Qualification standard	3	4
	Σ C	12	11
	Σ C / n	3	2.8
3.	**Self-representation specifications**		
3.1	Corporate identity	2	3
3.2	Product design	3	3
3.3	Corporate design	4	4
	Σ C	14	13
	Σ C / n	3.5	3.2
4.	**Corporate image specifications**		
4.1	Presentation on the market	5	4
4.2	Uniform appearance	4	4
4.3	Clear competitive differentiation	4	3
	Σ C	13	11
	Σ C / n	4.3	3.7
5.	**Corporate policy guidelines**		
5.1	Dealing with partners	2	3
5.2	Attitude to social problems	3	2
5.3	Relationship to social groups	2	4
	Σ C	7	9
	Σ C / n	2.3	3
	Total	16.7	15.7
	Total / n	3.3	3.1

Scale: 1 = low
6 = high

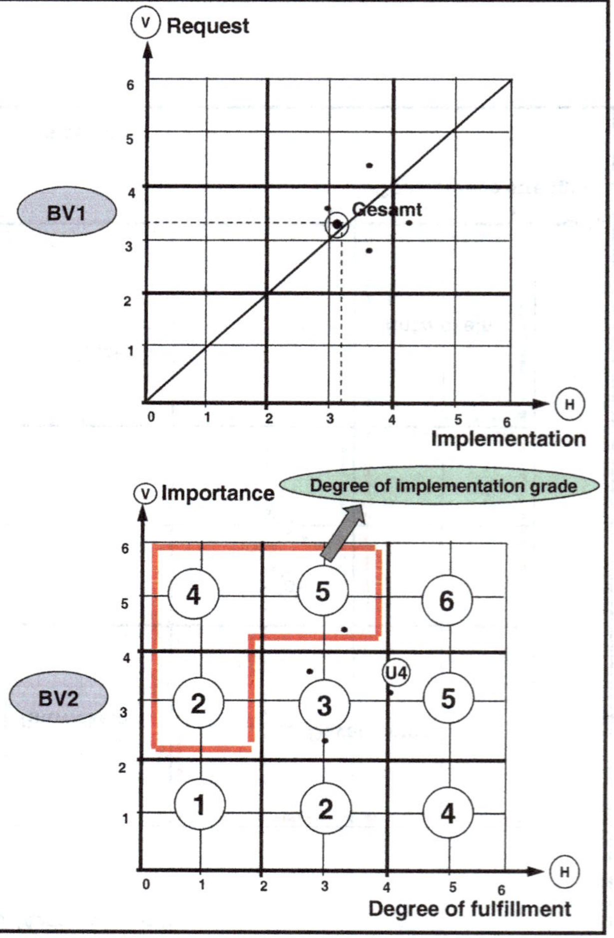

Fig. 2.9 Vision and mission statement assessment portfolio

2.4.2 Answers to Basic Question 2 "Who?" (Customer Value Proposition)

The central aspect of the business model consideration in basic question 2 "Who?" is the determination of the customer target group or the customer to whom the business idea refers. Customer benefit and customer target analyses are the focus here, but also the definition of the distribution channels for passing on the product and services to the customer must be answered in this basic question 2.

The value proposition to the customer is intended to motivate him to act as a customer for the products and services offered. This value proposition is made up of a whole number of the usage features shown in Fig. 2.10, which are to be fulfilled. For the analysis, these characteristics are transferred to a portfolio matrix in order to determine the degree of fulfilment.

The decisive factor here is that, in the customer's perception, these performance characteristics are actually fulfilled. This is, for example, a positive image of the company in terms of the level of performance, the management style, fairness, interaction with employees and customers, in other words, the overall external **appearance** of the company. Only with a positive image will the customer be willing to recommend the company to others. A further characteristic is the accessibility, i.e. if the contact from the customer to the enterprise is looked for it must be ensured that the customer can actually contact the persons desired by him in the enterprise without larger time losses and without much expenditure. The communication that is then possible or takes place is also an important point.

All the information that the customer wants about the company should be answered as comprehensively as possible. In this case, too, negative **feedback** results if the company as a communication partner lacks empathy and does not show caring behaviour. Product and service quality should not be discussed at all, because the customer takes them for granted. Complemented by reliability and professionalism, these are the decisive factors for long-term customer loyalty. Flexibility or **agility** with regard to responding to changes in expectations or products is almost a matter of course. It is particularly well received by customers when they are offered the opportunity to participate, e.g. in projects, developments and events.

A **portfolio analysis** in order to assess the benefits for the selected **customer target group** consists of determining the purchase criteria. This usually requires a group of experts who are familiar with the respective product and service market and thus have the necessary experience for the purchasing processes taking place. Figure 2.11 shows a MITO purchase decision portfolio checklist with the two evaluation variants BV1: "V = relevance, H = **degree of fulfilment**". Here, the need for action results in the upper left segment of the portfolio diagram. With BV2: "V = Requirement, H = Implementation" all purchase criteria above the diagonal are again not fulfilled.

The evaluations themselves can also be carried out by customers or, for example, by the marketing department. In this case, several columns can simply be added to the **portfolio matrix**. The need for action could also be specified for BV1 again via a purchase criteria

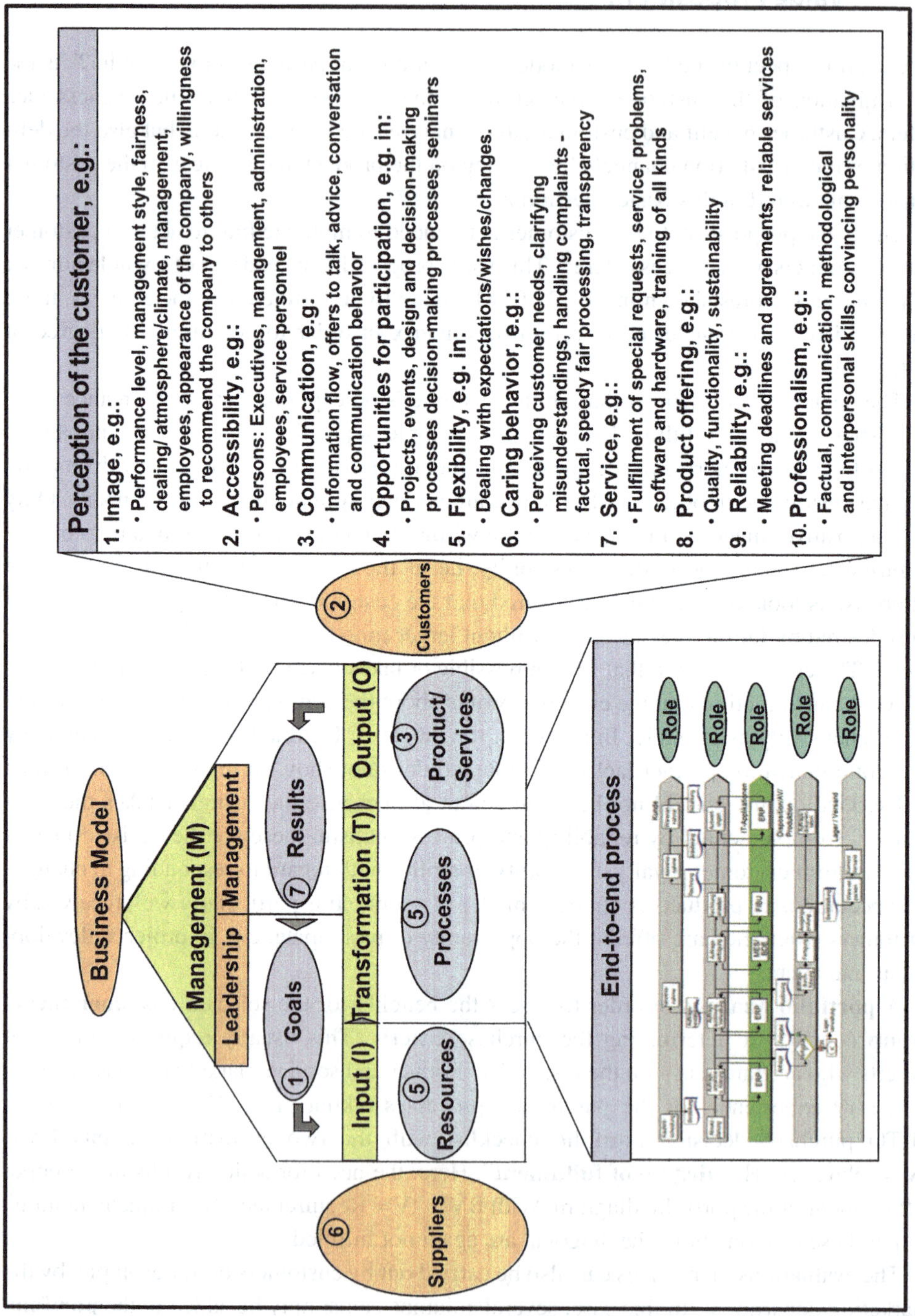

Fig. 2.10 Statements on basic question 2 in the business model: Who? (customer benefit verses)

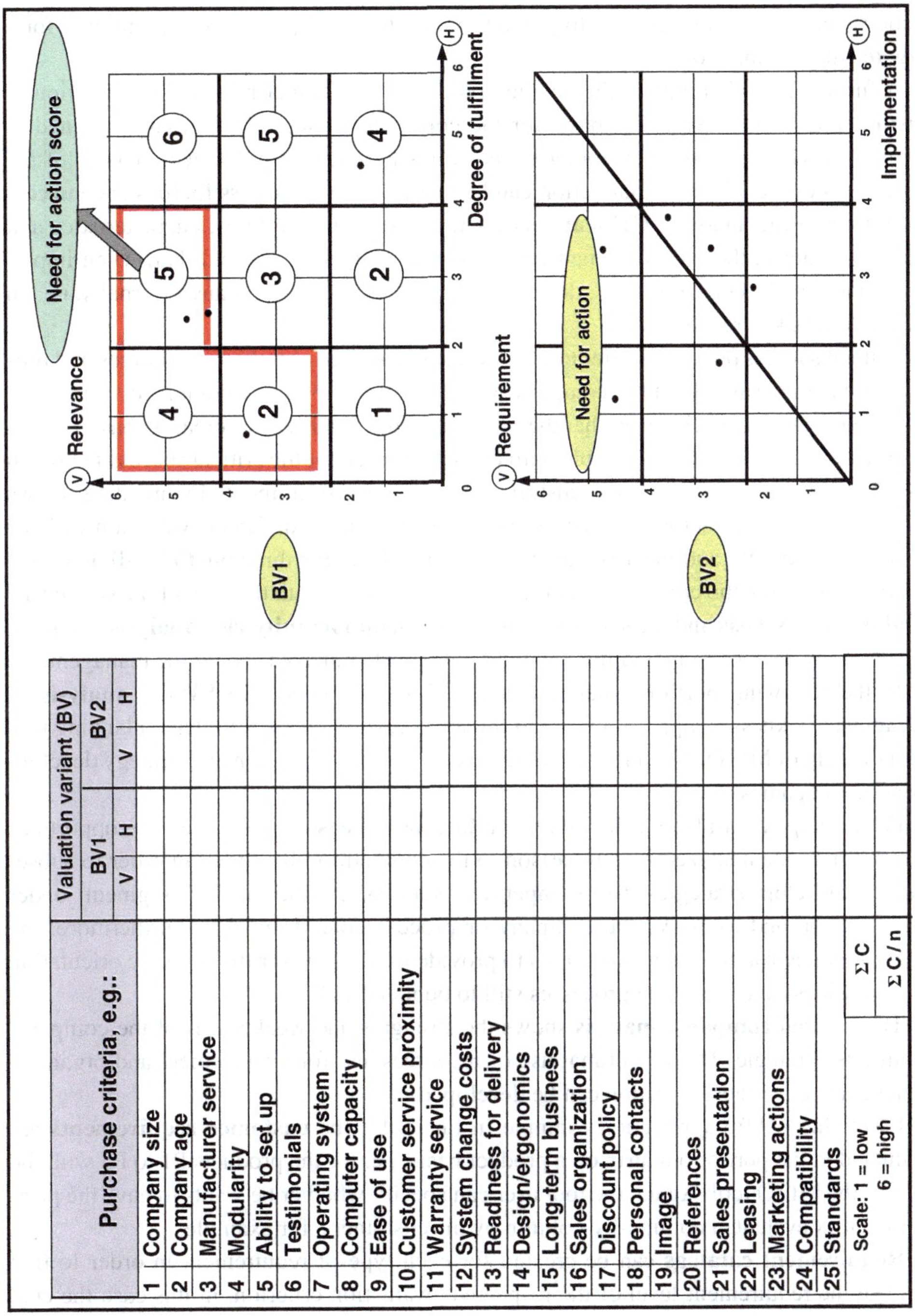

Fig. 2.11 Purchase decision criteria assessment portfolio matrix

grade specification from grade 1 to grade 6 within the BV1 portfolio diagram, e.g. for a target/actual comparison.

A further analysis refers to the detailed product- or customer-related determination of **customer expectations** as the basis for the corporate strategy derivations explained in point 1.10. The analysis of customer expectations is based on a detailed analysis of the customer's expectations. A distinction can be made between **success factors** and **success potentials** in the analysis. **Critical success factors** are the abilities, characteristics and features (criteria) that are important for achieving strategic goals and that, when implemented within the core processes, determine the success of the company externally, i.e. on the market, as key results.

Critical success potentials refer to the internal capabilities, methods, resources and production factors available in the company, which must be optimally combined by the process organization in such a way that the optimal product and service creation based on the existing core competence is possible with the achievement of the critical success factors in order to achieve comprehensive customer requirement fulfillment. Figure 2.12 shows examples of success factors and success potentials with three different evaluation variants BV1, BV2 and BV3 and the associated analysis results in the three **portfolio diagrams**.

By determining the company-specific success potentials with the help of the **strengths/ weaknesses analysis** and the success factors with an **opportunity/risk analysis**, the business strategy development and implementation is made much easier for the management.

In the following portfolio diagram in Fig. 2.13, a competitive **SWOT analysis** of strengths, weaknesses, opportunities and threats is carried out as a strategic planning tool with the help of MITO. The analysis serves to determine the position and strategy development of companies.

For a company or also for the individual **business areas** of a company, the opportunities and risks are analyzed in comparison to the competition K1 to K3 in order to subsequently develop strategies for competitive success in the market segment under consideration and to derive the company or process goals from this. Furthermore, the external or environment analysis serves to provide indications for the strategic orientation of the business and operating processes still to be identified.

The internal **company analysis** shows the strengths and weaknesses of the company. From this, strategies for the optimal use of resources and for management and organizational changes or reorganization can be developed.

In another MITO application example in Fig. 2.14, the **customer requirements** are evaluated in the portfolio matrix on a product basis, i.e. for the products P1 to P5 with the help of the MITO tool. Again, the tool user can specify whether he wants to have the portfolio matrix evaluated column-by-column by his customers, for example.

Requirement catalogs can be created for each type of requirement in order to first analyze the requirement level of the respective evaluation criterion, in this case the customer requirement, for example according to "V = importance, H = necessity" with software support using the MITO method tool. The requirement level can be taken in the form of a grade from the **portfolio result diagram**, here a requirement level grade is assigned

Criteria		K1 V	K1 H	K2 V	K2 H	K3 V	K3 H	K4 V	K4 H
1.	**Success factors (EF)**								
1.1	Low price	5	3	3	2	4	5	3	2
1.2	Low maintenance	3	2	4	4	3	4	4	2
1.3	Easy to operate	3	4	3	4	6	5	2	2
1.4	Environmentally friendly	2	3	5	3	4	4	2	2
1.5	High comfort	5	3	4	3	4	5	3	2
1.6	Safety	3	3	3	2	5	4	3	2
1.7	Image	5	3	3	2	5	5	3	2
1.8	Stockable	2	3	5	3	4	5	2	2
1.9	Meeting deadlines	3	2	3	5	4	4	3	2
1.10	Customer service	3	2	4	3	6	5	3	2
1.11	Information policy	3	4	5	2	6	4	3	2
1.12	Innovations	3	3	2	4	5	4	2	2
	Σ C	41	35	44	37	56	54	33	24
	Σ C / n	3.4	2.9	3.7	3.1	4.7	4.5	2.8	2
2.	**Potential for success (EP)**								
2.1	Product/service competence	2	2	4	4	4	5	3	2
2.2	Flexibility	3	4	5	2	4	4	4	2
2.3	Personnel qualification	5	3	4	3	5	5	6	2
2.4	Customer service level	2	3	3	3	5	4	4	2
2.5	Brand name	5	3	4	3	3	4	3	2
2.6	Sales organization	3	3	4	2	4	3	3	2
2.7	Advertising presence	5	3	5	3	3	4	2	4
2.8	Profitability	2	2	4	4	4	5	3	2
2.9	Product life cycle	3	4	5	2	4	4	3	2
2.10	Customer care	5	3	4	3	5	5	3	2
2.11	Positive image	2	3	3	3	5	4	3	2
2.12	Innovation competence	2	3	5	2	3	3	2	3
	Σ C	39	36	50	34	49	50	39	27
Scale: 1 = low 6 = high	Σ C / n	3.3	3	4.2	2.8	4.1	4.2	3.3	2.3
		80	71	94	71	05	104	72	51
K = Customer	Total. / n	3.3	3	3.9	3	4.4	4.3	3	2.1

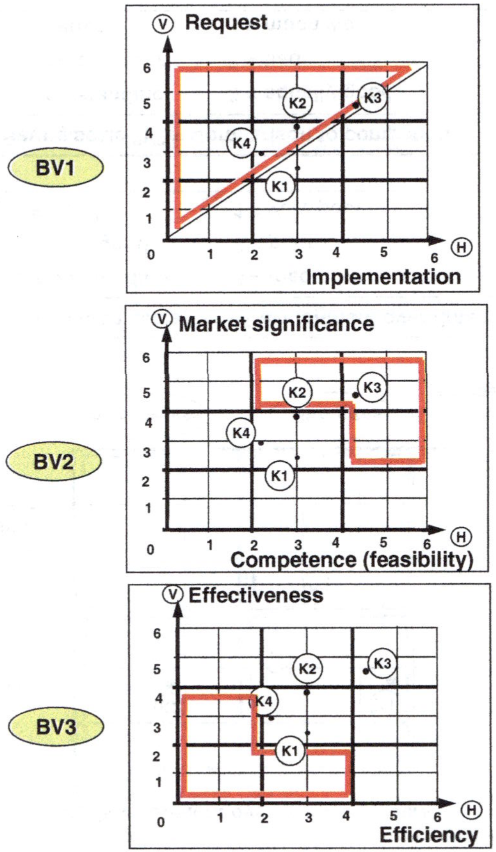

Fig. 2.12 Customer expectations portfolio

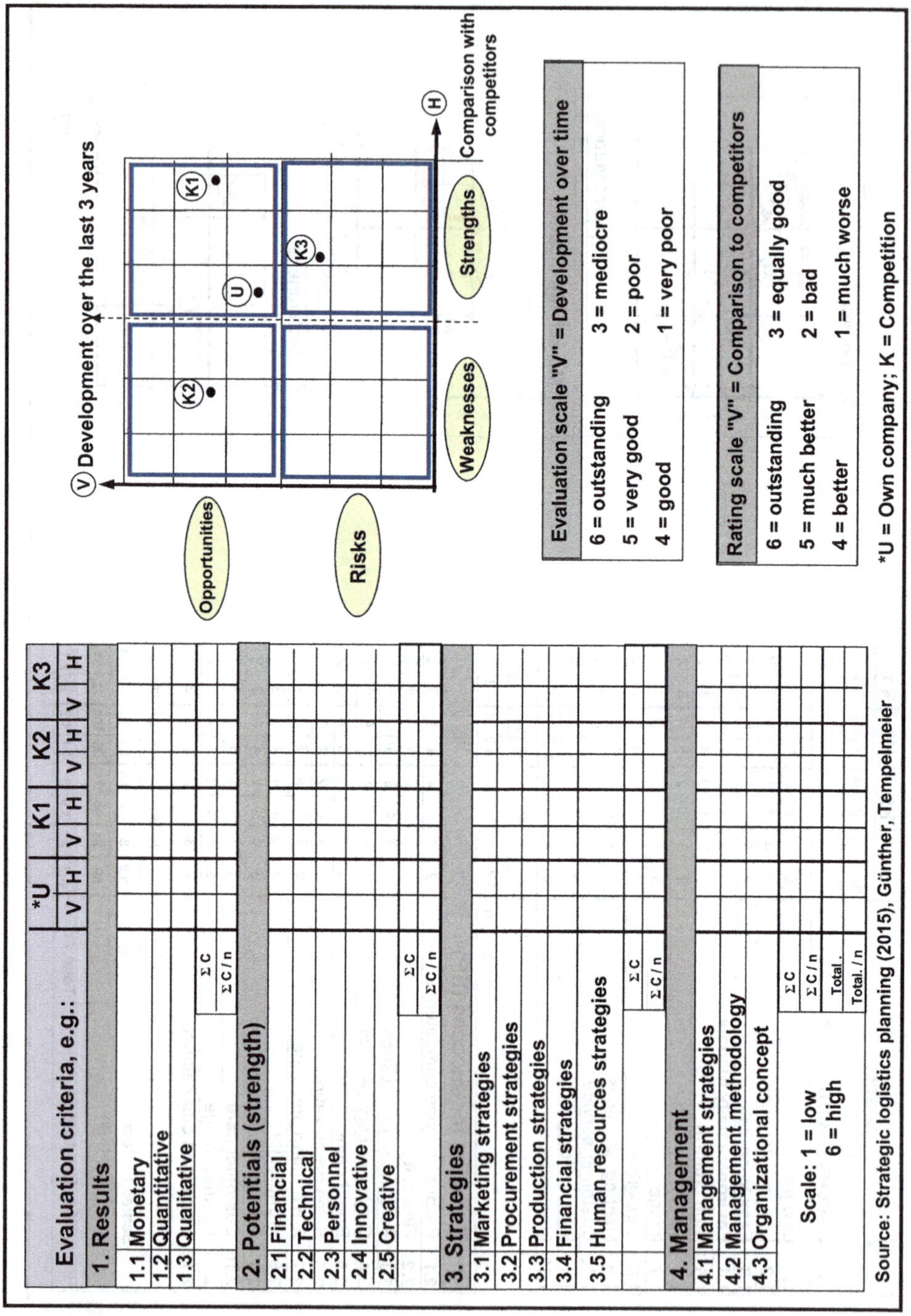

Fig. 2.13 MITO competitive SWOT analysis

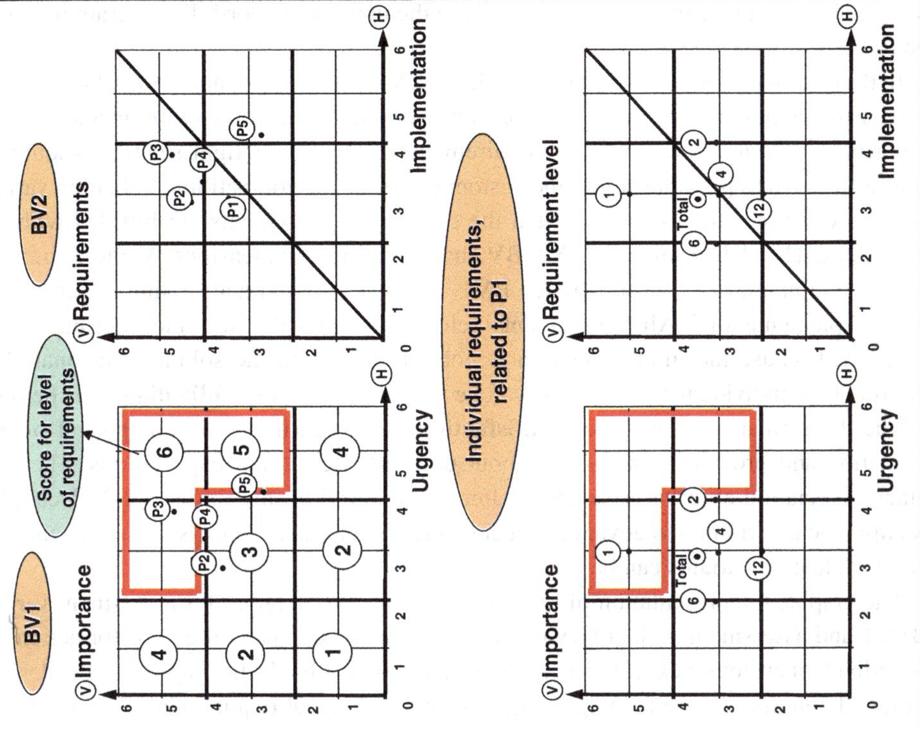

lfd Nr.	Customer requirements, e.g.:	*P1 V	*P1 H	P2 V	P2 H	P3 V	P3 H	P4 V	P4 H	P5 V	P5 H
1	Simple operation	5	3	6	2	5	4	5	3	3	4
2	Low training requirements	3	4	3	4	4	3	4	2	2	5
3	Low operating costs	5	3	4	3	4	4	5	4	2	4
4	Low follow-up costs	5	3	5	3	5	4	6	3	4	4
5	Compatibility	3	2	3	5	5	3	4	3	3	5
6	Recycling	3	2	5	3	4	4	4	2	2	4
7	Accessibility	3	3	5	3	5	3	4	3	3	4
8	Hotline	3	3	4	2	5	3	4	3	2	4
9	Service offer	3	3	3	2	6	4	3	4	3	4
10	Favorable price	5	3	3	2	5	5	3	4	3	4
11	High quality	2	3	5	3	4	4	2	4	2	4
12	Spare parts supply	3	3	4	2	4	3	4	4	2	4
Scale: 1 = low, 6 = high	ΣC	43	35	50	34	56	44	48	39	32	50
	$\frac{\Sigma C}{n}$	3.6	2.9	4.2	2.8	4.7	3.7	4	3.3	2.7	4.2

*P = Product

Fig. 2.14 MITO portfolio valuation variants using the example of "customer requirements"

to each of the 9 sub-segments. For example, in the upper right portfolio diagram field it is the grade 6.

In the example shown, in **valuation variant (BV) 1**, the requirement level of the respective customer requirement is determined on a product-specific basis by evaluating the importance and urgency. All target requirements in the upper right segment should be fulfilled as soon as possible before the customer goes to the competition. Valuation variant (BV) 2 determines the extent to which the customer requirements are fulfilled with the **requirement level** determined in BV1. BV2 has as valuation dimensions "V = Requirement level" (automatically taken from BV1 for the individual requirements) and "H = Implementation". All requirements below the diagonal still require **action** for the company, because the implementation is not fulfilled up to the solution diagonal. The **results** of the individual requirements can be seen in the two **portfolio diagrams** below.

The determination of **customer satisfaction** is also an important component of this evaluation and provides conclusions about unfulfilled customer expectations. The customer expectation criteria listed line by line in the portfolio matrix in Fig. 2.15 can, for example, be determined in advance in a customer requirements analysis. Here again, different evaluation variants can be used.

The graphical representation of results in the portfolio diagram for assessment variant (BV) 1 and assessment variant (BV) 2 clearly show the company the need for action for the individual customer expectation criteria. Here too, for BV1, the diagonal is the desired degree of solution, where the target requirements and actual requirements fulfillment are in balance.

For BV2, the need for action is in the upper left portfolio diagram segment for all assessment criteria that have not reached implementation level scores 5 and 6. Here, too, measures must be taken for these criteria to improve implementation via a **cascade of objectives and measures** with to-do list generation.

2.4.3 Answers to Basic Question 3 "What?" (What Products and Services)

The central aspect of the basic business model question 3 "What?" is the determination of the current and, derived from this, the answer to the future **product and service offering** that fulfils the customer benefit promise formulated in basic question 2. These product and service offerings, which must be clearly defined, must demonstrate the customer benefit to the customer target group previously determined in basic question 2.

A number of **MITO reference examples** are explained below. The focus here is on the interpretation of the customer-specific specifications and requirements that this product and service offering must meet.

	Evaluation criteria, e.g.:	K1		K2		K3		K4	
		V	H	V	H	V	H	V	H
1	Technical product quality	4	3	4	4	4	2	4	2
2	Service quality	3	3	5	3	4	2	5	2
3	Friendliness	3	5	3	4	3	3	3	3
4	Image	5	4	5	3	5	4	5	3
5	Personal support	3	3	3	2	4	4	5	3
6	Price/performance ratio	4	3	4	4	4	5	4	2
7	Additional benefits	4	5	4	3	4	2	4	4
8	Follow-up costs	5	4	5	2	5	4	5	2
9	Disposal	2	4	2	3	3	2	4	3
10	Communication	3	4	3	2	4	5	4	2
11	Accessibility	2	6	5	2	2	4	5	3
12	Complaints	2	2	4	4	4	5	3	2
13	Adherence to delivery dates	3	4	5	2	4	4	4	2
14	Compatibility	5	3	4	3	5	5	6	2
15	Qualification	2	3	4	5	3	3	5	4
16	Speed	2	1	6	4	5	3	5	4
17	Problem-solving ability	3	3	4	4	4	4	5	4
18	Availability	2	2	5	4	4	3	4	4
Scale: 1 = low, 6 = high	ΣC	57	62	75	58	71	64	80	51
	$\frac{\Sigma C}{n}$	3.2	3.4	4.2	3.2	3.9	3.6	4.4	2.8

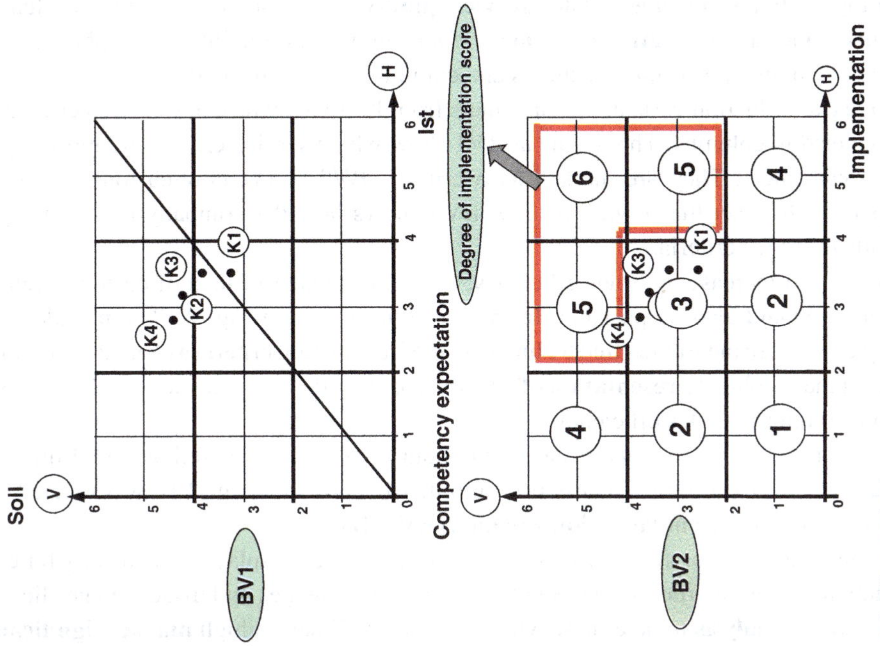

K = customer; BV = evaluation variant

Fig. 2.15 Portfolio-related customer satisfaction fulfilment rating

In Fig. 2.16, the customer-related **service quality** is analysed in 3 different evaluation variants. Important **evaluation criteria** are, for example, "availability by telephone, office equipment, politeness, critical faculties and communication/information".

For each evaluation variant, the customers from K1 to K4 who carry out this evaluation are assigned in columns. The results at BV1 show which service criteria are most important to customers. They are marked as A-criteria. BV2 shows how customers rate the competence to meet the service criteria. BV3 shows how the company implements the individual service criteria.

In order to increase the sales efficiency, a product-related instead of customer-related evaluation would also be possible. In the portfolio matrix in Fig. 2.17 some sales efficiency criteria are mentioned line by line with the 3 evaluation criteria assigned in columns.

From the graphical **presentation of results**, the sales department can see what needs to be done to improve sales efficiency.

In order to be able to make a statement about the **market attractiveness** of different products, the market attractiveness portfolio matrix shown in Fig. 2.18 was created and analysed over 4 different **valuation variants** (BV1–BV4).

In this example, too, the individual criteria results can be displayed graphically for each evaluation variant in order to see exactly where the advantages and disadvantages lie.

A **market analysis** to determine which products will have a high **market significance** in which countries in the future is shown in Fig. 2.19. Here, the products or sectors are named in rows, and the individual countries in columns. The graphical representation of the results shows which future markets require action on the supply side so that suppliers can focus on them.

The following Fig. 2.20 shows the **service level agreement** portfolio evaluation in relation to the requirement criteria for the 3 service providers available for selection.

The graphical representation of the results clearly shows that the service provider "D3" best meets the user's requirements.

2.4.4 Answers to Basic Question 4 "How?" (Which Processes with Which Roles?)

With regard to the answer to the basic question 4 "How?", it is about the aspect of how the optimization of the core and support processes within the value chain is to be realized, for example which costs, times, qualities are to be adhered to in the creation of products and services, i.e. the key activities.

Whereby it is clear from the answer to the previous basic question 3 "What?" what this product and service must look like in the result and what value contribution it must make in order to finally obtain in basic question 7 a clear statement about the economic success and the resulting sources of income for the company for this then completely described business model. Here, there is a wide range of process design and optimization analyses to make these processes error-free and waste-free. These include the standardization and

lfd Nr.	Evaluation criteria, e.g.:	Evaluation variant, e.g. BV1							
		*K1		K2		K3		K4	
		V	H	V	H	V	H	V	H
1	Availability by telephone	5	3	6	2	2	4	5	5
2	Communication/ Information	3	4	3	4	2	3	4	2
3	Qualification	5	3	4	3	3	4	3	4
4	Transaction processing	3	3	4	2	4	3	4	4
5	Office equipment	5	3	5	3	3	4	6	4
6	Politeness	3	2	3	5	3	3	4	3
7	Appearance	3	2	5	3	4	4	4	2
8	Critical faculties	3	3	5	3	3	3	4	3
9	Problem solving ability	3	3	4	2	3	3	4	3
Scale: 1 = low 6 = high	Σ C	33	26	39	27	27	31	38	30
	Σ C / n	3.5	3	4.4	2.9	2.9	3.4	4.1	3.2

*K = Kunde

BV = Valuation variant

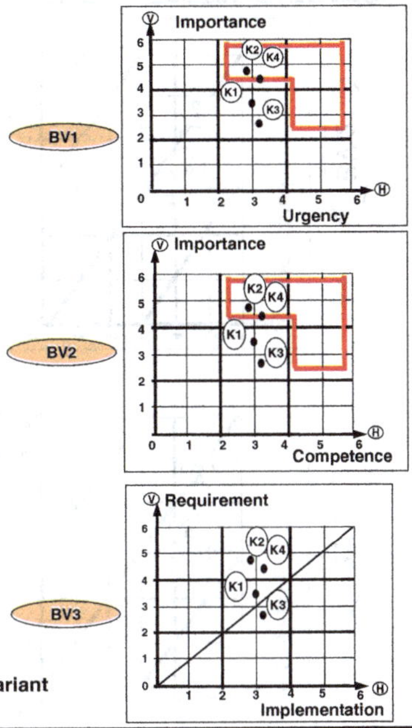

Fig. 2.16 Customer-related service quality portfolio

lfd Nr.	Sales efficiency, e.g.:	Valuation variant, e.g. BV1							
		*P1		P2		P3		P4	
		V	H	V	H	V	H	V	H
1	Offer management	4	3	4	4	4	2	4	2
2	Query/customer evaluation	3	3	5	3	5	2	5	2
3	Quotation tracking	3	5	3	4	6	3	3	3
4	Customer retention	5	4	5	3	5	4	5	3
5	Customer identification	3	3	3	2	4	4	5	3
6	Customer discussions	4	3	4	4	4	5	4	2
7	New customer acquisition	4	5	4	3	4	2	4	4
8	Establishing/Initiating Contact	5	4	5	2	5	2	5	2
9	After sale	2	4	2	3	3	2	4	3
10	Customer recovery	3	4	3	2	4	5	4	2
11	Order processing and follow-up	4	4	4	3	4	3	4	2
Scale: 1 = low; 6 = high	Σ C	36	38	38	30	44	31	43	26
	Σ C / n	3.6	3.8	3.8	3	4.4	3.1	4.3	2.6

*P = Product

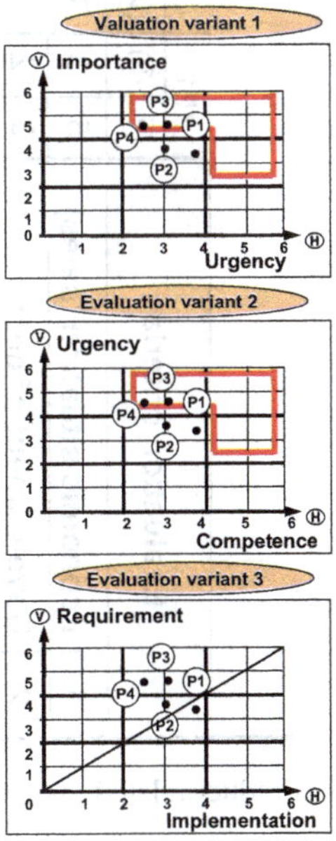

Fig. 2.17 Product-related sales efficiency portfolio assessment

	Evaluation criteria		*P1 V	*P1 H	P2 V	P2 H	P3 V	P3 H
1.	Economic situation (sales)		5	3	3	2	4	4
2.	Development of demand		3	2	3	3	3	5
3.	Availability of raw materials		3	4	4	3	5	4
4.	Environmental compatibility		2	3	5	3	3	4
5.	Competition		2	3	2	4	4	4
6.	Differentiation features		3	3	3	5	5	4
7.	Product innovation		4	2	3	5	5	4
8.	Product lifetime		3	4	2	4	4	3
9.	Product timeliness		4	2	4	4	4	4
10.	Product maturity		3	4	5	3	4	4
11.	Product investment		3	3	4	2	5	5
12.	Product profit margin		2	3	3	3	3	4
	Scale: 1 = low (poor) 6 = high (good)	ΣC	37	36	41	41	49	49
		$\frac{\Sigma C}{n}$	3.1	3	3.4	3.4	4.1	4.1

*P = products

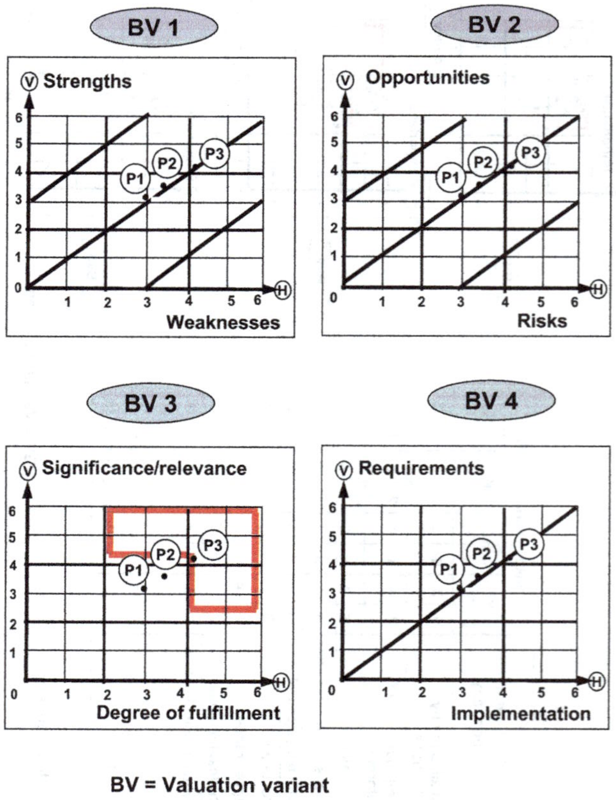

Fig. 2.18 Product-related market attractiveness analysis

	Future markets, e.g.:	A		B		C		D		E	
		V	H	V	H	V	H	V	H	V	H
1.	Machine tools and Manufacturing Systems	5	3	3	2	5	4	3	2	2	2
2.	Process engineering machinery and equipment	3	2	2	4	3	3	4	3	3	2
3.	Materials handling technology	3	4	3	4	2	3	2	3	2	2
4.	Drive technology	2	3	5	3	3	4	2	5	2	2
5.	Fluid technology	2	3	4	2	3	3	3	2	3	3
6.	Food processing and packaging machinery	5	3	4	3	3	4	3	2	2	2
7.	Construction and building material machines	3	3	2	2	4	3	3	2	2	2
8.	Printing and paper technology	5	3	3	2	2	4	3	2	2	2
9.	Pumps	2	3	5	3	3	4	2	5	2	2
10.	Plastics and rubber machinery	2	2	4	3	4	4	3	2	3	3
11.	Agricultural engineering	3	2	3	5	5	3	3	3	2	3
12.	Electrical engineering	3	2	2	3	4	4	2	2	3	2
13.	Medical technology	3	4	2	2	3	3	2	3	2	4
14.	Other	3	3	2	3	5	3	2	3	2	2
Scale: 1 = low, 6 = high	Σ C	42	40	44	41	50	49	37	39	32	33
	Σ C / n	3	2.8	3.1	2.9	3.6	3.5	2.6	2.7	2.2	2.3

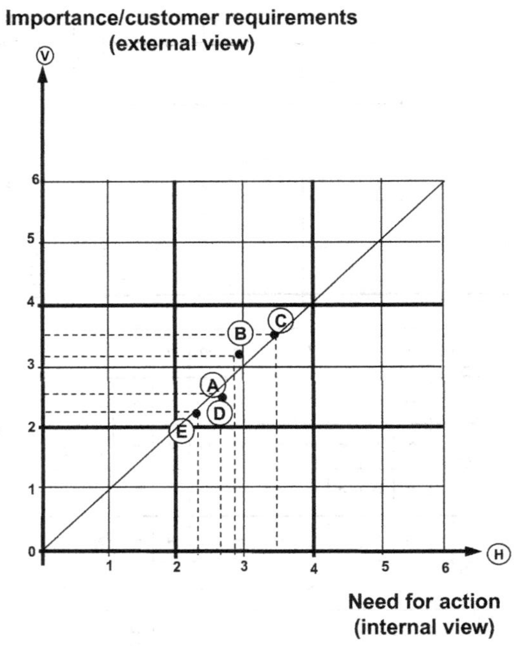

Legend:

A = Germany

B = Rest of Western Europe

C = North America

D = Central and Eastern European countries

E = Asia / Australia / Oceania

Fig. 2.19 Assessment portfolio on the importance of future markets

lfd. Nr.	Requirement criteria for service providers	D1		D2		D3	
		V	H	V	H	V	H
1	Accessibility	5	3	3	2	2	4
2	Flexibility	3	2	3	4	3	3
3	Response time	3	4	5	4	2	3
4	Reliability	2	3	5	3	3	4
5	Innovativeness	4	2	3	4	2	2
6	State of the art technology	2	3	4	4	2	3
7	Information management	3	3	5	2	4	5
8	Improvement management	4	2	4	4	3	3
9	Contribution to customer value	3	4	4	2	2	5
Scale: 1 = low 6 = high	ΣC	29	26	36	29	23	32
	$\frac{\Sigma C}{n}$	3.2	2.9	4	3.2	2.6	3.6

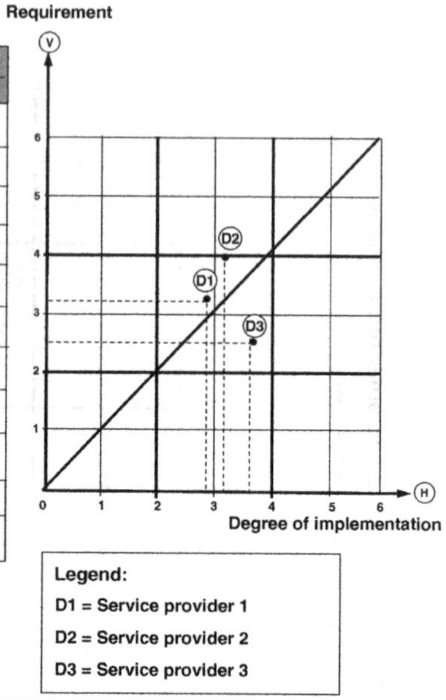

Fig. 2.20 Service Level Agreement (SLA) portfolio assessment

process potential activation analyses described in detail in Sect. 3.13. They are performed as part of a role-based **end-to-end process analysis**, for example with the BPM tool Sycat. Process digitization, which is also to be considered as a main point in this basic question 4, is a separate focus topic – dealt with in Chap. 5 – with a large number of different digitization analyses to be performed.

In order to analyze which processes have the greatest potential for improvement, the one-dimensional process potential prioritization assessment portfolio matrix shown in Fig. 2.21 can be used with V (importance for company) and H (potential for improvement).

All processes that are arranged in the upper right segment of the portfolio diagram are particularly suitable for the potential improvement view. In this case, the "P3" process and the "P3" process.

Another process improvement potential analysis, this time in public administration with the goal of reducing bureaucracy in conjunction with a benefit assessment, is shown in Fig. 2.22. The starting points for improvement shown in the portfolio matrix result from the actual process and weak point analysis with subsequent target concept development. As the graphical comparison between the target and actual process shows, the target process has far fewer roles and is therefore much simpler and faster to run through. In evaluation variant (BV) 1 with "V = potential for improvement" and "H = implementation", it is determined for the participants arranged in columns, in this case "citizen, authority, business", who benefits most from the localized improvements. For Assessment Variant (BV) 2 with "V = Effort, H = Benefit", it is determined who benefits the most from the above three stakeholders. In this example, it is then the regional business community.

lfd Nr.	(V) Significance for companies, e.g.:	*P1	P2	P3	P4	P5
1	Core competence	2	3	4	3	3
2	Competitive share	2	4	4	4	2
3	Process costs	4	3	4	5	3
4	Impact of process results	3	2	4	2	3
5	Tied up employee capacities	2	3	4	1	3
6	Support of the production network	2	2	4	3	2
7	Degree of innovation	3	2	4	4	3
Scale: 1 = low 6 = high	ΣC	18	19	28	22	19
	$\frac{\Sigma C}{n}$	2.6	2.7	4	3.1	2.7

lfd Nr.	(H) Potential for improvement, e.g.:	*P1	P2	P3	P4	P5
1	Responsibilities regulated	3	5	3	2	2
2	Decision-making authority define	2	4	2	2	2
3	High error frequency and possibility of errors	1	3	1	1	1
4	High process quality	3	5	3	3	2
5	Low number of interfaces	4	2	4	3	2
6	Shorter lead time	4	4	4	2	2
7	High standardization	2	4	2	3	2
Scale: 1 = low 6 = high	ΣC	19	27	19	16	13
	$\frac{\Sigma C}{n}$	2.7	3.9	2.7	2.3	1.9

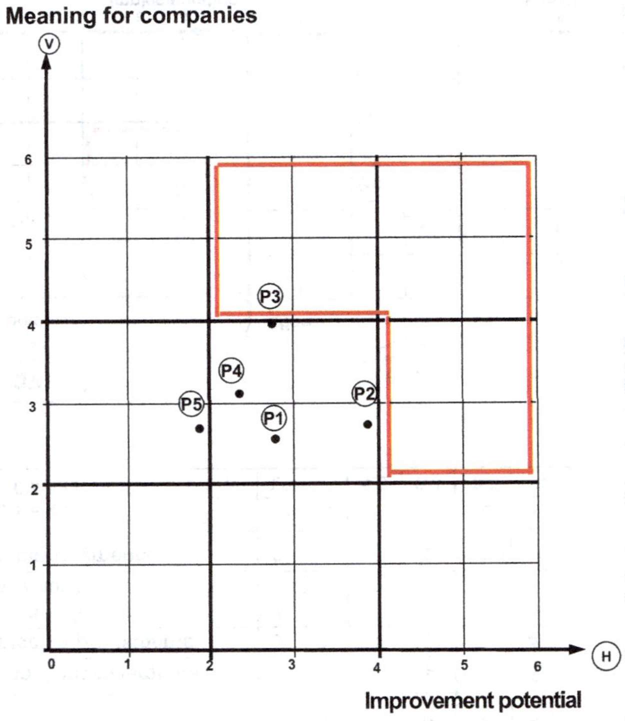

*P = Process

Fig. 2.21 Process potential prioritization assessment portfolio

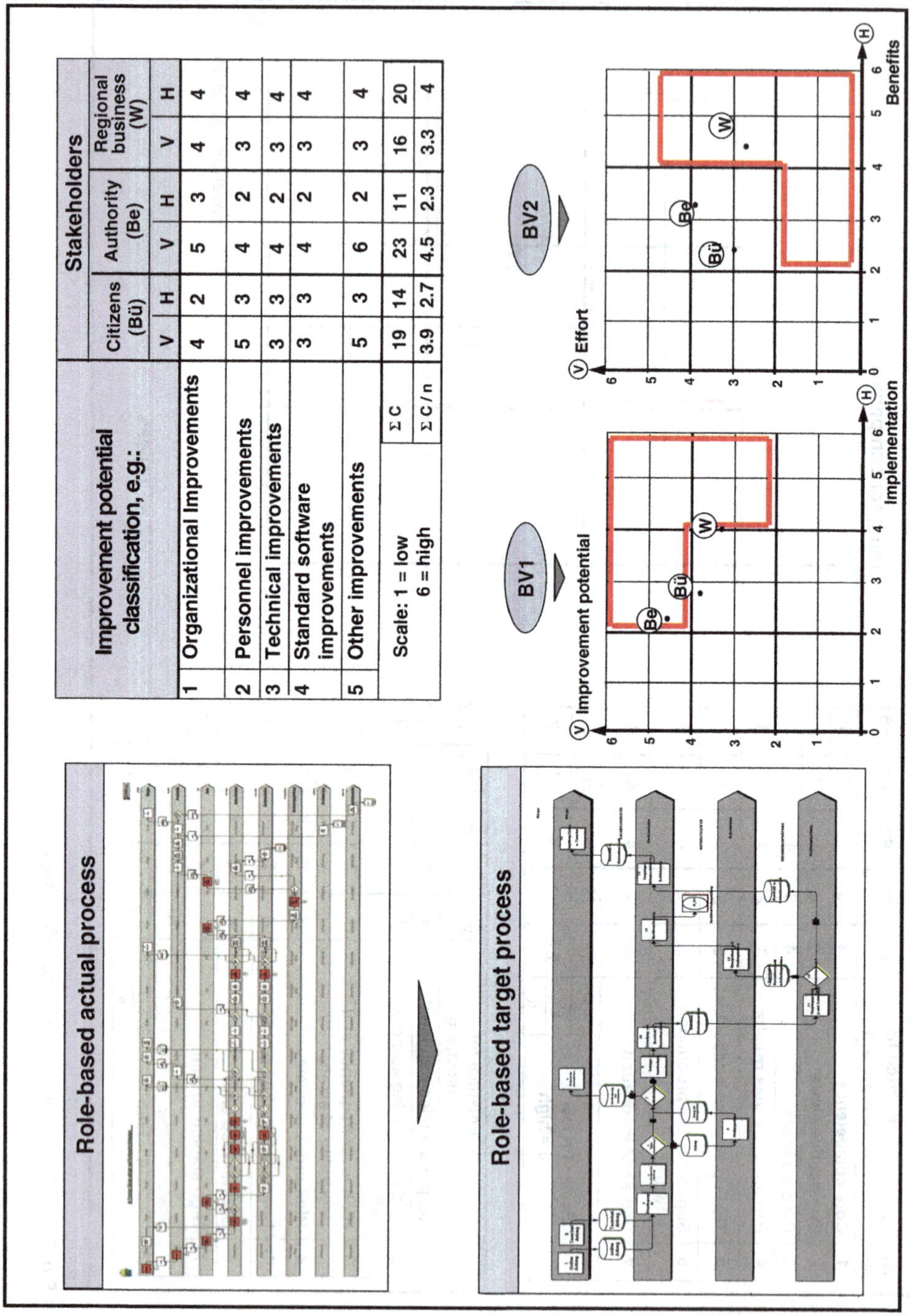

Improvement potential classification, e.g.:	Citizens (Bü) V	Citizens (Bü) H	Authority (Be) V	Authority (Be) H	Regional business (W) V	Regional business (W) H
1 Organizational Improvements	4	2	5	3	4	4
2 Personnel improvements	5	3	4	2	3	4
3 Technical improvements	3	3	4	2	3	4
4 Standard software improvements	3	3	4	2	3	4
5 Other improvements	5	3	6	2	3	4
Σ C	19	14	23	11	16	20
Σ C / n	3.9	2.7	4.5	2.3	3.3	4

Fig. 2.22 Process improvement potential and benefit assessment in administration

lfd. Nr.	Requirement criteria for service providers	Need for change (V)			
		P1	P2	P3	P4
1.	High employee turnover				
2.	High error rate				
3.	High process costs				
4.	Process errors are outside the tolerance limit				
5.	Customer satisfaction not sufficient				
6.	Process performance not stable				
7.	Process cycle time too high				
8.	Insufficient process standardization				
Scale: 1 = low	ΣC				
6 = high	ΣC / n				

lfd. Nr.	Requirement criteria for service providers	Knowledge requirement (H)			
		P1	P2	P3	P4
1.	High change service				
2.	High coordination effort				
3.	A lot of order-related information				
4.	High environmental dynamics				
5.	Use of complex work equipment				
6.	High customer and service orientation				
7.	High individuality of business transactions				
8.	High qualification requirements				
Scale: 1 = low	ΣC				
6 = high	ΣC / n				

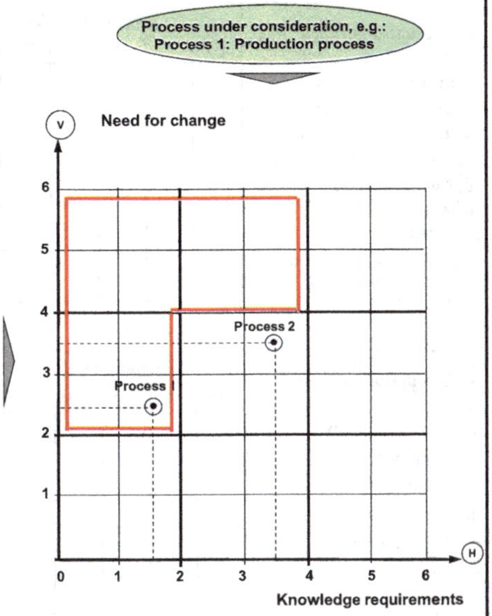

Fig. 2.23 Improvement- and knowledge-need-based business process prioritization via portfolio assessment

To determine which change and knowledge needs are present in the **process potential analyses**, the portfolio matrix shown in Fig. 2.23 can be used for business process prioritization. Preference should be given to improving the processes that have the highest change with the lowest knowledge requirement because these are the easiest to optimize.

Another portfolio-based process selection and prioritization evaluation in the context of **process optimization** is shown in Fig. 2.24. The processes arranged in columns are evaluated in terms of V = importance and H = feasibility. All processes in the upper right portfolio diagram have the highest priority for optimization. Using the available optimization goal and measure catalogs, goal-measure trees can now be cascaded using the MITO tool via the **MITO king path** to systematically implement the optimization. After implementation, a method-supported **evaluation** is carried out to determine whether the measures have actually become effective.

A further **process assessment** is made, as shown in Fig. 2.25, using the external assessment criteria shown in the one-dimensional portfolio matrix, which reflect the market view, and the internal assessment criteria, which show the feasibility of the **market requirements**. All processes that are in the upper left portfolio diagram have feasibility issues. Therefore, specific considerations should be made as to how the feasibility of the individual criteria can be improved in order to meet the external market requirements.

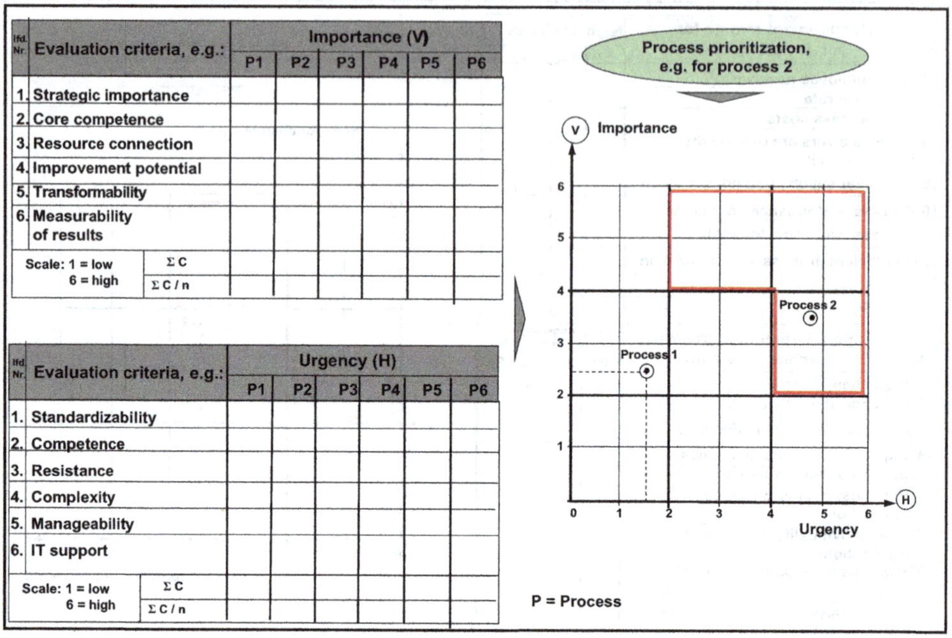

Fig. 2.24 Process selection and prioritization portfolio

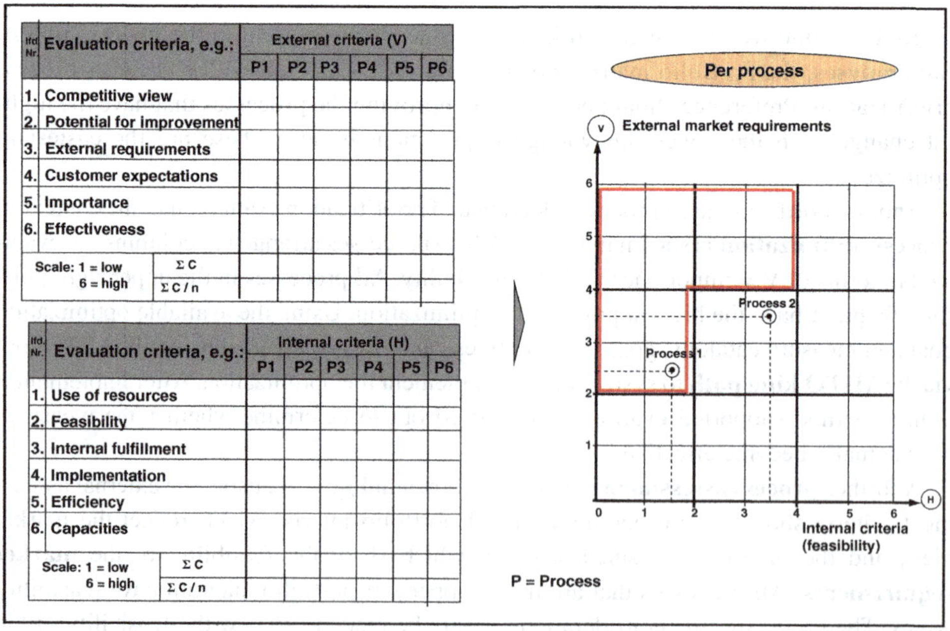

Fig. 2.25 Process assessment portfolio

There are a large number of other **design approaches** to this basic question 4 "How?", such as CIP, Lean, 6 Sigma, GPS, for which reference portfolio matrices have also already been created. This will be discussed in detail in Chap. 3.

2.4.5 Answers to Basic Question 5 "With What?" (What Resources, Staff and Infrastructure?)

Basic question 5 is about identifying the **key resources** required to carry out the core processes in the horizontal value chain of the processes described in detail in basic question 4. Particularly important is the selection of qualified employees in line with requirements by means of competence and **capability analyses**. The same applies to the selection of technology and systems for the required machinery, equipment and IT applications. On the basis of the documentation in the BPMN 2.0 Swimlane process representation carried out during the process analyses, the required resources and applications can be derived on a role basis.

In particular, within the framework of personnel management and **personnel development**, a **qualification needs analysis** with the MITO method tool can be used to determine which employees still need to be qualified for the tasks and process steps described in the roles.

Figure 2.26 starts with a **MOB analysis** of the parts and products, whether they should be bought (buy) or made (make).

The graphical representation of the results in the portfolio diagram can be used to clearly determine whether components should be manufactured externally or in-house for the parts assigned by column. All components below the diagonal should be produced in-house, all components above this diagonal should be produced externally.

Figure 2.27 shows a process-related **outsourcing analysis** using the outsourcing criteria arranged in rows. The service processes that may be outsourced are arranged in columns in the portfolio matrix. They are evaluated according to "V = outsourcing suitability" and "H = feasibility". All service processes located in the upper right portfolio diagram segment are particularly suitable for outsourcing. Here it should be checked how they can be outsourced to external service providers.

In order to find out in which processes the necessary specifications with regard to the planning, management and controlling of these processes are the most time-consuming or, conversely, the easiest, the portfolio matrix shown in Fig. 2.28 with "V = effectiveness and H = effort" can be applied. After the evaluation, the 5 processes with the least effort are located in the upper left portfolio diagram and, conversely, the processes that are the most time-consuming to perform are located in the lower right portfolio diagram segment.

A further evaluation of the evaluation results in addition to an automatically generated ranking calculation is the classification of the process criteria via an **A, B, C classification**. The user can create the classes himself in the MITO tool.

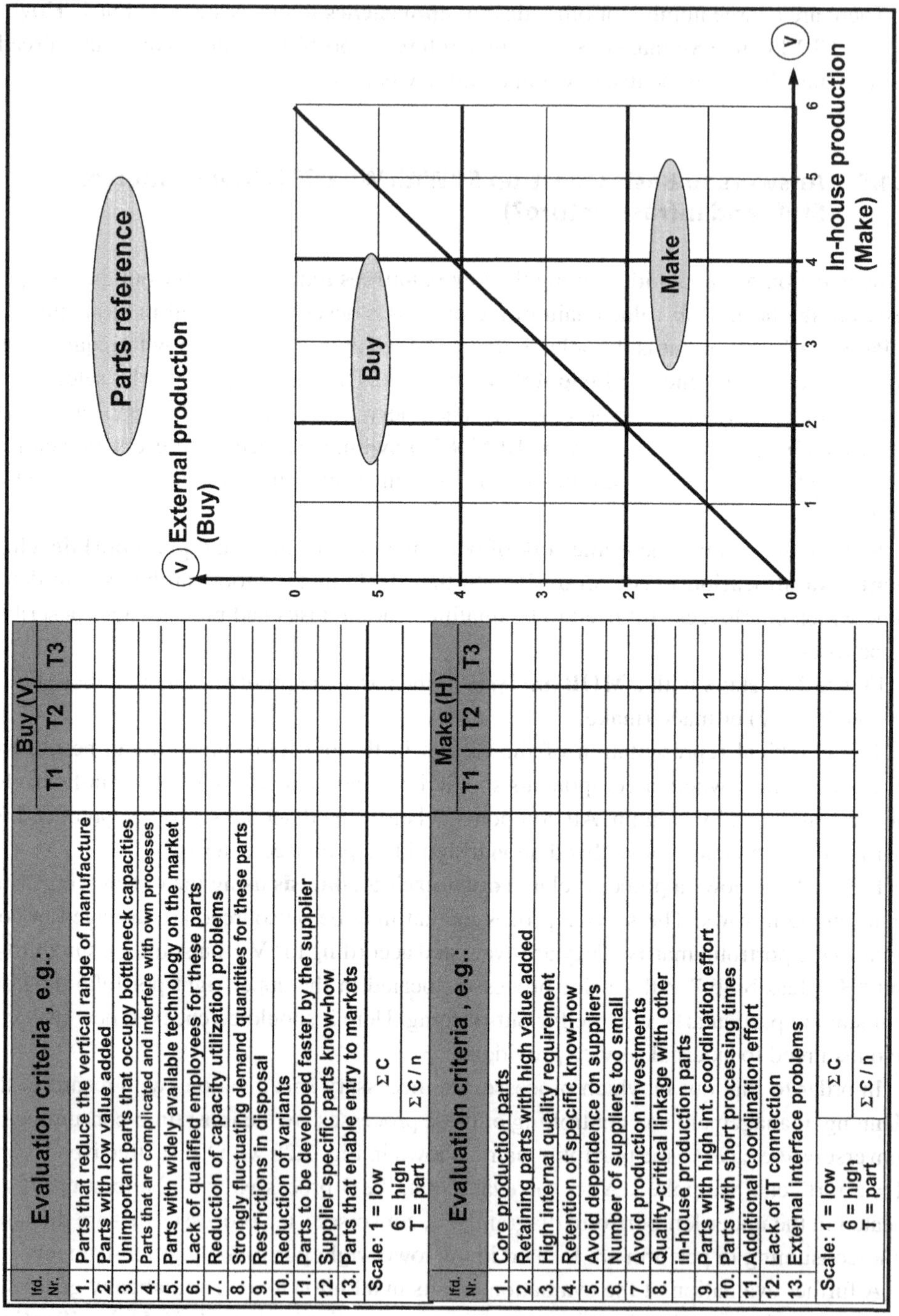

Fig. 2.26 Make or buy (MOB) portfolio

lfd Nr.	Evaluation criteria, e.g.:	*P1		P2		P3		P4		P5	
		V	H	V	H	V	H	V	H	V	H
1	Overhead cost reductions in indirect areas.	5	3	6	2	5	4	3	3	3	4
2	Variabilization of fixed costs	3	4	3	4	4	3	4	2	2	5
3	Creation of a new cost awareness	5	3	4	3	4	4	2	4	2	4
4	Reduction of follow-up costs	3	3	4	2	4	3	4	4	2	4
5	Cost advantages for external service providers	5	3	5	3	5	4	3	3	4	4
6	Increased core competence with external service providers	3	2	3	5	5	3	3	3	3	5
7	Leaner own processes	3	2	5	3	4	4	3	2	2	4
8	Building and space savings	3	3	5	3	5	3	4	3	3	4
9	Problem-free adaptation to increasing demand	3	3	4	2	5	3	4	3	2	4
10	Rapid availability	3	3	3	2	6	4	3	4	3	4
11	Increased flexibility in competition	4	2	5	3	4	3	4	3	2	5
12	Concentration on own core competence	2	3	5	2	3	4	2	2	3	4
Scale: 1 = low, 6 = high	ΣC	42	34	52	39	54	42	38	36	32	51
	$\frac{\Sigma C}{n}$	3.5	2.8	4.3	3.3	4.5	3.5	3.2	3	2.7	4.3

*P = Process

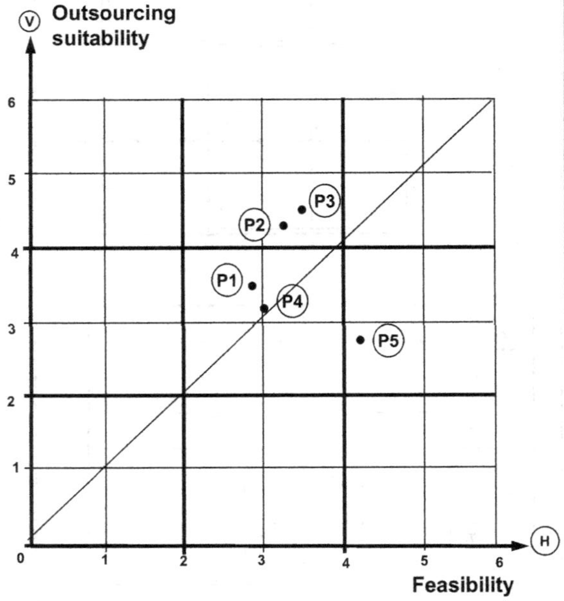

Fig. 2.27 Process-related outsourcing evaluation portfolio

Design fields (G), e.g.:		P1		P2		P3		P4	
		V	H	V	H	V	H	V	H
1.	Strategy specification								
2.	Target agreements								
3.	Planning								
4.	Control								
5.	Controlling								
6.	Visualization								
7.	Work and cleanliness								
8.	Value stream								
9.	PDCA cycle								
10.	Benchmarking								
Scale: 1 = low 6 = high	ΣC								
	ΣC / n								

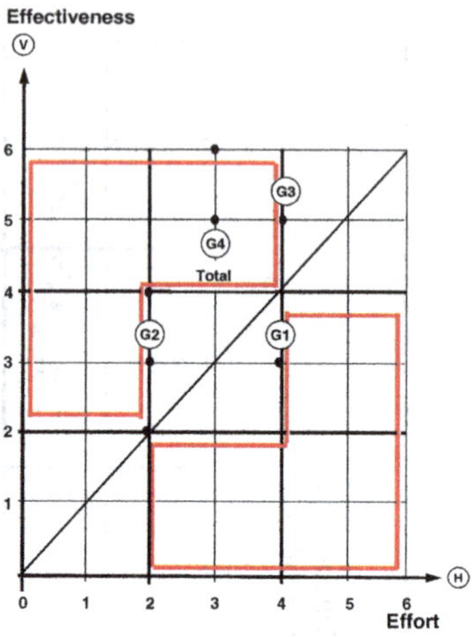

Fig. 2.28 ABC analysis method effectiveness assessment portfolio

Satisfied employees are the highest potential for success in a company. Supervisors play the decisive role here. Using the employee satisfaction portfolio matrix shown in Fig. 2.29 with the satisfaction criteria listed line by line, the employee satisfaction evaluation can be carried out according to different evaluation variants, both generally and in relation to specific managers. With evaluation variant (BV) 1 with the evaluation dimensions "V = requirement" and "H = implementation" as well as with evaluation variant (BV) 2 with "V = importance" and "H = urgency". Another variant would be "V = Target" and "H = Actual". The graphical representation of the results in the portfolio diagram clearly shows the need for action for the respective **satisfaction criterion** for the initiation of measures to improve employee satisfaction. For this purpose, prepared catalogues of objectives and measures are again available for the MITO King's Path.

Another evaluation variant for measuring the **satisfaction score** in the context of the corporate goal achievement review would be BV3 with "V = importance" and "H = degree of fulfilment". The result of the evaluation of the satisfaction criteria is shown in the portfolio diagram. Here, the satisfaction scores are entered within the 9 portfolio segments. The grade 6 is in the upper right segment. The grade 5 is assigned to the left of it as well as below it. In this way, there is a clear, reliable statement, e.g. in the case of an audit, as to whether the target value has been achieved or not. In the example shown, this is only the case for employee "M4".

lfd Nr.	Satisfaction evaluation criteria, e.g.:	M1		M2		M3		M4	
		V	H	V	H	V	H	V	H
1	Leadership behavior	4	3	4	4	3	2	4	2
2	Information transfer	3	3	5	3	3	2	5	2
3	Working atmosphere	3	5	3	4	2	3	3	3
4	Trust culture	5	4	5	3	3	2	5	3
5	Cooperation	3	3	3	2	2	2	5	3
6	Works council	4	3	4	4	1	2	4	2
7	Communication	4	5	4	3	3	2	4	4
8	Recognition	5	4	5	2	3	2	5	2
9	Remuneration	2	4	2	3	3	3	4	3
10	Working hours	3	4	3	2	2	2	4	2
11	Work content	2	6	5	2	2	2	5	3
12	Working environment	2	2	4	4	3	3	3	2
13	Qualification	3	4	5	2	2	3	4	2
14	Social facilities	5	3	4	3	2	2	6	2
Scale: 1 = low, 6 = high	ΣC	45	50	51	38	34	32	56	33
	$\frac{\Sigma C}{n}$	3.5	3.8	4	2.9	2.4	2.3	4.3	2.5

M = employees

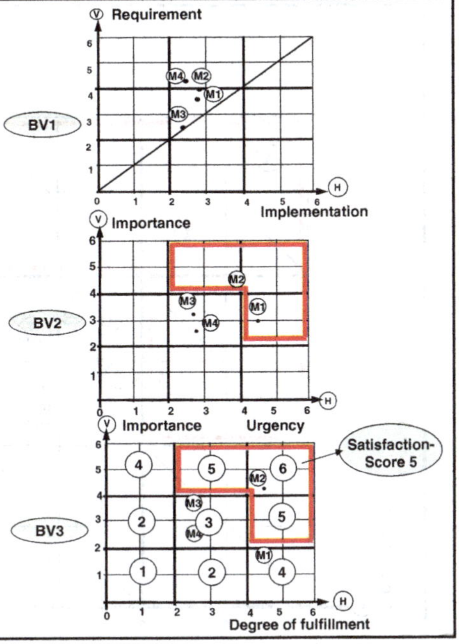

Fig. 2.29 Portfolio-related employee satisfaction rating

2.4.6 Answers to Basic Question 6 "With Whom?" (Which Partners and Suppliers?)

The aspect of selecting **key partners** is the focus of basic question 6 "with whom?", after the **key resources** have been determined in basic question 5, which are necessary within the key processes in basic question 4 for the creation of the product and service offerings previously defined for this purpose. Systematic supplier evaluations provide support here. However, since the procurement of the entire infrastructure is involved, all tangible and intangible resources for whose provision external partners are responsible are affected. IT, human resources and services, for example, are playing an increasingly important role.

Figure 2.30 shows a **supplier selection portfolio matrix**. Using several selection clusters, such as price, quality, logistics, partnership, innovation, technology, the evaluation criteria contained therein are evaluated for the suppliers assigned in columns with "V = importance" and "H = fulfillment level".

The portfolio diagram shows the evaluation results. At the same time, an additional **maturity assessment** is carried out in order to identify the delivery maturity level of the individual supplier.

The individual criteria evaluation can be used to determine exactly which requirements are not met by each supplier.

lfd Nr.	Evaluation criteria	L1 A	L1 B	L2 A	L2 B	L3 A	L3 B	L4 A	L4 B	L5 A	L5 B
1.	**Price**										
1.1	Price level	5	3	6	2	5	4	3	2	2	2
1.2	Price behavior	3	2	3	4	3	3	4	3	3	2
1.3	Risk of price increases	3	4	3	4	2	3	2	3	2	2
1.4	Cooperation in pricing	6	3	5	3	3	4	2	5	2	2
1.5	Price behavior vis-à-vis competitors	2	3	4	2	3	3	3	2	3	3
2.	**Quality**										
2.1	Quality indicators	5	3	4	3	3	4	3	2	2	2
2.2	Cooperation (quality)	3	3	4	2	4	3	3	2	2	2
2.3	Quality capability	5	3	3	2	2	4	3	2	2	2
2.4	Quality system	5	3	5	3	3	4	2	5	2	2
2.5	Compliance with technical specifications	2	2	4	3	4	4	3	2	3	3
3.	**Logistics**										
3.1	Adherence to delivery dates	3	2	3	5	5	3	3	3	2	3
3.2	Quantity adherence	3	2	5	3	4	4	2	2	3	2
3.3	Completeness	3	4	2	2	3	3	2	3	2	4
3.4	Level of service	3	3	5	3	5	3	2	3	2	2
3.5	Availability of information	2	3	4	3	4	5	4	2	2	2
4.	**Partnership**										
4.1	Service	2	4	3	2	2	3	3	3	5	2
4.2	Reliability	3	3	3	2	2	4	5	4	3	3
4.3	Openness	4	3	6	2	3	3	6	3	4	4
4.4	Credibility	5	3	2	5	4	3	2	3	4	3
4.5	Security	3	3	4	2	2	3	3	5	2	4
5.	**Innovations**										
5.1	Added value	5	3	2	5	4	3	2	3	4	3
5.2	Compatibility	3	3	4	2	2	3	3	5	2	3
5.3	Investment protection	3	3	4	3	3	2	4	4	4	3
5.4	Improvements	3	2	2	3	3	2	3	4	2	5
5.5	System supplier	3	5	3	4	2	4	2	2	2	2
6.	**Technology**										
6.1	Degree of automation	4	2	5	3	3	2	2	2	5	4
6.2	Use of EDV	3	2	3	3	2	3	3	4	2	3
6.3	Machinery	5	4	4	3	4	2	3	3	4	4
6.4	Flexibility	4	3	3	4	4	5	4	4	3	3
6.5	Documentation of measurement and test results	5	3	3	5	3	4	2	4	3	2
Scale: 1 = low, 6 = high	ΣC	108	89	121	87	96	99	88	94	83	81
	$\frac{\Sigma C}{n}$	3.6	3.0	4.0	2.9	3.2	3.3	2.9	3.1	2.8	2.7

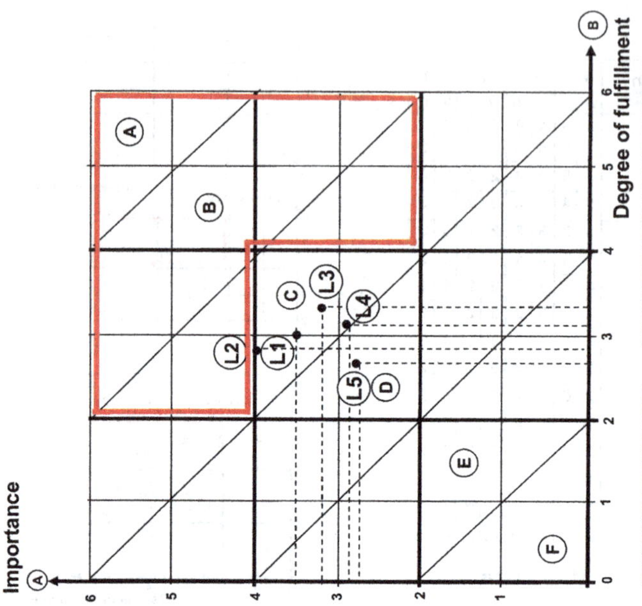

Legend:
L1 = Supplier1
L2 = Supplier 2
L3 = Supplier 3
L4 = Supplier 4
L5 = Supplier 5

Maturity levels:	
Ⓐ	Outstanding
Ⓑ	Good
Ⓒ	Satisfactory
Ⓓ	Sufficient
Ⓔ	Poor
Ⓕ	Very Poor

Fig. 2.30 Supplier evaluation portfolio

The following Fig. 2.31 shows the single-column **portfolio matrix** for the supplier-related portfolio evaluation with regard to the selection under the aspect of the dependency of the consumption value and demand regularity. The graphical result shows the classification according to A, B and C suppliers.

The systematic solution or selection evaluation for different problems, e.g. for process simplification or IT system introduction, is shown in the portfolio matrix in Fig. 2.32. In the analyses, the evaluation dimensions refer to the determination of the opportunities/risks or strengths/weaknesses for BV1 and to the determination of the solution costs/solution time expenditure for BV2.

The distribution of power between the supplier and the buyer can be determined using the portfolio matrix shown in Fig. 2.33. The result diagram shows the distribution of power. The result diagram shows the distribution of power. Here, the power of the supplier is in proportion to the power of the demander. The diagonal line shows the equilibrium between the supplier and the demander. Above the diagonal the supplier has more power, below the diagonal the supplier.

More and more companies that carry out their orders in the form of projects for their customers are endeavouring to carry out a project analysis with regard to the risks that may arise and the complexity inherent in the project before **accepting the project order**. In the following, a 2-step project classification analysis with the MITO method tool is described, which gives the user a clear statement regarding the degree of risk and the degree of complexity of the subsequent project, in order to obtain a clean decision-making about the project order acceptance.

The starting point for the project risk analysis are the possible risk types that can occur in this project and also risks that are analyzed 2-dimensionally in terms of their probability of occurrence and their impact. The user can modify this portfolio matrix according to his own ideas. Each of the line-by-line evaluation criteria stored in the portfolio matrices is also assigned a score scale of 1–6. Generally, the grade 1 = low, grade 6 = very high. However, it is also possible to develop a separate grading scale for each criterion. The results of this analysis are presented graphically in the portfolio diagram shown in Fig. 2.34 or in a radar diagram. At the same time, the project risk level is classified from 1 (not at all) to 6 (very high). A high risk level is in the upper right corner of the three MITO portfolio segments.

In the second step, a project complexity analysis takes place. Here, a MITO portfolio matrix is also the starting point. In this matrix, the complexity drivers are listed. They are evaluated according to "V = project coordination effort" and "H = implementation scope", again in 2 dimensions. Here, too, the graphical representation of results in the portfolio diagram shows which projects have the highest degree of complexity.

Subsequently, in stage 2, as also shown in Fig. 1.1, the projects can now be represented once again in the project portfolio matrix in relation to "V = risk class and H = complexity level". Whereby the scores for the respective project evaluations are taken from the previously graphically presented result portfolio diagrams project class and **project complexity** for the respective project. The overall result is a transparent project classification of all

lfd. Nr.	Evaluation criteria, e.g.:	Consumption value (V)		
		L1	L2	L3
1.	Degree of concentration of suppliers	3	4	4
2.	Position of the product in the production life cycle	2	5	3
3.	Market growth	4	4	4
4.	Market share of supplier	2	5	2
5.	Market entry barriers for new suppliers	3	6	3
6.	Market entry barriers for suppliers	2	3	3
7.	Uniqueness of the product	3	4	4
8.	Performance of the supplier	2	4	2
9.	Image of the supplier	4	5	3
10.	Capacity utilization	2	4	3
11.	Supplier switching costs	1	6	4
12.	Possibilities to become a system supplier	2	4	2
Scale: 1 = low, 6 = high	Σ C	29	54	37
	Σ C / n	2.4	4.5	3.1

lfd. Nr.	Evaluation criteria, e.g.:	Regularity of demand (H)		
		L1	L2	L3
1.	In-house production	3	5	3
2.	Flexibility of demand structure	4	2	4
3.	Procurement market share	4	4	4
4.	Supplier switching costs	2	6	3
5.	Image of the customer	2	4	2
6.	Continuity of demand	1	3	3
7.	Number of audited suppliers	2	4	2
8.	Economic forecast	2	3	4
9.	Company size	3	5	5
10.	Innovation potential	3	4	3
11.	Number of end customers	3	5	2
12.	Development potential	2	4	3
Scale: 1 = low, 6 = high	Σ C	31	49	38
	Σ C / n	2.6	4.1	3.2

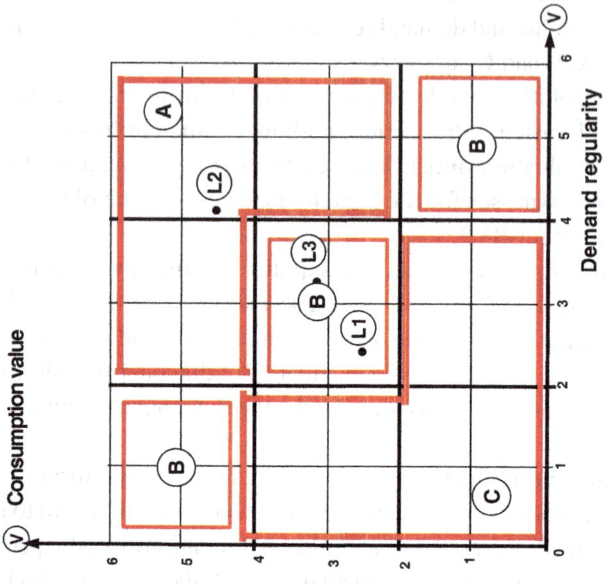

*L = supplier

Fig. 2.31 Supplier-related portfolio evaluation

lfd Nr.	Solution indicator, e.g.:	*L1		L2		L3		L4	
		V	H	V	H	V	H	V	H
1	Sustainability	4	3	4	4	4	2	4	2
2	Reduction of interfaces	3	3	5	3	4	2	5	2
3	Return on investment	3	5	3	4	3	3	3	3
4	Follow-up costs (1 = high)	5	4	5	3	5	4	5	3
5	Investment costs (1 = high)	3	3	3	2	4	4	5	3
6	Handling	4	3	4	4	4	5	4	2
7	Ease of maintenance	4	5	4	3	4	2	4	4
8	Training effort	5	4	5	2	3	2	5	2
9	Compatibility	2	4	2	3	3	2	4	3
10	Flexibility	3	4	3	2	4	5	4	2
11	Suitability	2	6	5	2	2	4	5	3
12	Customer satisfaction	2	2	4	4	4	5	3	2
13	Error reduction	3	4	5	2	4	4	4	2
14	Recyclable	5	3	4	3	5	5	6	2
Scale: 1 = low, 6 = high	ΣC	45	50	51	38	49	47	56	33
	$\frac{\Sigma C}{n}$	3.5	3.8	4	2.9	3.8	3.6	4.3	2.5

*L = Solution or area

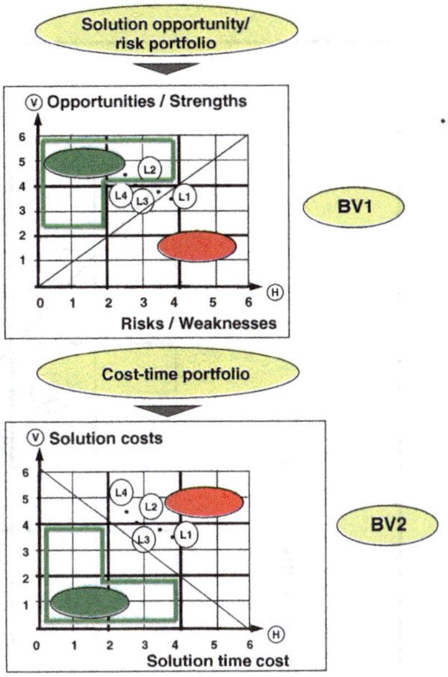

Fig. 2.32 Systematic solution evaluation and selection portfolio

projects in category A B C from which the degree of risk and complexity can be immediately read graphically. The management can see very precisely which decisions it has to make with regard to the project order acceptance.

2.4.7 Answers to Basic Question 7 "How Much?" (Revenue Model)

The final and ultimately decisive aspect in basic question 7 "**Value contribution**?" is the answer to the competitive success of the aforementioned business activities within the individual **MITO model segments**. For this purpose, the product and service offering must be completely transparent internally in terms of costs in order to assess whether the measurable and tangible value contribution created for the customer can also be provided economically by the company. This requires a clean pre- and post-calculation. The value proposition to the customer must pay off economically for the company through the resulting revenue sources, primarily through the product and service itself, but also through additional services, seminars, training or cooperations. The financial accounting and cost accounting applications available in the company can be used to provide detailed digital evidence of successful business activity. The method-supported **target fulfillment measurements** described in Chap. 6 for a wide variety of design specifications in the form of assessments, reviews, evaluations and audits also play an important role here.

lfd Nr.	Ⓥ Power of the provider, e.g.:		*A1	A2	A3	A4
1.	Total number of providers		3	2	4	3
2.	Market share of the provider		2	5	5	4
3.	Power of the supplier		2	4	4	2
4.	Countertrade		4	5	2	3
	Scale: 1 = low, 6 = high	Σ C	11	16	15	12
		Σ C / n	2.8	4	3.6	3

lfd Nr.	Ⓗ Power of the demand party, e.g.:		*L1	L2	L3	L4
1.	Performance of the buyer		3	5	3	5
2.	Image of the customer		4	2	4	5
3.	Capacity utilization		4	4	4	4
4.	Economic forecast		2	3	3	4
5.	Supplier switching costs		2	4	2	3
6.	Possibility of integration		1	3	3	4
	Scale: 1 = low, 6 = high	Σ C	16	21	19	25
		Σ C / n	2.7	3.5	3.2	4.2

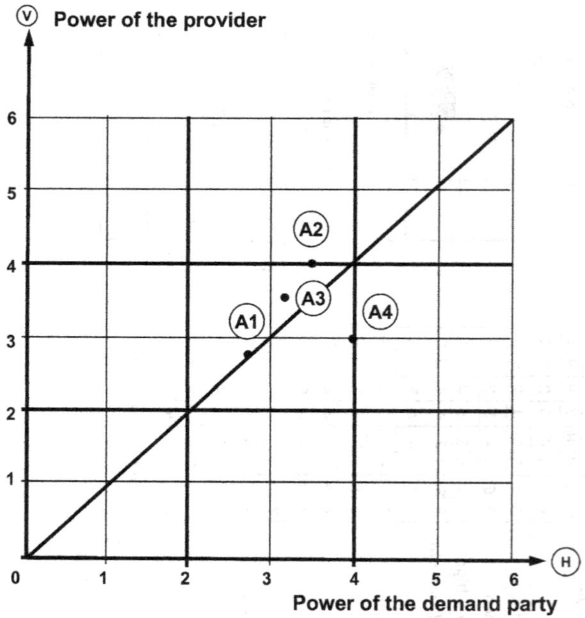

Fig. 2.33 Power question assessment portfolio

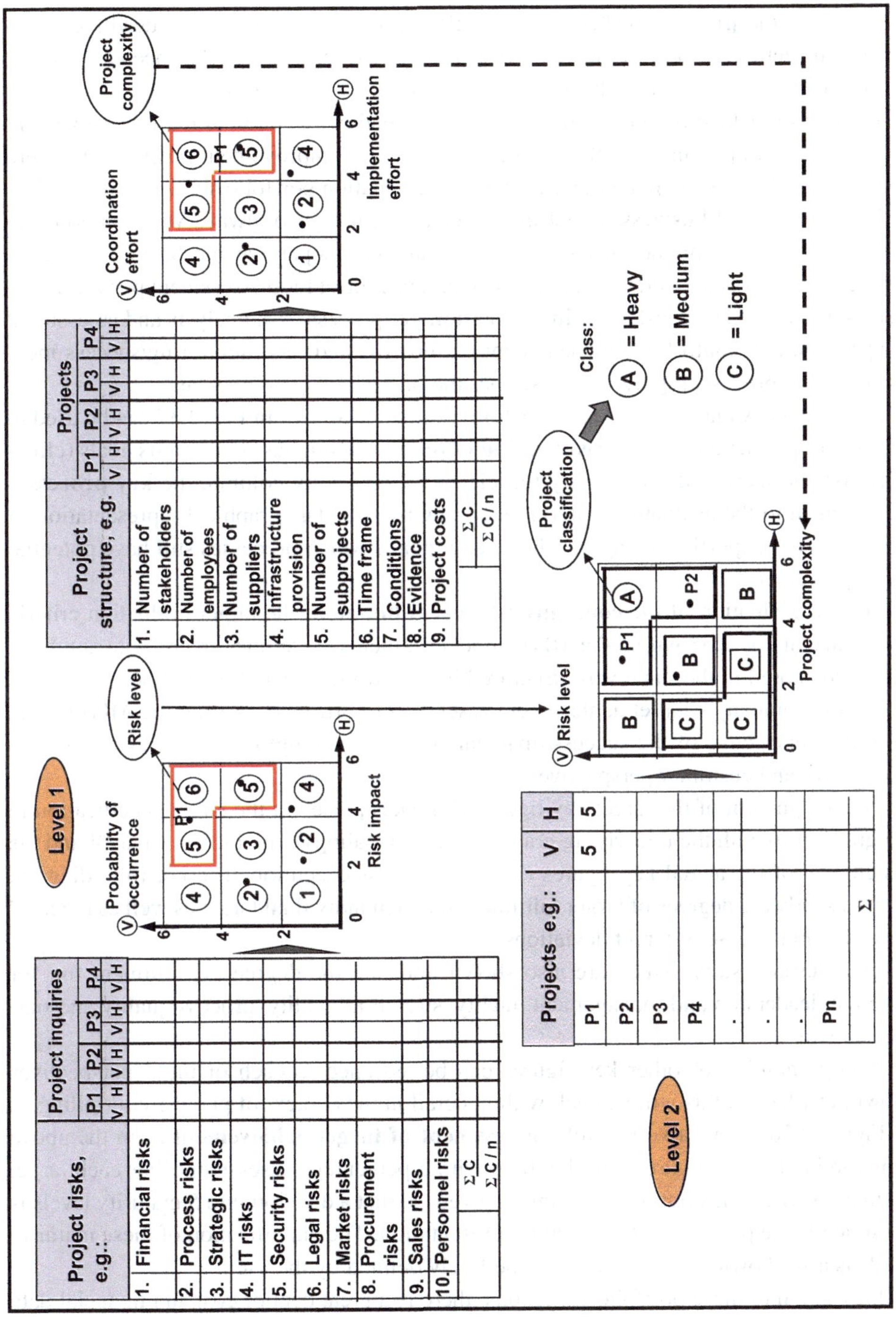

Fig. 2.34 MITO tool-supported 2-step project classification analysis

Based on the **process performance results** in terms of costs, times, deadlines, customer satisfaction, it can be assessed whether the end-to-end process has been carried out successfully and the specified business objectives have been achieved.

In order to make this analysis from the target/actual comparison of these improvement potentials, the importance for the company (V) and the improvement potential (H) were compared in the process potential prioritization evaluation portfolio shown in Fig. 2.35.

For a successful business model implementation, it is also always very important to determine the risks of the business activity that may jeopardize the business success. Figure 2.36 shows the operational risk management control loop assessment portfolio. The 4 steps are divided into **risk type identification** per process, risk analysis and assessment per process, risk control and management per process and risk monitoring/success measurement per process. Figure 2.36 describes the procedure again in detail.

The efficiency and effectiveness portfolio evaluation shown in Fig. 2.37 can be used to determine whether a **process organization implementation** has achieved its goals (effectiveness) and increased profitability (efficiency). Column by column, the **key processes** are assigned to the evaluation criteria listed row by row. The graphical representation of the results in the portfolio diagram shows at a glance which processes still have potential for improvement.

For the evaluation of the **company's target fulfillment**, the target evaluation criteria mentioned in Fig. 2.38 within the MITO model segments are applied in absolute numbers, which are stored in the same way structured in a portfolio matrix line by line. This figure shows the company's target achievement assessment portfolio based on the MITO cycle from the perspective of the success/financial perspective, employee perspective, process perspective and customer perspective.

The assignment of the target key figures (V) takes place via the target specification in the grades 1–6 with the underlying grade divisions (scaling) explained in Chap. 4 and the assignment of the actual key figures (H) after process execution. The portfolio diagram shows exactly the degrees of target fulfilment for each individual target as well as the need for action in the case of target deviations.

The cluster results, which are also shown, indicate the degree of fulfilment for, for example, leadership and management quality, structural quality, process quality and outcome quality.

A large number of other key figures can be assigned to each of the 5 perspectives shown. In Chap. 4, this will be dealt with in detail in the context of process controlling.

Figure 2.38 shows a very similar **assessment of target achievement** as in the above example in absolute figures, but this time with a percentage assessment. For each target evaluation criterion, a number of points is given, so that a division into 5 maturity levels is possible via the percentage total result representation. The classification of these maturity levels is also shown in Fig. 2.39. It can be freely defined by the user.

In addition to these portfolio valuations, there is a great deal of cost and financial data from financial and operational accounting available to answer basic question 7.

lfd Nr.	(V) Meaning for companies, e.g.:	*P1	P2	P3	P4	P5
1	Core competence	2	3	4	3	3
2	Competitive share	2	4	4	4	2
3	Process costs	4	3	4	5	3
4	Impact of process results	3	2	4	2	3
5	Tied-up employee capacities	2	3	4	1	3
6	Support of the production network	2	2	4	3	2
7	Degree of innovation	3	2	4	4	3
	Scale: 1 = low, 6 = high — ΣC	18	19	28	22	19
	ΣC / n	2.6	2.7	4	3.1	2.7

lfd Nr.	(H) Potential for improvement, e.g.:	*P1	P2	P3	P4	P5
1	Responsibilities regulated	3	5	3	2	2
2	Decision-making authority define	2	4	2	2	2
3	High error frequency and possibility of errors	1	3	1	1	1
4	High process quality	3	5	3	3	2
5	Low number of interfaces	4	2	4	3	2
6	Shorter lead time	4	4	4	2	2
7	High level of standardization	2	4	2	3	2
	Scale: 1 = low, 6 = high — ΣC	19	27	19	16	13
	ΣC / n	2.7	3.9	2.7	2.3	1.9

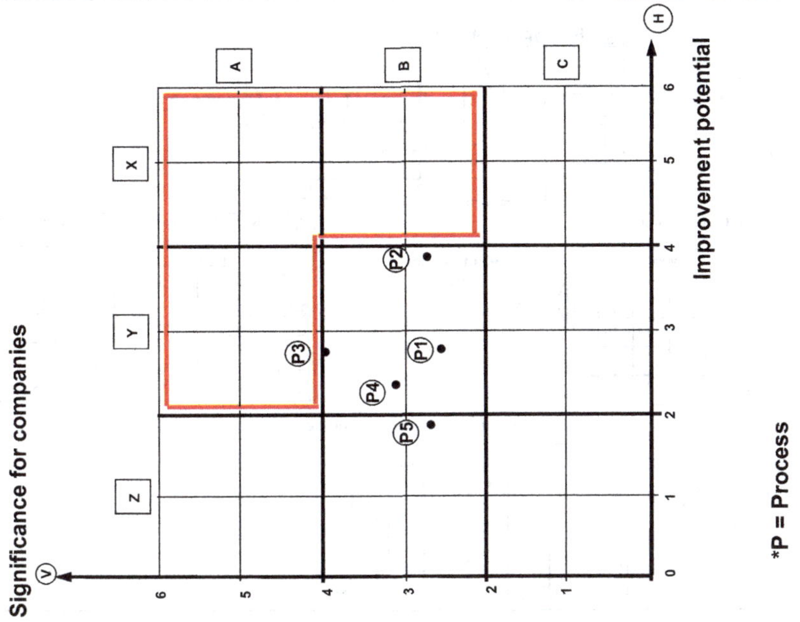

Fig. 2.35 Process potential prioritization assessment portfolio

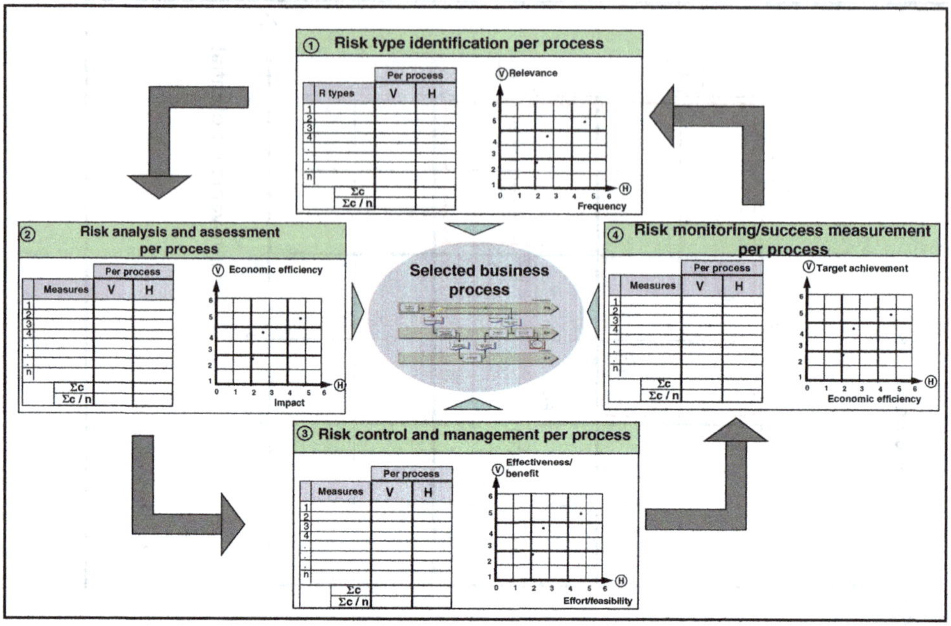

Fig. 2.36 Operational risk management control loop assessment portfolio

The portfolio matrices shown as examples for answering the 7 basic W-questions are only an excerpt from a number of approximately 3500 available reference checklists for approx. 70 organizational design topics that can be systematically processed with the MITO method tool. Further application examples are also shown in the following chapters.

2.5 MITO Business Model-Related Corporate Goal, Strategy and Action Requirement Analyses

After answering the 7 W basic questions, there is a clear idea among those responsible about the **business purpose** with a concrete statement about which customers with which products or services the customer benefit is to be achieved with the customer target group through an optimal value chain. To this end, it is now important to define a **corporate goal** and strategy. Different procedures are conceivable here, whereby the MITO business model is always used as a structural specification for the goal, strategy and action field derivation in the approach presented here.

In principle, a large number of different organizational design parameters with the underlying success potentials and success factors must be analyzed and linked to an overall optimum in order to achieve the corporate goals and implement the corporate purpose. The **business model tasks** are shown in Fig. 2.40. They are assigned to the five MITO model segments as follows:

Evaluation criteria	P1 V	P1 H	P2 V	P2 H	P3 V	P3 H	P4 V	P4 H	P5 V	P5 H	P6 V	P6 H	P7 V	P7 H
1. Success factors are known	3	4	2	2	4	3	4	4	3	4	3	3	4	4
2. Strategy is given	2	3	3	2	3	4	5	4	3	4	3	3	2	3
3. Goals are defined	5	3	3	2	4	4	5	3	4	3	3	3	2	5
4. Processes are identified	3	2	4	3	4	2	4	3	3	3	4	4	3	4
5. Processes are documented	4	2	3	2	5	2	3	4	4	3	5	3	2	4
6. Process management is implemented	2	2	2	3	5	4	6	4	4	3	4	3	2	5
7. KVP takes place	5	3	2	2	3	3	4	3	2	5	4	4	3	4
8. Process measurements and evaluations	4	3	3	2	4	2	5	2	3	4	4	3	2	5
Scale: 1 = low, 6 = high — Σ C	28	22	22	18	32	24	36	27	26	29	30	26	20	34
$\frac{\Sigma C}{n}$	3.5	2.8	2.8	2.3	4	3	4.5	3.4	3.3	3.6	3.8	3.3	2.5	4.3

Key processes:

P1 = Sales process
P2 = Development process
P3 = Procurement process
P4 = Planning process
P5 = Production process
P6 = Shipping process
P7 = Disposal process

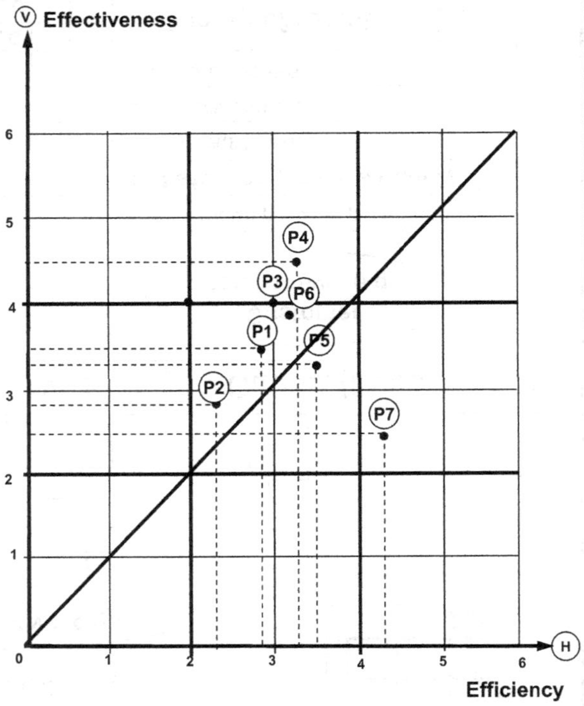

Fig. 2.37 Key process-related effectiveness and efficiency portfolio

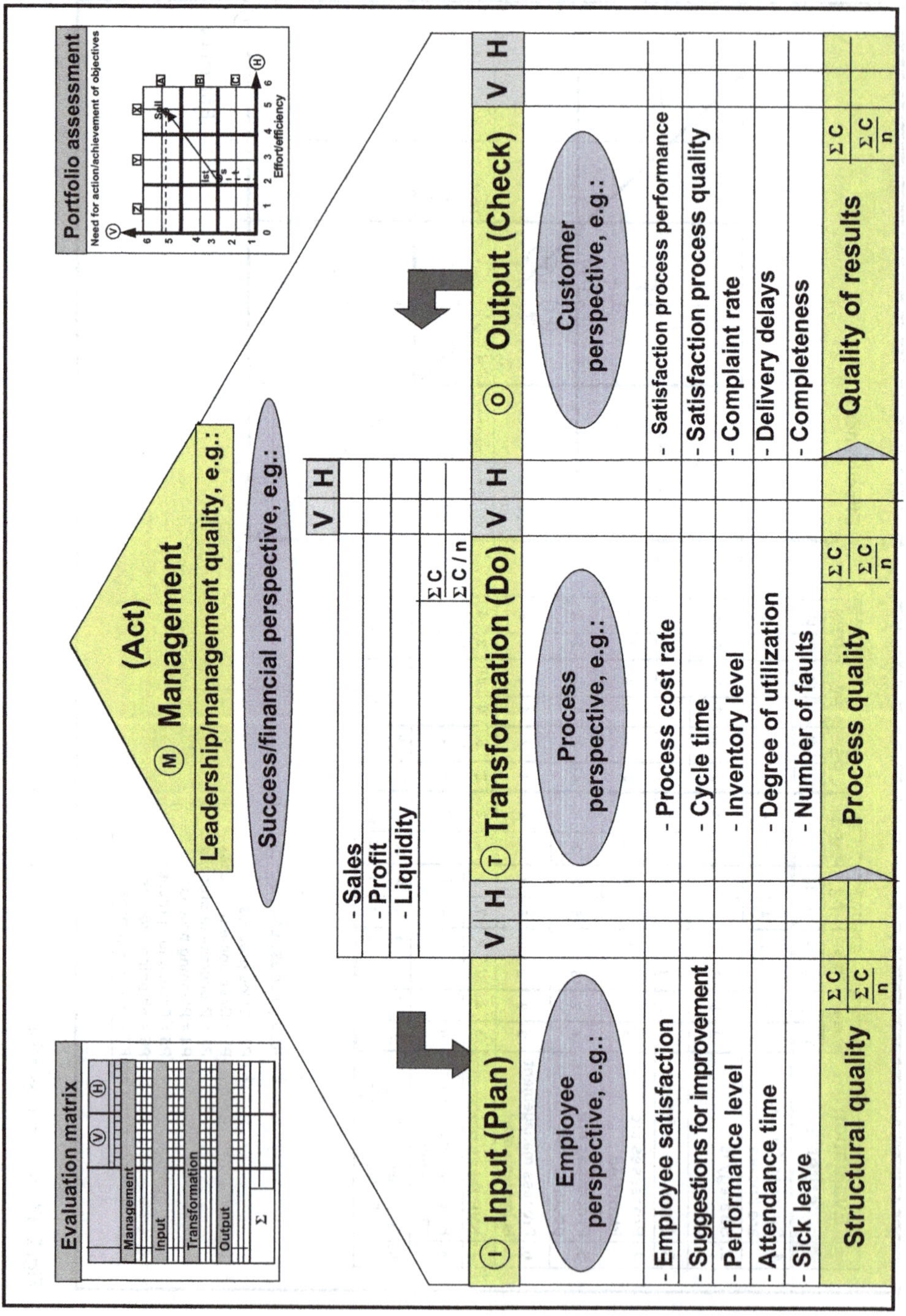

Fig. 2.38 Company target achievement assessment portfolio

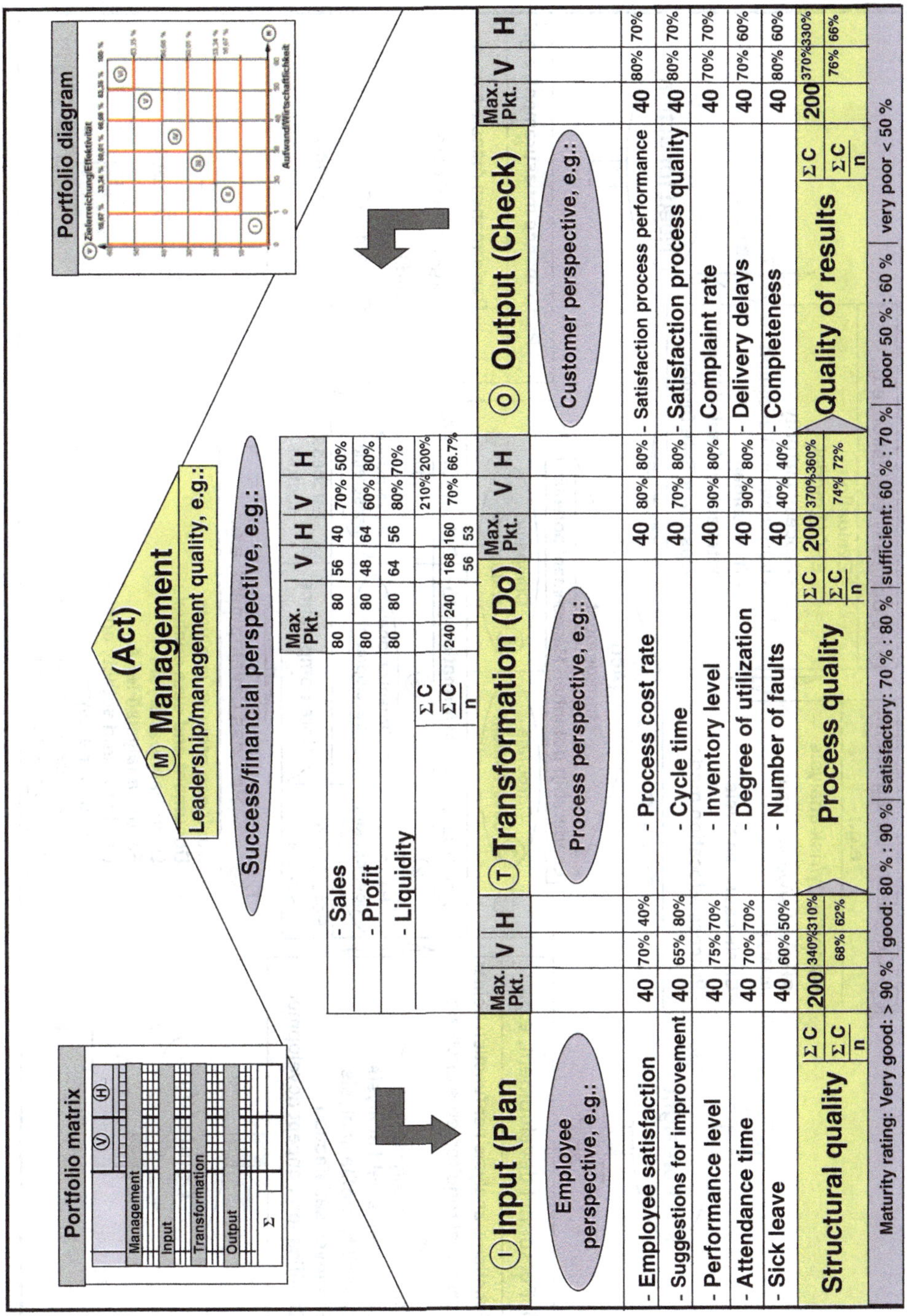

Fig. 2.39 Percentage company target achievement assessment portfolio

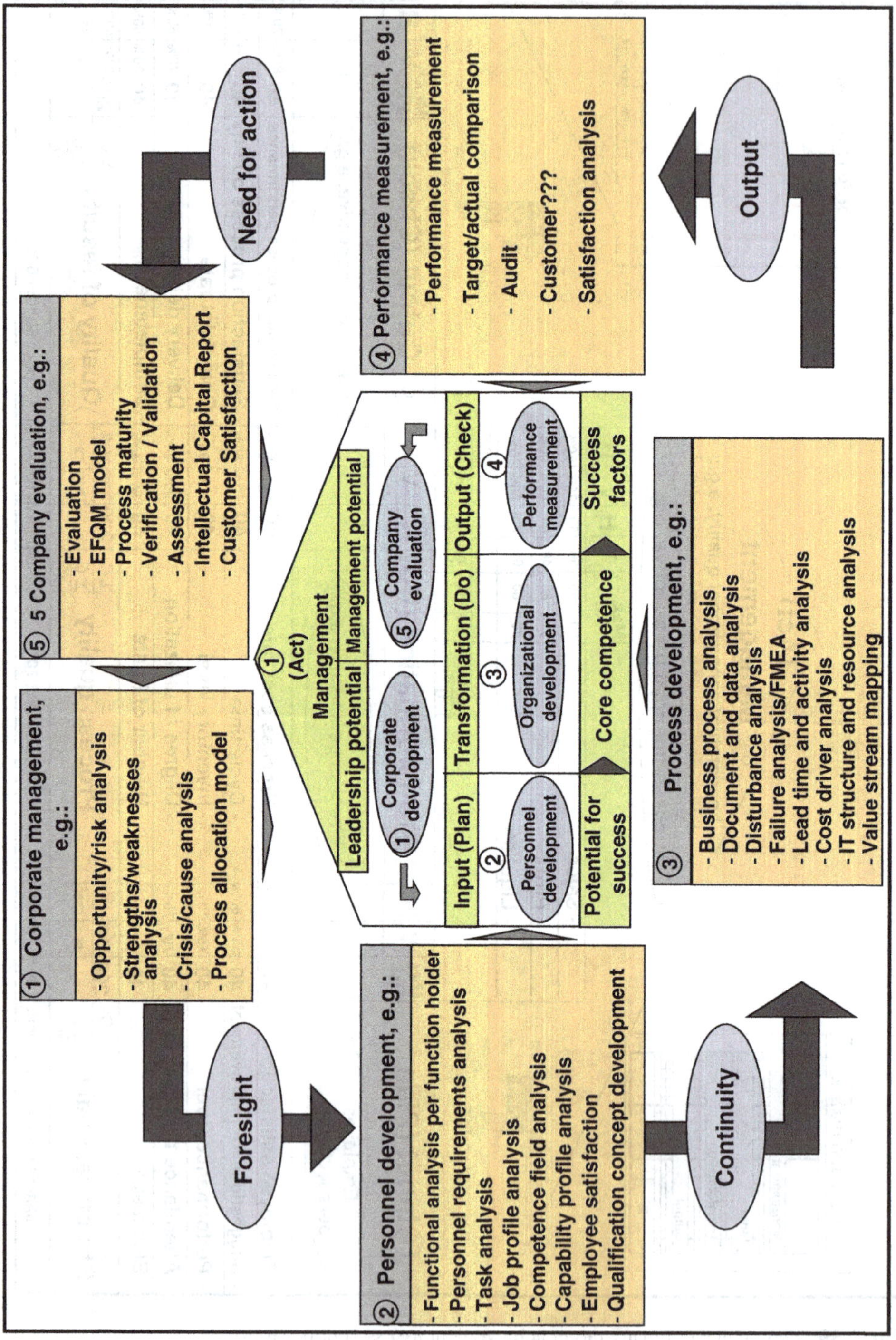

Fig. 2.40 MITO model-related company analysis, diagnosis and evaluation

1. MITO management segment with the core task of "corporate development".
2. MITO input segment with the core task "personnel development".
3. MITO transformation segment with the core task "core process development".
4. MITO output segment with the core task "Outstanding product or service offering".
5. MITO management segment with the main task of "business evaluation and improvement".

The business model task analysis also includes the customer segment upstream of the MITO model with the main task "customer benefit generation" and the supplier or partner segment with the main task "partner integration".

A high level of methodological competence is required for the necessary analyses, diagnoses, therapies and evaluations to answer the resulting questions of these five core tasks, which are very well covered by the MITO methodological tool. For each of the core tasks, Fig. 2.40 lists the analyses that management must perform in order to meet the requirements for implementing the business model. In relation to the management function with leadership and direction, these are, for example, opportunity/risk analyses, strengths/weaknesses analyses, crisis/cause analyses and others. The necessary analyses for the core tasks of personnel development, process development and evaluation are also listed – without claiming to be exhaustive. The reference and knowledge object for many of these analyses is the previously role-based documented business process. As described in detail in the following Chap. 3, the role here provides the process participants with the factual, temporal, and logical framework for action with regard to the flow of work, e.g., tasks, capability profiles, resources, and the flow of information, e.g., data, documents, IT applications with the associated rights and duties, together with the interfaces to the other roles in the process. The role-based process representation ensures that the analyses can be carried out in a context-related manner. In order to systematically determine the need for action for these design parameters and then to initiate suitable measures, an action requirement analysis can be performed in a targeted manner. In the portfolio matrix shown in Fig. 2.41, possible **action requirement starting points** are named within the 4 MITO model segments "Management, Input, Transformation, Output", which can be evaluated according to different evaluation variants BV1 to BV4.

As shown in Fig. 2.41, four **evaluation variants** (BV) are used here as examples, each of which evaluates a specific design view in two dimensions. Assessment variant 1 (BV1) with "V = target" and "H = actual" is concerned with determining the deviation in the individual portfolio criteria in order to subsequently derive targets and measures for closing the coverage gap. The ideal solution can be seen in the portfolio diagram on the diagonal. All action requirements that lie on this diagonal in the results diagram are optimally fulfilled because the "target" corresponds directly to the "actual". All criteria above the diagonal are not fully met and need to be improved. All criteria below the diagonal are more than fulfilled.

The evaluation variant (BV) 2 is concerned with determining the criteria for which the degree of implementation is not yet sufficient. These are all criteria that are assigned in the

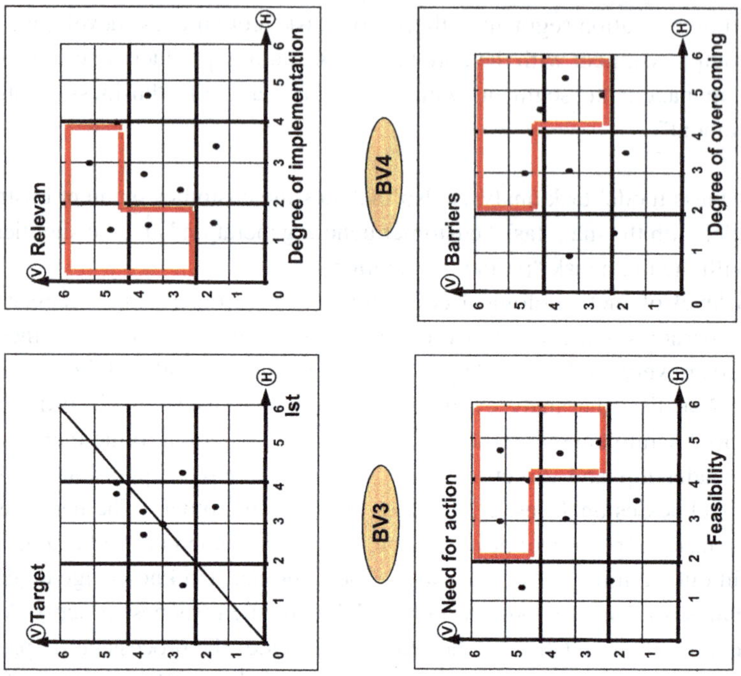

lfd Nr.	Need for action, e.g.:	BV1 V	BV1 H	BV2 V	BV2 H	BV3 V	BV3 H	BV4 V	BV4 H
1.	Management (leadership/management-related), e.g.:								
1.1	Profit/DB/Sales								
1.2	Legal compliance								
1.3	Return on equity								
1.4	Liquidity								
1.5	Capital structure								
1.6	Return on sales								
1.7	Risk minimization								
1.8	Creditworthiness								
2.	Input (employee/infrastructure-related), e.g.								
2.1	Job satisfaction								
2.2	Participation								
2.3	Income increase								
2.4	Motivation								
2.5	Social security								
2.6	Humanization								
2.7	Social/personal integration								
2.8	Qualification								
3.	Transformation (prozessbezogen), z. B.:								
3.1	Simplification								
3.2	Standardization								
3.3	Decentralization								
3.4	Normalization								
3.5	Functional integration								
3.6	Interface reduction								
3.7	Hierarchy reduction								
3.8	Job security								
4.	Output (customer-related), e.g.:								
4.1	Customer satisfaction								
4.2	Image								
4.3	Market share								
4.4	Customer communication								
4.5	Product reliability								
4.6	Returns								
4.7	Product defects								
4.8	Service level/offer								
Scale: 1 = low 6 = high	ΣC								
	ΣC / n								

BV = evaluation variant

Fig. 2.41 MITO model-related target field and action requirement portfolio

portfolio diagram in the upper left corner of the results display. These criteria have a high relevance for implementation, but this is not reflected in the degree of implementation. A further evaluation variant (BV) 3, which is not shown here, results from the relevance findings of evaluation variant 2. Here, the need for action for the individual criteria is evaluated again vertically. In the horizontal evaluation, it is checked whether the feasibility for implementation is also given. All evaluation criteria in the upper right corner of the portfolio diagram have a high degree of feasibility and should therefore be tackled. In contrast, all criteria that are located in the upper left corner of the portfolio diagram have a high need for action, but the feasibility is so low that one should not deal with these criteria unnecessarily. In evaluation variant 4, the possible barriers that prevent implementation are once again localized for the individual evaluation criteria. Therefore, these barriers are put in relation to the degree of overcoming. Here, the situation is such that all serious barriers assigned in the upper right portfolio diagram segment can be overcome by suitable measures.

However, the user can also consider many other evaluation variants in the business model action requirement analysis in order to localize even more necessary design views in this way. The result of the action requirement analyses is then further used in the MITO tool royal road, i.e. in the derivation of the interlinked objectives, measures and to-do lists.

2.6 Systematic Business Model Change Analysis

In the search for the right strategies for a successful implementation of the company-specific business model for sustainable competitive success, a business model change analysis could also be the starting point.

The goal is to determine the target, strategy, and action areas that must lead to a digital realignment of the business model due to the technological changes taking place. For this purpose, there is also a MITO reference checklist with the evaluation dimensions "V = change relevance, H = impact" for localizing the most relevant changes and their effects. The main starting points in the upper right portfolio segment result from the presentation of results.

Via a further two-dimensional evaluation with the MITO method tool in terms of "V = turnover/profit and H = costs/expense", the economic framework conditions can be determined for each individual change criterion. The results of the revenue and profit consideration/evaluation and the cost and expense consideration are shown in Fig. 2.42. The target field is located in the upper left portfolio diagram area. The changes made increase revenue and profit at low cost.

As Fig. 2.42 shows, process analyses should be carried out in the upper right portfolio diagram segment if sales are satisfactory, i.e. there are enough customers and they demand the products or services. However, if product or service manufacturing is done at too high a cost and no profits can be realized, processes should be simplified and accelerated. By using process analysis design as the main approach, an efficient and effective process

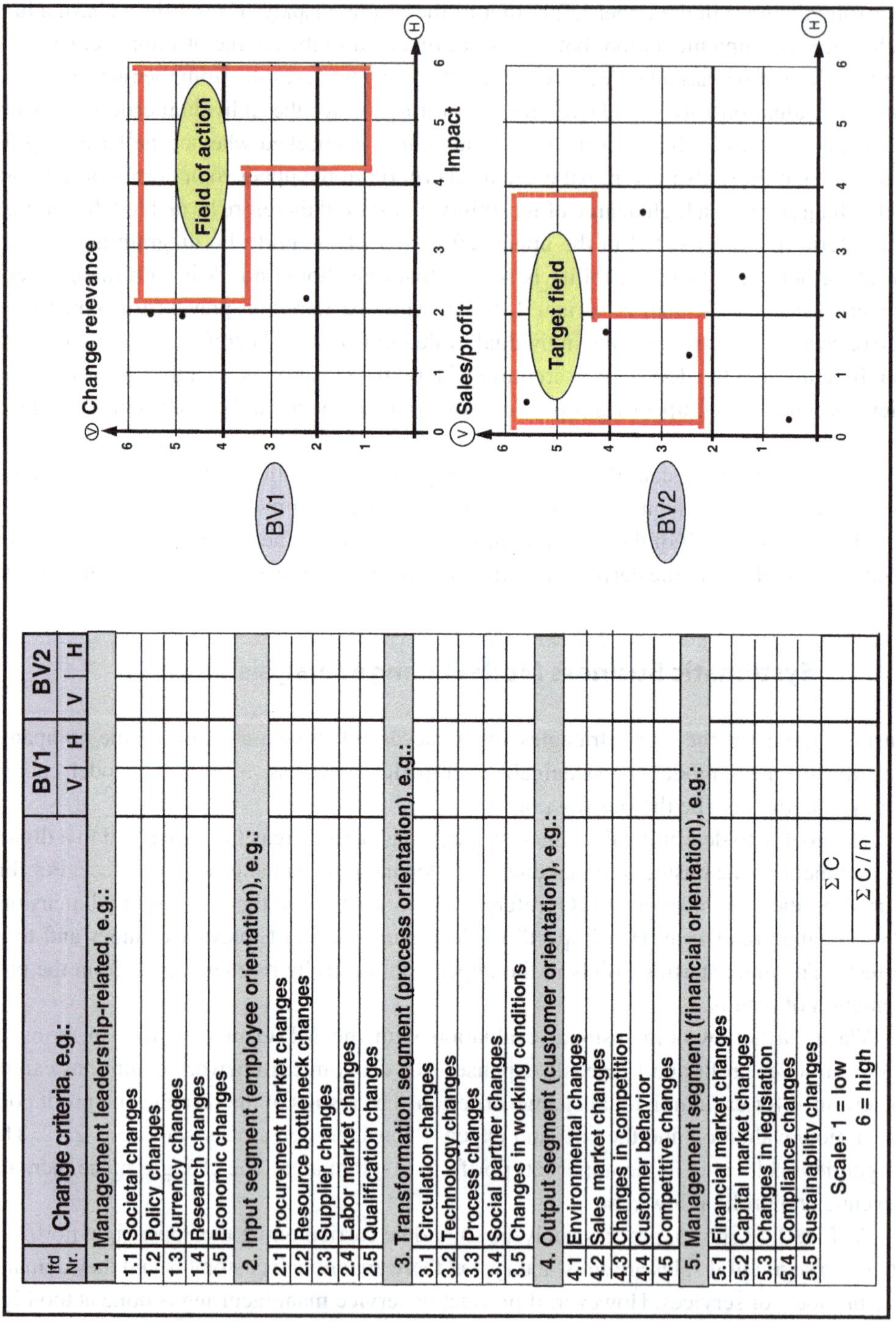

Fig. 2.42 MITO model segment-related change analysis

should be designed in such a way that it is wasteful and error free. However, if sales are very low and the costs for product creation are also in the low range, the primary objective here is to acquire new customers through new products and services. Therefore, in the lower left segment of the portfolio diagram, a product analysis is required here. The aim is therefore to generate greater customer benefits for the customer through improved products and services. In the lower right segment, process analyses should also be carried out in addition to these product analyses if the costs and expenses are too high in addition to the sales that are too low. An integrated process and product analysis should therefore be carried out here. The target range of the business model to be aimed for is, as shown, in the upper left segment, i.e. with high sales and profits and low costs and expenses. In this way, the competitiveness of the company is ensured. The product and process analyses should therefore change the competitive situation in such a way that the results can be assigned to the upper left target range shown.

2.7 MITO Tool-Supported Requirements Analyses

For the development of a successful business model, it is always particularly important, especially at the beginning, to find out the requirements of the customer or, more generally, the stakeholder requirements and expectations of the manufactured product or service. Even in many standards and regulations, the determination of customer requirements is the first priority. As already explained in Sect. 2.4.2 in relation to the answer to basic question 2 "What", such customer requirements analyses can be carried out very easily on a multidimensional basis with the help of the **MITO method tool**.

As an example, a specific customer requirements analysis matrix is shown in Fig. 2.43, which is subdivided according to different clusters. This matrix shows the requirements in the company differentiated by management/performance requirements, personnel-related requirements, procurement requirements and implementation policy requirements. The associated individual criteria per cluster are then assessed using the MITO tool.

This portfolio matrix can be supplemented by the user as desired. The systematic approach to the analysis is primarily described here. Also in the selection of the valuation variants shown, here the valuation variant (BV):

BV 1 with "V = Relevance", "H = Frequency".
BV 2 with "V = Target", "H = Actual".
BV 3 with "V = Importance", "H = Urgency".

The user can decide freely.

The results of the evaluations in the grades from 1 to 6 – for example by the customers or by the managers – are graphically displayed as a portfolio diagram or as a radar diagram. Using the selected valuation variants, different valuation views can be placed on

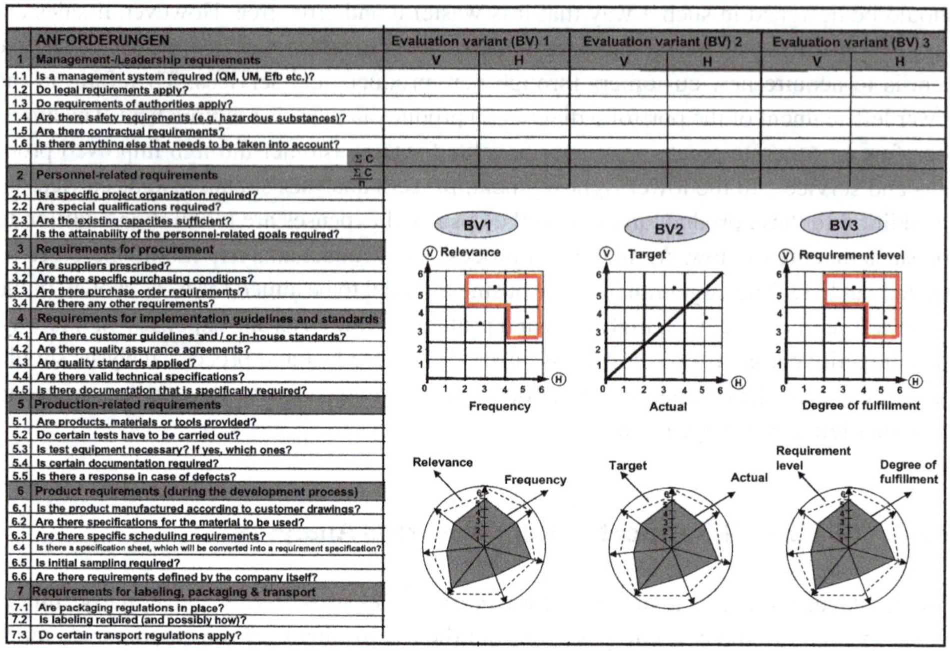

Fig. 2.43 Business requirement assessment portfolio

these requirements. For example, in valuation variant (BV) 1, it is clarified whether these requirements are to be included in the consideration at all with regard to relevance and frequency. The really important requirements are in the results display in the upper right area of the portfolio diagram. In valuation variant (BV) 2, a target/actual analysis is performed. In the portfolio diagram, the diagnosis represents the optimal solution because the target and actual statuses correspond here. Valuation variant (BV) 3 analyzes whether the existing requirements are met by the company. Here, too, all individual requirements above the diagonal are not fulfilled. The ideal degree of fulfillment lies on the diagonal. Here the requirement level corresponds exactly to the implementation carried out. All requirements below the diagonal are overfulfilled.

In addition to meeting customer requirements, there are a large number of other requirement types from a wide variety of organizational design views. For requirements evaluation, a clear grading scheme must be available that can be used uniformly by every user.

Using the example of the holistic requirements structuring in the MITO model in Fig. 2.44, this grading with the assessment scale from grade 1 to grade 6 together with the grading aids is explained by way of example.

From the graphical presentation of results in the portfolio diagram after the line-by-line V and H = evaluation (analysis) of the individual criteria and the subsequent localization of the need for action (diagnosis), the MITO method tool is now used to derive the measures for requirement fulfillment (therapy) in the form of goal-measure cascades. For the

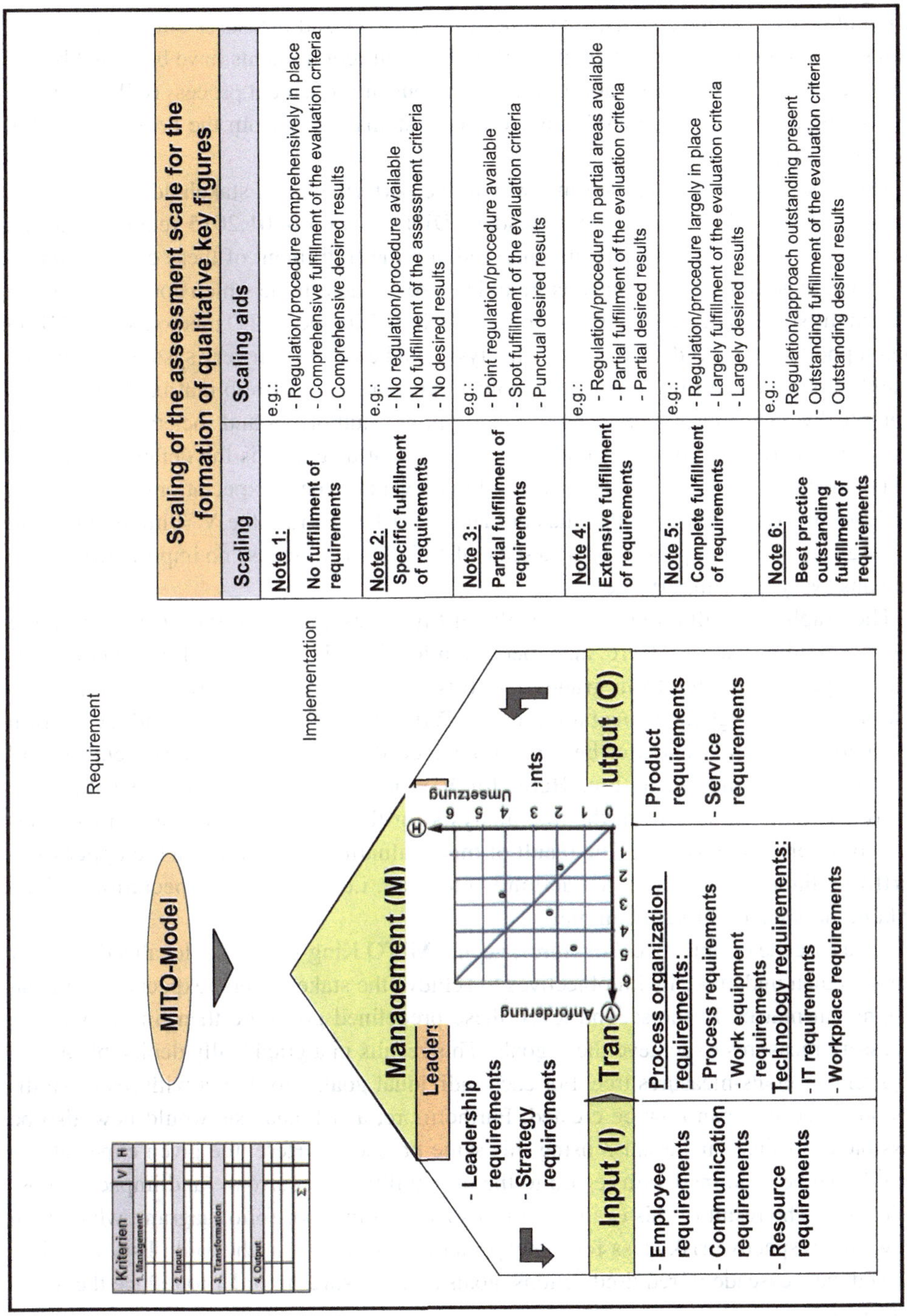

Fig. 2.44 Holistic MITO model-related requirements assessment

different types of requirements, catalogues of objectives and measures already exist. The final step is a method-based evaluation of whether all requirements have been met by the measures used. In case of deviations, the continuous improvement process (CIP), which is also required in many integrated management systems, starts from the beginning within the MITO model.

The procedure applies in the same way to the performance of stakeholder expectation analyses. The quality management standard DIN EN ISO 9001:2015 requires that the expectations of the stakeholders are analyzed and the fulfillment of these expectations is reviewed. In addition, a risk analysis should be used to determine which possible risks can prevent the stakeholder expectations from occurring. With the MITO method tool, a MITO tool-supported stakeholder expectation analysis can be carried out very systematically and quickly. As shown in Fig. 2.45, a stakeholder expectations portfolio matrix clustered, for example, by owner, customers, employees, suppliers, authorities and society, in which the expectations are entered, for example, on the basis of a survey, is the default. Using the MITO method tool, the first step can now be to evaluate these expectations according to the level of expectation, i.e. the stakeholders are asked to rate the V = importance and H = urgency of their expectations on a scale of 1–6. Score 1 means "no importance", score 6 means "very high importance".

The graphical evaluation of the results of this assessment variant 1 is shown in the upper portfolio diagram. Here, an expectation level grade scaling within the new portfolio diagram segments from grades 1 to 6 is also provided. A score of 6 would correspond to the highest expectation level. With these results, a second evaluation (evaluation variant 2) can now be carried out according to V = level of expectation and H = degree of implementation. Here, for V = level of expectation, the values are entered as they resulted from the first analysis for the respective stakeholder expectation considered line by line. The result of this evaluation then shows in the upper right portfolio diagram segment what action is required, i.e. where the expectations of the stakeholders have not yet been met.

Via a cascade of objectives/measures, i.e. the MITO King's Path, the localized need for action is then undertaken with objectives to achieve the stakeholders' expectations via an assignment matrix. In the second level, these predefined goals are then linked with the necessary measures to achieve these goals. This results in a graphically depictable action requirement-goals-measures tree. For each individual goal, a to-do list with responsibilities and deadlines can now be created. Furthermore, a risk analysis would now also be possible as evaluation variant 3 using this same procedure. Here, the given expectations would now be examined with regard to the probability of occurrence and impact of possible risks. The result of this evaluation is also shown in a portfolio diagram, which then shows the respective risk class for the expectations. Here again, the to-do lists would be derived via a cascade of required actions, goals and measures in order to reduce the localized risks.

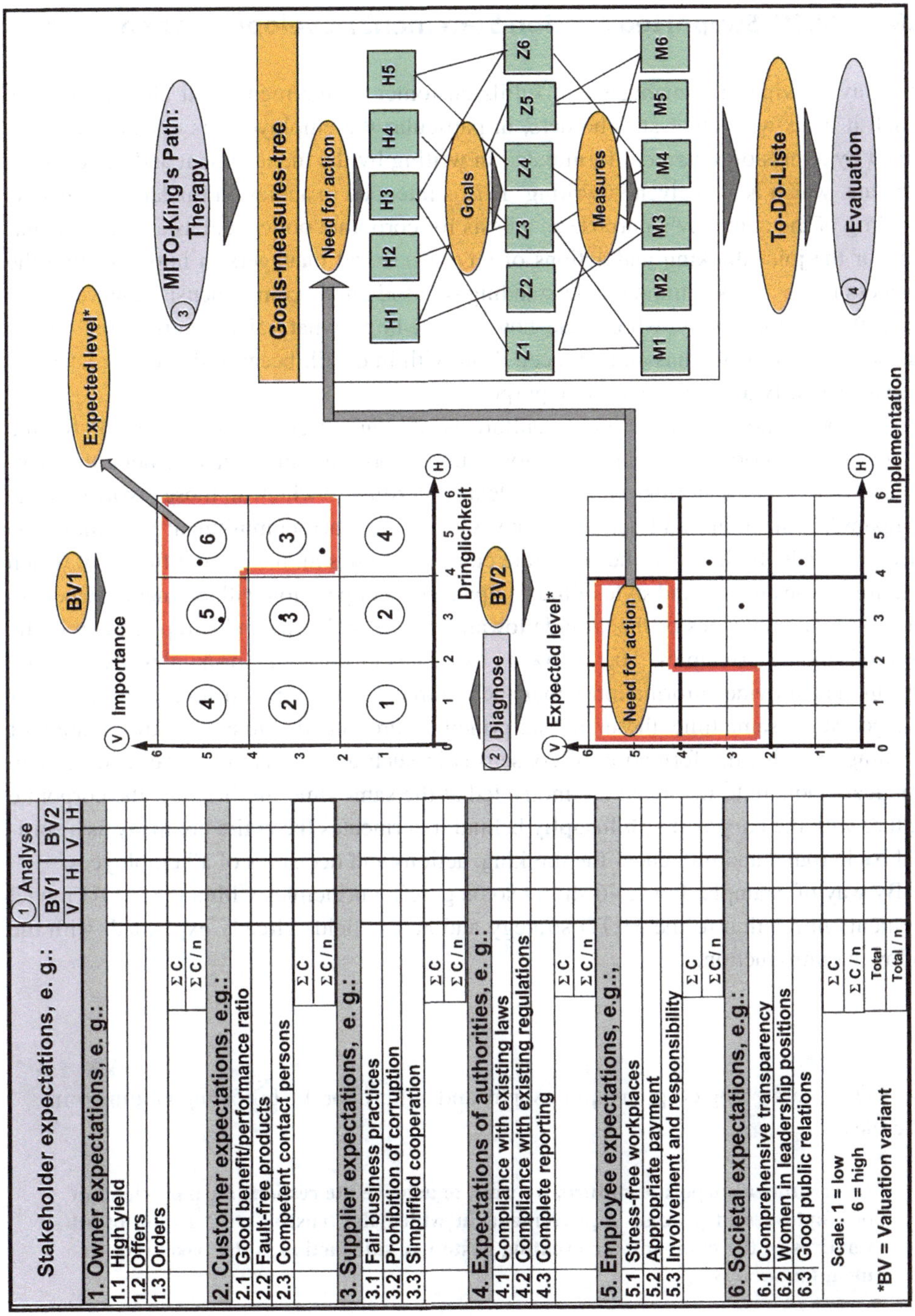

Fig. 2.45 MITO tool-supported stakeholder expectations analyses

2.8 MITO-Supported Mission Statement Development as a Basis

The way in which the management fulfils customer requirements, but also the way in which it deals with other stakeholders, in particular the employees, is essentially determined by a mission statement formulated in writing by the management and the Code of Conduct, which is also given in writing. This is intended to achieve a fundamental understanding of the company's purpose as a basis for corporate policy and as a value orientation for the joint thinking and actions of employees and managers in implementing the business model. This common understanding is based on the comprehensive answering of the 7 W-questions "why, who, what, how, with whom, what value contribution" of the business model, which has already been dealt with in detail, because this has created the necessary clarity about the corporate purpose.

The specification of a corporate culture is also an essential success factor for the achievement of corporate and process goals. In the form of a mission statement, the management specifies the norms, values and ideals according to which all those involved in the company should think and act on the basis of a voluntary commitment to achieve the specified goals. In this way, the corporate culture assumes an integration function, which determines the attitude and style of the company, the cooperation with partners, the behaviour towards employees or the attitude towards social problems and is represented in the form of guiding principles. The following examples of corporate principles also contain visions that provide information about the company's medium- to long-term goals for change. At the same time, these guiding principles are intended to convey the creation of meaning and also the formation of consensus in such a way that all those involved can practically adhere to them and are motivated at the same time. In this way, the corporate culture with the **corporate philosophy** behind it permeates the entire company as a spiritual background and influences the thinking, actions and decisions of all employees.

By way of example, Fig. 2.46 shows some guiding principles within the MITO model segments in relation to the MITO strategy and action fields already explained, with the following introduction.

Our overarching corporate philosophy and culture for the following guiding principles is:

By creating a corporate culture, we want to achieve the responsible participation of employees in process improvement, in which the trustful cooperation of all relatives in the company for creating customer satisfaction is the basic requirement for success.

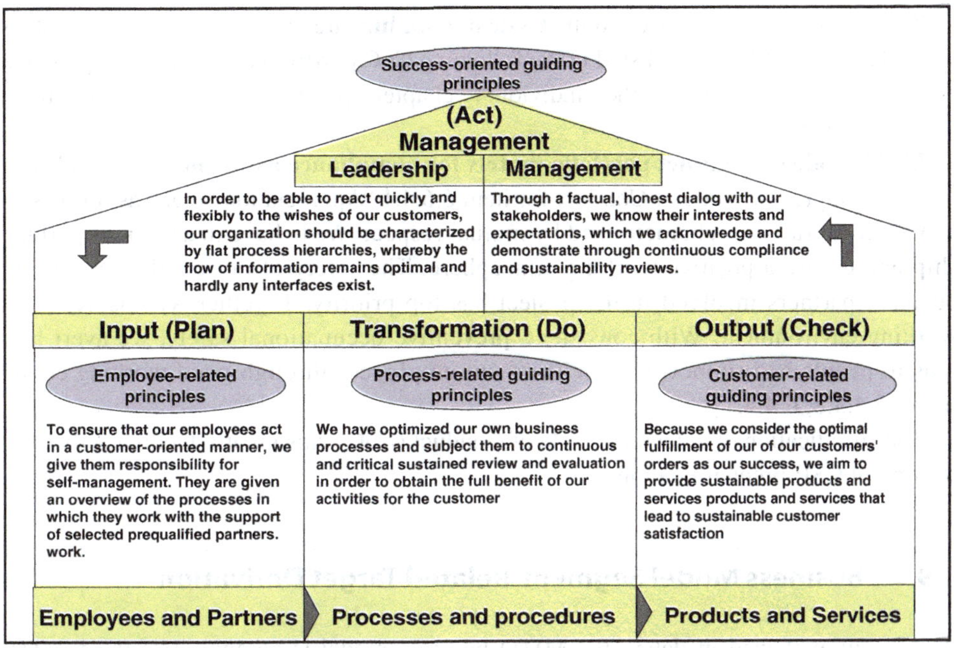

Fig. 2.46 Guiding principles for sustainable corporate culture (example)

The written evidence of corporate policy required in a whole number of Integrated Management Systems is derived from these guiding principles. This is a written declaration of intent, for example:

- Dealing with stakeholders and employees
- On the relationship with social groups
- On attitudes to social problems
- On the use of company capital
- On the assumption of social responsibility

The guiding principles are specified by predefined rules of conduct (Code of Conduct) as a central component of the lived corporate values. These codes of conduct are codes of conduct in general or instructions for action in specific situations. The Code of Conduct is the ethical guideline for the employees in the company. As a rule, the formulated behavioral instructions serve as orientation aids for employees in order to channel desired behavior or to avoid undesired actions. Supervisors have a special responsibility to communicate the content of this code of conduct to employees by setting an example. Employees can be trained, for example, through an intranet-based eLearning program. This helps to ensure that the rules of conduct are understood and internalized.

Topics that can be addressed in the **Code of Conduct** are based on the requirements of DIN EN ISO-26000 and are listed in the following CoC portfolio matrix as examples. The contents are assigned to the individual chapter points in the CSR reference documentation:

MITO-code of Conduct portfolio matrix for compliance assessment (Fig. 2.47)

For example, the Code of Conduct for item 6.6.4.1 "Appreciation" reads as follows.

Our cooperation is characterized by mutual respect. We behave in a spirit of partnership and ensure a positive working atmosphere. The safety of our employees and the business partners involved in the project has top priority. Together we ensure a safe working environment. With consistent, preventive occupational safety, we avert hazards to people and support the health of our employees through good working conditions [6.4.3.8, 6.4.4.1].

The specification of a detailed Code of Conduct (CoC) thus greatly facilitates the verification of CSR prequalification.

2.9 Business Model Segment-Related Target Derivation

As already explained in detail, the MITO business model is composed of the 5 MITO model segments supplemented by the customer and supplier segments, which, by including the hierarchical process level model in the graphical representation with the associated management and control system, represent an integrated company system and are linked to each other in the form of a control loop.

The **corporate objectives** can also be differentiated in relation to the MITO model segments according to the cultural, economic, social, technological and ecological target aspects or perspectives. In Fig. 2.48, the MITO model segment-related target aspects are named within the MITO model segments, from which the respective segment main target is derived.

The cultural system with its focus on value orientation is assigned to the integrated corporate target system in the management segment. The main objective here is image improvement and also employee loyalty via the value culture described in the previous point. In the input segment, the social system is assigned with the focus on employee needs orientation. Here, the objective is to increase the performance of employees, for example, through a company health system and ergonomic conditions at the workplace. In the transformation segment, technological systems are used in the production of products or services. Here the focus is on factual orientation with the aim of increasing productivity. This is followed by the MITO output segment with the ecological system assignment. The focus is on sustainability orientation and the main objective derived from this is customer satisfaction. More and more customers attach importance to resource-saving and low-polluting production and to recyclable products. In the MITO line segment, the economic

Nr.		Individual references to DIN ISO 26600, e. g.:	G	Dimensions	
				Requirement	Degree of fulfillment
1. Chapter 4: MITO-CSR basic principle assessment per stakeholder.					
1	4.1.1	Implementation and monitoring			
2	4.1.1	Behavior towards each other			
3	4.1.1	Behavior toward third parties			
4	4.4.1	Respect for human rights/responsibilities ethical principles/legislation and other internal other internal requirements			
5	4.6.1	Compliance with applicable law/compliance and law/compliance requirement			
6	4.6.2	Compliance Requirement/Conclusion of Contracts of business transactions			
7	4.6.2	Compliance Guidelines			
8	4.6.2	Minimum standards			
9	4.6.3	Compliance risk analysis			
10	4.6.4	Compliance Management System			
11	4.6.4	Compliance audit			
		C			
		∑ C/n			
2. Chapter 5: MITO-CSR - Safeguarding the Interests of Stakeholders Analysis					
1	5.1	Integrating the interests of owners			
2	5.1.2	Sustainable environmental and climate protection			
3	5.1.3	Laws and ethical principles			
4	5.1.4	Exclusion of forced labor/prohibition of child labor			
5	5.1.6	Use and security of IT systems			
6	5.1.7	Financial integrity			
7	5.1.8	Product safety			
8	5.2	Integration of management interests			
9	5.2.1	Environmental protection			
10	5.2.2	Sustainable environmental and climate protection			
11	5.2.4	Exclusion of forced labor/prohibition of child labor			
12	5.2.6	Data protection, confidentiality			
13	5.2.7	Relations with business partners			
14	5.2.8	Product safety			
15	5.2.9	Market transparency			
16	5.2.11	Guidance for decisions			
17	5.6.3.3	Handling waste and hazardous substances			
		C			
		∑ C/n			

Fig. 2.47 MITO Code of Conduct portfolio matrix

3. Chapter 6:Implementing the recommendations for action on the core issues of social responsibility					
1	6.1	Human rights			
2	6.3.3.1	Human rights/respectful behavior			
3	6.3.7.1	Equal opportunities and prohibition of discrimination			
4	6.3.7.3	Discrimination			
5	6.4	Labor practices			
6	6.4.3.5	Equal treatment and non-discrimination/Fair Working Conditions			
7	6.4.3.8	Selection of service providers and suppliers			
8	6.4.4.6	Fair remuneration			
9	6.4.5.1	Open discussion			
10	6.4.5.3	Right to organize and right to Collective Bargaining			
11	6.4.6.1	Safety and Health			
12	6.5	Environment			
13	6.6	Fair operating and business practices			
14	6.6.3.1	Acceptance of gifts and donations			
15	6.6.3.3	Donations policy			
16	6.6.3.3	Gifts and hospitality			
17	6.6.3.4	Anti-corruption (bribery and corruption)			
18	6.6.3.4	Conduct toward public officials and peers			
19	6.6.3.5	Compliance with antitrust regulations			
20	6.6.3.5	Donations and sponsoring			
21	6.6.3.5	Conflicts of interest and corruption			
22	6.6.3.5	Bribery and corruption			
23	6.6.3.5	Documentation of business transactions			
24	6.6.3.5	Handling company property/assets			
25	6.6.3.5	Respect for human dignity			
26	6.6.3.5	Rejection of child labor			
27	6.6.3.5	Corruption			
28	6.6.3.5	Transparency and openness			
29	6.6.3.5	Intangible benefits			
30	6.6.3.5	Accepting invitations			
31	6.6.3.5	Donations			
32	6.6.3.5	Money laundering			
33	6.6.4.1	Human rights			
34	6.6.4.1	Child labor			
35	6.6.4.1	Discrimination			
36	6.6.4.1	Ethical behavior			
37	6.6.4.1	Freedom of association			

Fig. 2.47 (continued)

38	6.6.4.1	Appreciation			
39	6.6.4.1	Occupational health and safety			
40	6.6.4.1	Environment			
41	6.6.4.1	Protection of personal data			
42	6.6.5.4	Price setting			
43	6.6.5.5	Handling company property and information			
44	6.6.5.5	Conduct in competition			
45	6.6.5.2	Compliance and implementation			
46	6.7	Consumer concerns			
47	6.7.3.2	Market sharing and customer protection			
48	6.7.3.2	Contacts with competitors			
49	6.7.3.2	Other restrictions			
50	6.7.3.4	Exchange of information			
51	6.7.6.4	Complaint mechanisms			
52	6.7.7.1	Confidentiality			
53	6.7.7.2	Treatment of confidential information			
		C			
		∑ C/n			
	Scale: 1 = low 6 = high	Total			

Fig. 2.47 (continued)

system is assigned with the focus on economic efficiency. Here, the goal is to align the company in terms of profit maximization. Figure 2.48 also shows that the soft-fact-oriented targets are located in the management segment and the hard facts are assigned more to the management segment.

After the derivation of the company-specific target system always in relation to the MITO model segment structure, considerations can now be made about strategy derivation. The strategies sought should ensure that the specified goals are actually achieved.

The separation of **corporate goals** into formal and material goals introduced by Kosiol, E. 1962 can also be depicted in the MITO model. The formal goals are assigned to the two MITO management segments “leadership and management” and refer to the company’s success, the material goals are subordinate to the formal goals and refer to the performance at the operational level, i.e. in the MITO model to the 3 MITO segments: “input, transformation, output”. This will be elaborated in more detail in the conception of the integrated operational management and leadership system in Chap. 4.

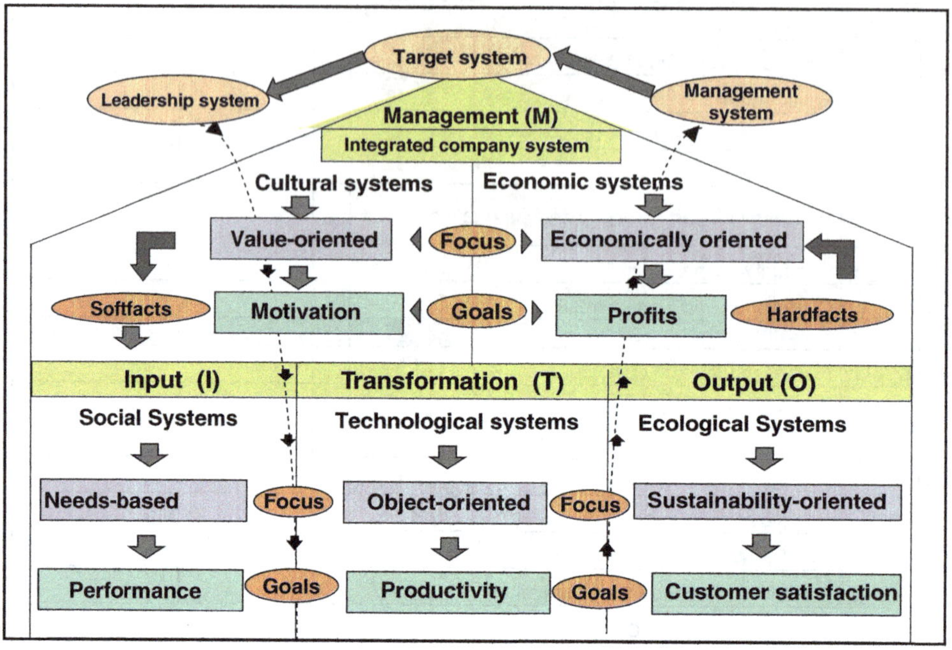

Fig. 2.48 MITO model-related cultural, economic, social, technological and environmental business model subsystem targets

2.10 Goal and Strategy Implementation Via the BSC Model

Targets are specified using key performance indicators. In the past, KPI systems often focused only on financial or cost-related KPIs and performance indicators. In the meantime, however, there are performance measurement systems that combine financial and non-financial aspects. First and foremost, the "**Balanced Scorecard**" (BSC) should be mentioned here.

The Balanced Scorecard (BSC) is a strategic management tool that provides a system of key performance indicators (KPIs) of interdependent objectives, metrics and target KPIs and enables a permanent review process via the feedback management system by recording the actual KPIs. Using the Balanced Scorecard, it is possible to determine the **key performance indicators** from various perspectives, i.e. in the case under consideration here from the five MITO segment target aspects explained in point 1.9:

- Success orientation (value culture perspective)
- Employee orientation (social perspective)
- Process orientation (technological perspective)
- Customer orientation (ecological perspective)
- Financial orientation (economic perspective)

Break down the visions and strategies as well as qualitative and quantitative goals and key figures to the various process levels. In this way, the generally overarching, sometimes abstract ideas from the corporate or top management levels are translated into operationalized **metrics** at the hierarchical process levels below, structured via the process level model, which are easily comprehensible and transparent for those involved in the process.

Figure 2.49 shows the interactions of the 5 BSC target and action areas with the KPIs used within the MITO business model structures.

From a strategic point of view, the objectives of the Balanced Scorecard application can be assigned to the end-to-end corporate process and main process level with the associated key figures and metrics. These are the following overarching organizational **objectives**, e.g. around:

- Functioning management and leadership instrument for strategic corporate management and control
- Specify corporate strategy and goals in a transparent and binding manner
- Measurement of changes in the internal area and in the environment
- Rapid responsiveness to change
- Improvement of productivity and efficiency in all processes through measurements, analyses and measures

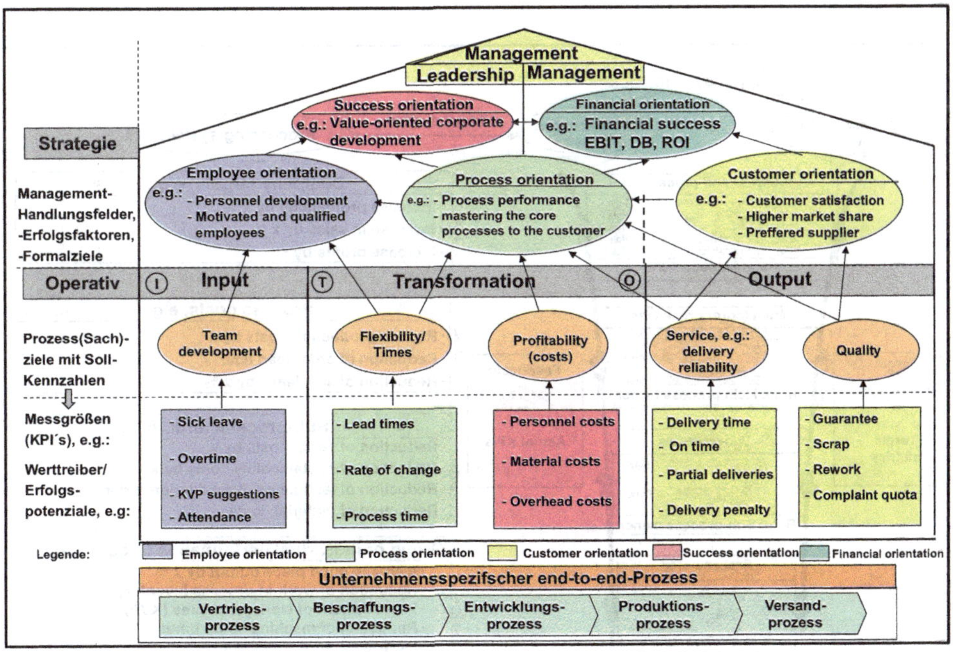

Fig. 2.49 Cause-effect chains for targets and metrics in the MITO business model

The operational **process objectives** refer to the sub-process and work system process level, they are:

- Mastery of dynamic business processes
- Coupling of process performance and team remuneration
- Optimization of processes through standardization
- Establish process comparability (benchmarks)
- Alignment of day-to-day operations with corporate strategies

The starting point for implementation is the development of a **process target system** that is derived from the overarching corporate goals for the management and leadership processes defined in the company-specific process model. This is the prerequisite for the development of a process management and guidance system for corporate management (specification) and controlling (feedback) described in detail in Chap. 4.

As shown in Fig. 2.50, a continuous **process level model** is specified as the organizational structure for this process management and control system, in which, starting from the top company level in relation to the end-to-end core process assigned there, the main or core processes on the following level are then derived in a magnifying glass function with an increasing level of detail once in level 2. The main and core processes in turn are composed of individual sub-processes one level lower, i.e. in level 3. Within the

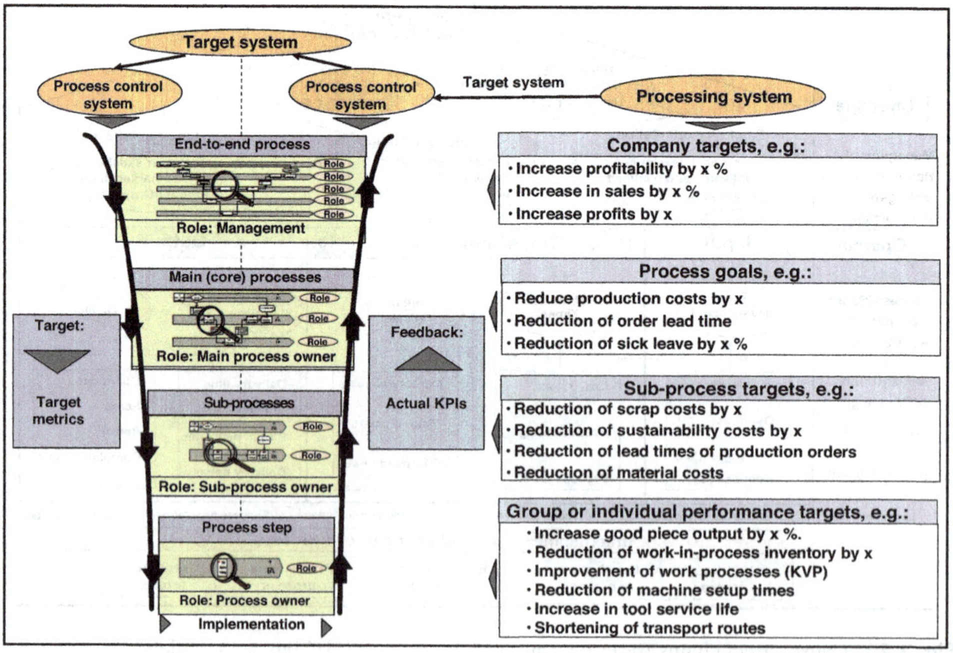

Fig. 2.50 Continuous process level model

subprocesses, the individual process steps and the work centers are specified in the role descriptions for the process employees at the lowest level.

Based on the target agreements, the person-related process management system is the basis for the employee management by the process owners in the individual process levels. Here it is the target key figures that specify the target agreement. They are broken down from the top level top down to the workplace in the lowest level. Here the soft facts dominate. After the process execution and performance measurement, an aggregation from the lowest level based on the actual key figures takes place in order to carry out a target/actual comparison in each level and to identify deviations. If deviations have occurred, measures to eliminate them are also initiated here immediately. Within the role-based Swimlane process representation, the measuring points for the recording of these actual key figures are also defined contextually based on the feedback. The process control system is the fact-based control with the verification of the hardfact-related compliance with rules, regulations and instructions. Furthermore, process controlling takes place across all levels with the examination of whether the agreed objectives have also been achieved in accordance with compliance. The process owners are responsible for managing their employees in such a way that the process objectives are achieved at every level.

2.11 MITO-Supported Company Structure Analyses

For the derivation of organization-specific, requirements and goals, but also for prioritization and standardization or for the selection and implementation of IT systems, it is usually necessary that company-related structural analyses are carried out in advance, which subsequently allow a differentiated consideration of possible solution variants in relation to the determined structural specifications.

As Fig. 2.51 shows, these structural analyses can relate, for example, to the analyses and evaluation of customer, sales, product, employee, organizational, communication, core or IT system structures. Using the portfolio analysis stored in the MITO tool, it is possible to map even complex structures in multiple dimensions, which then allow the recommendations for action to be implemented in a targeted manner from the two-dimensional portfolio diagrams. This is illustrated in Fig. 2.51 using the example of the customer structure analysis with the customer structure portfolio matrix shown. The customer groups that make a decisive contribution to competitive success are localized.

The two evaluation dimensions (V = vertical and H = horizontal) refer on the one hand on the vertical axis to the economic significance from the respective point of view, for example in this case with the customer structure from the competitive point of view, and on the horizontal axis in relation to the relative share or the percentage expression of the respective structure to be analysed.

The evaluation in the MITO portfolio matrix then enables a clear allocation in the portfolio diagram in this case once related to four quadrants instead of the 9 portfolio diagram fields considered so far. These quadrants contain the following recommendations for

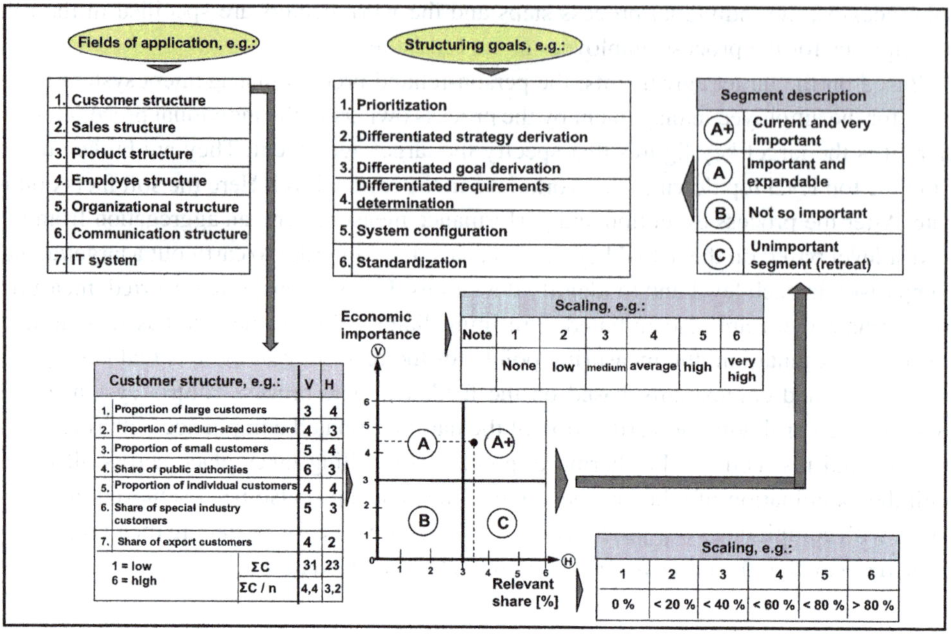

Fig. 2.51 MITO-supported structural analyses and evaluations

action: In the upper right segment, the A+ segment, the customer structure present there is quite important for competitive success due to its high relative share and importance, so this customer group must continue to be served with special care. For the segment in the upper left portfolio diagram, the importance is also high. However, the percentage is relatively small. There is still a great deal of activation potential here to transform this customer group into the A+ segment. In the lower left right segment B, the importance is not so high from a competitive point of view. No further special efforts should be made here. In the lower left quadrant C it is actually about very unimportant customer relationships. Possibly, a withdrawal should also be considered here.

In the same way, these structural analyses can of course be carried out for the fields of application mentioned above. It is only necessary that a detailed decomposition of the existing structural elements is carried out for each field of application in order to be able to carry out a clear evaluation afterwards.

2.12 Business Model Strategy Derivation

As already explained in the introduction, no sustainable competitive success can be achieved today on the basis of pure product and process innovations because, in particular, completely new and in some cases disruptive business models are emerging due to the new **cloud-based technologies** and the resulting networking on the basis of digital business platforms with the data streams that are thus recorded in real time and directly processed or evaluated. It is becoming increasingly clear that competition in the future will no longer be decided between products or processes, but between business models. That is why this book also focuses on digital **business model development** in companies. A study by BCG shows that over a period of 5 years, **business model innovations** were on average 6% more profitable than pure product and process innovations. Further, BCG's 2013 study revealed that 14 of the 25 most innovative companies in the world are primarily business model innovators. For the detailed implementation of the first 3 basic questions "Why?, How?, What?" it makes sense to include the classic competitive and business strategy considerations in the business model strategy development.

From the findings of the MITO method-tool-supported determination of the need for action with the SWOT, i.e. success factor, success potential and improvement potential analysis frameworks, different starting points for strategy determination with subsequent allocation of the target-target key figures according to the BSC system result for each individual MITO model segment with the strategy field behind it.

Every company has the choice between several different **competitive strategies** for its strategic orientation. This assumes, of course, that the business areas in which the company confirms itself in the market are clearly specified via the MITO business model analysis explained above. This is an upstream separate consideration, it is also called business or market behavior strategy definition.

The various competitive strategies can be differentiated according to Porter, as Fig. 2.52 shows, into **product leadership**, cost leadership, customer partnership and global leadership. They can be directly assigned to the individual MITO model segments and the process optimization starting points mentioned in Sect. 3.6. These are to be supplemented with the digital business model innovations described in Chap. 5, which are also MITO segment-related.

In terms of output, product leadership aims to differentiate the company from the competition by means of various characteristics. The goal is to position the company on the market through its product or service offering in such a way that it is seen as unique in the entire industry. The differentiation criteria and thus competitive factors are, for example, the technology used, the existing innovation potential, the flexibility offered, quality or the delivery service.

In terms of inputs, the company tries to become the supplier with the lowest costs in the provision of services when it comes to **cost leadership**. This naturally results in a strong focus on cost reduction approaches. The easiest way to achieve this is through large quantities with high productivity and optimal processes. For this reason, this strategy presupposes relatively large markets.

In the case of **customer partnership**, the company attempts to concentrate on certain submarkets or market segments as a supplier in a transformation-related manner. Within this segment or a group of segments, a long-term customer loyalty or relationship is to be built up on the basis of specializations by comprehensively fulfilling the individual needs of the customers on the basis of its specific problem-solving capabilities. The required

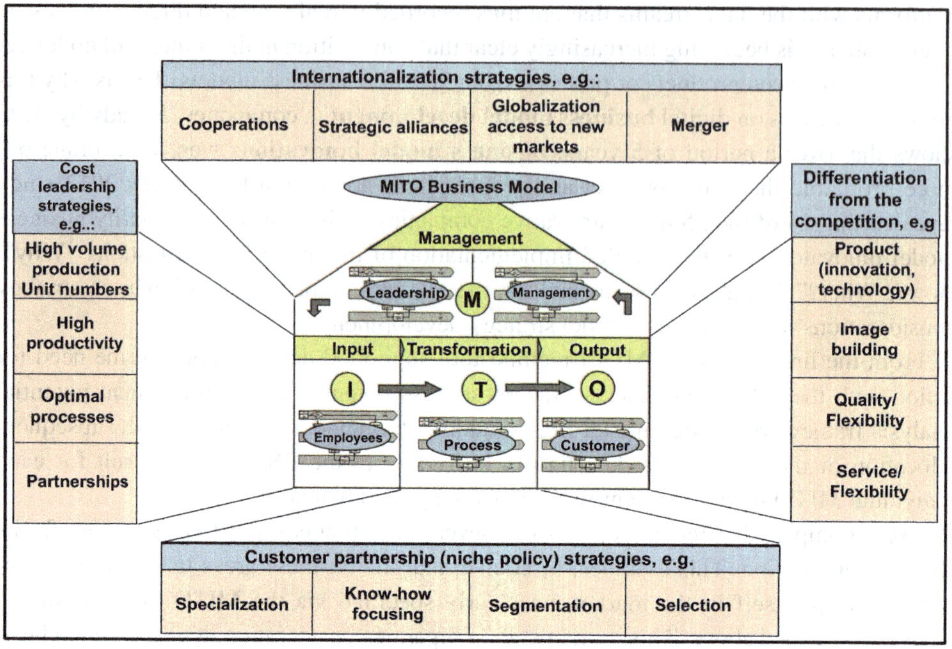

Fig. 2.52 MITO business model-related business strategies for successful company development

skills are the ability to produce small series economically as well as high flexibility and service quality.

From an overriding management perspective, the **internationalization strategy** aims to gain access and thus competitive advantages to worldwide sales and procurement markets through strategic alliances and cooperations in order to become a global player and world market leader.

2.13 Implementation of Competitive Strategies by GMS

In order to actually implement these **competitive strategies** successfully, suitable implementation strategies with the underlying implementation policy and implementation goals must be applied internally.

The implementation of the competitive strategies explained above with allocation to the MITO model segments is carried out one level lower through topic-specific individual management strategies, which are applied separately in the form of management tools with reference to a management system standard such as the quality standard DIN EN ISO 9001-2015, but which always focus jointly on a specified process and are linked with each other in this way.

These management system strategies are grouped together under the term "Integrated Management Systems" (IMS) and are uniformly structured according to the High Level Structure explained in Sect. 4.10. The integrated application of the individual management system management tools is referred to here as the **General Management Strategy (GMS)**. The framework for implementing this general management strategy is value-based management, also referred to as economic value added (EVA). In Fig. 2.53, the GMS is bundled into the MITO model segments with the assignment of the five strategy fields:

Customer orientation (output segment)	Employee orientation (input segment)
Success orientation (management segment)	Process orientation (transformation segment)
Financial orientation (management segment)	

The implementation of these Integrated Management Systems (IMS) is dealt with separately in Sect. 4.10.

Especially in the case of innovation management, which is assigned to the strategic field of "customer orientation", technology management always plays an important role. The term technology itself is not clearly defined. **Technology** is generally understood to be a complex interaction between material, technical components and systems as well as immaterial knowledge and skills (definition by Dr. Peter Meyer). From this definition it is already clear that the term technology can include several conceptual contents. Technology providers can offer both the acquisition and sale of a technology in the sense of a transfer

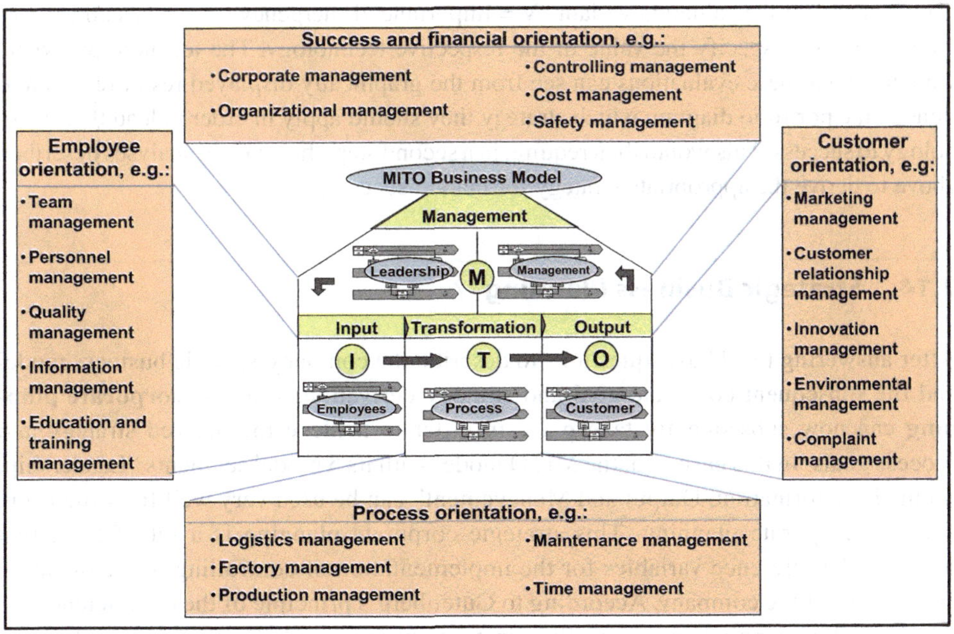

Fig. 2.53 General Management Strategies (GMS)

of action and the acquisition and sale of rights to use a technology for certain defined applications. From this perspective, technology is a good with a tangible value that can be traded on the market. However, the difficulty now lies in the precise determination of the value of this technology. There are different approaches to this. On the one hand, the value can be determined from the total development costs for the development of this technology. So here the cost principle is the basis of valuation. Another approach is the valuation of the technology by the market, i.e. it has to be analysed what proceeds can be achieved in case of an actual sale of this technology on the market. Another approach would be to determine the **value of the technology** on the basis of the amount in dispute, which would be open to legal discussion in the event of unlawful use of this technology.

The following describes a procedure model with the MITO method tool for a MITO technology positioning analysis, in which the technology value for different technologies is determined on the basis of market attractiveness and competitive position. For this purpose – as shown in Fig. 2.54 – a portfolio matrix is created in which the evaluation criteria for the subsequent evaluation according to market attractiveness (MA) and for the competitive position (WP) are stored line by line. The three different technologies shown, T1 to T3, are evaluated with scores ranging from 1 = low to 6 = high. Based on this evaluation, an ABC classification can then be used to determine whether a high, medium or low value is to be specified on the market for the technology under consideration.

The characteristic of the application of the MITO method tool is that different valuation variants can be applied for one and the same problem, i.e. in the considered positioning analysis case, for example, that one can also apply the valuation variant "V = Effort", "H = Benefit" or the valuation variant "V = Importance/Emergency" as well as other valuation variants to specify the value of the respective technology. The technology owners who carry out these evaluations can see from the graphically displayed result representations in the portfolio diagram which strategy they should apply in order to lead their technology to success. This would then require, in a second step, the strategy analyses described above to derive the appropriate strategy for market success.

2.14 Strategic Business Planning

After answering the 7 basic questions to describe the company-specific business model and the subsequent corporate goal and strategy derivation, strategic **corporate planning** can now subsequently take place in order to achieve the derived strategy and process goals. In this case, too, the MITO model with its 5 model segments "Leadership, Input, Transformation, Output and Management" can be used very well for structuring strategic corporate planning. This strategic corporate planning is a set of tools that provides the reference variables for the implementation of controlling in the planning and control of the company. According to Gutenberg's principle of the completeness of planning, this planning and controlling instrument must include all operational subareas in order to specify all goals with the corresponding measures that are necessary to

	Evaluation criteria, e.g.:	T 1 V	T 1 H	T2 V	T2 H	T3 V	T3 H
1.	**Market attractiveness (MA), e.g.:**						
1.1	Size of the market for the technology.						
1.2	Growth of the market for the technology						
1.3	Stability of the market in relation to the technology						
1.4	Experience of the company in the market in relation to the technology						
1.5	Technology competitors in the market						
1.6	Regulations and standards on the market						
	Σ C						
	Σ C/n						
2	**Competitive position (WP), e.g.:**						
2.1	Own resources available with regard to development and marketing of the technology						
2.2	Development status of own technology in relation to the competition						
2.3	Innovation strength of the company compared to the competition						
2.4	Degree of innovation of the own technology enterprise in relation to the competition						
2.5	Relations of the enterprise to users (customers) of the technology						
2.6	Protection of own technology by strategic únd legal measures						
T = Technology offerings on the market	Σ C						
	Σ C / n						
	Total						
	Total / n						

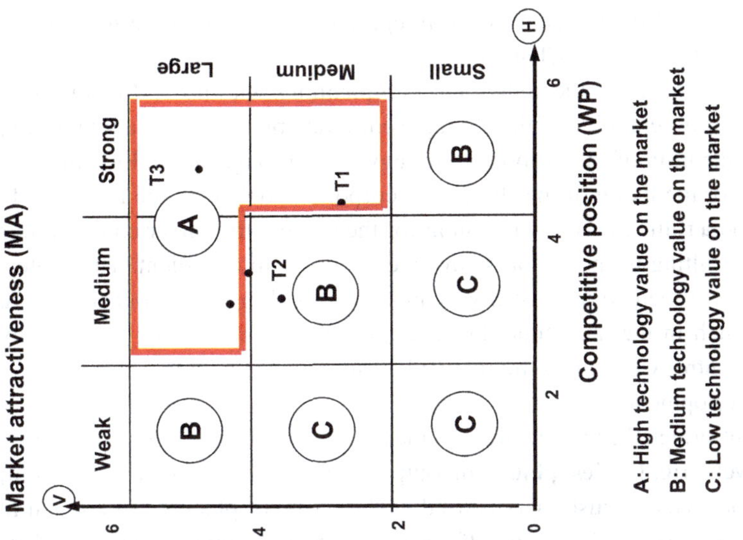

Source: Dr. Peter Meier, WEKA, QM according to the new ISO 9000 series

Fig. 2.54 MITO technology positioning analysis

achieve these goals. The results of strategic corporate planning are determined by the specifications of the concept of the integrated process-oriented management and control system discussed in Chap. 4.

Figure 2.55 shows the individual sub-planning within the MITO model segments, whereby a differentiation of the strategic corporate planning into a long-term planning for the determination of the corporate strategy over a longer period of time, a rigid annual planning for the fixing of the short-term corporate goals with the measures for their realization and a rolling monthly planning for the fine control under consideration of the data changes resulting from the course of time is often still expedient. The strategic corporate planning described below is still very much oriented towards input-oriented control principles, which in the meantime, however, are increasingly being replaced by an output-oriented control view due to market and customer changes, as is also the case in business model development.

In input-oriented corporate management, the focus is on resource planning on the basis of relatively rigid **sales plans**. In output-oriented corporate management, the actual demand behavior of customers is used as the basis for planning in a much more flexible manner. Agile principles with self-organization are applied in shorter planning cycles. Firstly, in order to meet customer requirements more quickly, and secondly, in order to reduce the planning effort and avoid permanent changes to the fixed target data.

The sub-plans mentioned in Fig. 2.55 can be described as follows. As an example, from an output-oriented control perspective, we start with the implementation plan or sales plan in the output segment. The sales plan involves the specification of the planned sales

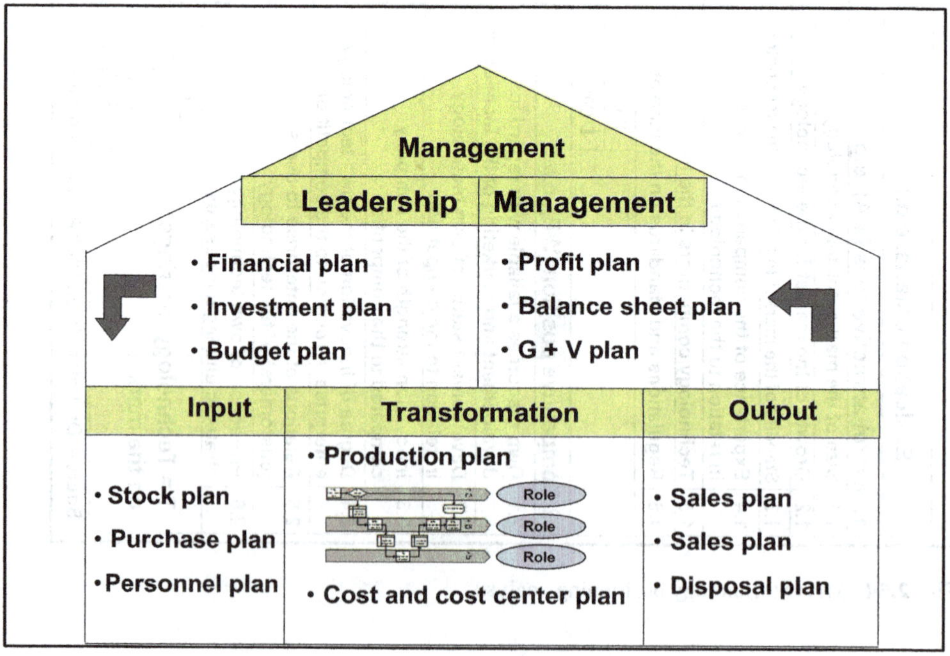

Fig. 2.55 MITO®-related strategic business model enterprise planning

quantity per article or article group with the planned sales price, which then results in the planned sales.

In the transformation segment, the production plan includes the articles or article groups to be produced with the planned production quantities, often also machines and group assignment.

In the input segment, the purchasing plan contains the planned procurement quantities for raw materials and materials as well as for auxiliary and operating materials with the planned purchase values. The stock plan contains the planned stocks of raw materials, article groups as well as auxiliary and operating materials, finished products and the sum of the total stocks. The investment plan includes the planned investment amounts for machines and equipment, land, buildings and other. The **personnel plan** can be divided into the planned headcount and the additional personnel requirements. The cost plan lists the planned, proportional and fixed costs by cost element and cost center. The profit plan in the management segment contains the planned contribution for the articles or article groups with the planned fixed costs and the planned operating results.

The finance plan in the management segment includes the planned incoming and outgoing payments and the planned changes with the financial status. The aim of the finance plan is to plan the liquid funds required to achieve the company's goals and to determine the origin and use of these funds. The **balance sheet plan** contains the plan fixed assets and the plan current assets, the plan equity and the plan liabilities. This data is to be compiled within the framework of the planning calculation for the entire year, but also for individual months. For this purpose, key figures can be determined and comparative data from previous periods can be added. This provides the controller with a comprehensive set of figures for annual planning. According to Gutenberg, there is an indissoluble connection between the subplans mentioned. Any change in data in any subplan has a direct or indirect effect on all other subplans of the company. To avoid this inevitability, a specific subplan can be chosen as the initial plan, for example, the sales plan or the finance plan. All the succession plans mentioned are then aligned with its plan data. Often, the highest business goal is taken as the planned result, that is, the profit plan. By means of rolling monthly planning, the controller is able to carry out a continuous update of the plan data that is tightly defined in the annual plan, and to show the effects that arise due to plan variances on the control values that are relevant for enterprise policy. The monthly plan update mainly covers the following data: Planned sales quantities, planned production quantities, planned procurement quantities, planned warehouse stocks, planned costs, planned profit/loss, and planned financial status. The aim of this rolling monthly planning is to be able to react quickly to data changes within the planning processes with suitable measures. As already explained in the introduction, the risk of input-oriented control is that customer behavior is not sufficiently taken into account and therefore plan adjustments have to be made again and again.

Within the framework of strategic corporate planning, a whole range of methods and tools are needed to support the execution of the individual planning tasks. These are usually the analysis methods already explained in Chap. 2 for answering the 7 W-questions, e.g.:

- Competitor analysis
- Strengths and weaknesses analysis
- Analysis of the product submarkets
- ABC markets
- Portfolio analysis
- Brainstorming
- Risk analysis
- Product market matrices
- Life cycle analysis
- Gap analysis
- Scenario method
- Sensitivity analysis
- Morphological box

As also explained above, the MITO method tool provides a large number of classical method tools within the framework of an overarching problem-solving cycle "analysis, diagnosis, therapy, evaluation", with which the aforementioned business planning tasks can be carried out.

2.15 Networked Initiatives for MITO Business Model Target and Strategy Implementation

The application of the described process models for holistic MITO business model development and design together with the systematic use of methods for optimizing the horizontal value chain for successful sustainable implementation of the MITO business model refer to a large number of strategic approaches that should be tackled by management in the form of networked initiatives. As Fig. 2.56 shows, these initiatives are assigned to the 5 MITO model segments with the subsequent objectives and strategies to be derived from them according to BSC aspects. It starts in the management segment with the value-oriented success factor focus, continues in the input segment with the employee focus, in the transformation segment with the process and quality focus and in the output segment with the customer and consumer focus. The control loop closes again in the MITO management segment, this time in the right half in relation to the controlling and CIP focus.

From the **management leadership** point of view – as shown – strategy initiatives for the promotion and improvement of cooperation, the training of change skills among superiors and employees, the assumption of the role model function by management, the

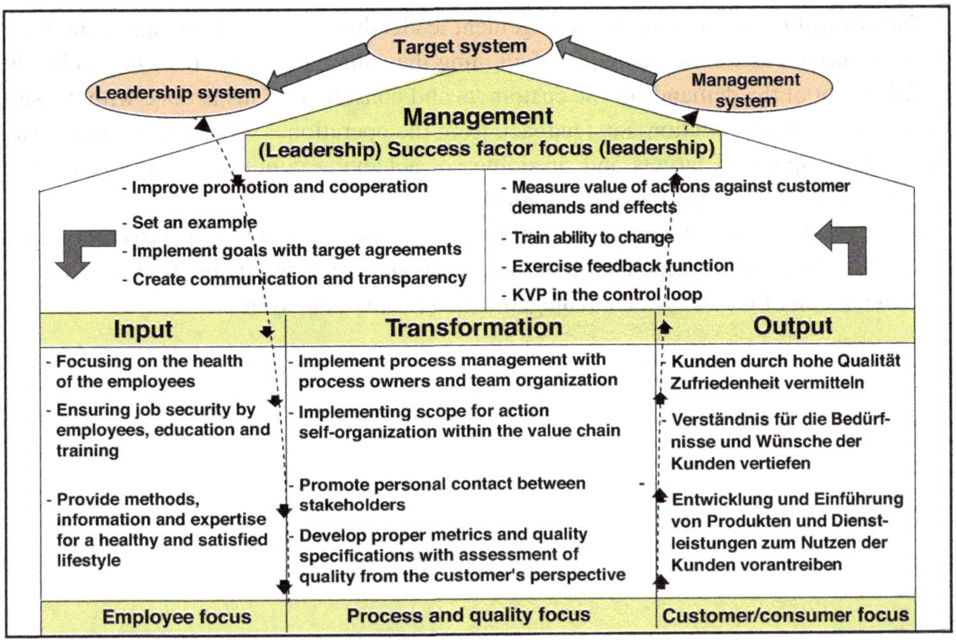

Fig. 2.56 Networked initiatives for sustainable MITO business model implementation

specification of goals with target agreements within a process level-oriented leadership system, in order to also create the necessary communication and transparency.

The input segment focuses on strategies to maintain the health of employees. Ensuring **job security** can be ensured through employee training. Further, methods, information and expertise for a healthy and satisfied lifestyle should be provided and also taught within the framework of health management. The **transformation segment** is concerned with the introduction of process management with process owners and team organisations, in order to enable the basis for the transfer of **room for manoeuvre** for self-organisation within the value chain. This is always done within the framework of the company-specific management and leadership system with the promotion of personal contacts with each other and from a controlling and compliance perspective with the development of the right measurement values and quality specifications with the assessment of quality from the customer's point of view.

In the output segment with the customer and consumer focus, **customer satisfaction** must be conveyed to the customers and consumers through high quality. The understanding of the customer's needs and desires must be deepened through market needs analyses in order to then also offer them the promised benefits. This in conjunction with the development and introduction of new products and services that further enhance the customer's benefits.

The **control loop** closes in the management leadership segment. Here again, the focus is on the success factor. It is a matter of aligning the value measurement of the trade with the fulfilment of the demands of the customers and consumers. This is done with the support of the feedback function, i.e. feedback from the operational value chain for comparison with the specified targets and, in doing so, achieving continuous improvement by anchoring CIP in all segments of the control loop.

In Sects. 4.6 and 4.7, the process-related targets in the associated BSC target indicators are explained for the implementation of these strategic targets within the framework of the implementation of the integrated management and leadership system.

Systematic Process Organization Development and Design

3

Abstract

A successful business model development and a business model transformation based on it is not possible in vertical function-oriented organizational structures based on the division of labor due to the lack of a horizontal value chain view. Therefore, an organizational business transformation must take place according to the process-oriented approach with "design, plan, execute, measure, improve processes" that has been required for the implementation of **integrated management systems (IMS)** for 20 years.

3.1 MITO Model-Related Process Anchoring Control Loop

The MITO model is also in this case the order and reference framework for the implementation of an effective and efficient **process organization** through the realization of a process anchoring control loop for successful and sustainable business model implementation. The **process anchoring elements** or main activities are assigned to the five MITO model segments "Management-Leadership, Input, Transformation, Output, Management-Leadership" – as shown in Fig. 3.1. From a systems engineering perspective, these 5 MITO model segments map the cybernetic organizational control loop, which is implemented by the process control elements of the integrated **management and leadership systems** described in Chap. 4.

The MITO management segment "Leadership" is about identifying the necessary processes for the implementation of the business model with the derivation of process goals and implementation strategies. As already explained in detail in Chap. 2, the business idea for a selected customer target group should always focus on the customer benefit as the

H. F. Binner, *Holistic Business Model Transformation*,
https://doi.org/10.1007/978-3-658-37367-2_3

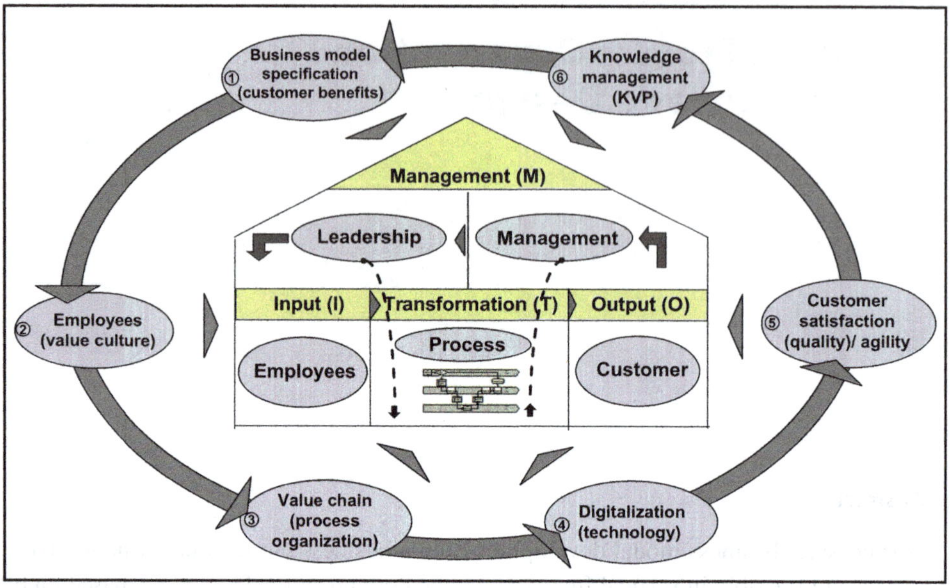

Fig. 3.1 MITO model-related process anchoring control loop

trigger for these activities, which ensures that successful company development takes place by fulfilling customer requirements.

With regard to the MITO input segment, employees are the most important resource for successfully implementing the business model targets within the operational level with the MITO model segments "Input, Transformation, Output" with the necessary qualifications on the basis of a new employee-related management culture described in Sect. 4.2, for example through transformational **leadership**. The prerequisite for this is that the underlying company-specific end-to-end process is mapped in a role-related manner. Factually-logically-temporally, all process participants in this value chain mapped according to the BPMN 2.0 process visualization standard are transparently assigned in a role-based manner with the documents and data required for this as well as the IT applications used. The analyzed, modeled and documented business processes within the company are then vertically and horizontally informationally networked with each other in the transformation segment via the most diverse digitization components across all process levels. This networking, which takes place within the framework of cloud computing with the provision of various IT services, ensures an effective and efficient order processing process in which the employee is increasingly integrated into the decision-making flow on a mobile basis in the future. The result of the interaction of these anchoring elements should then lead to the fact that as a result, i.e. process output, a product or service has been produced that leads to full customer satisfaction in terms of price, performance, quality and agility. In case of requirements, a continuous **improvement process** is initiated.

This continuous improvement process requires that all faults localized and documented in the process flow are analyzed with regard to their causes and that remedial measures are initiated. This is then also documented for further learning effects in the sense of an organizational process-oriented knowledge base. The described systematic approach to process anchoring is referred to as the Organization 4.0 concept and replaces the classic function-oriented organizational structures in favor of a process organization. This enables a holistic business model transformation taking into account all necessary business process design views. The overarching Business Process Management (BPM) as a management tool is responsible for ensuring that this business process fulfills the requirements and objectives mentioned above in a compliant manner.

These design views include, for example, the integrated management systems mentioned in Fig. 3.2, which are intended to be used effectively as management tools for specific design requirements specified by the standards. These process-oriented management systems also focus on the end-to-end business process, but broken down into the relevant core or sub-processes, such as the marketing, procurement, development, production or sales process, using the process level model.

These core processes, described in detail, are also always the basis for holistic process optimization concepts, such as SWOT analyses, CIP management, lean management, TQM or 6 Sigma.

The main drivers for the changes in this end-to-end business process are the new information technologies – discussed in detail in Chap. 5 – such as cloud computing, enterprise mobility, big data, Industry 4.0, social business and supply chain logistics. These information technologies enable completely new business model approaches, particularly through the use of AI, for example in procurement processes, in sales via e-commerce, in automation or in the service offering over the product lifetime. Based on the customer requirements of the customer target groups selected for the business models, the end-to-end business processes must be designed with these new technologies and the stakeholders involved in such a way that competitive success is ensured under the above-mentioned framework conditions.

Because this chapter focuses on the implementation of a process organization in line with requirements, the difference between a functional and a process-oriented organization will be briefly highlighted again below.

3.2 Characteristics of Function- and Process-Oriented Organisational Development

The most common form of design currently encountered in practice is the application of the first **organizational design paradigm** with the classic function-oriented organizational development and design.

As shown in Fig. 3.3, function-oriented organisational development is composed of two consecutive steps 1.1 and 1.2. In step 1.1, the organizational structure is structured.

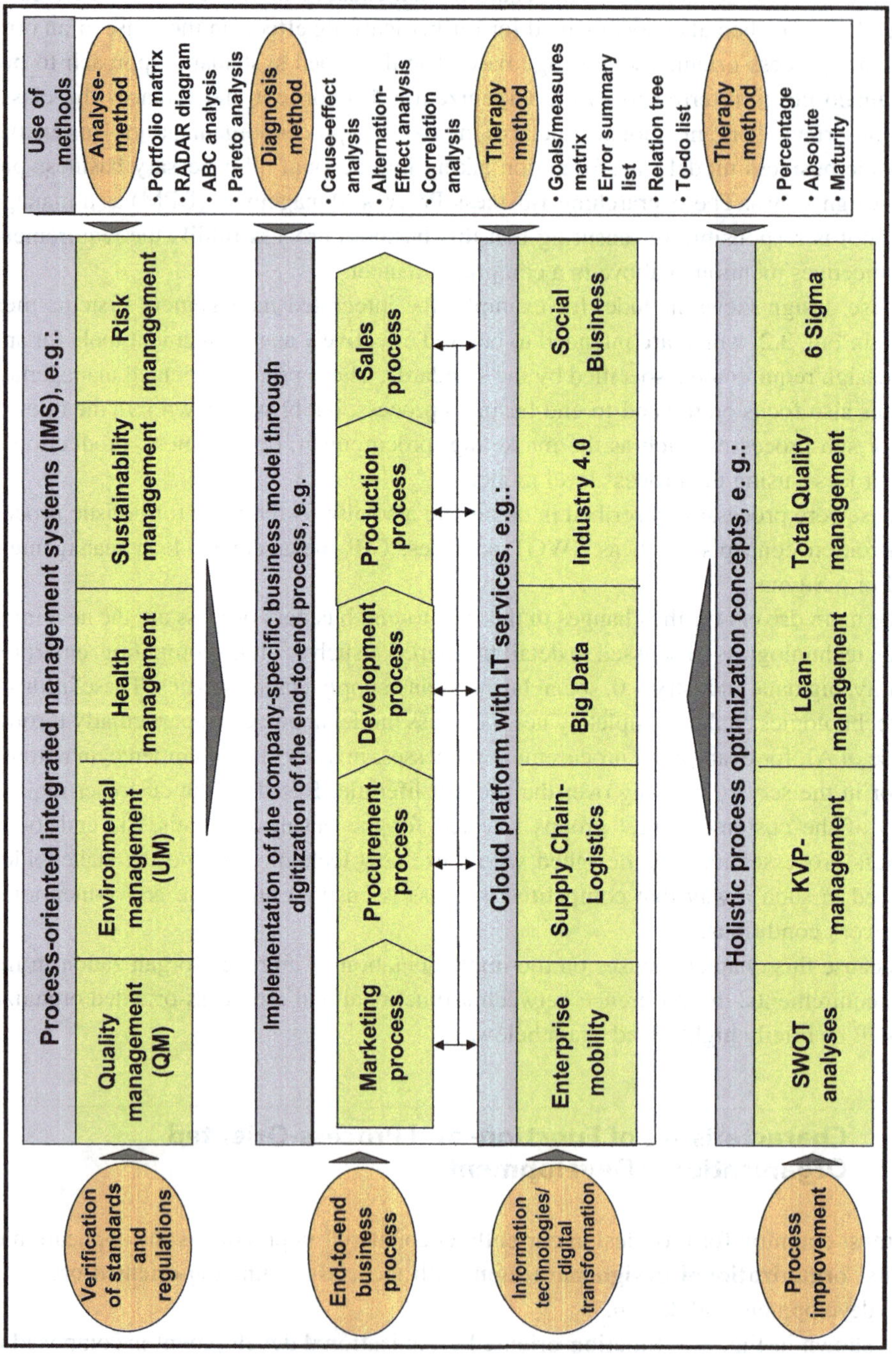

Fig. 3.2 Business process design views

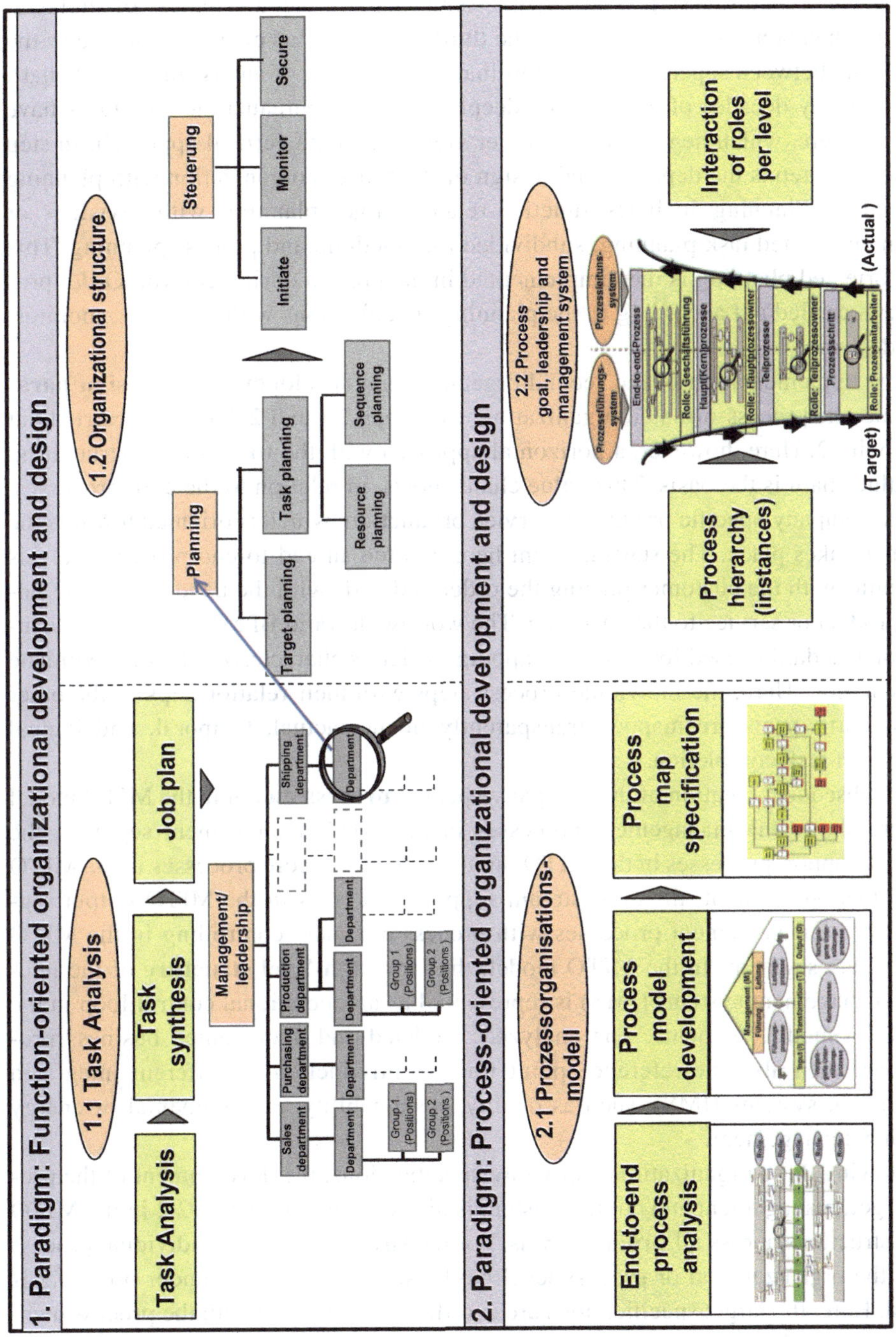

Fig. 3.3 Systematic approaches to organisational development and design

It is divided into the 3 sub-steps shown in Fig. 3.3. First, a task analysis is performed. Then, as the second sub-step, a task synthesis takes place, i.e. a summary of subtasks, which are then bundled in a job plan in the third sub-step. This position plan shows the relationship between superiors and subordinates in the form of an organizational chart. Over the many decades of application, deeply staggered bureaucratic structures have developed here, which neglect the customer view due to the vertical approach. In step 1.2, the next step is the departmental design of the process organization with planning and control. Planning includes function-related target planning with division- or department-related task planning, subdivided into medium and process planning. This future-oriented planning is then implemented in the present during control. Order processing is carried out according to the planning specifications with initiating, monitoring and saving.

In the implementation of the second organizational development and **design paradigm**, i.e. the process-oriented organization, two steps 2.1 and 2.2 are also carried out under point 2. Here, however, a horizontal approach with the focus on the structuring of a value chain is the basis. This value chain shows, in relation to the core processes, how the company-specific product or service production, which is oriented towards the customer, takes place. The starting point here is often an end-to-end process analysis that begins with the customer placing the order and ends with the handover of the finished product or service to the customer. The worldwide valid BPMN 2.0 process visualization standard is used for process mapping, which is characterized by the swimlane representation. Here, the individual process steps with their relationships to the other process participants are mapped transparently in the factual, temporal, and logical sequence of task completion.

The subsequent creation of the company-specific **process model** in the MITO model structure shows the management processes in the MITO management segment, the upstream support processes in the MITO input segment, the core processes in the MITO transformation segment, the downstream support processes in the MITO output segment and the management processes with process company controlling in the MITO management segment. In the MITO model, the new **high-level structure** of the integrated management systems (IMS) is represented as an operational control loop in the five MITO model segments. The analyzed, modeled and documented business processes are then also the reference point for the introduction of different integrated management systems (IMS), such as quality, sustainability, environmental or energy efficiency management.

Following these organizational structure specifications, the development of the process target, management and control system is also carried out in step 2.2 in the MITO model structures across all **process levels**. For the structuring of the individual process levels, the organizational or process level model shown in Fig. 2.2 under point 2.2 is applied. Here, the target specifications are coordinated top-down with the process owners at each level in the form of **target agreements** explained in Sect. 4.5. Through process performance measurement at each level, which is also structured in a role-based manner, feedback is provided bottom up across all four levels with increasing compression back to the company-specific end-to-end process level after process execution. In this way, it can be determined very precisely at each level whether target/actual deviations occur and which measures are to be introduced for improvement. In this way, the individual views can be linked with each other in the form of a MITO layer model based on segments. If all business processes in a company are analyzed and documented in the described manner, the naming of process owners can replace the function-oriented, i.e. job-related, view in favor of a horizontal, i.e. role-related, value chain view. The department heads become process owners, and the job description is replaced by a detailed role description.

3.3 Role-Based Process Organisation Structure and Design

As described in point 2.2, for more than 100 years organisational structuring and design has been based on the division of labour in structuring the overall task into subtasks, which are combined into jobs in a **task synthesis** and are subject to a hierarchical structure with superordination and subordination. The disadvantages of this function-oriented organizational structure have been known for a long time. Deeply staggered hierarchies are bureaucratically controlled. This means long processing and turnaround times, with employees aligning themselves with their superiors rather than the customer, who is often completely out of the picture. In contrast, a process-based organizational structure and design is oriented towards optimizing the horizontal **value chain**, which is focused on the customer. The processes are mapped in the globally valid BPMN 2.0 process visualization standard of the Object Management Group (OMG) in America.

Even with a process-oriented organizational structure, the basic business functions must of course be processed without errors and waste. However, in a process-oriented organization this does not take place with the positions documented in the organization chart, but through the roles defined within the processes. About the MITO model as a reference and regulatory framework for the introduction of a process-oriented organization with the 5 MITO model segments:

1. Process target in the management guidance segment
2. Infrastructure and resource provision in the input segment
3. Process execution in the transformation segment
4. Process performance measurement in the output segment
5. Continuous process improvement in the management line segment

These basic functions can be mapped in a process-oriented manner in the form of an operational **control loop**, which is shown in Fig. 3.4. The reference point is the analyzed and documented **end-to-end process**.

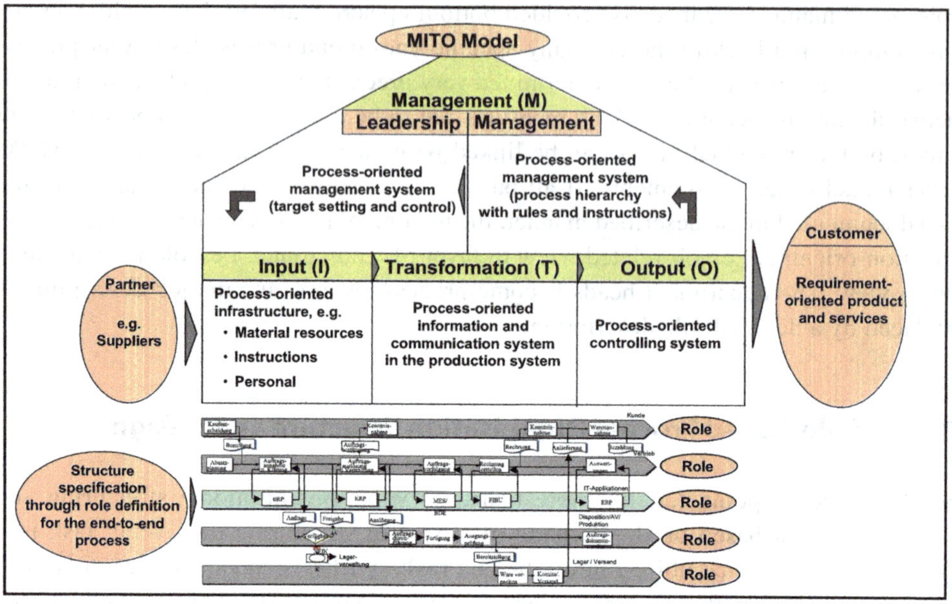

Fig. 3.4 Process organization structure

However, each basic function itself is now designed and documented as a process with the associated roles. These are the following basic functions or processes assigned to the MITO model:

- The management segment includes the corporate management with specification of the mission statement and the strategy and process target setting process.
- The input segment includes the provision of infrastructure with the procurement process with the procurement and provision of the means of production and production aids.
- The personnel development process, also in the input segment, includes the procurement, training, promotion and deployment management of personnel.
- The input segment also includes the provision of services, equipment and IT infrastructure.
- The transformation segment includes the production and assembly process responsible for creating the service or products.
- Another is the product development process, which precedes the production process within the transformation segment. The aim is to develop technically feasible and economically viable products. The design and development process is also integrated into this product development process.
- The sales process in the output segment is concerned with the sale of the products and services produced, i.e. the delivery of the orders to the customers in accordance with the logistics.

- The finance and controlling processes with the monitoring of the financial resources required for the provision of services and the continuous improvement process (CIP) are assigned to the management segment.

These are each separately considered processes that are also analyzed, modeled and documented in the swimlane representation. The linking of these processes within the operational control loop in the form of a process map is intended to ensure that external and internal disturbance variables are eliminated as far as possible. Via the feedback functions, i.e. feedback to the management segment through the control system, deviations are detected and countermeasures are initiated. It is now crucial for the organizational design that the roles within the processes under consideration are described transparently with the fields of activity and tasks assigned to them.

The process-oriented organizational structure is mapped using the role-based Swimlane representation. Here, the role provides the process participants with the factual, temporal, and logical framework for action with regard to the work flow, e.g., tasks, capability profiles, resources, and the information flow, e.g., data, documents, IT applications with the associated rights and duties, together with the interfaces to the other roles in the process.

On the basis of the process organization-related organizational chart development with the associated documented processes across all process hierarchy levels – as Fig. 3.5 shows – the management and leadership system contents and structures discussed in detail in Chap. 4 are developed in detail and documented in their interactions. On the management side, it is a matter of clear objectives and values with the

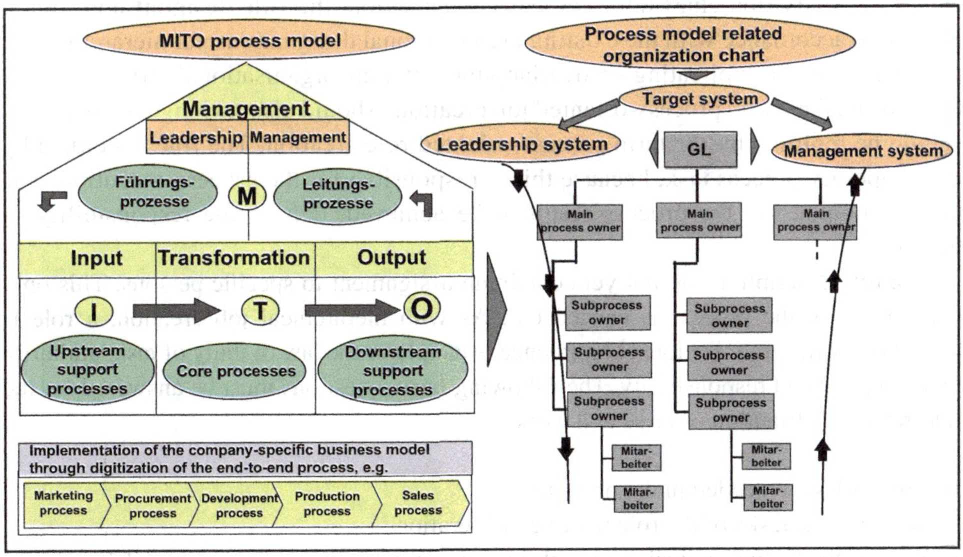

Fig. 3.5 Process organization-related organizational chart development

associated target key figures and regulations across all process levels. On the management side, i.e. on the feedback side, this applies in the same way to the measurement of results with a target-performance comparison and the resulting impetus for improvement. This is combined with continuous learning through the creation of a process-related knowledge repository.

3.4 Implementation of an Integrated Process Organization

The decisive difference in process-oriented organisational design compared to function-oriented organisational design is that the classic task analysis, synthesis and job creation mentioned above do not take place at the beginning, but rather the processes that are necessary to generate the individual customer benefits are identified first. For this process or for the customer-related value chain, the roles required for this – as already described in Sect. 3.3 – must then be defined with the defined process input and output. The process level model provides a standardized process hierarchy with defined process levels, e.g.

Level 1 = Higher-level end-to-end process
Level 2 = Main process level
Level 3 = Sub-process level
Level 4 = Work system processes (process functions)

When converting an existing function-oriented organisational structure with an existing organisation chart into a process organisation, the **role designations** should be used in accordance with the existing organisational designations per hierarchy level in order to avoid duplicating or overlapping different organisational structures. For this reason, the term "process-oriented job creation" should also no longer be used and should be replaced by the term process-oriented role creation. The role is defined by the temporary process task, because this is responsible for the process execution. The process output, i.e. the process result to be achieved, defines the responsibility of the role.

The role descriptions do not yet contain an assignment to specific persons. This only happens when the process is carried out. As with hierarchical job creation, a role is described by the organizational congruence principle or the law of unity of task, authority (competence) and responsibility. The following basic questions must be answered for the role-related distribution of tasks and work:

1. What roles are needed in the process?
2. What are the tasks of the role under consideration?
3. What is the factual-logical-temporal sequence of task completion in the role?
4. Which management and implementation competencies are assigned?

5. Which management and result responsibility is assigned?
6. Which interfaces to other roles exist?

The detailed answer to these basic questions, shown in Fig. 3.6, is provided by the continuous swimlane (role)-related process documentation according to the BPMN 2.0 standard, which shows the business processes in a role-based manner in the temporal, factual and logical relationships to the other process participants. Figure 3.6 shows the role contents to be described in process documentation. They replace the job descriptions used in the functional organization.

By assigning **process owners** to these processes at the top level, the foundation is laid for a process organization, which then completely replaces a functional organization, usually described by organizational charts. Process organization also has a hierarchical structure – as shown in Fig. 3.6 – with the end-to-end enterprise process mapping at the top level of authority. This end-to-end process shows the core processes that are run through from customer order entry to delivery to the customer according to his service specifications. Level 2 below focuses on the core processes, level 3 on the sub-processes within the core processes. Finally, in level 4, the individual process function at work system level.

For compliance reasons, the process description itself contains a context-related compilation of all valid regulations and rules as well as the standard requirements together with procedural and work instructions, applicable documents and interface agreements across all 4 **process levels**. Furthermore, the entire IT infrastructure is also

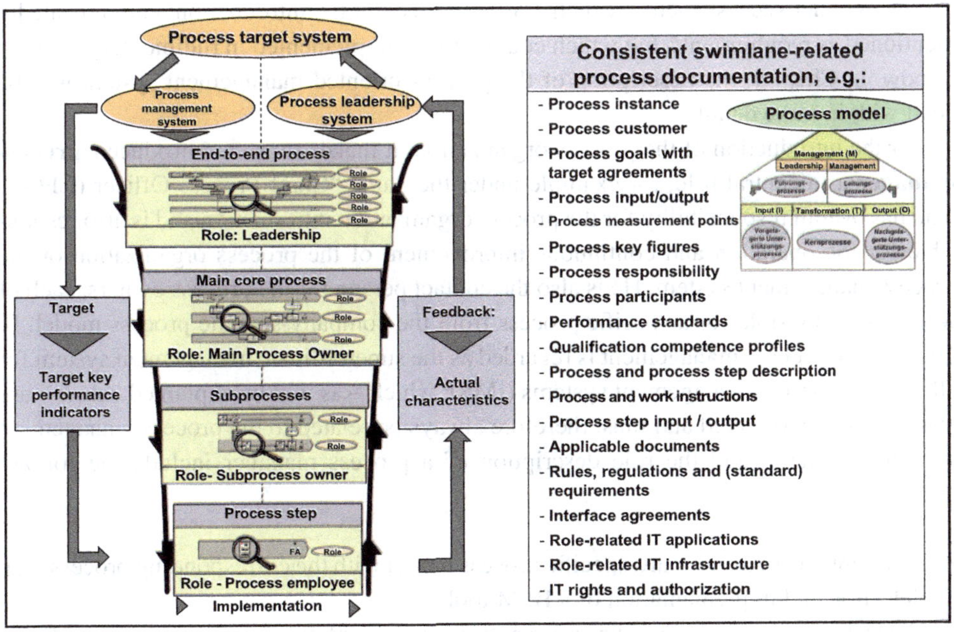

Fig. 3.6 Consistent role-based BPMN 2.0 process description, documentation and design

mapped on a role-related basis with assignment to the process steps. The IT applications used and the role-related IT rights and authorizations are also mentioned here. In contrast to the job description in the function-oriented organizational chart description, the Swimlane representations allow many more process parameters to be mapped in networked form, which then also enable a holistic process digitization view for further process design.

At the same time, the **process documentation** is also the basis for process digitization because the existing or planned IT applications and digitization components are also represented as individual roles within the process documentation. They must now be optimally networked vertically and horizontally as part of the company-specific **digitization strategy**. However, the implementation of many other management system requirements is also based on the documented processes, for example the entire **controlling management** with the mentioned key figures or also the personnel management with the description of the individual process functions and the assigned skill and **qualification profiles**. It was already mentioned in the introduction that this process documentation also serves as an essential component of every management system as proof of the process-oriented implementation.

The decisive factor is that the introduction of a process organization can also enforce the value-oriented **corporate culture** already described in Chap. 2, which is based on participative employee management. This corporate culture, which can only be implemented in process-oriented structures, supports qualification, motivation, freedom from stress, health promotion, well-being, attentiveness, team building, personal responsibility and many other success factors which – as mentioned in the introduction – are repeatedly mentioned as requirements, but which could only be implemented in rudimentary form up to now. In Chap. 4, the description of the process-oriented management system will be dealt with in more detail.

For the introduction of the process organization, it makes sense to introduce a **process manager** as a central role, for example under the name "Chief Process Officer (CPO)", who has overall responsibility for the process organization introduction and is also responsible for the operation and continuous improvement of the process organization or the process management system. He is also the contact person for the process owners, each of whom is responsible for a specific process from the company-specific process model. In this context, process management is regarded as the superordinate management system for all other integrated management systems (IMS), which – as will be explained below – are also all process-oriented and must therefore always be related to the process management system. The tasks and the role description of a process manager include the following tasks:

- Development of a company-specific process model with the corresponding process map
- Selection and implementation of a BPM tool
- Control and coordination of process analysis, documentation and improvement of processes by the process owners

- Continuous improvement of the process organization or the process management system with selected BPM tool
- Specification of conventions for process modeling and process documentation
- Creation of cross-process management standards
- Reviews for the evaluation of the continuous process improvement measures implementation
- Coordination and support of the process owners in the performance of their tasks
- Qualification of those responsible for the process in terms of methods and expertise
- Initiation of the process manager with regard to potential analyses, CIP and lean management concepts with control of the results
- Overall control of the continuous improvement process (CIP)

The **process manager (COP)** and the process owners must work very closely together. While the process manager rather takes over the strategic task within the process organization, the process owners are responsible for the daily business within their process. In coordination with the process manager, the process owner must embed their process goals from the overall business goals and then take over the ongoing management of the processes. This also includes supporting and reporting on the achievement of process goals during process execution, developing suggestions for improvement with the process participants, ongoing coordination and interface optimization with the other process owners, and initiating the adaptation of process documentation in the event of process changes. Furthermore, the process owner is responsible for the coordination and convening of regular internal process team meetings – as described below for shop floor management in Sect. 3.14. The process owner is also responsible for the coordination and convening of regular internal process team meetings.

3.5 Hierarchical Process and Task Distribution Within the MITO Control Loop Model

The task content of process execution by the process owners depends very much on the respective **process hierarchy level**. The **process level model** shown in Fig. 3.7 can be used to classify the analysis priorities and design tasks. Starting at the top level from the end-to-end process, i.e. from the receipt of the customer's order through all operational processes to the delivery of the product or service to the customer, different MITO method-tool application focal points are set at the subsequent levels.

The company-specific target system with the management, employee, process, customer and compliance targets assigned within the MITO model segments is used via the process level model shown for structuring the process management system, i.e. breaking down the individual role-based targets across all process levels down to the workplace, and after process execution for structuring the process control system, i.e. process

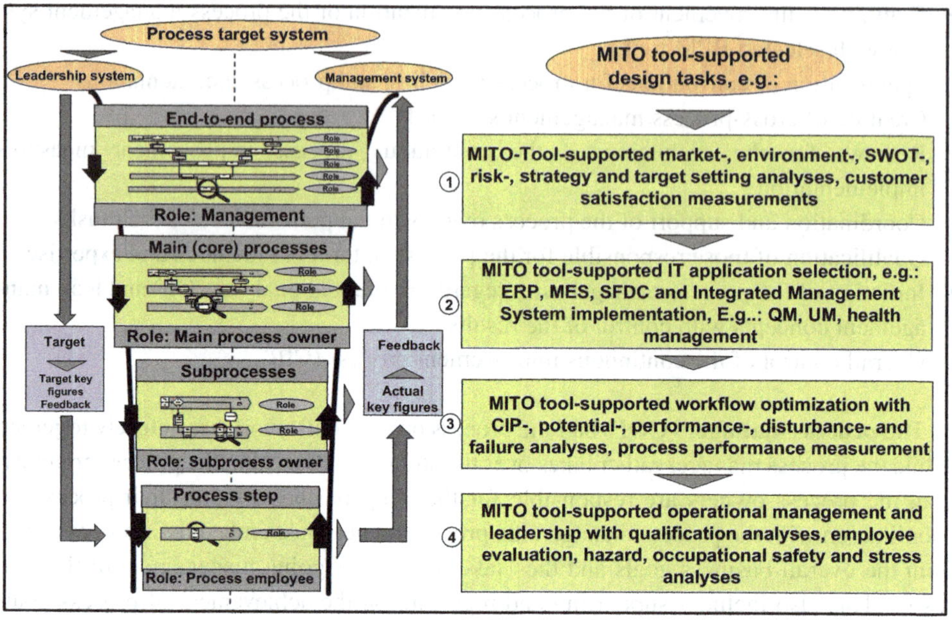

Fig. 3.7 MITO tool-supported design tasks within the process level model s

measurement and evaluation to assess process target achievement. These objectives are then also assigned the target key figures for the target agreement with the process participants.

For the end-to-end process with process ownership in terms of process governance and management, the top level is about comprehensively answering the questions for an optimal business model design. Therefore, the method-tool applications mainly refer to market, environmental, SWOT, risk strategy and target derivation analyses. However, they also include stakeholder analyses, customer satisfaction measurements, trend analyses or scenario analyses.

The main or core processes considered at the following level within the end-to-end process have the MITO method tool application focus, for example, in relation to the MITO tool-supported IT application selection, for example, for ERP, PPS, MES, BDE systems as well as for the integrated management system introduction, such as quality, environmental, health, sustainability, compliance management. There are reference audit checklists for the underlying standards, which are used with the help of the MITO method tool for the fulfillment and implementation evaluation of the respective standard requirements.

The sub-processes considered one level deeper within a core or main process refer to the MITO method tool-supported work flow optimization with CIP, potential, malfunction and error analyses as well as process performance measurements and evaluations. A large number of standard reference checklists are also available for this purpose, which localize the need for action.

At the lowest process model level, i.e. the consideration of the process functions or the individual process step, the focus is on MITO tool-supported operational management and qualification analyses, employee evaluations, hazard, occupational safety and stress analyses. For this purpose, too, there is a large number of standard reference checklists that allow the user to immediately perform very precise analyses and evaluations using the freely selectable two-dimensional evaluation variants with the evaluation dimensions "V = Vertical" and "H = Horizontal". The evaluation results, which show the need for action, can be graphically displayed in portfolio diagrams, radar diagrams or pie charts. This covers the diagnosis phase. In the therapy phase, the goals, measures, target key figure processes or employees are cascaded to the respective localized need for action in order to obtain transparent statements in the form of to-do lists via a goal/measure tree, which show the user how to work through the need for action. The final step is then formed by evaluation, assessment and maturity methods, which can be used to measure the implementation of the measures carried out, the achievement of objectives or the fulfilment of the need for action. The MITO-Method-Tool supports the **methodological competence** of the participants to a great extent. With the provided MITO checklists a target-oriented working off of the necessary tasks and analyses over all process levels becomes efficiently possible. This makes a valuable contribution to achieving corporate, organizational and process goals across all process levels.

3.6 Starting Points for the Implementation of Process Orientation in the Organisation 4.0 Concept

When introducing a process organization, for example in the context of a company-specific business model development, there are a large number of starting points to realize a successful company development. From a holistic perspective, these starting points can be presented in a structured manner in the MITO model within the five MITO model segments. They complement the process-related interlinked initiative and strategy approaches for MITO business model implementation described in Sect. 2.15 and are used to specify the MITO BSC targets discussed in Sect. 4.6.

Subsequently, the digital business model innovations explained in Chap. 5 are assigned to them on a MITO segment basis for further implementation or target achievement.

Furthermore, the **quality components** of a comprehensive corporate quality are named within the MITO model segments, i.e. management, structural, process, result and leadership quality, for which quality-related improvement measures can also be specifically planned within the framework of strategy specifications.

As Fig. 3.8 shows, the starting points in the management segment relate to a reduction in hierarchical levels with the transfer of responsibility to the employees. This may take the form of a team organization based on clearly defined targets. In the final result, the organization chart with the vertically assigned positions there is replaced by a process model with the horizontally mapped processes and the assigned process owners.

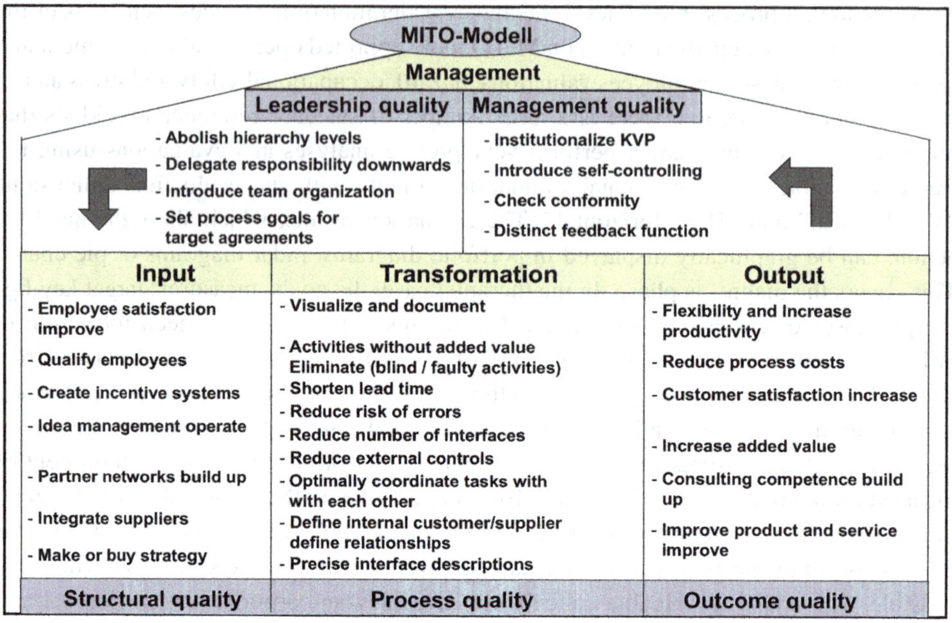

Fig. 3.8 Starting points for the implementation of process orientation in the Organisation 4.0 concept

In the MITO input segment, the aim is to improve employee satisfaction, to qualify employees, to create **incentives for innovation** through room for manoeuvre and thus to raise idea management to a higher level. This is always done in conjunction with the development of **partner networks** and the integration of suppliers. In the transformation segment, the focus is on process quality. Processes must be visualized and documented in order to localize activities that do not add value during process execution. In this way, throughput times can be shortened and the risk of errors reduced. The reduction of interfaces is also an essential starting point, because in this way, the interface errors that frequently occur in practice are reduced. The employees should be able to measure and assess this process quality through self-controlling, so that any deficiencies that are identified can be eliminated immediately.

In the output segment with the focus on the **quality of results**, the aim is to increase customer satisfaction through added value, as well as to improve product and service quality. This is always based on the transparently mapped processes and an integrated process management and control system developed on this basis to assess process performance.

In the MITO management segment, the starting points are a CIP institutionalization and the conformity or compliance check, i.e. whether all instructions, rules and regulations have been adhered to. What is necessary here is a pronounced feedback function with the associated error culture, i.e. that errors can certainly occur and that superiors also take on a role model function here, i.e. that they can also admit to errors themselves.

There are many more starting points for the implementation of process orientation through process organization that are not mentioned here. It is crucial that processes are aligned with the customer, that employees assume responsibility for the execution of their work in a team organization, and that superiors give employees the scope to act on their own responsibility within the framework of target agreements.

3.7 Process-Related Organizational Structure: Quantity Structure Analysis

In a holistic process-oriented organizational development project, but also in the selection of IT applications such as the introduction of ERP/PPS systems, an organizational structure/quantity structure analysis should always be carried out at the beginning in order to determine in detail a whole series of important parameters, such as the number of business transactions, existing asset and cost structures, personnel data, design, work preparation and production data, customer and supplier data, plant and product data, also for **benchmark purposes**, in order to determine the decisive framework conditions and facts of the company. The point of reference here – as Fig. 3.9 shows – is the continuous end-to-end process with the linking of the value chain-related **core processes**. The financial framework conditions can be obtained without much effort from the existing balance sheets, profit and loss accounts and operating statements. This also refers to the supplier and

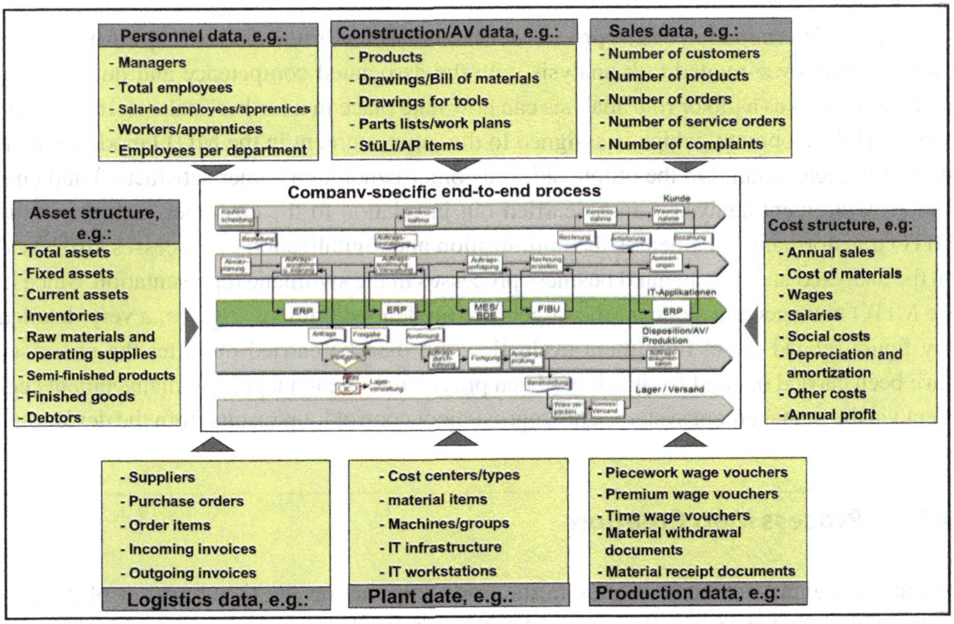

Fig. 3.9 Process-related organizational structure – quantity structure analysis

customer data with the material stocks and product deliveries from the CRM, logistics and ERP systems.

The organization-specific organizational or **process level model** can be used to derive an ever more extensive level of detail across several organizational levels. Starting, for example, at the strategic level via the tactical level to the dispositive and operational level down to the workstation. It is also very important to determine the volume of data to be processed in terms of master and inventory data for customers, suppliers, products, materials, number of orders, purchase orders, invoices, etc. per period. The machines and equipment used as well as the infrastructure equipment should also be determined by key figures. Here already exist in the MITO method tool a whole number of prepared analysis portfolio matrices for the determination of the customer, supplier and product structures etc., in order to specify with it a relatively exact statement for the requirement-fair organization development and organization organization. These analysis structure lists include, for example:

- Customer structure checklist
- Sales Organization Checklist
- Type of order triggering checklist
- Operating mode checklist
- Area Size Checklist
- Order structure checklist
- Location checklist and much more

After the determination of this process-related **organizational structure quantity structure**, the employee-related task analysis with the associated competence and qualification analyses as well as a job or role analysis can now take place in a further analysis. In this way, personnel development, which is assigned to the input segment in the MITO model, is considered in great detail. On the output side, customer benefit, customer satisfaction and customer requirement analyses can be carried out in relation to the customer. A focus in the MITO transformation segment is the optimization and digitalization of processes also based on the analyzed and documented business processes in the swimlane representation. Since in the MITO management segment the targets are predefined with key figures, a very detailed key figure-related target fulfillment evaluation can then be carried out after the processes have been carried out and feedback has been provided to the management management segment via the management system. The improvement control loop results from the deviations.

3.8 Process Map Creation

Again and again, one finds articles in the trade journals on the development of process maps, which, however, usually represent nothing more than a process model in which the management, core and support processes are defined, but without showing the linkage between these processes. Therefore, this process model cannot be called a process map.

The organization-specific process model contains – often also referred to as a **process manual** – the business processes described in detail. Based on the specified high level structure of Integrated Management Systems (IMS), the MITO model distinguishes between the following 5 process types, which are linked together in the MITO model as a control loop. These are:

- Leadership processes in the management leadership segment (Chapter 5: Leadership, Chapter 6: Management)
- Upstream support processes in the input segment (Chapter 7: Support)
- Core processes in the transformation segment (Chapter 8: Operations)
- Downstream support processes in the output segment (Chapter 9: Performance evaluation)
- Controlling processes in the management control segment (Chapter 10: Improvement)

A process map is based on this process model and the business processes it contains. The decisive factor here is that it shows the links between the processes and thus the interaction between them as required by the standards. It thus creates the prerequisite for end-to-end process optimization. This avoids the risk of only dealing with the partial optimum of a separately considered process. Most BPM tool providers create this process map automatically, using the single-process-related input and output connectors stored in the process notation. Only then is a cross-departmental process view possible and replaces the departmental view.

In analogy to maps with different scales, the level of detail can be adapted to the problem at each level of the organizational level model already described. Starting from the strategic view with a large scale, the overview perspective assigned there can be detailed top-down with each level, whereby the mapping scale becomes smaller and smaller and thus the statement becomes more and more precise. In order to determine the flow and interaction of the process named in the process maps, it is necessary to determine the respective process input and process output. In the input/output investigation it is important to find out what the process under consideration requires from the upstream processes or what the downstream process expects from the process under consideration. For this purpose, not only demands on material and personnel, but also on information have to be determined.

If the inputs/outputs and thus also the demands of downstream activities on the process under consideration are known, the task, the purpose and the goal of the process under consideration can now be defined. This can be done in the form of a standardized **process description**.

As shown in Fig. 3.10, the individual processes are linked to each other via a **connector overview** in the form of a map. Only this linkage and interpretation of the interaction enables the potential activation in favor of the overall optimum instead of the partial optimum.

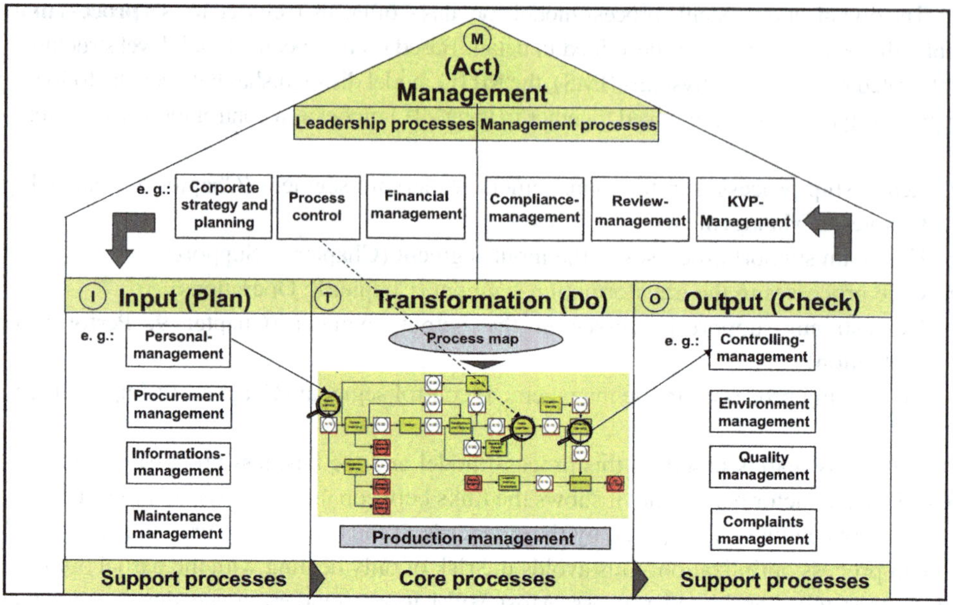

Fig. 3.10 The process map

3.9 Process Connector and Interface Description

As explained above, the **process map** shows how the business processes defined in the process model within the five MITO model segments

> Management processes, upstream support processes, core processes, downstream support processes, governance processes

Are interconnected at the top level via process connectors. In accordance with the process hierarchy view in four levels already explained, this process map can be increasingly detailed across all four levels. Each process level shows how the business processes or sub-processes defined there are related to each other and what output they provide as input via the process connector in terms of an internal or external **customer-supplier relationship**. The individual description parameters within this process map are named in Fig. 3.11.

It begins with a process overview of all four levels in the form of a tree structure and the associated **process characteristics** for the respective process under consideration. The process characteristics include process input, process output, process owner and other **process description characteristics**. Furthermore, a standard-compliant role-based process flow description exists for each selected process. In addition, the connector identification number is named, which is only uniquely defined for one process link in each case.

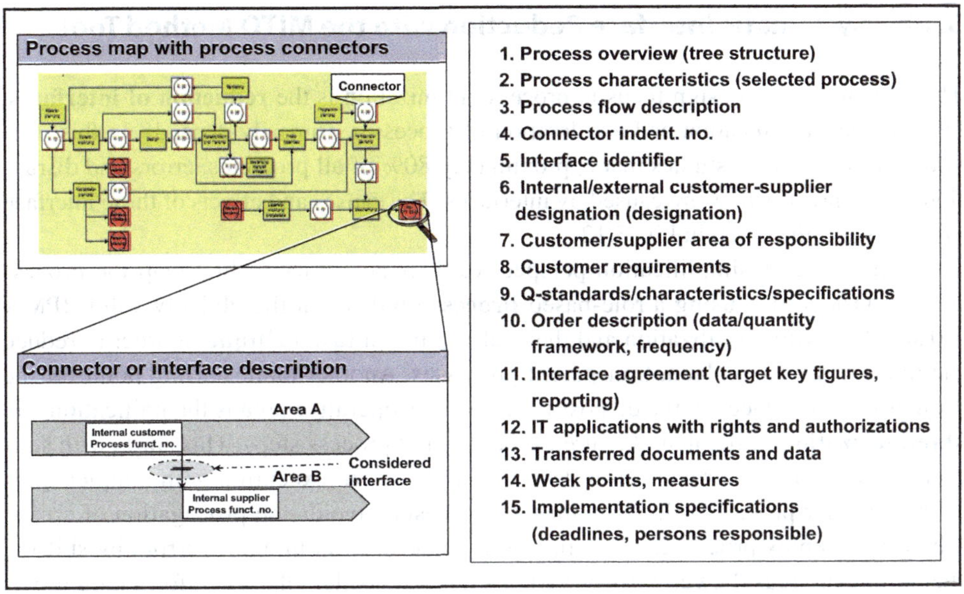

Fig. 3.11 Levels of detail for the process connector or interface description within the process map

The same applies to the internal interfaces located in this process, which are also defined by an interface identification number based on roles. Using a software-supported BPM program, each process can now be opened or mapped in the process map in its individual swimlane representation on a role-based basis. With regard to the connector or interface description, the internal and external customer/supplier relationships are now assigned. This includes the respective area of responsibility, customer or process requirements, quality standards or specifications for these connectors or interfaces.

If applicable, there is also an assignment of the **data quantity framework** it with the frequency at this interface. The internal or external interface agreement describes in great detail which requirements are placed on the internal or external supplier or customer. This is combined with target key figures for interface controlling, in addition to the specifications for reporting. Further information includes the assignment of the IT applications used with this connector or interface with rights and authorizations, documents and data to be transferred. For **potential analyses**, the localized weak points are documented at the connectors or interfaces and suitable measures for the elimination of weak points are stored. Furthermore, there are implementation specifications with regard to deadlines and responsibility in order to initiate a controlled improvement process within this process map representation.

3.10 Systematic Interface Reduction with the MITO Method Tool

The most important design focus in process optimization is the **reduction of interfaces**, because the simplification and acceleration of processes primarily depends on this. It is known from practical studies that approximately 80% of all problems, errors and disruptions in the process flow are caused by interfaces. The causes and effects of these interface problems are illustrated in Fig. 3.12.

From a process simplification perspective, it is necessary to first map the process under consideration using a role-based **process analysis** in the globally valid BPMN 2.0 standard with visualization and then subject it to a **task critique** in order to reduce the interfaces through lean, transparent processes. Another main starting point for the reduction of interfaces in the dispositive as well as operative area is the unification and **standardization** of the manufactured products and process steps. This starts with simpler preparation and organization design, simpler work execution with simpler tools within simpler processes. In particular, this measure avoids the propagation of errors, which in complex processes often increases the cost of eliminating errors by shifting them to other areas. Fewer parts or variants mean considerably less information provision with fewer routings, parts lists, order and stock items. With the correspondingly lower creation, planning and control effort in conjunction with the transfer of greater scope for action to employees in group work structures, it is often possible to dispense

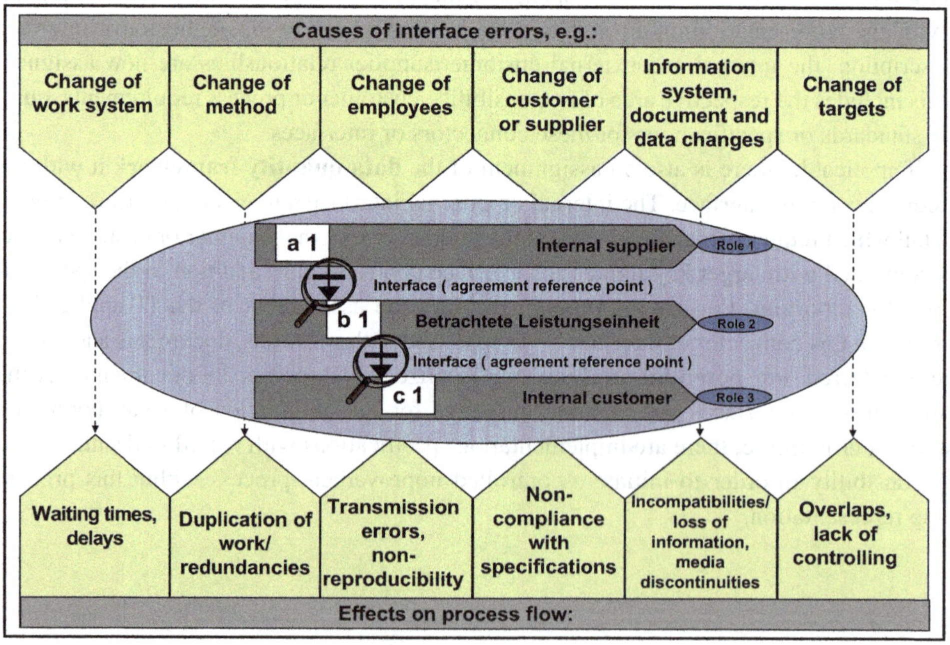

Fig. 3.12 Illustration of the interface problems

with the elaboration of detailed work specifications because the employees act on their own responsibility and do not wait until they receive an order from their supervisor. Due to this reduction in interfaces, completely unnecessary stress situations are reduced for all those involved. There is more room for creativity and innovation. For these reasons, a precise consideration and design of the process interfaces makes a significant contribution to process optimization.

As Fig. 3.13 shows, a comprehensive set of interface design tools for the optimization of the command and control and feedback control system discussed in detail in Chap. 4 is derived from the **interface descriptions** with the help of the **MITO assignment matrix**.

In the case of the management system, for example, these interfaces are the point of reference for clear target agreements within a consistent key figure system with the specification of certain standards, which can relate to costs, time, quality or many other potentials. Furthermore, a defined information and work input and output with clear competence and responsibility allocations is established. The remuneration parameters for the subprocess under consideration can be determined from the targets or target values, and it is also possible to delimit or allocate the necessary resources. In addition, the measurement of results at the work center is facilitated with regard to the control system over the entire process hierarchy. Error assignments and evaluations for building up the company-specific knowledge store are also carried out in relation to interfaces, as are the definition of project milestones and documentation in the form of interface quality or delivery agreements. Furthermore, these interfaces are reference points for monitoring and controlling activities with the associated targets and key figures.

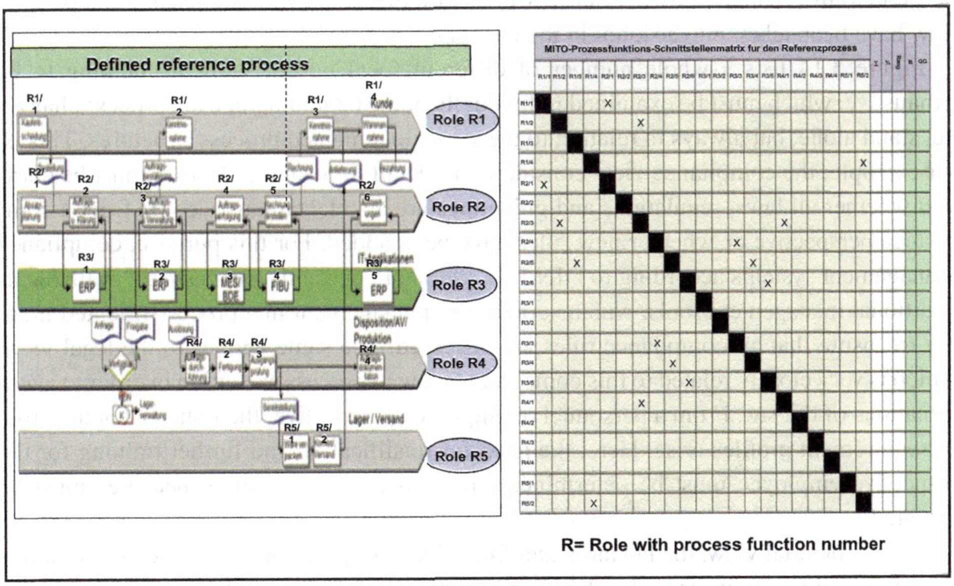

Fig. 3.13 MITO process function interface matrix for the reference process

The progress measurements refer to these reference points and, if necessary, support the definition of **process benchmarks**. All other management views and characteristics can also refer to these interfaces with their starting points and measures. Finally, an essential aspect is the coordination, synchronization and harmonization with other operational parallel, partial or sub-processes, which is also oriented temporally and factually-logically to these interfaces.

The clear interface representation enables a clear role-related assignment of the process parameters, whereby this process representation is company-neutral and has a freely selectable level of detail. In each role, it is graphically displayed when and where actions take place with which documents and data and which office or function holders are directly or only indirectly involved, for example by way of information. For the process digitization discussed in Chap. 5, the networking concept can be created using the IT integration levels shown.

3.11 Process Design Priorities for Change

As described in the introduction in Chap. 2, **process changes** occur in practice for various external reasons due to new product developments, new technologies or new customer requirements. However, from an internal perspective, the starting point for process changes is often the optimization of processes due to identified weaknesses or in potential analyses in order to activate as yet unused cost, time, or quality potential. From a holistic process design perspective, however, it is important to apply as many different design views as possible to the changed process in order to ensure that all factors influencing the process flow have been taken into account in the changes.

Figure 3.14 lists a whole number of different focal points, without claiming to be exhaustive, which must be examined individually at the beginning of each process change, i.e. stand alone, but always in relation to the same documented process structures. This is, for example, the compliance view considered in detail in Sect. 6.3. Here it must be clarified whether all laws, regulations and guidelines are also taken into account from a compliance perspective or whether new rules have been added. For this purpose, compliance management systems according to DIN ISO 19600 are currently increasingly available as additional management tools, which support the management in a process-oriented manner to ensure that all compliance rules are observed. The same applies to the legal view, which is very closely related to this compliance view in process execution in order to avoid violations of the law. From a personnel or employee perspective, the issue is that new role or requirement profiles arise. Here, the need for qualification and further training for the respective employee must be determined and, if necessary, training measures must be initiated.

In the potential view, the business and financial key figures must be redefined in terms of measuring points in order to obtain information about the trend via the recording of these key figures during process execution. The process view involves documenting the

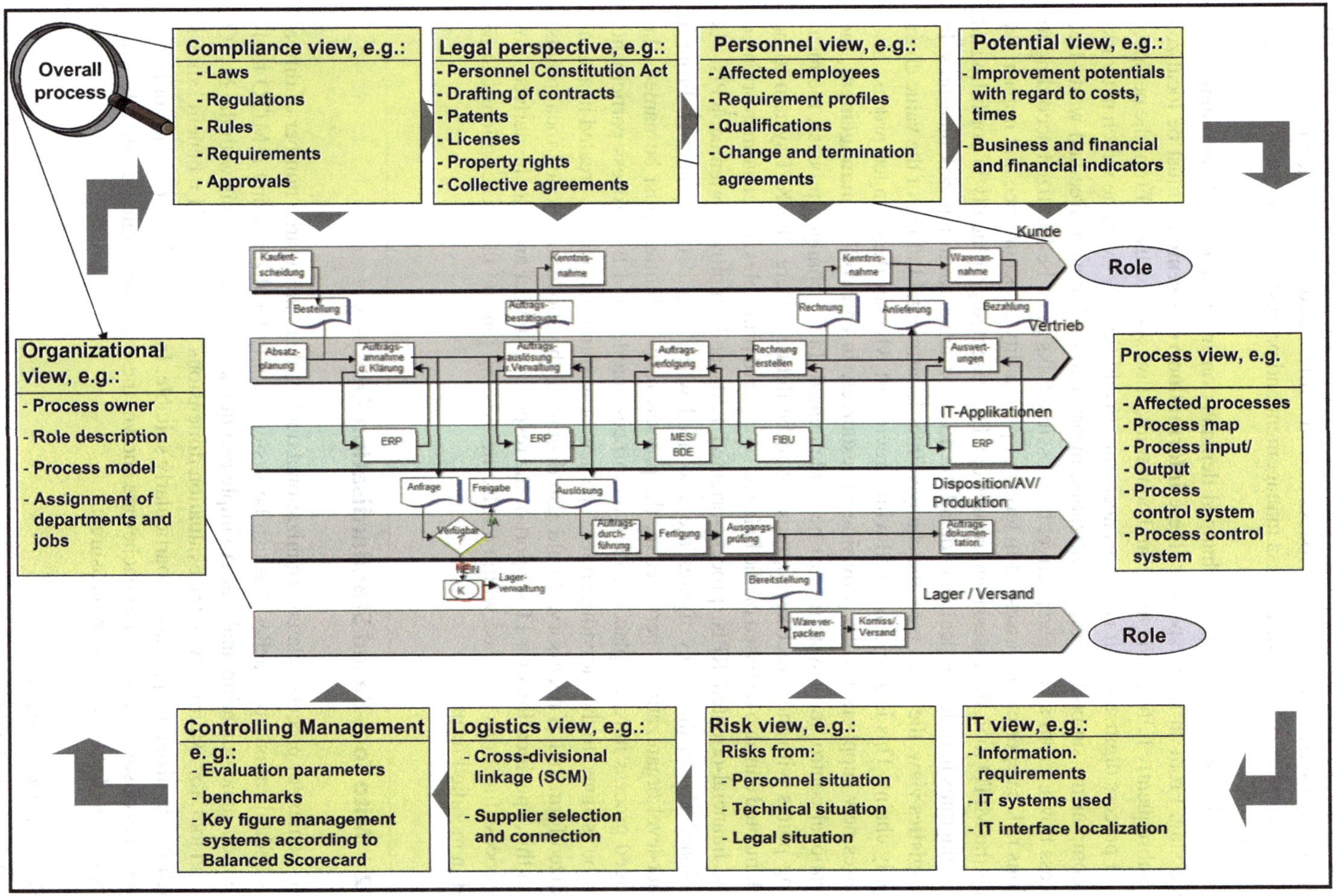

Fig. 3.14 Main points of consideration for process changes

affected processes, describing the process flow in a role-based manner, adapting the process maps, and modifying the process management and process control system across the process levels.

Changed processes also place changed demands on information and communication processing. From an IT perspective, these **information requirements** must be localized and subsequently fulfilled via the IT and communication systems used. From the perspective of process digitization, it is always necessary to additionally examine which networking components support process digitization in order to enable error-free and waste-free process flows. From a risk perspective, the possible risks must be localized according to various risk categories and assessed in terms of probability of occurrence and impact. By using the MITO tool, the assessment results can be presented graphically in portfolio and radar diagrams in order to localize in detail the need for action to initiate risk measures. In the **logistics view**, the focus is on the changed interdepartmental linking of the value chain (supply chain). This is also combined with a review of whether the changed process also requires new suppliers for the provision of resources. In **controlling management**, the operational control loop system must be implemented. In the changed process, the measuring points with the target key figures are to be defined. Here, the KPI system to be implemented can also be based on the balance-score-card principles, i.e. customer-oriented KPIs, financial-oriented KPIs, process-oriented KPIs and employee-oriented KPIs. As mentioned above, these key figures are also used when considering potential. From a higher-level organizational perspective, the process responsibilities must be named, the changed process must be placed within the process model, and the process participants must be assigned to the individual roles. The new descriptions should be created in a standardized form and, if necessary, should also document the above-mentioned focal points. From this, **specifications** for IT support of the respective subject area can be derived. For the process functions assigned within a role, the existing job and task descriptions can be used in modified form.

3.12 Mito Tool-Based Standardisation Analysis

In the context of process-related organizational design, there are a large number of different standardization approaches that can be systematically localized using a MITO tool-supported standardization analysis. A simple and quick portfolio analysis with the MITO method tool, for example, with the evaluation dimensions "V = effort, H = benefit" shows which standardization approach is particularly suitable. In Fig. 3.15, all contents or reference points of some of these approaches are shown; these are, for example, the following process-related standardization measures:

- Performance standards
- Process time standards
- Process cost standards

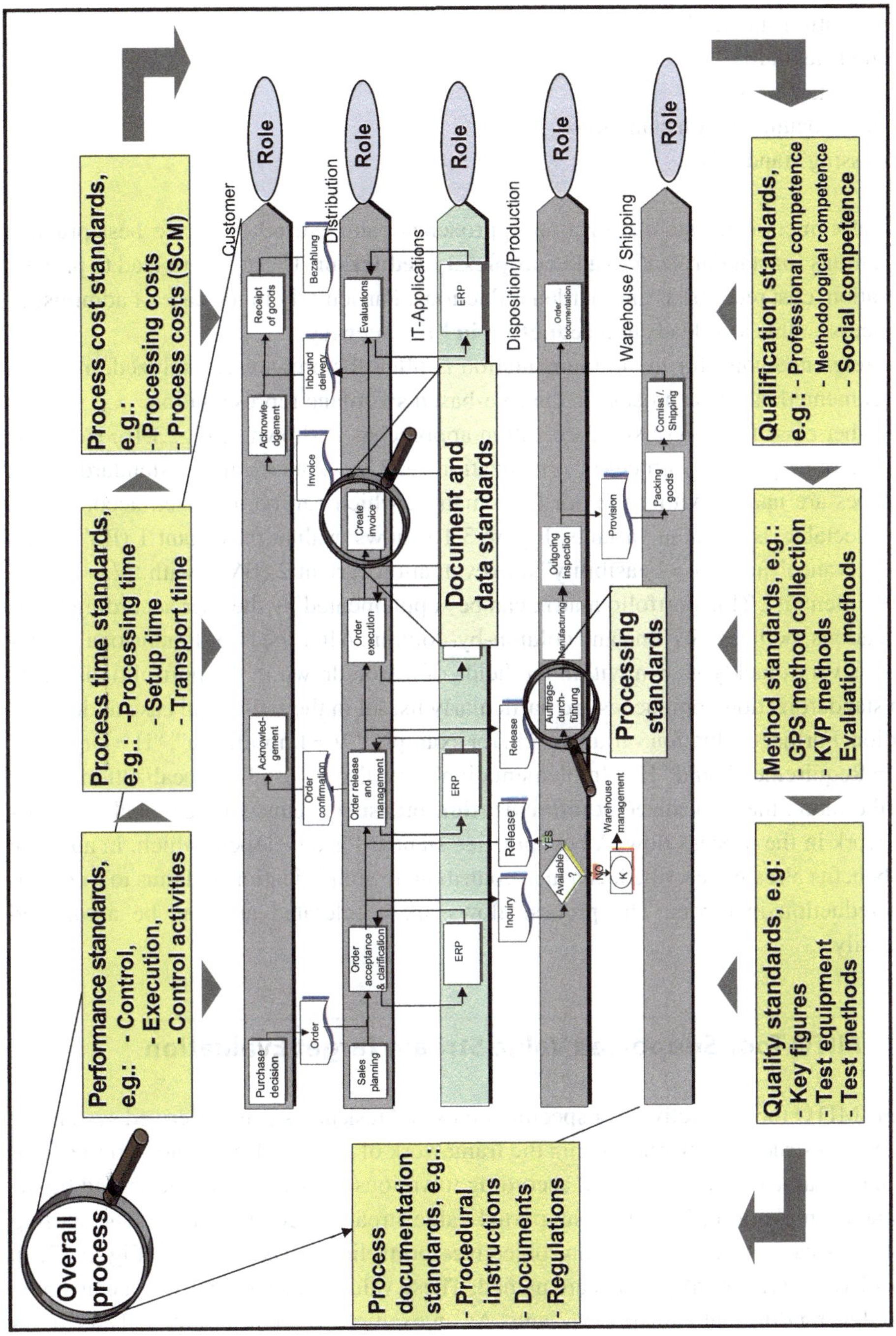

Fig. 3.15 Process-related standardization approaches

- Qualification standards
- Method standards
- Quality standards
- Process documentation standards
- Processing standards

The aforementioned standardization approaches can be used to derive best practice specifications for standardization and **complexity reduction**. These in turn lead to process acceleration, cost reductions and burden reductions. Particularly in the case of administrative processes, this also leads to a **reduction in bureaucracy**.

The reference point for the implementation is often the previously analyzed, modeled and documented business process in the role-based swimlane representation.

A further classification of standardization approaches is shown in Fig. 3.16. Here, the four clusters of product-, process-, organization- and workplace-related standardization approaches are named within the portfolio matrix, which can be localized according to freely selectable assessment variants. Figure 3.16 shows evaluation variant 1 (BV1) with "V = Relevance" and "H = Feasibility" and evaluation variant 2 (BV2) with "V = Effort" and "H = Benefit". This portfolio matrix can be supplemented by the user according to his specifications, both line-by-line and column-by-column. After the two-dimensional evaluation, it is very quickly shown within the fields of action drawn in the portfolio diagrams which standardization approaches are particularly useful in the individual case under consideration. Further evaluation variants with, for example, "V = Importance", "H = Urgency" or "V = Requirement" and "H = Implementation" can also be used for localization.

Furthermore, these localized **standardization measures** reduce a great deal of preparatory work in the process flow. A best practice standard is developed, which, in addition to the benefits already described, can also contribute to simplification and thus to a considerable reduction in errors. The process flows are accelerated and can be automated more easily.

3.13 MITO Tool-Supported Value Stream Target Evaluation

With the MITO tool, objectives for specific topics and task areas can be derived systematically and in a structured manner within the framework of process design and optimization, and can be evaluated and prioritized according to various aspects. This is described below using the example of a MITO tool-supported value stream target evaluation. The starting point in this case is the value stream objectives portfolio matrix shown in Fig. 3.17, in which 14 **value stream objectives** are named. These value stream objectives can again be analyzed using different valuation variants. As an example, three different analysis views with the associated three valuation variants (VV) and the assigned valuation dimensions are mentioned here:

Standardization approaches, e.g.:		BV1 V	BV1 H	BV2 V	BV2 H
1. Product-related, e.g.:					
1.1 Inquiries					
1.2 Offers					
1.3 Orders					
1.4 Parts lists					
1.5 Invoices					
	Σ C				
	Σ C / n				
2. Process-related, e. g.:					
2.1 Key figure definitions					
2.2 Routings/work sheets					
2.3 Production plans					
2.4 Defect recording sheets					
2.5 Stock overviews					
	Σ C				
	Σ C / n				
3. Organization-related, e.g.:					
3.1 Role descriptions					
3.2 Qualification standards					
3.3 Interface descriptions					
3.4 Rules/regulations					
3.5 Reports					
	Σ C				
	Σ C / n				
4. Work organization-related, e.g.:					
4.1 Cleaning standards					
4.2 Job space/arrangement standards					
4.3 Work methods					
4.4 Procedures					
4.5 KVP standards/ergonomics standards					
	Σ C				
Scale: 1 = low	Σ C / n				
6 = high	Total				
	Total / n				

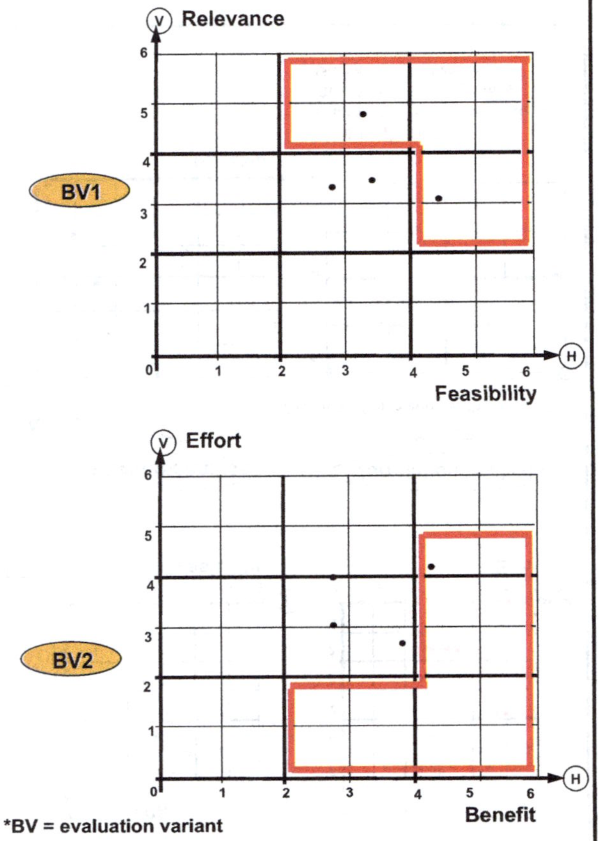

Fig. 3.16 MITO tool-supported standardization analysis

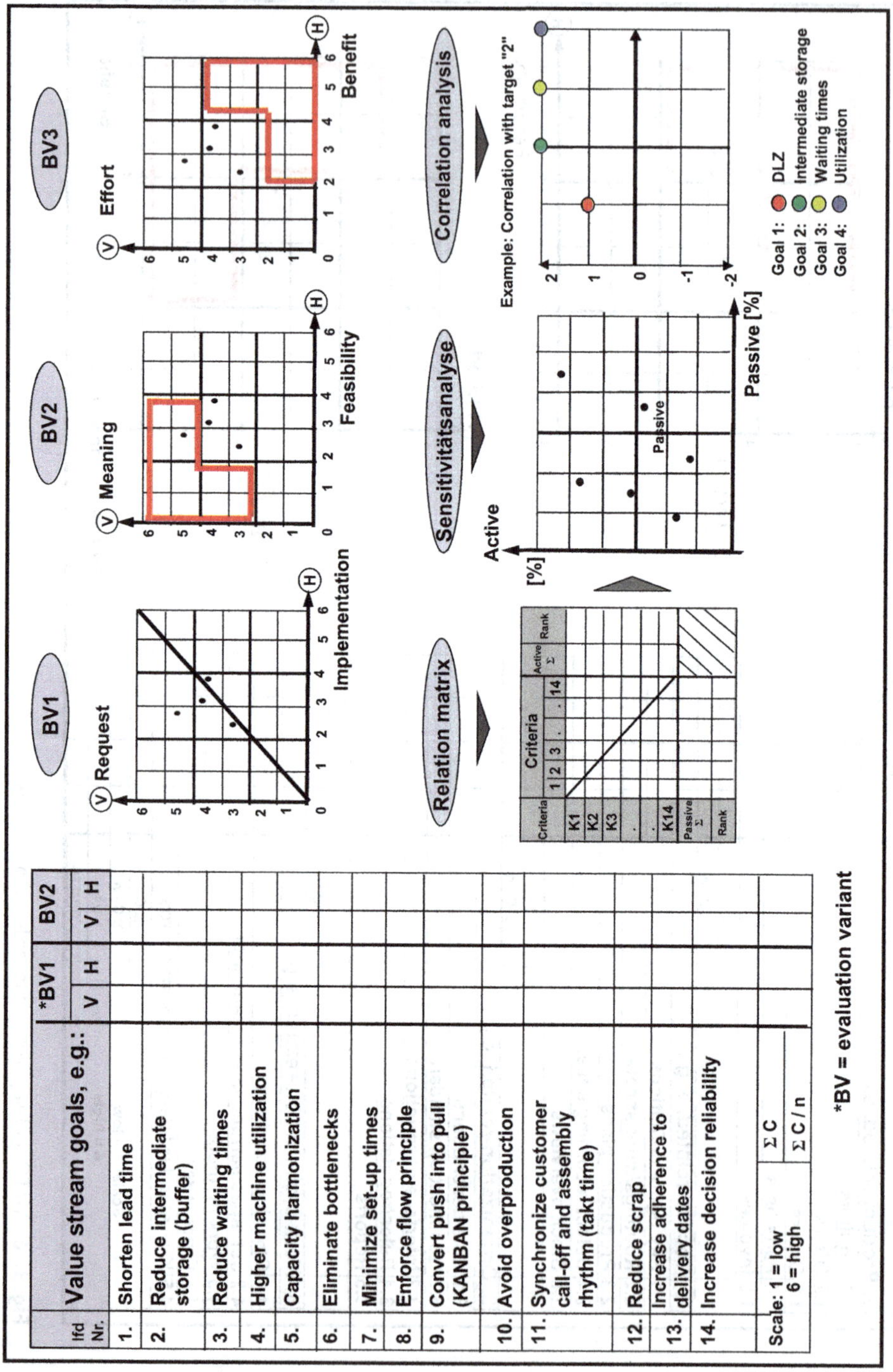

Fig. 3.17 Value stream targets portfolio matrix

For the achievement of objectives	BV1:	V = Requirement	H = Conversion
For the implementation of objectives	BV2:	V = Meaning	H = Feasibility
For the target-expenditure-benefit analysis	BV3:	V = Benefit	H = Effort

Here there would be other possible assessment variants, such as BV4: "V = probability of occurrence", "H = impact" for the identification of risks that endanger or prevent the achievement of objectives. From the evaluation of each individual objective with the scores from 1 = low to 6 = high for the above-mentioned evaluation dimensions with "V" and "H", the graphical representation of results in the portfolio or radar diagram already yields clear process-related statements as to which objective still requires action.

In order to prioritise values and objectives, the sensitivity analysis can be used to determine the influence of the individual objectives on each other using the relationship diagram also shown in Fig. 3.17 and to rank them in order of importance. Using the MITO-supported correlation analysis, it is then determined for each individual goal which other named goals have either a reinforcing or reducing effect. Furthermore, a pairwise comparison can be carried out to specify the ranking of the objectives. These analyses provide the user with a comprehensive statement on the sequence to be followed in the processing of objectives for all processes together or for each individual process under consideration.

In order to determine whether there is any need at all for a **value stream analysis** in a company and which value stream objectives are to be achieved in the process, the MITO value stream requirements analysis described below can be used. The portfolio matrix shown in Fig. 3.18 lists questions that, when answered, give the responder an indication of whether there is a need for action. For example, question 1 refers to whether the company-specific end-to-end processes are documented in a role-based manner. The degree of fulfillment of this question can be answered via the scaling of grades from 1 to 6 stored for each question; in this case, via a percentage rating. From the description or determination of the actual state by the actual grade assignment, the target value to be achieved can be specified at the same time for a possible target specification with the MITO method tool, also by means of a grade assignment. The complete answering of all questions with the actual evaluation and target specification then shows the user very clearly in which questions there is a need for action. At the same time, the user has already set a company-specific value stream target. The radar chart evaluation now graphically shows the discrepancies between the actual and target values. At the same time, the deficits to be eliminated are clearly localized (see Fig. 3.18).

With the MITO method tool, targets and measures for eliminating these **target-actual deviations** can now be derived via a target/measure cascade. As a result, this so-called MITO royal road provides automatically generated to-do lists with measures and responsibilities for meeting the value stream targets.

Another possibility is the generation of submatrices per target or also per main weak point. As explained below, tool-supported cause/effect chains can be formed one

Nr.	Evaluation criteria	Dimensionen		Scaling: Grade assignment					
		Target	Actual	Grade 1	Grade 2	Grade 3	Grade 4	Grade 5	Grade 6
1	Are the end-to-end processes documented in a role-based manner?	5	2	0%	30%	50%	70%	90%	100%
2	On-time delivery performance in % against confirmed delivery date known?	5	3	<60%	<70%	<80%	<90%	<95%	100%
3	Product-related end-to-end lead time known?	5	2	>40Tg	40Tg	35Tg	30Tg	25Tg	20Tg
4	Variation of average lead time per product known?	5	3	>20%	20%	15%	10%	8%	5%
5	Employee-related processing time per product known?	6	4	>14Std	12Std	10Std	8Std	6Std	<4Std
6	Current material cost share in the company known?	4	3	>80%	<70%	<60%	<50%	<40%	<30%
7	Number and trend of product variants known? (number)	5	2	3	5	8	10	15	>15
8	Lot size- anticipation horizon in pre-production/production known?	4	2	>20Tg	20Tg	15Tg	10Tg	5Tg	1Tg
9	Are the stocks of semi-finished parts in the production process (WIP work in process) known?	2	5	Very Low	Low	ange-messen	Etwa höher	hoch	Sehr hoch
10	Are the causes of the existing production problems known?	2	6	Very Frequent	Frequent	ange-messen	weniger	selten	Very selten
11	Are the top 10 production and logistics problems in the company known?	3	5	Compl-etely	Frequent	ange-messen	weniger	selten	Very selten
12	Are value stream targets set by management? (number)	5	2	0	3	5	8	10	>10
	C								
	ΣC/n								
Scale: 1 = low 6 = high	Total								

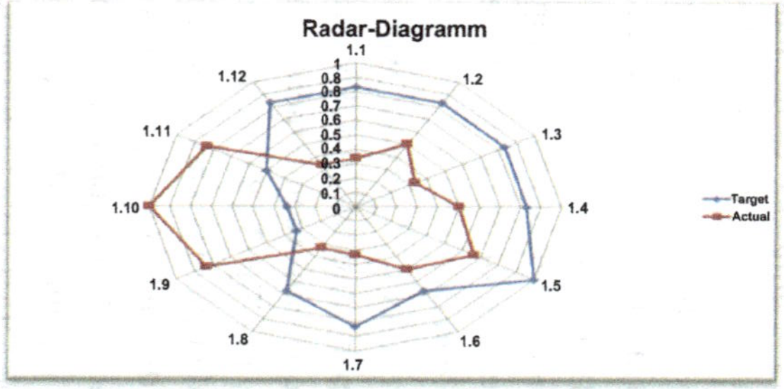

Fig. 3.18 MITO value stream demand analysis with target derivation

observation level lower, following the example of the **Ishikawa diagram**, in order to also analytically record all causes that lead to the identified weakness or target deviation via this systematic observation of the main influencing variables output portfolio matrix and to provide them with measures.

The Ishikawa diagram (cause-effect diagram) developed by the Japanese Ishikawa is commonly used for the systematic approach to identifying the causes of weaknesses and problems. Because the analysis model graphically resembles the shape of a fishbone, it is often referred to as a fishbone diagram.

When creating the cause-effect diagram according to Ishikawa, for the given main effect, all main and secondary causes are assigned that produce this negative main effect. These main causes collide with the horizontal arrow pointing in the direction of the main problem effect. This results in the herringbone pattern mentioned above.

This Ishikawa diagram can also be used in digital form for the successful implementation of a **target-measure analysis**. In Fig. 3.19, the cause-effect diagram is now replaced by the target-measure diagram. In this example, with the classical main influencing variables (clusters) man, machine, material, as well as environment. The starting point is a value stream target portfolio matrix, which can be analyzed from different analysis views according to the 4 evaluation variants BV1 to BV4 shown, in order to determine the need for action. The main goal to be achieved from Ishikawa's point of view is No. 6: Eliminate bottlenecks.

In the MITO method tool, a first sub-matrix for 4 main clusters is created line by line for each value stream target (in this case no. 6) in accordance with the Ishikawa approach. For each main cluster, a second sub-matrix is again created one level down, in which the individual measures per main cluster are stored. These measures can be evaluated for all 4 clusters together, for example – as shown – with BV4 according to "V = Effort and H = Benefit", in order to determine which measures bring the greatest benefit in the value stream vulnerability elimination "Eliminate bottlenecks". This is followed by the generation of a to-do list for processing the localized measures. The final step is an **evaluation of the measures**.

3.14 Systematic Process Potential Analyses

The process targets focus on the primary potentials. This refers to the performance indicators such as costs, times, qualities, services, and capacity utilization that link the critical success potentials on the input side with the critical success factors on the output side during the transformation process. Figure 3.20 lists the target variables of **potential analyses**. In the consideration in this chapter, it is a matter of assessing the achievement of these potential target values via the primary potentials. In the **recording of potential values, it** is important to determine the adjusting screws for the primary potentials within the considered business process easily and quickly in order to achieve the mentioned target values. These adjusting screws refer, for example, to the process parameters and potential target values mentioned below.

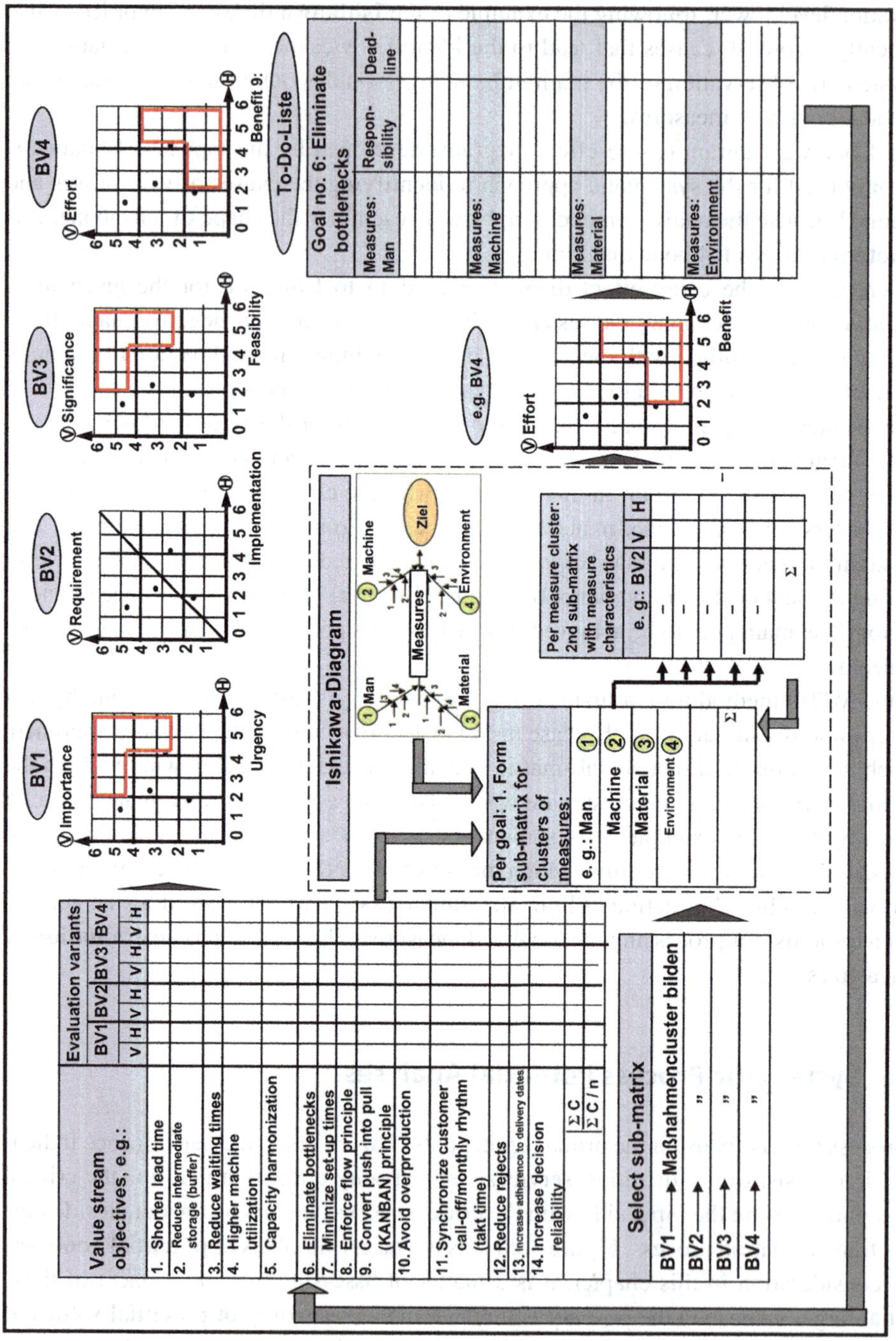

Fig. 3.19 Continuous Ishikawa value stream target and measure analysis

Further results of these process-related potential assessments are, for example, statements about:

Number of process functions	Actual/target
Number of process participants	Actual/target
Number of process areas	Actual/target
Number of process levels	Actual/target
Number of interfaces	Actual/target
Process costs per process function	Actual/target
Process times per process function	Actual/target
Process participants per process function	Actual/target
Quality standard per process function	Actual/target
Process utilization per process function	Actual/target
Process area per process function	Actual/target
Resource consumption per process function	Actual/target
Share of value added per process function	Actual/target
Share of non-value added per process function	Actual/target.

For better understanding and classification, this information must always be supplemented by the structural data described in point 2.7, i.e. production quantities, number of cases, available capacity of existing resources, logistics data, etc. The potential analyses can be applied in all processes defined in the MITO model. In the management and leadership processes as well as in the core and support processes.

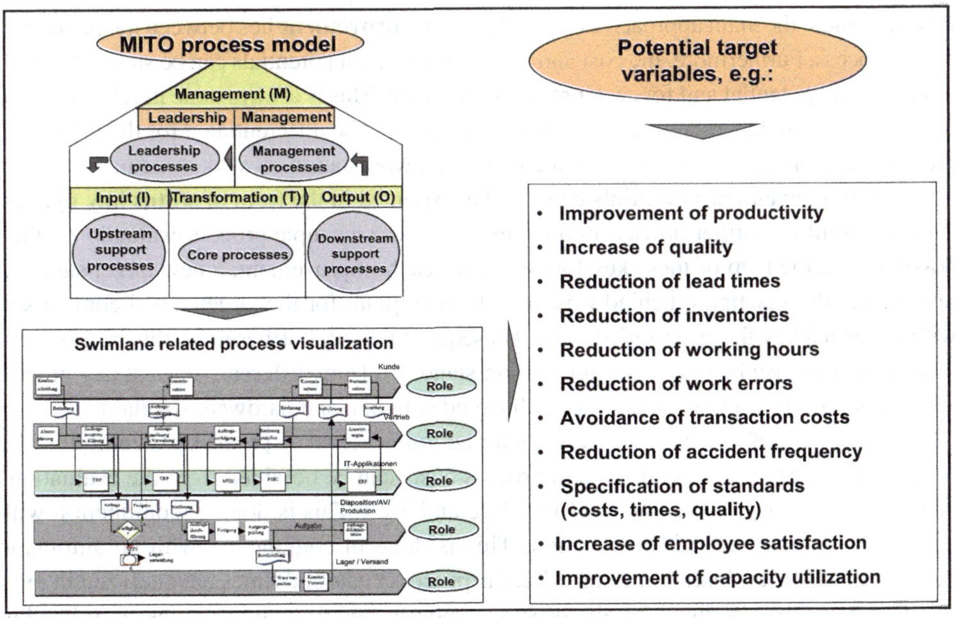

Fig. 3.20 Process-related target values for potential analyses

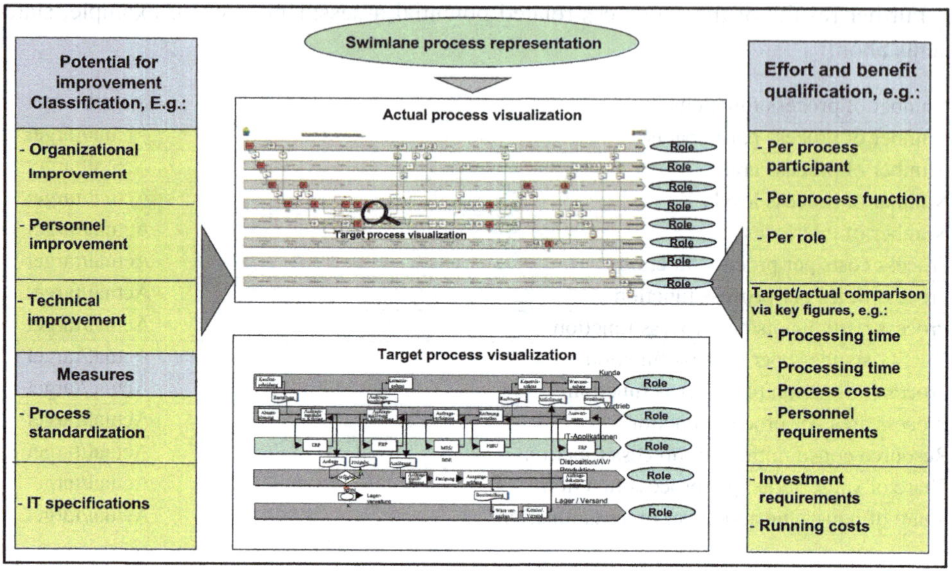

Fig. 3.21 Process-related improvement potential and benefit assessment

Figure 3.21 graphically illustrates the desired result of an improvement potential and benefit assessment by means of a direct **comparison of the actual and target process representation**. As this figure shows, the improvement potentials can be differentiated according to organizational, personnel, technical, IT or other improvements in order to find out in this way where the main approach of the **potential improvement** lies between the actual and target process. Furthermore, the cost and time improvement potentials can be shown for each improvement potential and for each process participant. This is always done in relation to the respective role in the process representation, but can also be differentiated for the individual process function, i.e. broken down to the individual workstation or work system.

These **improvement potentials** can also be presented in the form of **status key figures**. This is helpful for further process improvement because a simple process evaluation is then possible with the help of these key figures. After each improvement, a new target standard results, and the key figure behind it is the reference point for the target/actual comparison with the actual key figure recorded in the subsequent period. Furthermore, this process representation can also be used to assign certain standards from different views at any point – here, as an example, IT specifications with stored software and hardware standards.

An indication of which processes require action in terms of process expenditures and process revenues or process times and process costs can be obtained from the evaluations of the portfolio diagrams shown in Figs. 3.22 and 3.23. This is done in conjunction with automatic ranking and ABC evaluation. This is done in conjunction with an automatic ranking and ABC evaluation. In Fig. 3.22, the process costs and times are analyzed in relation to the process. In Fig. 3.23, the process expenses and process revenues are related to each other.

Lfd. Nr.	Processes	(V) Prozess-kosten			(H) Prozess-zeiten		
		Kosten	%	Rang	Zeiten	%	Rang
P1	Marketing process	0.2 Mio	3.5	6	0.2 J	7.1	5
P2	Development process	2.5 Mio	43.5	1	0.5 J	17.7	2
P3	Planning process	0.4 Mio	7	5	0.4 J	14.2	4
P4	Procurement process	0.6 Mio	10.4	3	0.5 J	17.7	2
P5	Production process	1.5 Mio	26	2	1 J	35.5	1
P6	Spare parts supply process	0.05 Mio	0.9	7	0.02 J	0.7	7
P7	Recycling process	0.5 Mio	8.7	4	0.2 J	7.1	5
	Total	5.75 Mio	100		2.82 J	100	

Cumulated and sorted

Rang	Pro-zess	Prozesskosten %	kummuliert
R1	P2	43.5	43.5
R2	P5	26	69.5
R3	P4	10.4	79.9
R4	P7	8.7	88.6
R5	P3	7	95.6
R6	P1	3.5	99.1
R7	P6	0.9	100

Rang	Pro-zess	Prozesszeiten %	kummuliert
R1	P5	35.5	35.5
R2	P2	17.7	53.2
R2	P4	17.7	70.9
R4	P3	14.2	85.1
R5	P1	7.1	92.2
R5	P7	7.1	99.3
R7	P6	0.7	100

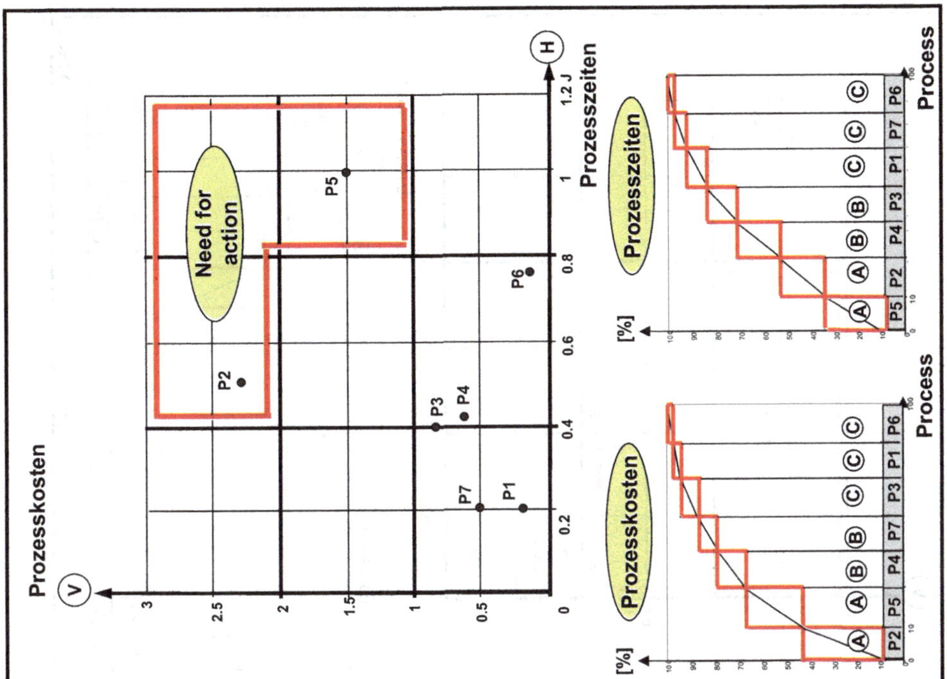

Fig. 3.22 Process cost and time portfolio diagram related ABC analysis

Lfd. Nr.	Processes	Ⓥ Expenditures			Ⓗ Revenues		
		Expenditures	%	Rank	Revenues	%	Rank
P1	Marketing process	0.5	9.8	4	0.2	4.2	4
P2	Development process	1.5	29.4	1	1.7	36	2
P3	Planning process	0.4	7.8	6	0.2	4.2	4
P4	Procurement process	0.6	11.8	3	0.6	12.7	3
P5	Production process	1.5	29.4	1	1.8	38	1
P6	Spare parts supply process	0.1	2	5	0.12	2.5	6
P7	Recycling process	0.5	9.8	4	0.1	2.1	7
	Total	5.1	100		4.72		

Cumulated and sorted

	Expenditures	
	%	Cumulated
Rank 1	29.4	29.4
Rank 1	29.4	58.8
Rank 3	11.8	70.6
Rank 4	9.8	80.4
Rank 4	9.8	90.2
Rank 6	7.8	98
Rank 7	2	100

	Revenues	
	%	Cumulated
Rank 1	38	38
Rank 2	36	74
Rank 3	12.7	86.7
Rank 4	4.2	90.9
Rank 4	4.2	95.1
Rank 6	2.5	97.6
Rank 7	2.1	100

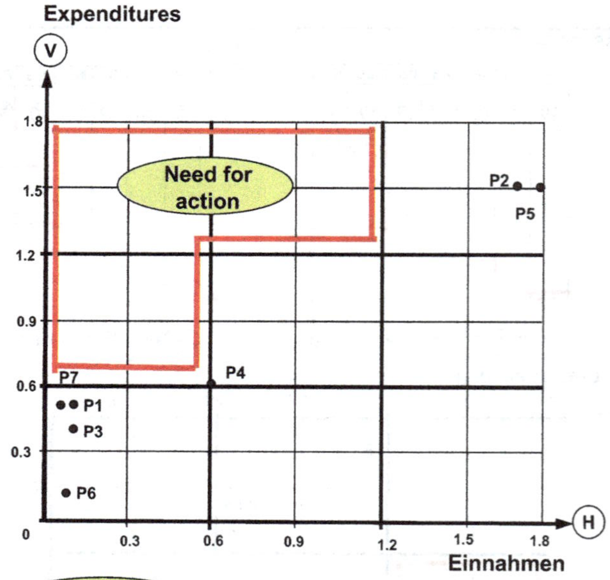

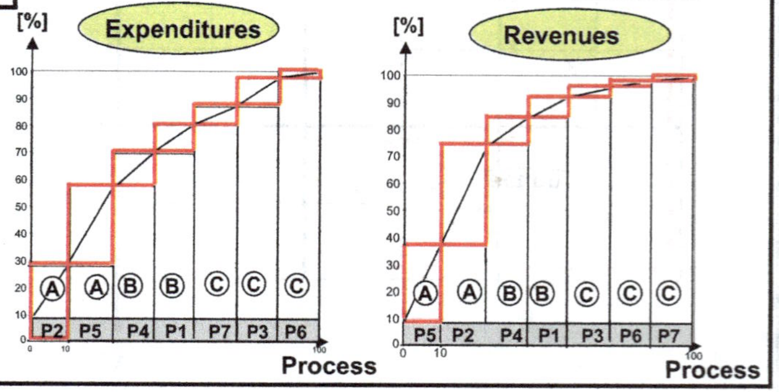

Fig. 3.23 Expense/revenue portfolio chart related ABC analysis

3.15 Process Design Tasks in Shop Floor Management

Many companies have recognized that they need to align their **value chain** with the customer throughout with process-oriented organizational structures. Faultless and wasteful process execution on site improves customer satisfaction. **Shopfloor management** is designed to support managers in optimally guiding employees in the operative execution of processes at their workplace. The activities required for this can be depicted as a cybernetic control loop model within the MITO model segments "Leadership, Input, Transformation, Output, Management". In Fig. 3.24, these operational shop floor design tasks are named within the overall framework of management tasks. They are assigned to the individual MITO model segments.

In the **management segment,** the process owners must agree on clear process goals with their employees. For this purpose, process target key figures must also be specified, which are assigned to specific measuring points in the previously analyzed, modeled and documented process in the swimlane representation. Furthermore, guidelines (**Code of Conduct**) must be specified for managers as a management instrument, which prescribe participative employee management. In the **input segment**, the focus is on the process- or role-related qualification of employees and on the standardization of processes, for example through KATA. Kata is a term from the Japanese martial arts and specifies behavioral routines that enable error-free work at the shop floor level even under stress and pressure. Here, movement sequences, i.e. work execution routines, are passed on from teachers to learners, which lead to employees continuously improving their processes. At the car

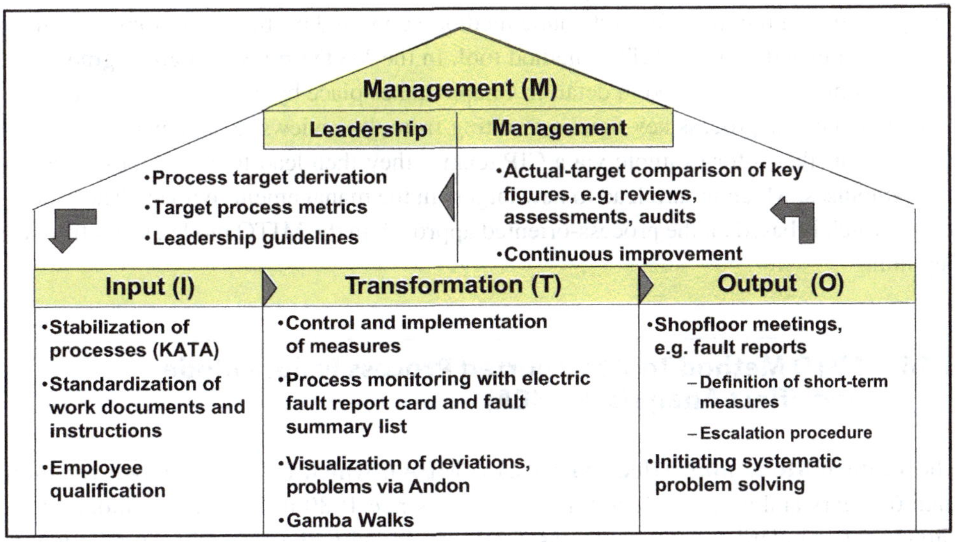

Fig. 3.24 MITO model-related shop floor management

manufacturer Toyota, Kata is used as a coaching concept and as an improvement strategy for the production system.

The **KATA philosophy** is supported by the standardization of work documents and rules. In the **transformation segment**, the manager controls the measures and monitors the implementation of these planned measures by the employees. The process monitoring leads to the fact that disturbances, deviations, errors or other problems are recognized and reported up-to-date. Here, for example, there is an electronic **fault report card** or also an electronic fault summary list as support, with which occurring faults in the process are immediately documented and after the cause localisation for the elimination of these faults the necessary measures can be quickly initiated. (Cause-effect chain mapping).

The detection of the malfunction is facilitated by Andon. Andon is a visualization methodology developed by Toyota and used in the Toyota Production System, e.g. optical signals on a machine to indicate problems and malfunctions at the problem location on the shop floor level. The Andon Card (rip cord) can be used to automatically or manually initiate a conveyor or line stop when problems occur.

The hallmark of **shop floor management** s is the increased absence of managers on the shop floor in order to carry out regular routines such as gemba walks. The Japanese term "Gemba" refers to the exact location of value creation in production. Gemba walks are designed to have management directly look for optimization opportunities through observation, understanding the full impact of the problem. Gemba walks are not fixed, but highly interactive and situational.

The shop floor meetings mentioned in the **output segment are** also intended to help establish close contact between employees and supervisors, which increases motivation and improves the problem-solving and improvement capabilities of all involved. This always results in impulses for systematic method-supported problem solutions, which are then implemented with the MITO method tool. In the **MITO management segment,** the process controlling explained in detail in Chap. 4 takes place by means of an actual-target comparison of the process key figures resulting from the reviews, gemba walks, audits or andons. Together – for example via a CIP team – they then lead to continuous improvement impulses, which in turn lead to new targets in the management segment. The process cycle, which is based on the process-oriented approach in the MITO model, starts from the beginning.

3.16 MITO Method Tool Supported Process Failure Mode and Effect Analysis (PFMEA)

The **Failure Mode and Effect Analysis** (FMEA), which has been known for more than 60 years and was developed in America – since 1980 it has been included in the catalog of standards in Germany as DIN 25448 with the title "Failure Sequence Analysis (Failure Mode and Effect Analysis)" – has the goal of avoiding potential failures from the outset through systematic evaluation instead of discovering and correcting them after the fact. Before the implementation phase of an error-prone product or process, this FMEA is carried out in order to localize potential risks of products or process errors, then to analyze the cause and consequences of such errors and risks, and finally to document avoidance and detection measures for risk and error reduction. Especially in the automotive industry, many suppliers have to evaluate their products and processes within the framework of FMEAs on the instructions of the vehicle manufacturers. This is in accordance with the specifications of, for example, the VDA (Verband der Automobil Industrie, German Association of the Automotive Industry) or also the Automotive Industrie Aktion Group (Automotive Industry Action Group, AIAG). Both associations, i.e. VDA and AIAG, have now developed a joint FMEA guideline which enables suppliers in the North American and German markets to apply a uniform FMEA procedure model. The goal of this guideline is to produce an accurate complete and robust FMEA that meets all customer requirements. Some changes to the previously known FMEA procedure have been worked out, among other things, 6 FMEA steps are now carried out instead of the 5 steps previously used by the VDA. The determination of the risk priority number (RPN) is omitted, instead a task priority (risk matrix) is used. This is done in a standardized FMEA form with new evaluation catalogs.

In the following, a process failure mode and effect analysis (PFMEA) carried out with the MITO method tool is described as a variant to this procedure, which can be carried out easily and quickly just like a process risk mode and effect analysis (PRMEA). This MITO-specific 2-dimensional risk assessment with a portfolio matrix can now be integrated very well into the 6-step procedure currently presented by the VDA and AIAG. The FMEA manual procedure prescribed by VDA/AIAG involves the following 6 steps:

- Step 1: Define the scope of observation.
- Step 2: Process structure analysis
- Step 3: Process Function Analysis
- Step 4: Error analysis
- Step 5: Risk analysis
- Step 6: Process-FMEA-goals-action-tree-derivation

Figure 3.25 illustrates these 6 steps with the methods and procedures as applied to the MITO tool-supported process failure mode and effects analysis.

Step 1 "Determine scope of consideration" is about delimiting the scope of the investigation, in this case the definition of the process to be considered for which the process FMEA is to be performed.

The MITO process model is used to define the scope of consideration in step 1 of the process FMEA. Here, according to the High Level Structure of the Integrated Management Systems (IMS), the processes are divided into the five MITO model segments:

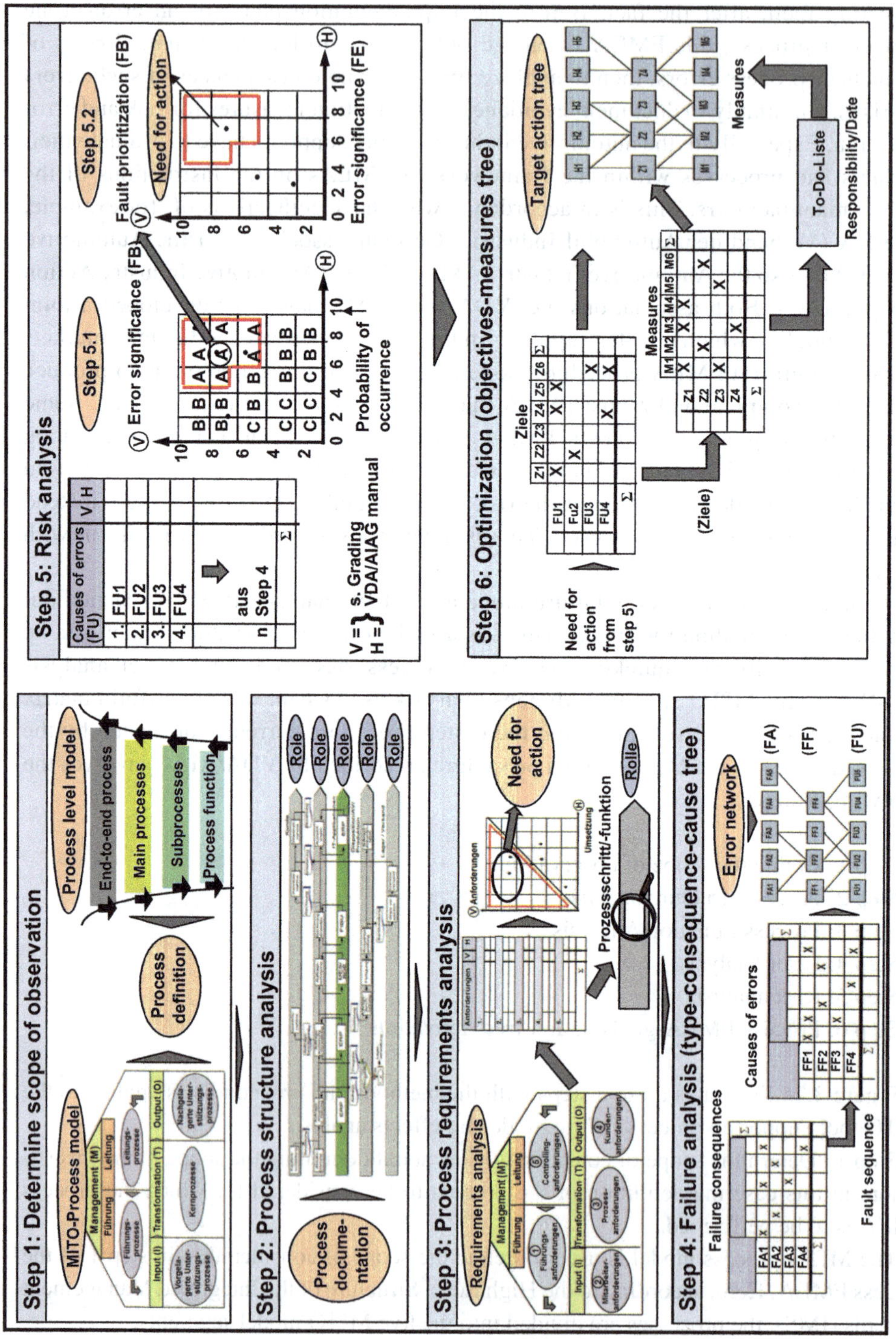

Fig. 3.25 MITO tool-supported process failure mode and effects analysis (FMEA)

1. Management processes in the MITO management segment
2. Upstream support processes in the MITO input segment
3. Core processes in the MITO transformation segment
4. Downstream support processes in the MITO output segment and
5. Controlling and CIP processes in the MITO management segment

A further delimitation takes place via the process level model shown. Here, the process hierarchy is mapped via four levels. The end-to-end process is on the top level, the main process on the second level, the subprocess on the third process hierarchy level, and the process function or process step view on the lowest, i.e. fourth level. Furthermore, this step 1 also includes the creation of a project plan with the assignment of potential team members as well as the project schedule with the milestones.

In step 2 "Process structure analysis", a process analysis and description takes place according to the already described valid BPMN 2.0 process visualization standard in the role-related swimlane representation. If no process documentation, for example from the quality management system manual, is available, the first thing to do is to create this process documentation in the swimlane representation. All relevant standards, rules and design views can then be clearly assigned and described to this process in a context-related manner, i.e. factually-logically-temporally.

The process function analysis in step 3 refers to the role-based process structure documented in step 2. With the support of prepared MITO requirements portfolio matrices, a requirements analysis is now performed per process step. In these MITO requirements reference checklists, a large number of requirements are also clustered again according to the MITO model structure, i.e. differentiated according to

- Leadership requirements
- Employee Requirements
- Infrastructure requirements
- Legal requirements
- Process requirements
- Customer requirements
- Compliance requirements
- Controlling requirements and others

The graphical representation of the results in the portfolio diagram shows the need for action, i.e. which requirements still need to be met with which measures.

This is followed in step 4 by an **error analysis**, also supported by the MITO method tool. This involves determining possible errors per process function or process step with the identification of possible **error causes** and the visualization of error relationships, i.e., error sequence, error type, and error cause. This can then be mapped graphically in a fault network. Based on the determination of possible defect types, again with the support of MITO portfolio checklists, the defect sequence and defect cause are then determined via an assignment matrix cascade formation. For the assignment of defect sequences to the defect type and defect causes, there are prepared defect sequence and defect cause catalogs in the MITO method tool. For the creation of the failure cause catalogue, it is useful to carry out a failure cause analysis beforehand with the MITO method tool. Here, typical failure causes are clustered in the MITO portfolio matrix, for example, according to the classic 4 M's methods of Ishikawa, i.e. analysed in relation to the cause of the failure to the human being, to the machine, to the material and to the environment.

After the assignment in the assignment matrices, the fault network – also referred to as the sequence cause tree – can be mapped graphically with software support. It shows the interrelationships between which defect types, which defect sequences and which defect causes can occur in a network.

In step 5, the localized failure causes from step 4 are subjected to a risk analysis. The purpose of this risk analysis is to localize possible risks by evaluating significance, occurrence, and detection with subsequent assignment of avoidance and detection measures. Avoidance measures are intended to facilitate optimal process planning to minimize the possibility of defects occurring. Detection measures are intended to locate existing failure causes or failure modes either automatically or manually before the component leaves the process or is shipped to the customer. The risk analysis performed in the following Step 5 using the MITO Method Tool to locate and prioritize risks by evaluating significance, occurrence, and detection is performed in two analysis substeps.

In step 5.1, the risk assessment for significance focuses on the failure consequence. In the VDA-AIAG guideline, a total of 10 evaluation levels are defined for the consequence of failure significance. These evaluation levels defined there are also used in the MITO portfolio failure consequence significance analyses. The evaluation of the occurrence of risks represents the cause of the defect. Here, too, the VDA-AIAG guideline defines 10 occurrence levels, which are also adopted.

The risk assessment in step 5.2 refers to the discovery of the defect cause and/or defect type that has occurred. The task priority AP described further in the VDA-AIAG guideline, which is intended to replace the risk priority number RPN from the classic FMEA analysis, results, as explained below, from the graphical representation of the results of the risk assessment in step 5.1 in the portfolio diagram.

The starting point is therefore, as also shown in Fig. 3.25 in step 5.1, a defect cause or defect type portfolio matrix. It is now evaluated with the help of the MITO method tool according to the evaluation dimensions: "V = importance of the defect" and "H = probability of occurrence" with the given scales of 1–10 of the VDA-AIAG manual. The portfolio result diagram now shows the defect priority, this is once again subdivided into an ABC classification. A risks have the highest defect priority. Therefore, further risk analyses must be carried out here in order to also detect these errors. This is done in step 5.2, where the initial portfolio matrix is also evaluated again, now according to the "V = error priority" and "H = error detection" determined in step 5.1. Where with score 10 fault detection is hardly possible and with score 9 fault detection is very unlikely. Here, too, it can be seen in the presentation of results in the portfolio diagram for step 5.2. that the greatest need for action to eliminate the possible errors exists in the upper right segments.

The optimization follows in step 6 of the process FMEA. This is again MITO tool-supported via the MITO royal road, i.e. through the derivation of an objectives/measures tree with the graphical representation of the measures derivation similar to the error network representation in step 4. As shown in Fig. 3.25, the need for action for risk elimination localized in step 5.2 is linked in the first assignment matrix on the top level with the objectives that are to be achieved when the risk is eliminated. Again, there is a risk objectives catalog in the MITO method tool for this purpose, which can be freely configured by the user. After assigning the risk objectives from this objective catalog in the assignment matrix on the first level, the assignment matrix on the second level is activated. Here, the previously assigned column-wise objectives in level 1 are now arranged row-wise in this assignment matrix in level 2 and the measures required to achieve these objectives are listed column-wise.

These measures for risk elimination are also stored in a **risk/measure catalogue** and can be transferred from there to the objectives/measure allocation matrix. In this risk/measure catalogue, the measures are further differentiated according to avoidance and detection measures. For each goal, a to-do list is then created with the assigned measures with responsibility and deadline. Furthermore, this need-for-action-goals/measures tree is graphically depicted. The final step is an evaluation of the implementation of the measures, also in the MITO method tool. Here an evaluation according to efficiency and effectiveness takes place again 2-dimensionally via a portfolio matrix evaluation. Since the entire implementation of all 6 steps is carried out with the support of the MITO method tool, the FMEA results are available in digitalized form and can always be used in modified form.

The very extensive and detailed described procedure in the FMEA VDA-AIAG manual is replaced by the MITO method tool supported procedure with less effort but equally good results.

3.17 MITO Tool-Supported Design of Work Systems According to DIN EN ISO 6358-2016

Another important standard specification for human-oriented process design and optimization is DIN EN ISO 6385. This standard is the basic ergonomic framework for the design of work systems, for example in production, offices, transportation, trade, health care or other areas with the main objective of humanizing and improving the efficiency of work. This international standard lays down basic principles of ergonomics in the form of guidelines for the design of work systems and standardizes the relevant principles and terms. In December 2016, the third, revised and modernized edition replaced the previously valid version of the international standard from 2004.

The aim of DIN EN ISO 6385 is to assist in the operational redesign or reorganisation of work systems by providing the necessary basic ergonomic knowledge and principles. The working person is the main factor and integral component at the centre of the system to be designed. The work result, the productivity as well as the well-being and health of the employee are decisively influenced by the technical, organizational and personnel factors of the work system. The ergonomic findings formulated in the standard are therefore aimed at the humane and economical design of work systems.

The term "**work system**" is used in DIN EN ISO 6385 to describe a wide range of work situations and workplaces. Work systems include the interaction of people with work equipment within an environment and a work organization. This includes both fixed and flexible or temporary (mobile) workplaces in production, logistics, production-related areas (e.g. maintenance), administration and trade, as well as in other areas (e.g. care, teaching).

For the practical implementation of DIN EN ISO 6385:2016, a systematic procedure in Six Phases for the Design of an Ergonomic Work System with implementation of the MITO Method Tool was developed, which significantly facilitates the design of work systems for users, i.e. in detail the ergonomic design of equipment and machines, work environments and personal protective equipment.

The main component of DIN EN ISO 6385 is the definition and explanation of the phases for designing an ergonomic work system. Figure 3.26 shows the individual phases of ergonomic work design adopted from the MITO procedure model with

- Phase 1: Requirement and goal analyses of the work system
- Phase 2: Task analysis with function assignment
- Phase 3: Ergonomic design concept
- Phase 4: Ergonomic design detail concept implementation
- Phase 5: Testing and implementation
- Phase 6: Assessment and monitoring (evaluation)

Phase 1, "Requirements and objectives analyses", is concerned with concretely determining the work design requirements for the work system in terms of the design of socio-technical systems by means of several different method-based portfolio analyses. Examples of this are the already explained CIP, hazard, potential or weak point analyses. The characteristic of the MITO method tool in the analysis phase is the 2-dimensional evaluation of the portfolio checklist, whereby the user can specify the evaluation variants (BV) for the checklist criteria. This is always done in the two dimensions "V = vertical" and "H = horizontal". These are the coordinates of the portfolio diagram in which the results are displayed. Possible evaluation variants (BV) for one and the same problem are, for example, BV 1: "V = Requirement", "H = Implementation", BV 2: "V = Relevance", "H = Frequency", BV 3: "V = Importance", "H = Urgency", BV 4: "V = Effort", "H = Benefit" and many more

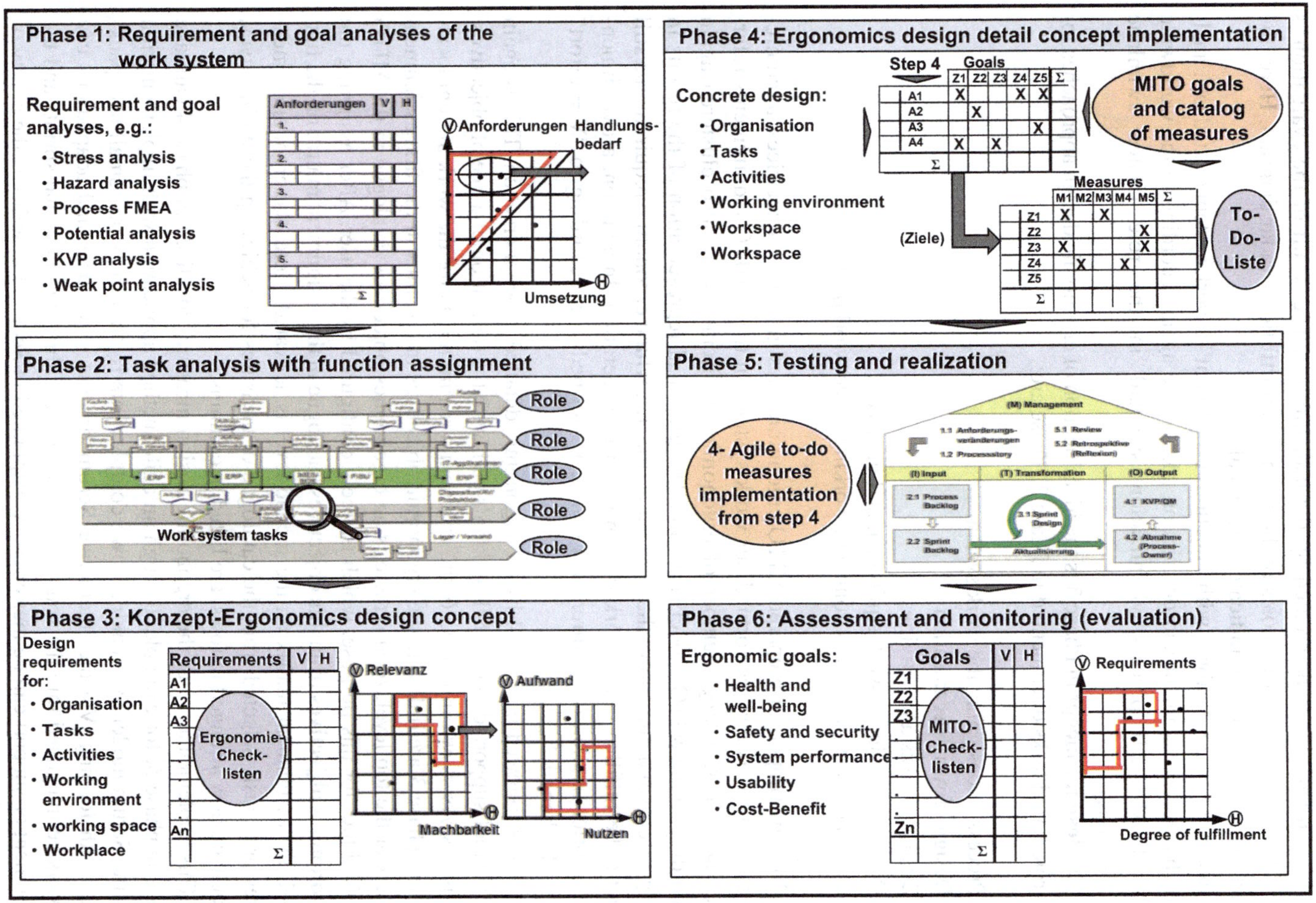

Fig. 3.26 Process of designing a work system according to DIN EN ISO 6385-2016

evaluation variants to be created by the user himself. The result of the evaluation is then displayed for the diagnosis in the form of a portfolio or radar diagram. Here, the need for action is clearly indicated graphically.

In phase 2 "Task Analysis with Function Assignment" a work system related task analysis, function assignment and description takes place again according to the worldwide valid BPMN 2.0 process visualization standard in the role related swimlane representation.

The **design concept** in Phase 3 is the identification of ergonomic design approaches for the role-based tasks documented in Phase 2. These are:

- Process of designing the work system
- Design of work organisation
- Design of tasks and activities
- Design of products, work equipment and interfaces
- Design of the working environment, working space, workplace

With the support of prepared MITO ergonomics design portfolio matrices, a requirements analysis is now performed per work system. In these MITO requirements reference checklists, a large number of ergonomic requirements are also clustered again according to the MITO model structure. The graphical representation of the results in the portfolio diagram shows the need for action, i.e. which ergonomic requirements still need to be fulfilled in the work system under consideration. In addition, a two-dimensional prioritization of requirements can be performed, e.g. according to "V = effort" and "H = benefit".

This is followed in phase 4 by the ergonomic detailed concept creation. This is again MITO tool-supported via the MITO king's path with the derivation of a tree of objectives/measures. As shown in Fig. 3.26, the ergonomic requirements for the work system localized in phase 3 are linked to the ergonomic objectives in columns in the first assignment matrix at the top level. Again, there is an ergonomics objectives catalogue in the MITO method tool for this purpose, which is freely configured by the user. After assigning the **ergonomics objectives** from this objectives catalogue in the assignment matrix on the first level, the assignment matrix on the second level is activated. Here, the ergonomic measures previously selected from the catalogue of measures for achieving these objectives, which are now arranged in rows, are listed in columns.

This implementation of the ergonomic design measures localized in phase 4 can take place in phase 5, for example, through an agile method application with implementation via the Scrum model by breaking down complex interrelationships into small task packages with looping. Via the interactive Scrum process, new ideas and adaptations can always be integrated into the solution development within the individual sprints and the fulfilment or support can be measured. As explained in Sect. 4.14, agility is the ability of an organization, or the people in it, to respond to unplanned changes, e.g., changes in the way things are done:

- New requirements
- Malfunctions, failures
- Lack of resources
- Rules/rules
- Customer expectations

To react quickly, correctly and appropriately under uncertain, turbulent, complex, ambiguous conditions.

After the implementation of the **work system design** measures, DIN EN ISO 6385 recommends in phase 6 a continuous evaluation and monitoring of the ergonomic target achievement with regard to:

- Health and well-being
- Security
- System performance
- Serviceability
- Cost/Benefit

This method-based assessment, e.g. with "V = requirement" and "H = degree of fulfilment", results in further approaches for the continuous improvement and further development of the work systems. These evaluation procedures are – as already mentioned in phase 1 – for example the identification of hazards, risks, potential and productivity analyses, utility models, psychosocial stress analyses and others. The control loop closes for the assessment procedures. Here, there are separate MITO tool-supported procedures with the associated standard reference portfolio checklists for the two-dimensional assessment of the respective problem.

Method-Based Integrated Process-Related Leadership and Management System Development

4

Abstract

The MITO corporate goal system depicted in Chap. 2 after answering the 7 W-questions for the description of the company-specific business model with allocation of the sub-goals within the MITO model segments

- Performance targets in the management segment,
- Employee goals in the input segment,
- Process goals in the transformation segment,
- Customer targets in the output segment,
- Compliance goals in the management segment,

As well as the differentiation in Sect. 2.9 according to value, cultural, social, economic, technological and ecological target aspects is now the starting point for the development of a continuous integrated management and leadership system as an essential control loop component of the MITO business model and the prerequisite for the cultural transformation that now follows.

4.1 Balanced End-to-End Business Model-Target System Implementation

Due to the **balance requirements** explained below, this process-oriented management and control system is a further development of the higher-level management system that was previously considered as a unit, without the subdivision now made into the management system on the input side and the control system on the feedback side. This subdivision is also appropriate because the requirements to be placed on the

H. F. Binner, *Holistic Business Model Transformation*,
https://doi.org/10.1007/978-3-658-37367-2_4

ERP/PPS systems on the input side with the target data specifications and the MES solutions on the feedback side with the associated actual data are to be formulated more clearly in the course of digitization. For this reason, the management segment in the MITO model is divided into the management and control segments from a control loop perspective.

The essential prerequisite for success, i.e. the achievement of objectives, is that there is a balance between people-based management and subject-based management, i.e. that there is a balance between the soft facts practiced in the management system by the responsible process owners and the hard facts also applied by these process owners in the subject-based management system.

The point of reference for the conception of the management and control system is the continuous **process level model** described in Chap. 3, which maps the process hierarchy, starting from the end-to-end process via main and sub-processes down to the process function on the lowest, i.e. shop floor level. The overall context is shown in Fig. 4.1 with the continuous process level mapping and the assigned five company-specific target and action areas within the MITO model segments.

The five entrepreneurial target and action fields"**success orientation, financial orientation, employee orientation, process orientation and customer orientation** are interconnected via the MITO model to form a cybernetic control loop". At the beginning there is the success orientation with the specification of the visions and objectives from a strategic point of view. They are the reference point for the subsequent operative

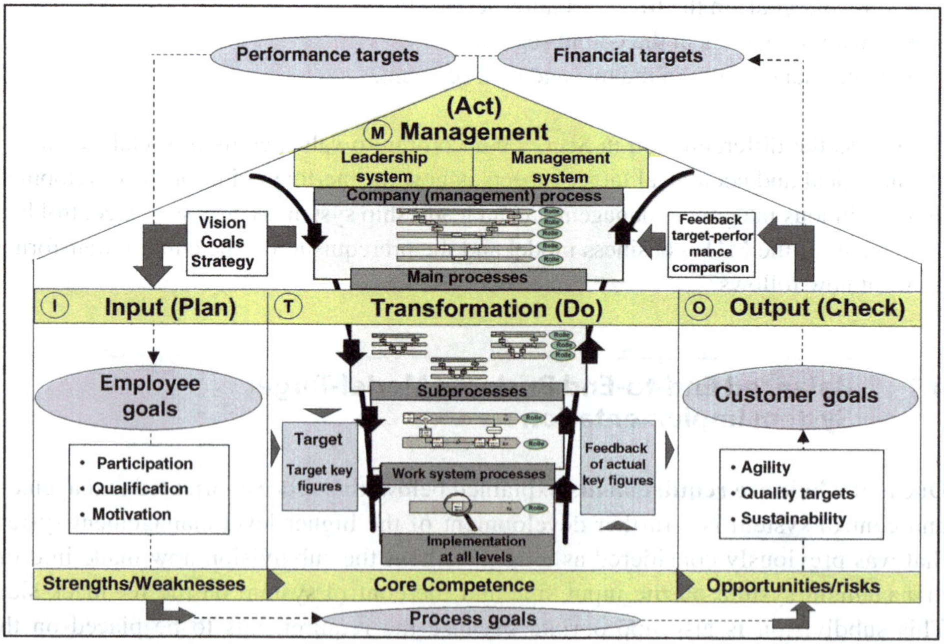

Fig. 4.1 Integrated MITO business model and process level model action field representation

implementation, which begins in the input segment. Here, the employees must be qualified and motivated in order to use their abilities responsibly within the given scope of action during the process implementation in the transformation segment. In the transformation segment with the field of action "process orientation", the creation of products and services is about optimally using the existing core competence, i.e. the differentiating feature of the company against competitors, in the execution of the process. This is followed at the operational level in the output segment by the connection to the customer in the "customer orientation" field of action. This customer is served with a high degree of agility, i.e. adaptability to its customer requirements with high quality. This is also an outstanding success factor for sustainable organizational development. Here it is very important that a feedback culture in the company enables a target/actual comparison via feedback to the management segment in order to obtain starting points for improvements.

For the description of the company-specific MITO business model, the MITO model – as Fig. 4.1 shows – is linked to the process-related **organizational level model**. In the process level model, the hierarchical process levels assigned to each other are mapped within the funnel shape with increasing detail of the process steps. Starting from the end-to-end management process, the next level focuses on the main processes, then on the sub-processes, and at the lowest level on the work system processes, i.e. on the individual workstation-related process function.

These processes are each described in a role-based manner in the Swimlane representation according to the BPMN 2.0 standard. Using this model specification, the corporate objectives are broken down with the support of the management system in the form of detailed process objectives with the associated target-target key figures top down over these four levels with an increasingly higher degree of accuracy down to the workplace. After the process has been executed, feedback on the process results is provided bottom up via the management system by aggregation across all four levels. In this way, it can be verifiably checked throughout the company whether the five overall objectives mentioned at the beginning, i.e. the five target and action areas mentioned, have also been successfully implemented. Precise and detailed role descriptions at each level also ensure that employees are selected in line with requirements, while at the same time structuring the company-specific leadership (specification) and management system structure (feedback) for management.

4.2 Cybernetic Management and Control System Structure

The MITO business model design approach **"Organization 4.0"**, which is the focus here, refers to the introduction of a process-oriented organization with the replacement of function-oriented, deeply staggered organizational structures based on the division of labor within the framework of a goal-oriented change management process. This requires the introduction of a process-oriented integrated **management and leadership system**

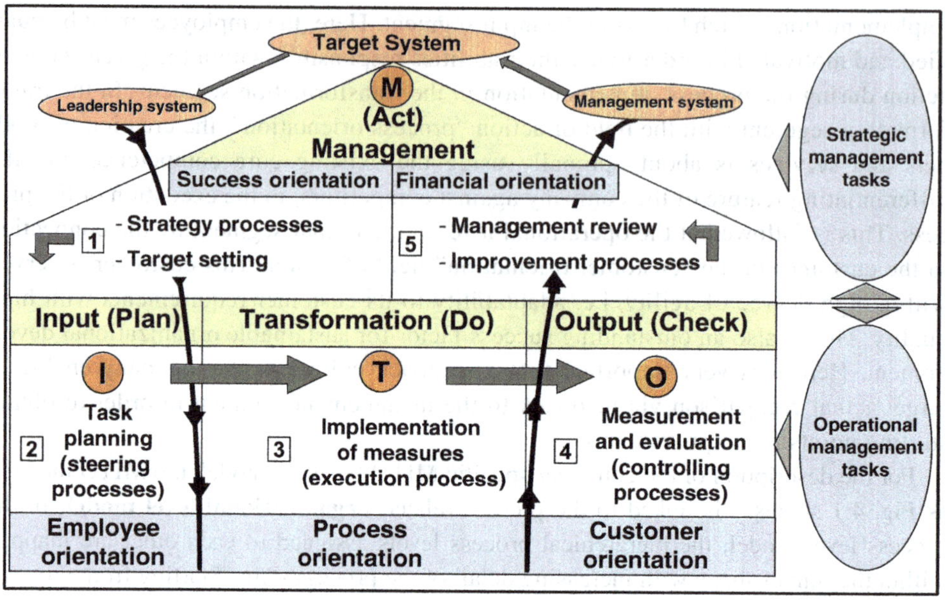

Fig. 4.2 Cybernetic MITO management and control system structure

that successfully implements this change management process. The starting point at the top process level is the role-based horizontal value chain, which is focused on fulfilling customer requirements and in which all process activities within the end-to-end process execution should run without errors or waste. In the MITO model shown in Fig. 4.2, the main tasks of the cybernetic management and control system are depicted in the form of a cybernetic control loop with assignment to the five target and action areas.

From a strategic point of view, the management with its people-related leadership and subject-related management is responsible for setting the goals for the organization that were previously formulated jointly in the management circle, which are then agreed with the process participants in the operative process implementation. The process organization enables the transfer of room for maneuver and **personal responsibility** to the employees at all hierarchical process levels, so that they can autonomously carry out their process tasks and are able to recognize and eliminate deviations at an early stage through self-controlling. The challenge for management is to strike a balance between the leadership and management functions. This means, on the one hand, to motivate and qualify employees to perform with empathy and appreciation in a softfact-based leadership. On the other hand, however, this must always take place on the feedback side, i.e. hard-fact related in a clear order structure, in order to give the persons involved also a security with the execution of work. For this purpose, the role-based swimlane representation is excellently suited for the graphical process representation, which transparently depicts the activities between the participants in a role-related, factual, temporal and logical manner. Without pressure and repression, however, hardfacts must be used to ensure that the instructions and rules are fulfilled in accordance with compliance. Hard facts and soft facts must therefore be in balance in order to optimise the management function, i.e. to motivate employees.

Closely linked to these process-oriented organisational structures, the participation of employees in the implementation of the business model is often also referred to as democratic co-determination.

Employees have an increasing demand for more **participation** in the company. The new process-oriented management system to be installed must meet these demands for democracy, participation and autonomy within the organization. This with the chance to achieve a faster employee identification and participation. In this context, the manager assumes an outstanding role model function by exemplifying democratic values and thereby acquiring the loyalty and trust of the employees. The advantages for the superior result from the reduction of coordination activities, the workload is reduced by the self-control of the employees. Consensus leadership style refers more to facilitation and orchestration and not so much to clear orders and commands. It is particularly suited to encouraging employee ownership. A prerequisite for this is to ensure the transparency of the process goals, the processes and the structures in order to thereby also enable a seamless flow of information and communication, which in particular also leads to agility implementation.

This is also the successful execution of the leadership and management tasks to implement Deming's **PDCA improvement cycle**. This lies in the fact that the replacement of a job-related, i.e. division of labor hierarchical organizational order structure in favor of a role-based order structure oriented to the horizontal value chain enables a participative leadership behavior, to which the employees on the basis of the transparently documented role-based processes with the associated role descriptions of the process participants receive a great deal of security and transparency in the autonomous execution of tasks. This also strongly supports the currently discussed holocratic forms of organization, which are set up in conjunction with the democratic co-determination discussed above as a counter-concept to the classic patriarchal structures. Holocratically organised companies no longer define the tasks to be solved on the basis of the person and hierarchical levels, but through the formation of process-related dynamic roles within the defined business processes. Through the scope of action transferred to the employees, the tasks become richer in content and, through self-management, undesirable developments are reduced. The existing corporate culture, which tends to be externally controlled, controlling, patronising and planning everything in advance, is to be replaced. Holocratic structures are to be used to establish an appreciative culture with autonomous work.

Successful **corporate cultures** are characterised not only by highly motivated employees who are taken seriously, valued and who identify with and are involved in the task, but also by the fact that they feel connected to the company because they are led by the employer or the responsible management through talent promotion, social support, participation in decision-making, extended scope for action with personal responsibility, fairness, credibility, clarity and a role model function.

	Corporate ethics values, e.g.:		F1			
			*BV1		BV2	
lfd Nr.	Weakness (1-3)	Strength (4-6)	V	H	V	H
1.	Disrespectful	- Respectful				
2.	Irresponsible	- Responsible				
3.	Wasteful	- Frugality				
4.	Undisciplined	- Discipline				
5.	Disobedience	- Obedience				
6.	Immodesty	- Modesty				
7.	Gluttony	- Frugality				
8.	Insecurity	- Self-confidence				
9.	Cowardice	- Courage				
10.	Impatience	- Patience				
11.	Carelessness	- Perseverance				
12.	Disrespectful	- Respectful				
13.	Creativityless	- Creativity				
14.	Distrustful	- Confidence				
15.	Dishonest	- Honest				
Scale: 1 = low 6 = high		ΣC				
		ΣC / n				

Source: Toyota Production System

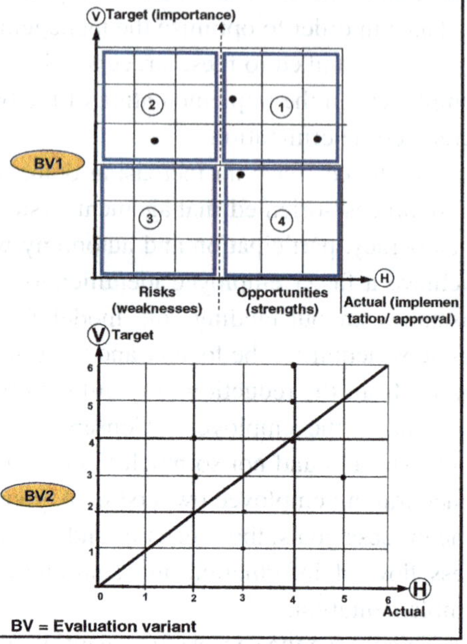

Fig. 4.3 MITO-related leadership strengths and weaknesses analysis

The extent to which managers fulfil these leadership aspirations can be determined using the MITO leadership analysis shown in Fig. 4.3. In the portfolio matrix, a whole number of leadership attributes are named line by line in the form of pairs of terms, which are rated in the grades from 1 (not fulfilled) to 6 (fully fulfilled) in the assessment dimensions V and H. In the assessment variant (BV) 1, there are no leadership attributes in relation to the assessment dimensions V and H. In the assessment variant (BV) 2, there are no leadership attributes in relation to the assessment dimensions H. In assessment variant (BV) 1, with respect to assessment dimension “V”, if marks are given from 1 to 3, there are indications of leadership weaknesses, while marks given from 4 to 6 show leadership strengths. The evaluation dimension “H” in BV 1 refers to the importance or relevance of the respective leadership characteristic. In the evaluation variant BV 2, the leadership characteristics are evaluated with “V = Target and H = Actual”. In the portfolio matrix shown, the leaders to be evaluated F1 to Fn are arranged in columns.

The graphical evaluation for BV 1 clearly shows the need for action for each individual manager in the upper left portfolio segment. In the case of evaluation variant 2, all the leadership characteristics mentioned line by line above the diagonal are not fulfilled.

In a very similar way, this **managerial analysis** can also be applied to the assessment of ethical values or to the implementation of mission statements or corporate culture discussed in Sect. 2.6.

The superordinate leadership and management tasks of the **process owners** within the MITO model segments are named in Fig. 4.4. In this way, the implementation of the

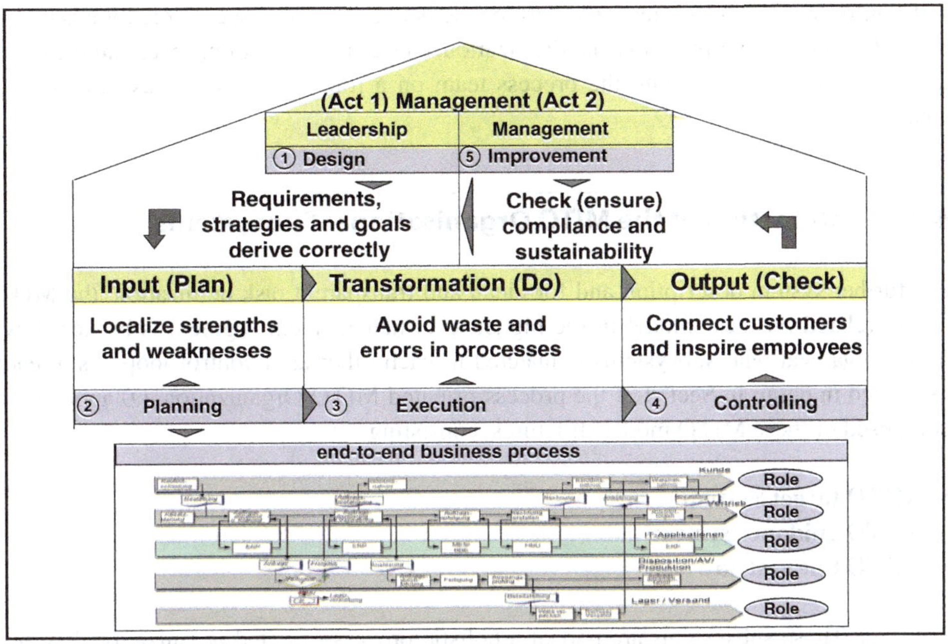

Fig. 4.4 Method-based execution of management and leadership tasks in the MITO model

process-oriented approach in the five steps "design, planning, implementation, controlling, improvement" is ensured. This process-oriented approach is – as already mentioned – a standard requirement and thus a basic prerequisite for the implementation of all Integrated Management Systems (IMS).

In accordance with the requirements of the process-oriented approach, the person responsible for the process must now transparently and completely derive or specify the requirements, strategy and process goals for the respective process under consideration. In the operational control loop sense, he must plan the process infrastructures in the second step and thereby work out the strengths and weaknesses of the organization. In the transformation segment, errors and waste must be avoided during process execution by the appropriately qualified process participants so that the process performance meets customer requirements and the employees also complete their process tasks in a customer-oriented manner with a high level of motivation. The control loop closes in the MITO Management segment with process step 5: "Improvement". The aim here is to determine whether the company and process goals have been achieved by providing feedback on process performance to management via reviews and audits. In the event of deviations, suitable measures for improvement must be initiated. This closes the control loop of the process-oriented execution of management and leadership tasks, and the review of the implementation or fulfillment of strategies, requirements and goals begins anew.

Within the **end-to-end process**, the **measuring points** forthe assignment of the target indicators are defined in each role in order to give the employees feedback via self-controlling and self-management as to whether successful process execution is taking place. For process optimization and digitization, a large number of improvement measures are then also developed with the process team on a role-based basis – as described in Chap. 3.

4.3 Interaction of the MITO Organisational Subsystems

For further system description and for clean and transparent task delineation, the MITO model-related business model in the higher-level management segment is broken down into 3 organizational subsystems connected to each other as a control loop. As already explained in detail in Sect. 1.3, the process-oriented MITO Organization 4.0 approach is composed of these MITO model structures, consisting of:

- **MITO target System**
- **MITO guidance system**
- **MITO line system**

Together. These subsystems are part of a holistic process-oriented organizational system and are each structured uniformly, i.e. separately, according to the MITO model. As shown in Fig. 4.5, the 3 organizational subsystems are in turn inserted into the superordinate MITO business metamodel structure in order to ensure in this way, from a strategic point of view, the integrative linking of these 3 subsystems for the implementation of the operational control loop principle.

At the strategic level, the focus is always on the company-specific end-to-end process. The upstream support processes, core processes and downstream support processes involved in the operational implementation in the ITO model are also structured via the MITO model. Each process has a target, a resource allocation, a process execution (transformation), a process result measurement and the feedback function provides impulses for process improvement. Management, supervisory, upstream support, core and downstream support processes together form the company-specific process model.

Based on the holistic MITO target system, the respective process targets are to be derived from the process model within the MITO model segments for the business processes assigned there as the basis for process target agreements with the process participants. In preparation for this, it is necessary to specify a detailed performance description on the basis of the process-related role definition, to which the bonus system then also refers. Since target key figures for measuring the achievement of objectives are also to be created in this context, the measurement procedures and evaluation processes must be assigned for this purpose within the framework of a continuous management and control system to be developed separately. All of these design elements always relate to the business process previously mapped on a role-based basis. In this way, the process performance is defined in detail for each role.

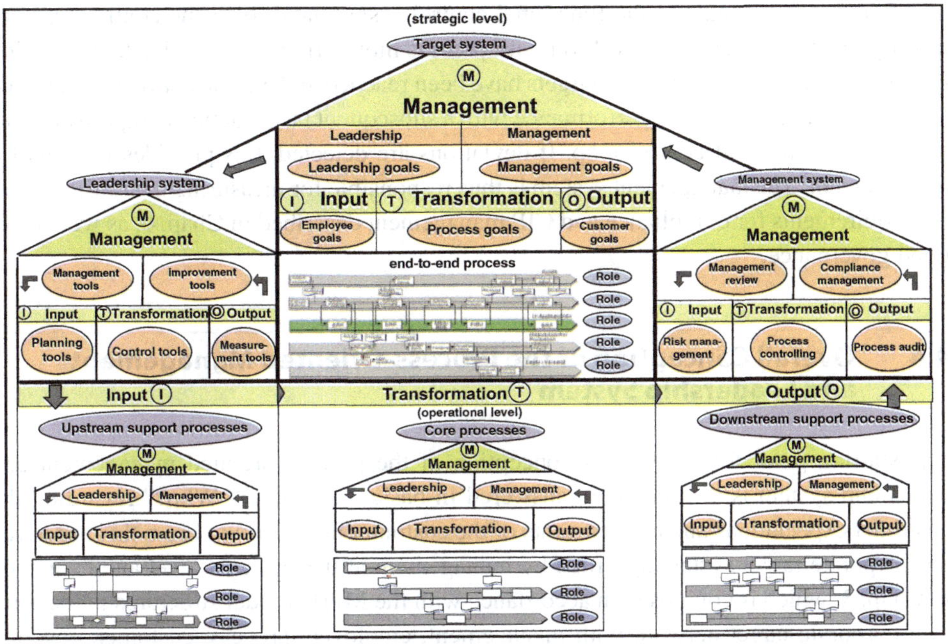

Fig. 4.5 3 subsystems of the process-oriented organisational subsystem

As explained above, the business processes themselves are arranged company-specifically in a process model and subdivided according to the five MITO segments into management processes, upstream support processes, core processes, downstream support processes and management processes. Furthermore, there is a process level model, starting from the end-to-end process via main process, sub-process to the process step on the lowest level. Each individual process in this process hierarchy is structured according to the MITO model. Through standardization, formalization and further process optimization measures in connection with CIP and potential analyses, the processes depicted in the process model are continuously improved according to the specifications of the management and feedback system to the control system.

Within the MITO model structures, the process-related **MITO leadership system** defines the design content for the managers across all hierarchical structured process levels. In addition to the objectives, this includes the guiding principles for the management culture mentioned in Chap. 2 with clear assignments of responsibility and authority. By specifying the management span with the management tools for employee management, but also the coaching program for managers, it is ensured that participative employee management can take place, which ensures a high level of employee satisfaction among those involved in the process.

After process execution, the functional control system takes over the continuous controlling function at each process level with process monitoring and actual data acquisition in order to determine whether all targets have been reached and all rules have been adhered to by measuring the process performance with a subsequent target/actual comparison. This closes the operational control loop. If deviations are detected, this provides impetus for improvement. The management system is thus responsible for measuring the fulfillment of the requirements for compliance and CIP management described in Chap. 6, as well as for good governance.

4.4 Overall Conception of the Process-Oriented Management and Leadership System

The starting point for the overall conception of the process-oriented management and leadership system is the statement answered in basic question 2: "Who?" regarding the customer expectations and requirements of the customer target group. From this is derived the corporate target system specified by management at the strategic level and explained in Chap. 3, which is composed in accordance with the MITO model structures in the form of a corporate target network with management, employee, process, customer, cost and compliance targets. This is the basis for the development of an end-to-end hierarchical process management and process control system. Figure 4.6 shows the overall concept of a company-specific process target and process management and control system across all defined process levels down to the individual process function at the lowest level. A functioning management and control system seamlessly maps the operational control loop across all process levels, provides impetus for continuous improvement throughout and is the basis for good governance. The starting point is the detailed determination of requirements from various requirement views, which are structured using the MITO model.

The task of the people-based process management system is to support the responsible process owners as a management tool so that the employees are highly motivated and highly qualified to carry out their tasks as instructed and to achieve the process goals agreed with them. Employee management by the process owners must be soft-fact based, i.e. based on appreciation. These appreciation components are the already mentioned democratic and holocratic concepts with the characteristics, for example, respect, tolerance, politeness, attentiveness, empathy and, above all, trust towards the subordinate employees. This appreciation is a basic human need. The employee strives to confirm the trust placed in him or her through performance. However, leadership also requires the superior to act as a role model and to create a positive culture of mistakes, i.e. to take away the employees' fear of punishment, because mistakes are unavoidable and employees may resist taking responsibility if they are not allowed to make mistakes. Here, managers must also set a good example and admit to mistakes.

As a management tool, the functional process control system supports the monitoring of compliance with planning targets by management on the feedback side. The focus here

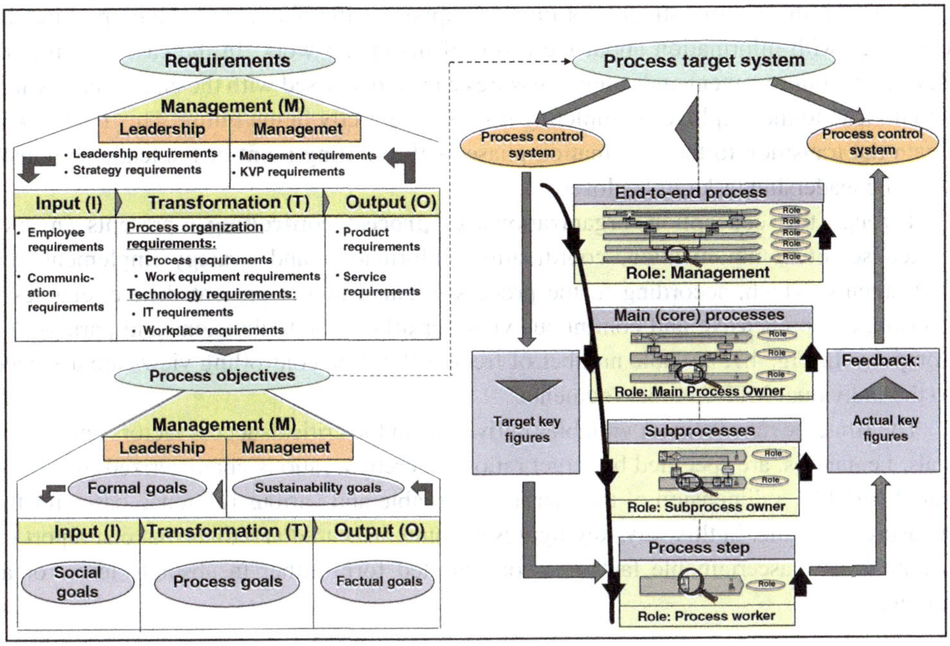

Fig. 4.6 Concept of the process-oriented management and leadership system

is on the implementation of controlling, compliance, performance and review management via the feedback function with the target/actual comparison. This also includes checking compliance with all relevant regulations, rules and instructions. The management system also covers the requirements specified in DIN EN ISO 9001-2015 in Chap. 9 "Assessment of performance", which are to be fulfilled by pt. 9.1 "Monitoring, measurement, analysis and evaluation" and pt. 9.2 "Internal audit" as well as pt. 9.3 "Management review". This creates the prerequisites for fulfilling the requirements in Chap. 10: "Improvement" in the QM standard.

The management system is thus the equivalent counterpart to the leadership system, because it uses process controlling to check whether the specifications have been executed accordingly. Process controlling is understood to be an integrated set of management instruments that is networked across all hierarchical levels in the organizational level model, with which all company activities as well as process performance and costs are controlled in accordance with the specifications from the management system. The main objective of this process-oriented enterprise controlling is therefore to provide all participants at every level with the management information with which the correct entrepreneurial or process-related decision can be made. From a superordinate point of view, controlling is therefore to be understood in general as the target-related support of management and decision-making tasks on the basis of ICT-supported information procurement and processing.

However, this control should not turn into apportioning blame, but should provide the employee with information about the result of his or her work. In the case of errors or deviations, improvement and safety measures can be discussed with the employees, which should lead to the employee completing his tasks correctly in the future. This feedback is again the transition to the information phase as the starting point of the leadership task, here the leadership task circle closes.

Through this conception, organizational or **process controlling** represents an integrated set of communication, coordination, information and strategy implementation instruments, which, according to the process-oriented model presented here, enables a holistic, comprehensive and continuous view for all corporate divisions and parts of the company. In Fig. 4.7, a whole number of freely selectable controlling views are assigned to the individual MITO model segments.

The strategic management variables derived from the criticalsuccess factors and potentials, i.e. targets, are specified by target ratios, whereby a ratio is characterized by a measured variable, a dimension of the measured variable and various reference bases for the measured variable. In this way, key figures become measured variables that can report on a numerically ascertainable fact in a concentrated form either in absolute terms or as a ratio.

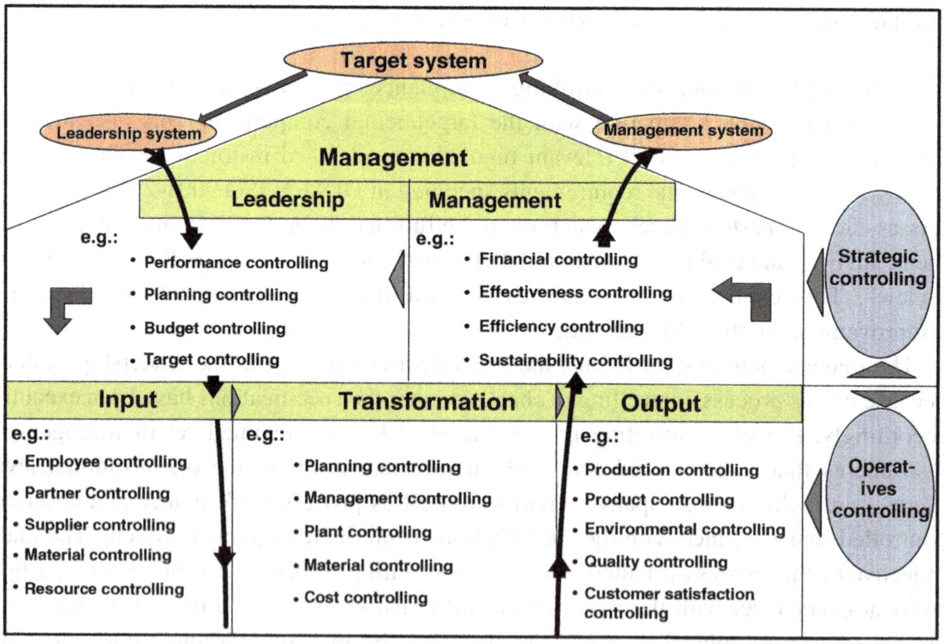

Fig. 4.7 Contents of the MITO model-related integrated process controlling platform

The process controlling view uses these key figures in the form of target specifications throughout the hierarchy levels in the processes running there, applying the control loop principles already explained. After measuring and evaluating the actual key figures, the loop is closed by providing feedback to the process management.

The overarching tasks of the integrated management and leadership system are:

- Measurement of the company and process development by means of numerically ascertainable business management and process-related facts and figures.
- Comprehensive enterprise and process cost and enterprise and process performance transparency.
- Argumentation and decision support at all levels.
- Consistent implementation of corporate and process goals through the specification of planning and control variables.
- Specification and review of company and process target fulfilment (Control loop enforcement).

The **management system** in particular has the following tasks:

- Complete target setting with target key figures and information provision at all levels.
- Development of measurable targets.
- Identification of decision-making needs.
- Reference point for the development of incentive schemes.
- Provide self-management and motivational incentives.
- Support process orientation.

The control system tasks necessary to achieve the goal are, for example:

- Determination and structuring of the information needs of management.
- Management, planning, control, data and information procurement.
- Development of measurable targets.
- Structure and maintenance of the key figure system.
- Setting up measuring systems.
- Design and maintenance of the reporting system.
- Carrying out target/actual comparisons.
- Variance analyses and documentation.
- Identification of decision-making needs.
- Identification of alternative solutions.
- Continuous control and improvement of processes.
- Comprehensive documentation of results in the organisational knowledge base.

4.5 End-to-End Target Agreement Process

The very important task within the management system is the management with goals via goal agreements, which are carried out via employee discussions between process managers and employees in consensus. Figure 4.8 shows the target agreement process. The reference point are the objectives derived from the answers to the 7 basic questions of the MITO business model explained in C2.

These target agreements with the associated target agreement key figures play an important role because the employee is to be guided in the execution of his activity in a success-oriented manner. The implementation of employee interviews for the concretization of process goals is part of the core, whereby the manager does not formulate the specifications alone, but develops the specifications together with the employee within the framework of the specified corporate goals and their guiding principles and this leads to an agreement accepted by both sides.

Employee appraisals are a management tool in their own right, focusing on advice and support, with the aim of promoting motivation through recognition and helping to improve performance through constructive criticism. These discussions can be held on a one-off basis or on a regular basis as individual or group discussions, depending on the occasion. In these discussions, the manager should use the statements of the employees to find out about their views, problems and interests. In particular, the individual performance in the past period should be discussed. Furthermore, this discussion should contribute to the fact that, for example

- The employee becomes aware of how his or her tasks and goals can make an optimal contribution to the success of the whole.
- The wishes, needs, goals, ideas and perceptions of the employees become known.
- The modality is discussed how the employee can best identify with the company.
- The expectations placed on the management employee become clear, that the criteria for assessing the results are applied equally by both sides and that a discussion takes place as to whether and how mutual communication and information can be made more productive.
- Tt becomes clear to the manager in which points of his leadership behaviour the employee makes an inhibiting or promoting assessment.
- The appropriateness of the organisation of work using the tools is examined jointly from the point of view of economy and efficiency.
- The further professional development of the employee with regard to his or her special skills and personal interests and, if necessary, concrete support measures can be derived from this.

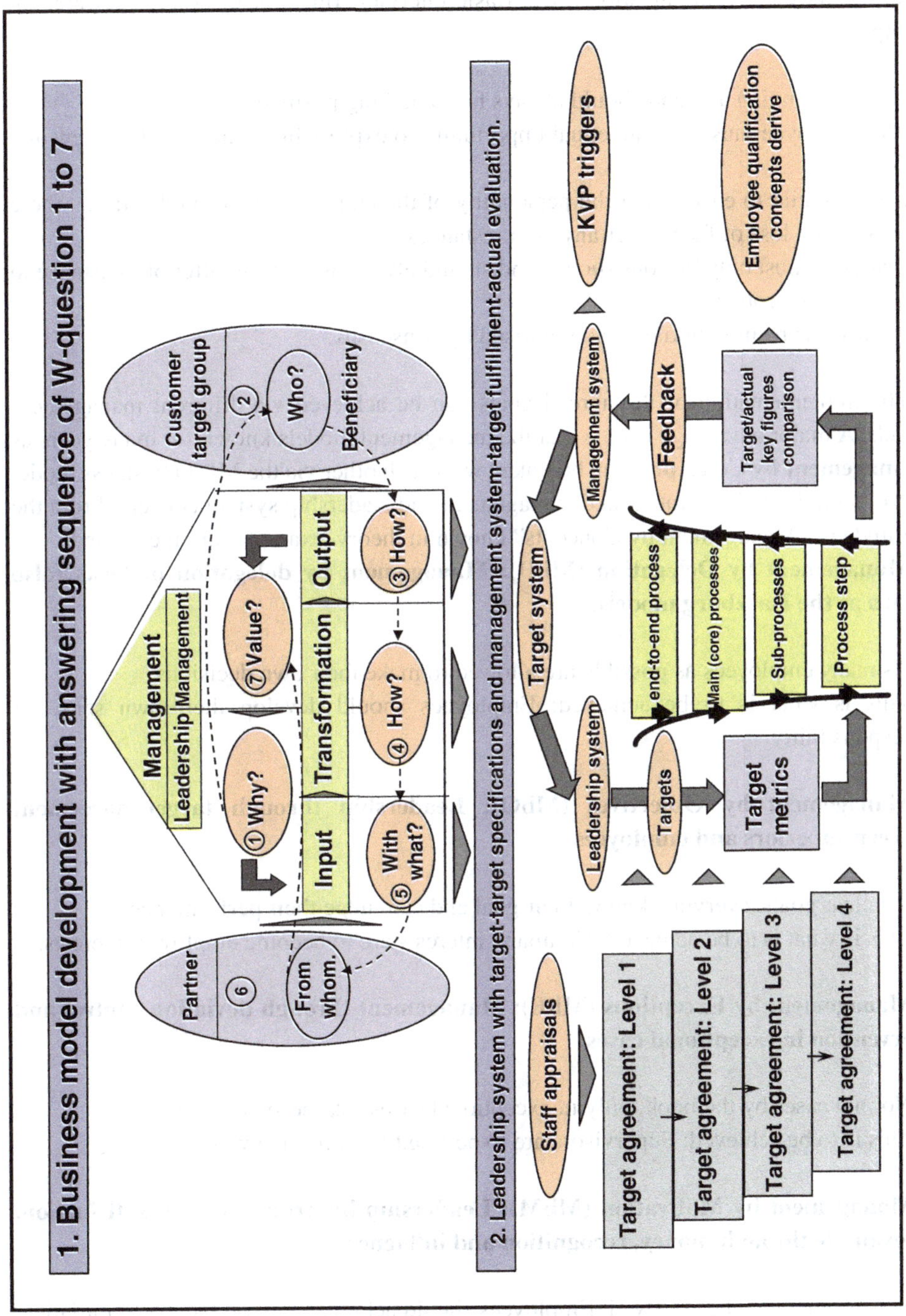

Fig. 4.8 End-to-end MITO business model-related target agreement process

These appraisal interviews require thorough preparation of a structured approach while adhering to basic communication rules. Basic interview rules for the supervisor are, for example:

- At the beginning and end should always be something positive.
- The employee must have an equal opportunity to express his or her point of view and assessment.
- It is essential to ensure that the personality of the employee is not violated, i.e. there must be no loss of face under any circumstances.
- Criticism must only be constructive and should always include an offer of assistance to remedy the problem.
- Finally, the results should be summarised by consensus.

The implementation of the agreed goals can be achieved via different management models. A major advantage here is that the management models known for many years as "**Management by Concepts**" can be linked with each other via the MITO business model control loop through the integrated management and leadership system concept. From the multitude of "Management by Concepts" known in theory, examples are mentioned:

Management by Delegation (MbD): Management by delegation of tasks (also known as the Harzburg model):

- As many employees as possible are allowed to make their own decisions.
- This is what is to be achieved: Employees should develop their own sense of responsibility.

Management by Objectives (MbO): Leadership through target agreement between superiors and employees

- Set clear goals, everyone knows their goal and can judge their performance.
- This is what is to be achieved: Company interests are to become employee interests.

Management by Exceptions (MbE): Management through deviation control and intervention in exceptional cases

- Normal cases by the book, only in exceptional cases ask the supervisor.
- This is to be achieved: Supervisors are to be freed from routine work.

Management by Motivation (MbM): Leadership by promoting job satisfaction, for example through money, recognition and influence.

- This is what is to be achieved: Employees should achieve more on their own initiative.

Management by Results (MbR): Leadership based on results achieved

- This is what is to be achieved: Employees should control themselves.

Management by Participation (MbP): Leadership for consistent employee information and gathering of employee knowledge

- Employee is informed and asked for advice.
- To be achieved: Use special contact of employees.

Management by Communication (MbC): Management by communication or contacts

- Almost everyone is informed about everyone.
- This is what is to be achieved: Better work through better information.

Management by Innovation (MbI): Leadership through innovation or continuous improvement

- Wanting to do everything better than before.
- This is what is to be achieved: Make or maintain companies competitive.

Management by Systems (MbS): Management through system control or management with delegation and the greatest possible degree of self-regulation on the basis of IT-supported information control systems.

- Want to do everything better, faster and more error-free – based on the latest technology.
- This is what is to be achieved: More effective and efficient work through the use of state-of-the-art IT technology.

The main content of the target agreement process is the development of the target indicators described below as target specifications.

4.6 MITO-BSC Targets in the Management System

As already described in Sect. 2.10 "Goal and strategy implementation using the BSC model", the BSC is a comprehensive communication, process management, planning and control instrument for strategy derivation and implementation that can be used comprehensively and consistently for all corporate divisions and organizational levels. The BSC is intended to depict, make measurable and communicate all success factors that are important for the company's success. At the same time, the current state of the company is mapped. The "Balanced Scorecard" is regarded as a strategic key figure management system because it provides a **key figure system** of interdependent objectives, measured variables and key figures – in the sense of a process controlling key figure systematization – which enables a permanent review process by the management system.

Because individual key figures, if they stand alone, are often limited in their information, they are combined in akey figure system. A system of key figures is understood to be a number of systematically developed, meaningfully coordinated, complementary and explanatory key figures, which are oriented, for example, in their structure to the already explained target hierarchy of a company. This hierarchy of objectives is aligned with a common overarching network of corporate objectives. In this way, this key figure system covers the information requirements of the various participants in the enterprise, independent of the process level and hierarchy. The relationships in a KPI system or the process controlling KPI systematization can be of a factual or mathematical nature; they are usually structured hierarchically. For example, the key figures "rate of incorrect deliveries" and "rate of customer evaluations" are related to each other both hierarchically and mathematically. If, on the other hand, you look at the key figures "employee satisfaction" and "attendance rate", there is only a logical link and the hierarchical order is not as pronounced.

The MITO model-related strategic **corporate objectives** in the BSC are linked, as Fig. 4.9 shows, in accordance with the MITO strategy, objective and field of action model, building on each other via the control loop through the following indicator perspectives:

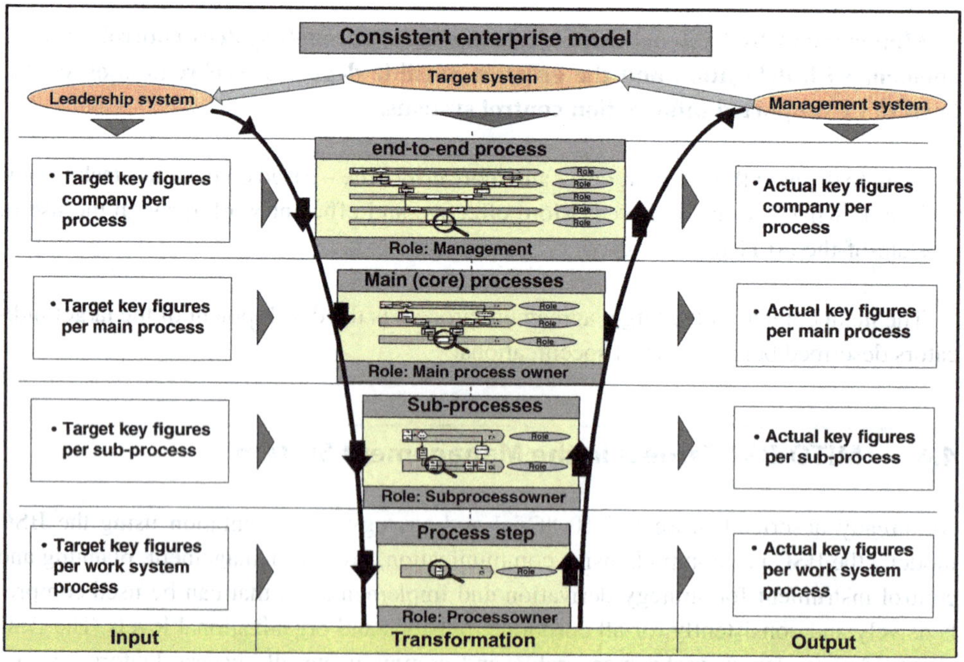

Fig. 4.9 Consistent BSC-based key performance indicator system

- Prospects for success in the MITO management segment.
- Employee and development perspective in the MITO input segment.
- Internal process perspective in the MITO transformation segment.
- Customer perspective in the MITO output segment.
- Financial outlook in the MITO line segment.

The individual **Balanced Scorecard perspectives** have the following contents:

The success perspective in the MITO leadership segment is focused on sustainable corporate success, i.e. that the underlying business model connects with customers and achieves corporate goals in terms of market share growth, revenue growth, flat hierarchies and lean processes through a clear mission, vision, guiding principles and policies.

The employee learning and development perspective in the input segment is aimed at the ability and potential of employees but also at the use of information technologies. Key performance indicators are used to assess the success, continuous improvement processes and innovative ability of employees. Late indicators include key figures on employee satisfaction, employee loyalty or employee productivity. Early indicators refer to training and further education, employee motivation and the performance of information systems.

The internal process perspective in the transformation segment identifies the critical processes in which the organization must be further developed via improvement proposals. The key performance indicators describe the efficiency and effectiveness of these processes, for example on the basis of productivity throughput times or quality indicators. Furthermore, the success of innovation processes is also assessed here.

The customer perspective in the MITO output segment is focused on the customer and market segments in which the company operates. General metrics here refer to profit, contribution margin and market shares in the segments of customer loyalty, customer satisfaction or customer profitability. Specific key figures show whether and to what extent customers remain loyal or migrate, i.e. information is provided here on how the external customer assesses the company's performance.

The financial perspective in the MITO management segment, which is considered the most important in practice, enables insight into whether the realization of the corporate strategy means an improvement in results. Here, classic business and financial economic ratios, such as profitability, return on sales, cash flow, ROI, amortization, turnover rate of capital or liquidity are used.

Frequent weaknesses in BSC target derivation in practice are a limitation to the company balanced score card, which cannot be broken down to the underlying company hierarchies or process levels. For this reason, strategy implementation is also not possible. Often, in this enterprise balanced scorecard approach, the strategic goals and metrics are also formulated too generally and globally and contain inconsistent and hidden conflicting goals.

Furthermore, there is often a lack of acceptance on the part of managers. A consistent target system implementation is only possible if the top management stands behind the implementation of this concept as a power promoter. It is not enough for specialists from the controlling departments to develop a solution that is supported by management but not actively advocated. However, this is often also due to the fact that management does not receive any support in the concept specification for the target system development due to the lack of BSC implementation tools.

It is particularly serious if the target system is not integrated into existing strategic management instruments. In this case, standard key figures are simply used for performance control, for which there is no concrete reference to strategy. Through this pure focus on standard key figures, the cause-effect relationships between the strategy as well as the consistent linking of key figure trees to connect the strategic goals with the workplace goals are not developed.

Another weak point is when the existing IT solution determines the effect of the BSC KPI system or when the IT specialists design a target or target system concept according to their own ideas without communication and often without coordination with management.

4.7 Consistent BSC-Target-Key Figure Linkage in the Horizontal Value Chain

The integrated management and control system is intended as the overriding goal in product and service creation to ensure that customer requirements are met in terms of effectiveness and efficiency. It is important that the core processes within the company-specific end-to-end process are consistently linked with each other with few interfaces in order to generate the product or service without errors and waste. By means of the assigned target key figures at the defined measuring points within the role-based process documentation, it is measured after the end-to-end process execution on the basis of the actual key figures whether the processes have also been executed in accordance with their **target specifications** without errors and wastage.

The requirements for **key figures** for strategic and operative process management and control and thus also for target agreement discussions are shown in Fig. 4.10 in relation to the target figures (target figures) and to the measured figures (actual figures).

This subdivision is based on the principles of the organizational control loop model. The key figures must be clearly identifiable with regard to their objectives and allow for an unambiguous derivation from higher-level corporate objectives. Furthermore, key figures must record the facts as completely, clearly, and uninterpretably as possible. They must be able to establish a reference to the past, but also a reference to the future, and must be able to depict differentiated observations, for example, process and function-related, but also overarching relationships, and must be structured as simply as possible. Therefore, key figures should only be given in a clear number. It is crucial that the metrics can be used in a way that is practicable in the long term under economic conditions.

Figure 4.11 shows this consistency and horizontal linking of the core process indicators via input and output connectors, with the sales, development, procurement, production and

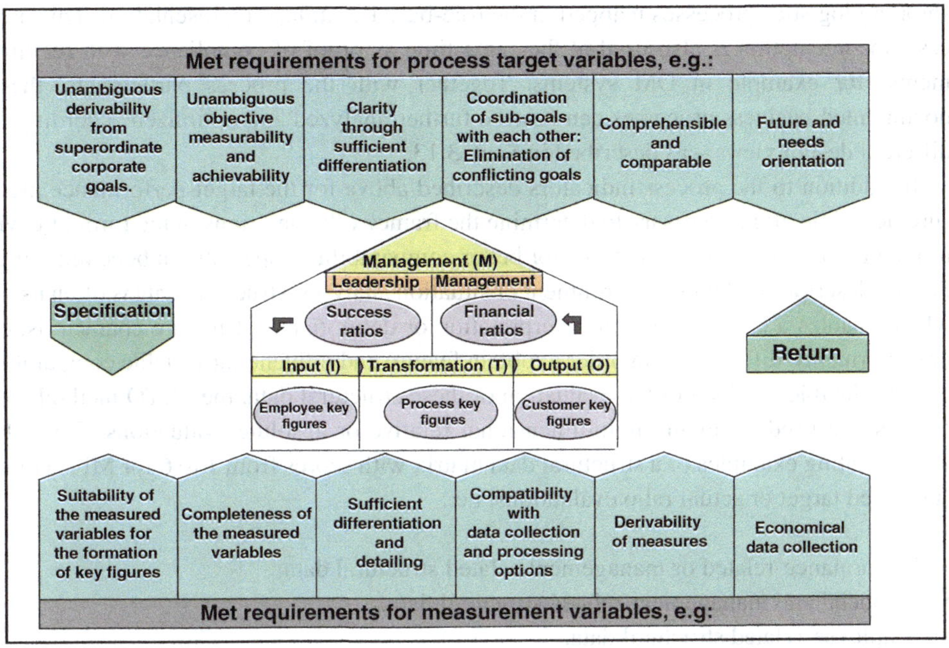

Fig. 4.10 Requirements for key figures

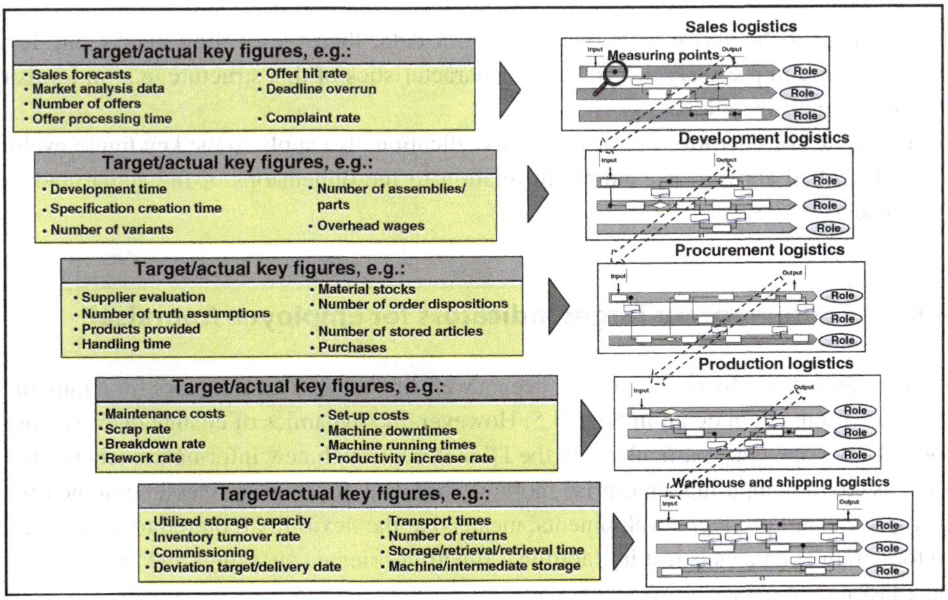

Fig. 4.11 Target-performance ratio linkage of individual logistics processes

shipping logistics processes mapped in the role-based swimlane representation. This process documentation is also used at the same time as proof of compliance with requirements, for example in QM systems. Together with the process participants, these documented business processes can now be further analyzed and optimized according to different design views – as described in Sect. 3.13.

In addition to the process indicators described above for the target-performance measurement, it is often necessary to determine the framework conditions in the form of environment or initial situation analyses for better comparability, especially in benchmarking. For the description of these environment or situation analyses, structural data is often used, which enables a characterization, interpretation or delimitation of feature characteristics or performance differences, in order to obtain feature and influencing variable comparable or reproducible results. For the evaluation of these structural data, the MITO method tool can also be used to obtain multidimensional relative or absolute evaluations. Fig. 4.12 shows scaling examples of a structural data matrix with scores from 1 to 6 for MITO tool-supported target or actual ratio evaluations, i.e.:

- Performance-related or management-related structural data.
- Financial and management-related structural data.
- Employee-related structural data.
- Process-related structural data.
- Customer-related structural data.

For each of the above-mentioned structural data, there is ascaling matrix one level down in order to precisely determine the characteristics of this structure, e.g. in terms of importance and share level.

The same considerations of a scaling specification also apply to the key figure evaluations described above, for example in relation to the dimensions of the actual and target values.

4.8 Contemporary Target Indicators for Employee Appraisal

Leading employees by objectives has been a well-known management tool for a long time and was discussed in detail in Sect. 4.5. However, the dynamics of change due to technological developments, particularly in the IT sector, through new information technologies such as cloud computing, enterprise mobility, big data or social business, combined with disruptive smart product developments, means that the flexibility required to adapt targets to these rapid changes is lost in traditional function-oriented structures and the associated bureaucratic processes.

Furthermore, it is important that these targets not only focus on the classic financial targets, but that a whole number of other targets within the entire value chain up to delivery to the customer should be included in the target system. The prerequisite for this, which

MITO-gestützte Skalierung der Strukturdaten (Kennzahlen)							
	Note:	**1**	**2**	**3**	**4**	**5**	**6**
1. Finanzkennzahlen z. B.:							
1.1	Umsatz [%]	<10	<15	<25	<40	<60	>100
1.2	Gewinn [%]	<15	<30	<50	<65	<80	>100
1.3	Investition [%]	<15	<30	<50	<65	<80	>100
1.4	Budget [%]	<15	<30	<50	<65	<80	>100
2. Prozessdokumentation z. B.:							
2.1	Arbeitsanweisung [Anzahl pro Periode]	<5	<10	<30	<50	<100	>100
2.2	Zielvereinbarung [Anzahl pro Periode]	<5	<10	<30	<50	<100	>100
2.3	Schnittstellenbeschreibung [Anzahl pro Periode]	<5	<10	<30	<50	<100	>100
2.4	Anzahl Wechselbeziehungen	<15	<30	<50	<65	<80	<100
2.5	Anzahl Prozessfunktionen	<15	<30	<50	<65	<80	<100
3. Personalkennzahlen z. B.:							
3.1	Leistungsgrad [%]	<50	<60	<70	<80	>90	>100
3.2	Überstunden [%]	<10	<15	<25	<50	>50	< 80
3.3	Direkte Lohnkosten [%]	<10	<15	<25	<50	>50	> 80
3.4	Lohnnebenkosten [%]	<20	<50	<75	<100	>100	>120
4. Ressourceneinsatzkennzahlen z. B.:							
4.1	Betriebsmittelauslastung [pro Periode]	<100	<250	<500	<700	<800	<1000
4.2	Leistungskennzahlen [%]	<15	<30	<50	<65	<80	<100
4.3	Kapazitäten [h/Periode]	<15	>15	<30	<50	>80	>100
4.4	Energiekosten [€/h]	>150	<150	<120	<90	<60	< 40
4.5	Instandhaltungskosten [%]	<15	<30	<50	<65	<80	<100
5. Wertgestaltungskennzahlen z. B.:							
5.1	Nutzleistung [%]	<20	<30	<50	<60	<80	>100
5.2	Stückleistung [%]	<20	<30	<50	<60	<80	>100
5.3	Blindleistung [%]	<20	<30	<50	<60	<80	>100
5.4	Stillstandzeiten [%]	<20	<30	<50	<60	<80	>100
5.5	Störungskosten [%]	<20	<30	<50	<60	<80	>100
6. Innovationskennzahlen z. B.:							
6.1	Umsatz aus neuen Leistungen [%]	<10	>10	>12	>15	>20	>50
6.2	Anzahl Einführung neuer Leistungen im Plan-Ist-Vergleich [X/Jahr]	<3	>3	>6	>8	>10	>12
6.3	Anzahl Einführung neuer Leistungen im Konkurrenzvergleich [X/Jahr]	<3	>3	>6	>8	>10	>12
6.4	Potenziale im Leistungserbringungsprozess [Anzahl Ideen/Periode]	<10	>10	>12	>15	>20	>50
7. Logistikkennzahlen z. B.:							
7.1	Anzahl Teile [Anzahl pro Periode]	<10	<30	<60	<100	<200	<300
7.2	Anzahl Behälter [Anzahl pro Periode]	<10	<30	<60	<100	<200	<300
7.3	Anzahl Transport [Anzahl pro Periode]	<5	<10	<20	<30	<40	<50
7.4	Anzahl Kommissionierungen [Anzahl pro Periode]	<5	<10	<20	<50	<100	<200
8. Prozesszeiten oder Kostenkennzahlen z. B.:							
8.1	Transport x Kostensatz [€/h]	>100	<100	<60	<40	<20	<10
8.2	Lagern x Kostensatz [€/Tage]	>100	<80	<40	<30	<20	<10
8.3	Rüsten x Kostensatz [€/h]	>60	<30	<20	<10	<5	<1
8.4	Bearbeiten x Kostensatz [€/h]	<90	>90	>120	>150	>180	>200
8.5	Instandhalten x Kostensatz [€/h]	>120	<90	<60	<45	<30	<15
8.6	Warten-/Stör Zeit x Kostensatz [€/h]	>60	<30	<20	<10	<5	<1
8.7	Prüfen x Kostensatz [€/h]	>120	<90	<60	<45	<30	<15
8.8	Nacharbeit x Kostensatz [€/h]	>120	<90	<60	<45	<30	<15

1 = schlecht; 6 = gut

9. Servicekennzahlen z. B.:							
8.1	Lieferzeit [Tage]	>5	<5	<4	<3	<2	<1
8.2	Termintreue [Tage]	>5	<5	<4	<3	<2	<1
8.3	Flexibilität [Tage]	>5	<5	<4	<3	<2	<1
8.4	Vollauslieferung [Tage]	>5	<5	<4	<3	<2	<1
9. Qualitätskennzahlen z. B.:							
9.1	Fehler an Produkt [pro Arbeitseinheiten]	>10	<8	<6	<3	<1	<0
9.2	Nacharbeit [min]	>120	<90	<60	<45	<30	<15
9.3	Rücklieferungen [Tage]	>10	<8	<6	<3	<1	<0
9.4	Prozessfähigkeit	>10	<8	<6	<3	<1	<0
10. Kundenkennzahlen z. B.:							
10.1	Preiselastizität [%]	<5	<10	<25	<50	<80	<100
10.2	Neukunden [%]	<5	<10	<25	<50	<80	<100
10.3	Leistungsangebot [%]	<5	<10	<25	<50	<80	<100
10.4	Kundenzufriedenheit [%]	<15	<30	<50	<65	<80	<100
1 = schlecht, 6 = gut							

Fig. 4.12 MITO-supported scaling of structural data (key figures)

has already been mentioned several times, is to replace the classic hierarchical organizational structures in favor of a process-oriented organizational structure in order to obtain a comprehensive picture of the current situation regarding the status of target achievement within the process execution in the creation of products and services by means of rapid feedback from those involved and, if necessary, to update target changes.

Figure 4.13 shows a number of different contemporary objectives for employee appraisal and compensation within the MITO model. They relate to the implementation of the process at the operational level and are subdivided according to the MITO model segments shown into input targets, transformation targets and output targets.

The management segment arranged above this from a strategic point of view with the management and leadership functions has the task of agreeing these targets with the employees in the leadership segment. In the management segment, the controlling function must then determine whether the objectives have been achieved and, in the event of deviations, initiate the successful corrective measures. In this context, it is an important prerequisite that the process under consideration is also mapped in the graphical process representation in a role-based manner and documented in detail with all potential variables such as costs, times, qualities as well as applications, rules and standards. Within this depicted process, the measuring points are then defined, which provide the actual key figures for the employee evaluation and remuneration in the respective role for the process participant.

By using the MITO model with the mapping of the process-oriented approach, it is avoided that only one-sided, e.g. financial criteria are defined, but that the process performance can be measured and evaluated comprehensively. It is important to note that managers need to be trained in relation to the feedback function, thereby providing the necessary up-to-date transparency in their process. These targets shown in Fig. 4.13 are not only suitable for the individual process participant, but can also be applied to process teams. Feedback cycles should be firmly agreed upon.

4.9 Role-Based Employee Qualification

The findings of the employee-related target-key figure evaluations are the reference point for another effective **management tool** for systematic process-oriented employee qualification. The qualification control loop procedure model in 6 steps described below refers to this. As shown in Fig. 4.14, the prerequisite for this is again the role description within a defined business process in the Swimlane representation, which was carried out in Chap. 3 in the context of the process organization implementation.

In step 1, the individual industry-specific qualification requirements are determined on the basis of this role profile description. For upstream and downstream support processes, a comprehensive reference process model development is already available, in which the tasks to be performed there are differentiated according to management, performance and support processes and the associated qualification requirements are described.

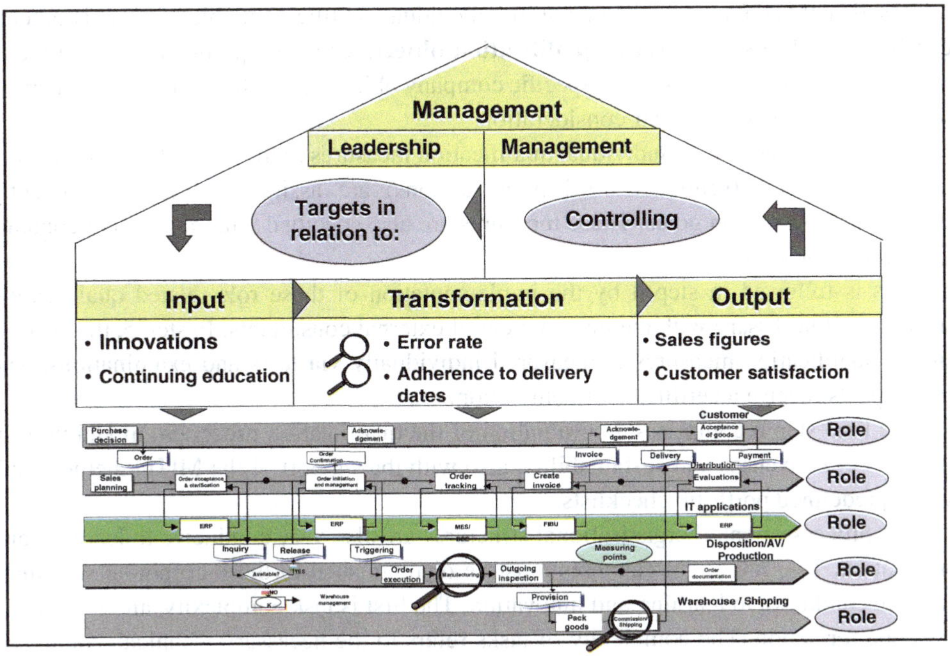

Fig. 4.13 MITO model-related targets for employee appraisal

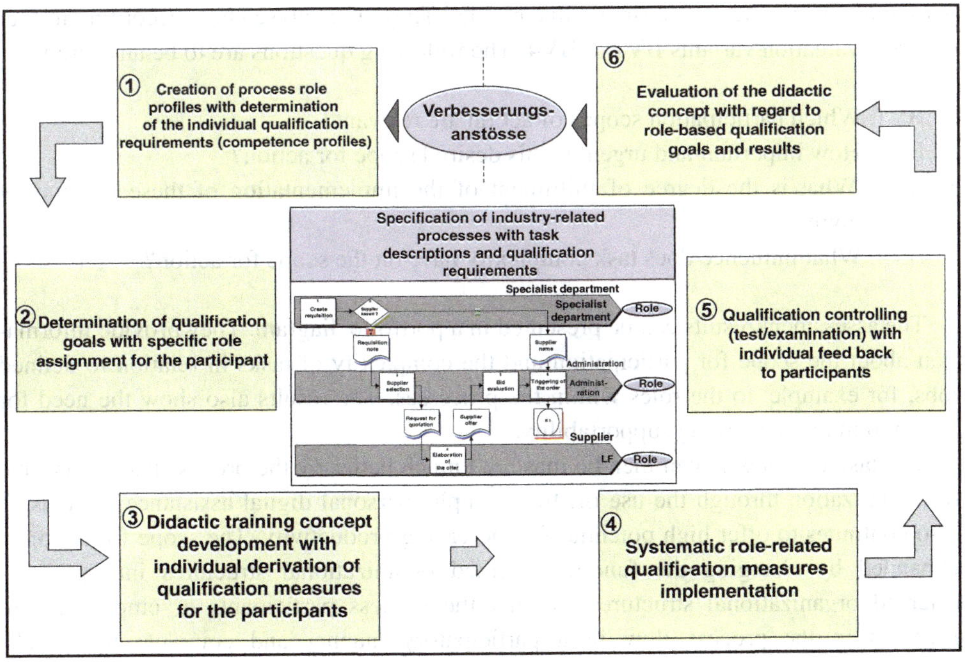

Fig. 4.14 Qualification control loop procedure model

Based on this reference documentation, individual qualification objectives and contents can be derived in step 2. These **qualification objectives** of the participants are directly interrelated with the organisation-specific company objectives of the respective industry or the respective company under consideration.

In step 3, the necessary individual qualification measures in the form of adapted further training measures (seminars, workshops, lessons) are assigned to the transparently described qualification goals. These measures are also specified with targets and contents as well as time scope.

This is followed in step 4 by the implementation of these role-related qualification measures, if necessary with the involvement of external consultants. In step 5, the success of the qualification measures is measured individually via tests and examinations. The participants receive a certificate of completion.

The final step 6 comprises an evaluation of the qualification procedure model used in terms of effectiveness and sustainability, also with the support of the MITO method tool, using predefined portfolio checklists.

The process-oriented organisational structures are also very conducive to learning and innovation. Two important elements must be distinguished in these corporate structures that are conducive to learning and innovation. The first is task complexity, and the second is scope for action. The complexity of tasks refers to the necessary technical, social and learning competences, from which the necessity of new learning also arises again and again. The second aspect, "scope for action", shows the possibilities for participation inshaping one's own work. In the portfolio matrix shown in Fig. 4.15, a whole number of participation approaches are shown line by line. They are analysed here according to four different valuation variants BV1 to BV4. The following questions are to be answered:

- BV1: Which participation scopes of action are relevant?
- BV2: How important and urgent is this desired scope for action?
- BV3: What is the degree of fulfilment of the implementation of these margins of manoeuvre?
- BV4: What influence does task complexity have on the scope for action?

The assessment results can be presented in a portfolio diagram. They provide information about the scope for participation and the complexity of tasks in relation to defined jobs, for example, to the roles within the processes. The results also show the need for action to improve learning supportability.

The task complexity can then be mastered much better by the process participant due to digitalization through the use of, for example, personal digital assistance systems. It also continues to offer high potential for increasing productivity. The scope for action is expanded by changing the function-oriented organizational structures into process-oriented organizational structures, so that the process participants or employees are involved in the process flow in a participatory manner and complete their tasks

lfd No.	Participation approaches, e.g.:	Process 1							
		BV1		BV2		BV3		BV4	
		V	H	V	H	V	H	V	H
1.	Self-assess own work								
2.	Working in a team that is allowed to organize the common tasks itself								
3.	Influencing important decisions for one's own work								
4.	Taking a break when you want								
5.	Participation, with whom one works together								
6.	Involved in optimization of work processes/work organization								
7.	Determine the speed of work determine								
8.	Determine working methods determine								
9.	Order of tasks determine yourself								
10.	Learn new things by yourself								
11.	Complex tasks								
12.	Solve unexpected problems solve								
Scale: 1 = low	ΣC								
6 = high	ΣC / n								

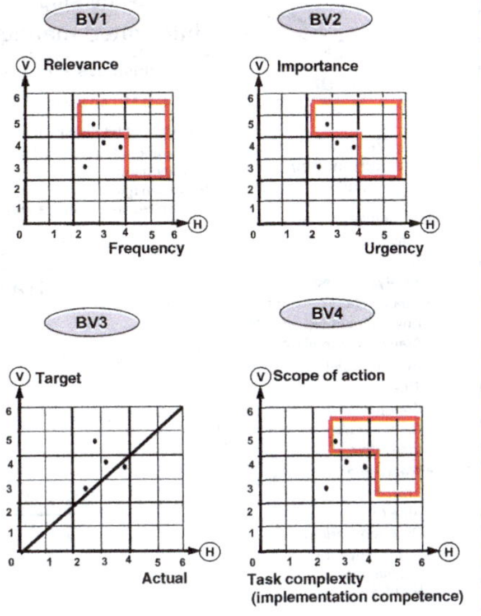

Fig. 4.15 Assessment of the learning supportiveness of the workplace

autonomously and independently. Management and leadership are required to transfer this leeway to the participants.

4.10 Implementation of Integrated Management Systems (IMS) as Further Management Instruments of the Management and Leadership System

In order to fulfil the integrated process requirements from many different design perspectives, various integrated management systems (IMS) are used as further management tools to support management. These are designed to help managers meet the process requirements shown in Fig. 4.16 and to provide evidence of compliance. These IMSs were grouped together in Sect. 2.13 under the heading "**general management strategy approach**". In all Integrated Management Systems, the enforcement of the process-oriented approach with:

Identify, plan, execute, measure, improve processes.

Required. The point of reference is therefore always the business process mapped in a role-based manner according to the globally valid BPMN 2.0 process visualization standard in the factual, temporal and logical sequence of task processing. This is done by assigning the required IT applications as separate swim lanes and by depicting the

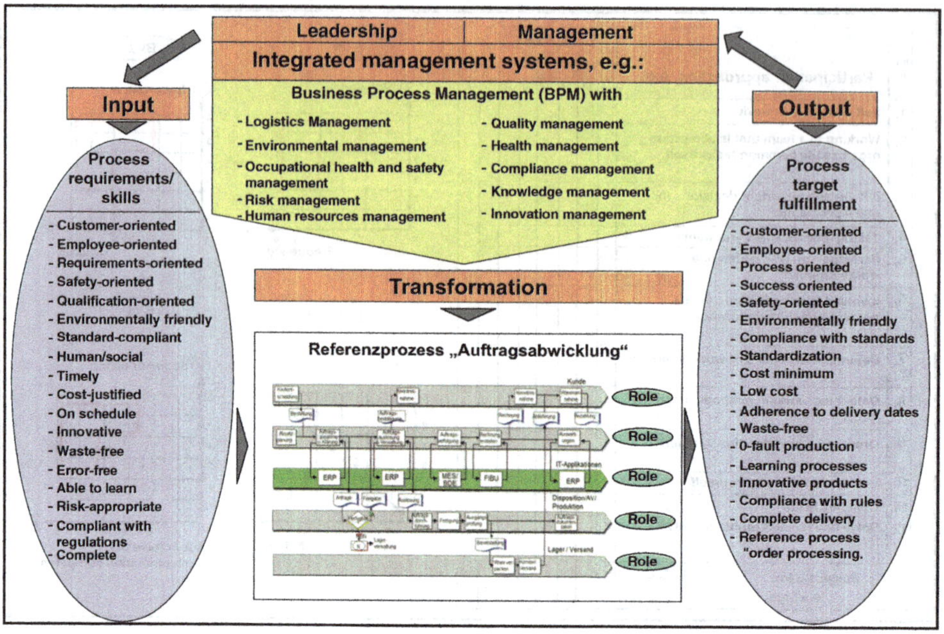

Fig. 4.16 Integrated management system deployment to meet process requirements and objectives

relationships between the participants within the roles. For this purpose, Business Process Management (BPM) provides – as explained in Chap. 3 – the process-related order structures in the form of a company- or organization-specific process model as a higher-level management system.

In this case, too, the principles of the process-related business model transformation control loop already explained several times apply. On the input side, the process execution (transformation) with the target specifications or target requirements. After the process has been executed, the method-supported measurement of results is performed on the output side with digital verification of the fulfillment of or deviations from the standard specifications in the form of assessments, reviews, or audits.

The process-related management system-specific requirements to be fulfilled from the perspective of the management system are many and varied. Figure 4.16 lists these requirements on the input side, without claiming to be exhaustive, which must be fulfilled during process transformation in order to meet the management system goals on the output side, which are also listed.

The integrated implementation approach for the individual management systems is important. The focus is always on the visualized business processes in order to achieve the process objectives in accordance with the requirements. Evaluations, reviews, assessments or audits are used after process implementation to determine whether these various management system-related process objectives have been met.

4.11 Integrated Management System Activity Matrix

As explained in the introduction to this chapter, there are a large number of different management system standards and regulations that are intended as management tools to support management in fulfilling the respective specific requirements. These include, for example, quality, environmental, sustainability, health and energy efficiency management and other management systems that must be implemented and applied in accordance with compliance requirements.

In the assignment matrix shown in Fig. 4.17, these management systems are listed in columns. Within each individual management system, a whole number of activities are to be demonstrably performed as standard specifications, which are listed line by line in Fig. 4.17. The order of these activities from 1 to 12 also corresponds to the contents or specifications of the process-oriented approach, which are interlinked in the form of a cybernetic control loop model.

The basis for the implementation of these IMS activities is the introduction of a process organisation with the MITO model as a structural and regulatory framework for the allocation of the respective management system requirements, objectives, tasks, key figures, weak points and measures.

For the implementation of the measures, the MITO method tool described in Sect. 2.4 is available with a large number of linked methods for the analysis, diagnosis, therapy and evaluation of the 12 BPM activities mentioned. At the beginning, there is usually a requirements portfolio analysis, which has also already been explained, for a

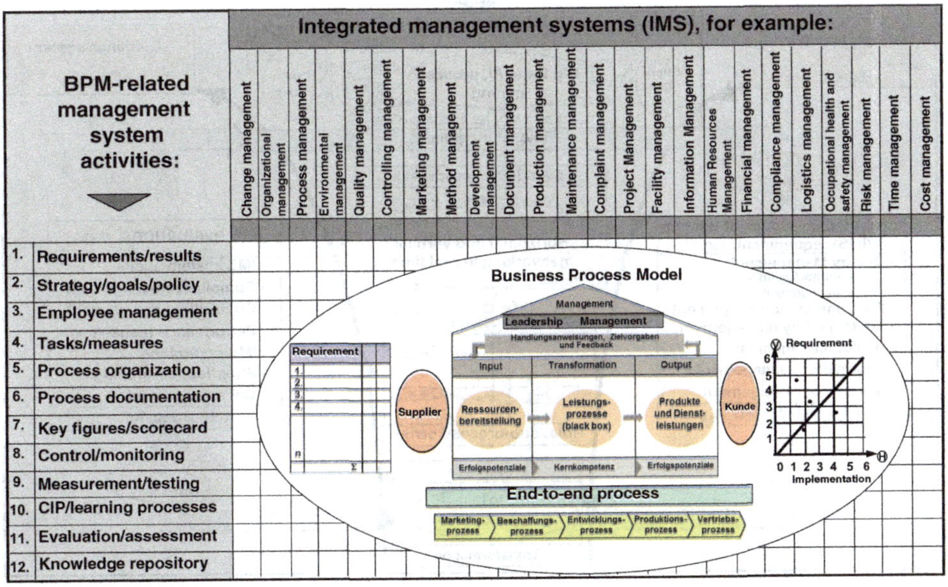

Fig. 4.17 Integrated Management System (IMS) activity matrix (I)

two-dimensional evaluation with different evaluation dimensions. Further assistance is provided by the portfolio checklists given for each activity, for example requirements checklists, strategy goals policy checklists, employee management checklists and so on. They enable a two-dimensional assessment, for example, according to BV1: "V = effort, H = benefit" or BV2 with "V = requirements and H = implementation" with the subsequent derivation of measures via the MITO royal road. The results are made available in digitized form.

4.12 Role-Based Process Description Is the Basis for the Introduction of Integrated Management Systems (IMS)

When **implementing integrated management** systems as management tools within the MITO business model control loop shown in Fig. 4.18 – which has already been explained several times – a distinction can be made between input-related and output-related focal points of use. Figure 4.18 shows the assignment of the individual integrated management systems referred to in Sect. 2.14 as general management strategy (GMS), arranged according to input and output function.

Due to their function-oriented, vertical organizational structures based on division of labor, many companies have problems meeting these standard requirements because all

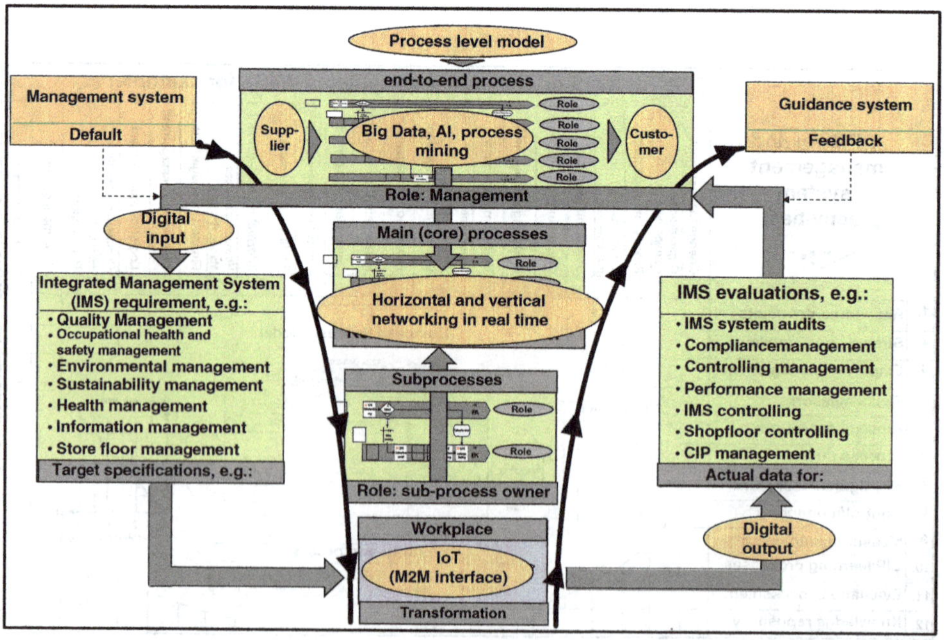

Fig. 4.18 Integrated Management System (IMS) control loop

processes assigned in the process model on a role-based basis actually have to be analyzed, modeled and documented again.

Figure 4.19 shows the models mentioned, which also represent the reference framework for the IMS management documentation. In addition to the MITO process model and the **swimlane representation**, this also refers to the process level model, which maps the process hierarchy or process instance from the strategic level through the tactical, scheduling, and operational levels. In each instance, the processes are also mapped in the BPMN 2.0 swimlane representation and interlinked within a process map. The entire process documentation is provided in digital form by the BPM tools used. Special document analysis software is available for the creation, distribution and control of the documents.

In order to comply with the **process-oriented approach** in accordance with the standard, it is necessary to have a detailed process description. The contents of the process description are also shown in Fig. 4.19. The role description, which replaces the job description of the function-oriented organizational structure in the process organization, is important here. As described in Chap. 3, the objectives, process steps, target key figures, and the tasks and competencies of the process participants are stated in this role description, as are their relationships to the other roles. This in connection with the IT applications used in this role with rights and authorizations.

Since the measuring points for the assignment of the target key figures are also stored within the **BPMN 2.0 process representation**, the foundation for a functioning process controlling is laid right away. Continuous maintenance of this process description then

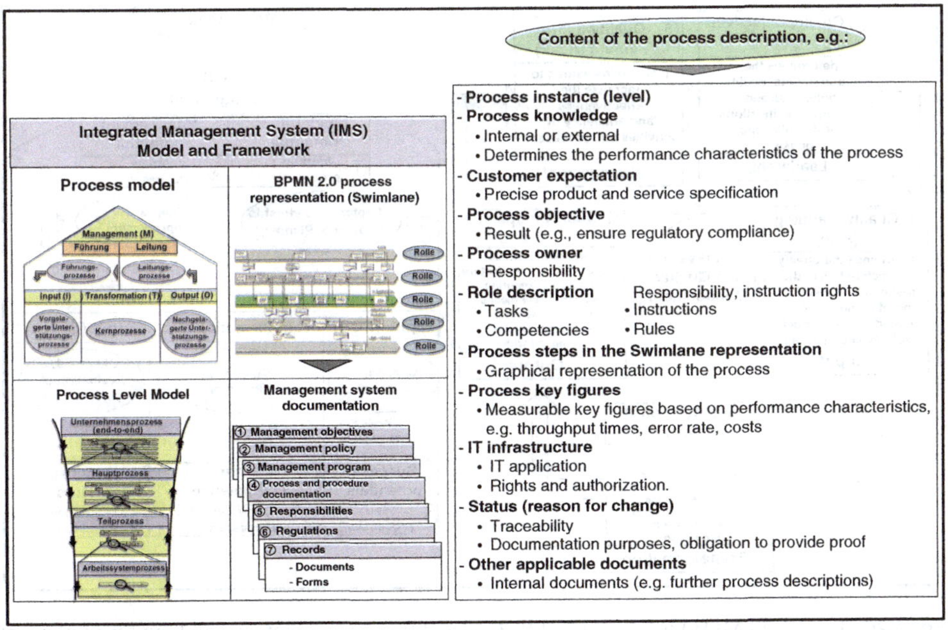

Fig. 4.19 Role-based process description within Integrated Management Systems (IMS)

also shows the changes that have taken place and the respective valid document status over the life of the process. With regard to the implementation of integrated management systems, the role descriptions are then also the reference point for the audits and evaluations to be carried out for the respective management system under consideration. In the following chapter points, some IMS contents are explained in more detail by way of example.

4.13 Systematic Process-Oriented QM System Implementation According to DIN EN ISO 9001:2015

The best known and most frequently used management system in the world is the quality management system currently according to DIN EN ISO 9001:2015. Since the year 2000, the process-oriented approach already described in detail has been prescribed in the MITP model structures to meet the QM system requirement. This requirement is now valid for all IMS with the specification and introduction of the High Level Structure for Integrated Management Systems (IMS). Figure 4.20 shows a comparison of the 5 phases of quality management according to the PDCA cycle with the higher-level MITO model structure with assignment of the DIN EN ISO 9001:2015 chapters according to the new High Level Structure for Integrated Management Systems (IMS) to the 5 MITO model segments. The 5 steps of the prescribed process-oriented approach are also integrated in this.

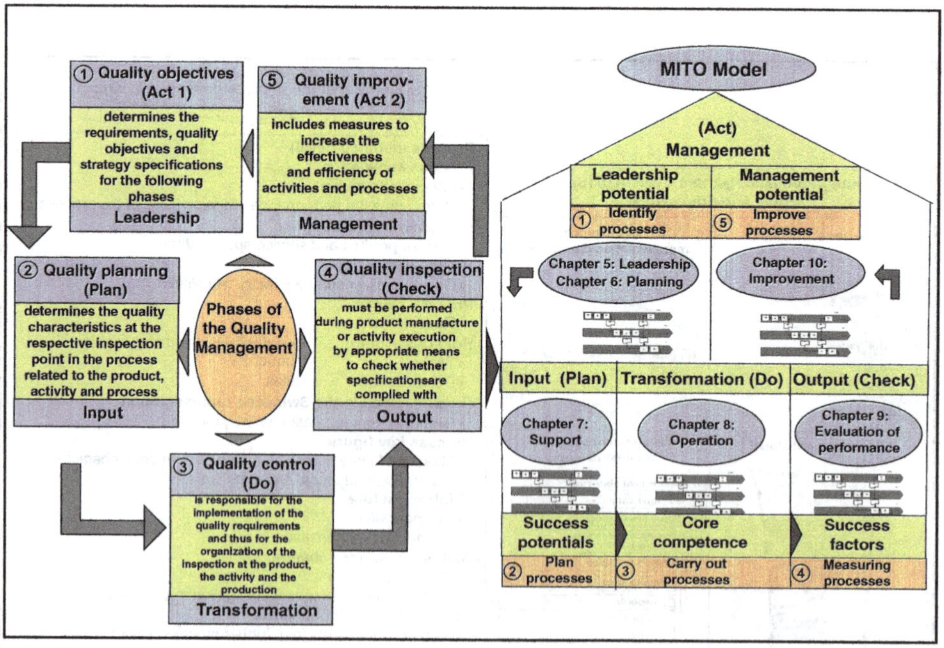

Fig. 4.20 Integrated MITO model-related PDCA quality management control loop for implementing the approach according to DIN EN ISO 9001:2015

For the evidence required in DIN EN ISO 9001:2015, e.g. on the topics of

- Context of the organization to point 4.1 of the standard.
- Stakeholder analysis for point 4.2 of the standard.
- Customer requirements analysis for point 4.2 of the standard.
- Customer satisfaction analysis for point 5.1.2 of the standard.
- Risk analysis for point 6.1.2 of the standard.
- Analysis of measures and evaluation for point 6.1.2 of the standard.
- Competence analysis for point 7.2 of the standard.
- Key figure management to point 7.1.5.1 of the standard and further.

Analysis checklists are prepared as standard, which are systematically processed via the MITO method tool.

4.14 Process Organisation Facilitates the Application of Agile Principles

In publications on the topic of "agility", one increasingly finds the indication that the rigid inflexible process structures prevent the application of agile principles and thus a fast flexible adaptation to changed customer product or legal requirements is not possible. The opposite is the case. Such theses do not mention the existing function-oriented hierarchical organizational structures, in which the self-controlling teams – as they are a natural prerequisite for the application of agile methods – cannot develop at all. Surprisingly, these existing work processes based on the division of labor are not even questioned, but rather the process organization required by standards and regulations, which is usually not even implemented in the company, is used as a killer argument for the failure of agile methods.

The process organization with its transparent and detailed processes is a prerequisite for agile behavior because it provides security and orientation for the employees involved. The hallmark of agile organizations is the transfer of self-management and self-organization to the employees without being restricted by hierarchical, i.e. vertical, organizational structures. The process-oriented scope for action must now be filled by the employees with commitment and a high sense of entrepreneurial responsibility. Of course, this also requires the necessary qualifications of the employees.

In general, agility is understood as the ability of an organization or the people in it to react quickly, correctly and appropriately to unplanned changes, such as new market requirements, disruptions, failures, lack of resources, new regulations, rules, new customer expectations under uncertain turbulent, complex, ambiguous framework conditions. In contrast to flexibility, where changes that can be planned for are already responded to from the outset during project planning or are taken into account during the planning phase.

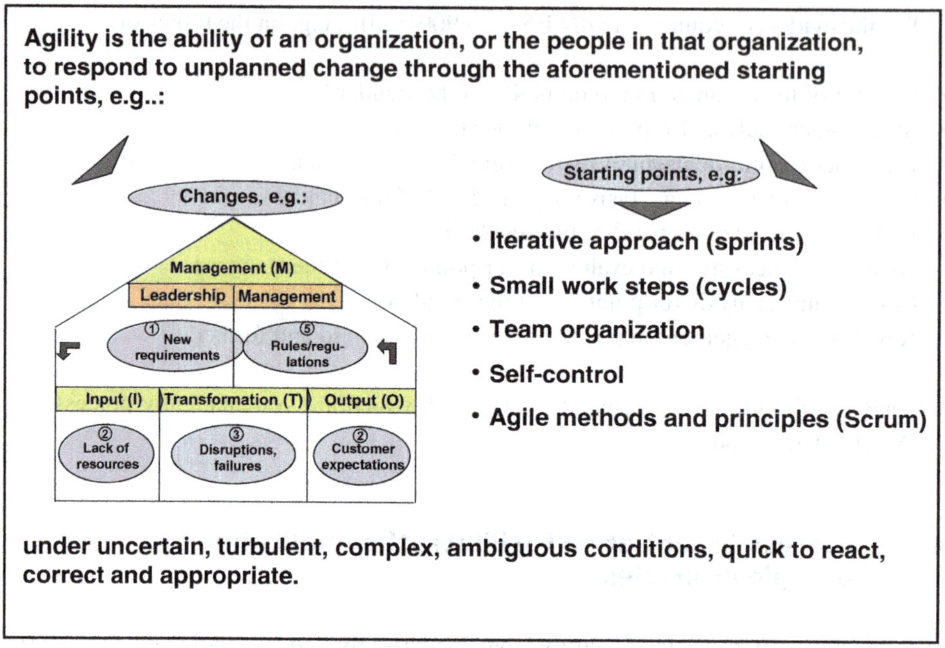

Fig. 4.21 MITO model-related agility solution approaches

From a holistic perspective, the various unplanned changes in the MITO model can be assigned to the individual five MITO model segments, as Fig. 4.21 shows. The required agility characteristics can then also be assigned to these changes, i.e. leadership agility in the leadership segment, employee agility in the input segment, process agility in the transformation segment, product market agility in the output segment, and management agility in the management segment. A further subdivision can also be made into operational agility and strategic agility.

Process orientation aligns all activities in product and service creation with the horizontal value chain, which is focused on the customer. The role-based value chain documentation shows in its factual-temporal-logical relationships with each other how the process participants must work together in flat hierarchies with few interfaces without errors or waste in order to achieve customer benefit and thus customer satisfaction.

This horizontal regulatory framework provides the guard rails with the assigned rules, work instructions, and regulations that are necessary so that the process participants can also act without errors and waste without restricting the scope of action. It is precisely the depiction of these process-oriented structures in the globally valid BPMN 2.0 process visualization representation that shows the network of relationships to the other roles involved in connection with the IT applications used in the process and gives the process participants the security to react to unplanned changes in requirements in an agile manner through self-organization. Without this Swimlane-related organizational structure, the risk of disorientation or even chaos would be pre-programmed, because the process participants would not even know among themselves how they would have to coordinate their activities in a goal-oriented manner within the value chain for the benefit of the customer.

A transparently documented company-specific process documentation with the business processes documented in the **swimlane representation** via a **process level model**, subdivided into end-to-end, main, sub, work system process as well as the process map with the showing of the interactions between the individual business processes and specifies the model spectrum in which the agile principles and methods must be applied. Figure 4.21 shows this method spectrum, which is mentioned in the following point 3.13 when describing the Design Thinking method. Here, there are also no distortions, as is the rule in function-oriented organisational structures, where self-organising groups are repeatedly thwarted by the intervention of hierarchically determined management structures. The feedback function is usually not at all or only very weakly developed in such organisational structures. However, it is the hallmark of successful agile principles application. In the iterative steps with the project team, the goals and measures are derived and implemented in the short term in sprints in order to prevent negative influences from taking effect in the first place.

4.15 MITO Method-Tool-Supported Design Thinking

Since the fulfillment of the agility requirement is currently an outstanding management topic in the holistic business model transformation, this chapter concludes with a discussion of this topic. In this context, design thinking is highlighted as the most important agile method in many current specialist articles. **Design thinking** is an innovation method developed in Silicon Valley that is very well suited to analyzing and testing digital products and services together in a team in an agile manner due to its iterative approach. The method, developed by the two Stanford professors Winograd and Leifer, focuses on the three components of design thinking.

technological feasibility, economic viability, human desirability.

Is the focus. The decisive factor here is that the customer's wishes are comprehensively analysed in order to innovatively develop future products or services. The Design Thinking method is divided into six individual steps, which are also repeated in loops. The first three steps deal with the understanding of the customer's wishes and the systematic analysis. The other three steps deal with the actual idea generation and implementation. The special thing about this is that after each phase you can jump back into a leading phase to achieve the best possible result.

The MITO method tool, which links a large number of known analysis, diagnosis, therapy and evaluation methods via an overarching problem-solving cycle, is very well suited for the application of the Design Thinking method. Different methods stored in the MITO method tool are used in each of the six design thinking steps. Figure 4.22 identifies these six steps. Further information is also given on how to work through them with the MITO method tool.

Step 1 "Analyze problems" involves using several different analyses to concretely determine customer requirements. Examples of this are SWOT, customer satisfaction, requirements, potential or weak point analyses. The result of the evaluation is then presented for diagnosis in the form of a portfolio or radar diagram. Here, the need for action is clearly marked graphically. The point of this first step in the design thinking method is to develop an understanding of the customer problem, which is then continued in the second step through detailed observation of people in the actual real situation.

Through targeted dialogues in this 2nd step, as many relevant details as possible should be discovered that are important for the later idea development phase. It is helpful to document the process with the roles involved in step 2 "Process observation" in order to make a factual-temporal-logical assignment of the localized requirements.

In step 3, "Problem description", a synthesis of all the collected information and needs for action from the first two steps now follows. For the following brainstorming, it should be clarified what is to be prioritized and what the customer places the greatest value on.

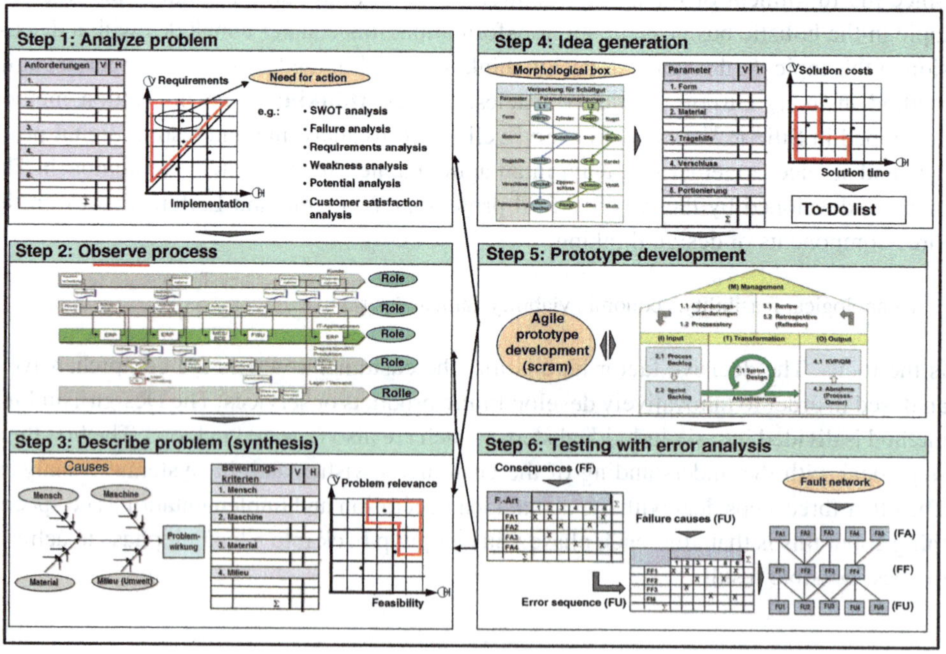

Fig. 4.22 MITO method tool-supported design thinking

This also includes the innovation search fields for new digital products and services. As shown in Fig. 4.22, the MITO tool-supported application of the Ishikawa method can provide very good support for this problem description (synthesis). Here, the clusters relevant for the localized problem description, i.e. for the main effect desired by the customer, are deposited as main influencing variables in the form of a fishbone. For example, 4 M's "Man/Machine/Material/Environment", in order to then assign the individual requirements to the individual main influencing variables or main requirements.

The **Ishikawa diagram** itself, with its clusters and the associated individual criteria, can again be mapped in a MITO portfolio matrix for a 2-dimensional evaluation. This enables the user to prioritize, for example, according to the evaluation variant (BV): "V = importance", "H = urgency" or "V: problem relevance", "H = feasibility".

Thus, after a sometimes lengthy preparation in the steps described, the prerequisites are now fulfilled to carry out the idea generation in step 4. The morphological box stored in the MITO tool can be used very well as a method here, which can also be mapped again in the form of a MITO portfolio matrix after the assignment of the respective solution options to the main parameters, in order to evaluate the individual ideas according to the evaluation variant (BV): "V = solution effort", "H = solution costs" or the evaluation variant (BV): "V = benefit", "H = effort", for example, and to display the result in the portfolio diagram. In this way, the most promising solution approaches are again graphically identified. The specifications for a to-do list are derived, which finally leads to a **prototype development** in step 5.

Thisprototype development in step 5 could, for example, take the form of a use case analysis with implementation via the Scrum model as an agile software development method with the decomposition of complex contexts into small task packages. Via the interactive Scrum process, new ideas and adjustments can always be integrated into the solution development within the individual sprints.

This is followed by the last step 6, testing. The aim here is to try out the developed prototype in a practical test and, following a Failure Mode and Effects Analysis (FMEA), to simultaneously determine the type of error, error sequence and error cause in the form of a MITO cascade. This is always done in direct dialogue with the users for further improvement. The customer must be intensively involved so that he can give further impulses, which are then applied again in the form of a loop formation in step 3 "Synthesis". This feedback can already take place in step 5 "Prototype development". A loop to step 1 "Understanding" can also be created.

This is also the particular success of Design Thinking, that looping repetitions of the individual steps are constantly possible as needed in iterative form. The decisive factor here is that there must always be an intelligent leap into the right phase. An open error culture is also important. Every discovered and communicated error should then be in one of the six steps to complement the considerations documented there. This supports teamwork at eye level between the participants. Design Thinking promotes teamwork and collaboration. This is always in conjunction with the necessary methodological competence provided by the MITO method tool and the open management culture.

5 Systematic Digitisation Master Plan Development and Implementation

Abstract

After the description of the procedures for the organizational business model transformation in Chap. 3 and the cultural business model transformation in Chap. 4, the foundations for the digital business model transformation, which is now the focus, have been created. The point of reference here is the current, i.e. not yet digitized, business model described in Chap. 2 by answering the 7 basic questions. This is also the current challenge for companies. The question here is how the digital transformation can be anchored in the current business processes in a way that meets requirements in order to reduce transaction costs and optimize communication and collaboration between the process participants in the manufacture of smart, i.e. networked, products over the product's useful life. The main problem here is the complexity of the various digitization solutions for the horizontal and **vertical networking** of business processes within the process level model. Horizontally, from an external perspective, these digitization solutions relate to the electronic inclusion of stakeholders in the horizontal value chain, such as customers, suppliers and other stakeholders. Vertically, i.e. internally to the mobile connection and collaboration of the process participants within the process hierarchy, starting at the top level related to the horizontal end-to-end process via the main and sub-processes down to the individual process step at the lowest process level, i.e. the shop floor management. Vertical networking also serves to optimize the horizontal value creation process and increase customer benefits.

The point of reference and the core for horizontal and vertical networking within the company-specific business model is the conception of a company-specific cloud-based digital business platform as the technological basis for the **data integration** of the IT

H. F. Binner, *Holistic Business Model Transformation*,
https://doi.org/10.1007/978-3-658-37367-2_5

applications used in the company, which all process participants can access barrier-free and mobile in real time. Also integrated into this digital platform are AI and machine learning tools for an automated production process and for predictive action based on real-time evaluations. However, it was necessary – as described in Chap. 3 – to create the organizational conditions beforehand in order to guarantee a smooth implementation of the digital business platform.

For the uniform structuring of this digital platform – as shown in Fig. 5.1 – the MITO business model with its 5 model segments "Leadership, Input, Transformation, Output, Management" and additionally the customer and partner segment is applied. The description of the existing business model as the starting point for the necessary change management process for digital business model transformation was covered in detail in Chap. 2. The focus in Chapter 5 is now on the holistic digitization of the company-specific end-to-end business process together with the business processes defined in the hierarchical process level model within the control loop-based MITO model segments.

The digital business model transformation is implemented through **the digital master plan** explained below.

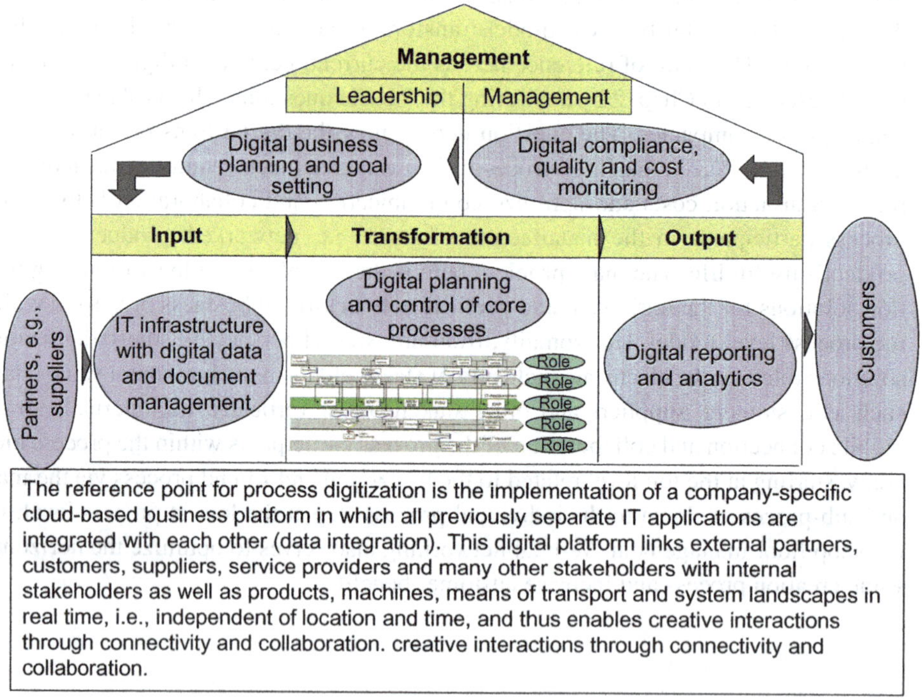

Fig. 5.1 Contents of a cloud-based digital business platform

5.1 Connectivity and Interoperability Requirements for the Digital Business Platform

The fulfillment of the **interoperability** and connectivity requirements, i.e. the ability to network applications and systems (data integration) with comprehensive information provision to all process participants via networking with the digital infrastructure (connectivity) in real time, is decisive for the success of digitization. The applications affected by the connectivity and interoperability requirements are assigned to the processes that have expired within the 5 MITO segments according to their area of application and use without claiming to be complete. As Fig. 5.2 shows, for example, in the MITO input segment it is personnel management and facility management software, in the MITO transformation segment it is ERP/PPS or MES software, or in the MITO output segment it is QM, testing, complaints, transport logistics software. This in conjunction with the planning and financial applications used in the management and leadership segment.

The benefits of connectivity and interoperability due to data integration in the digital business platform are many, e.g.:

- Dissolution of vertical data silos.
- No double entries with additional data maintenance effort.
- Central master data management.

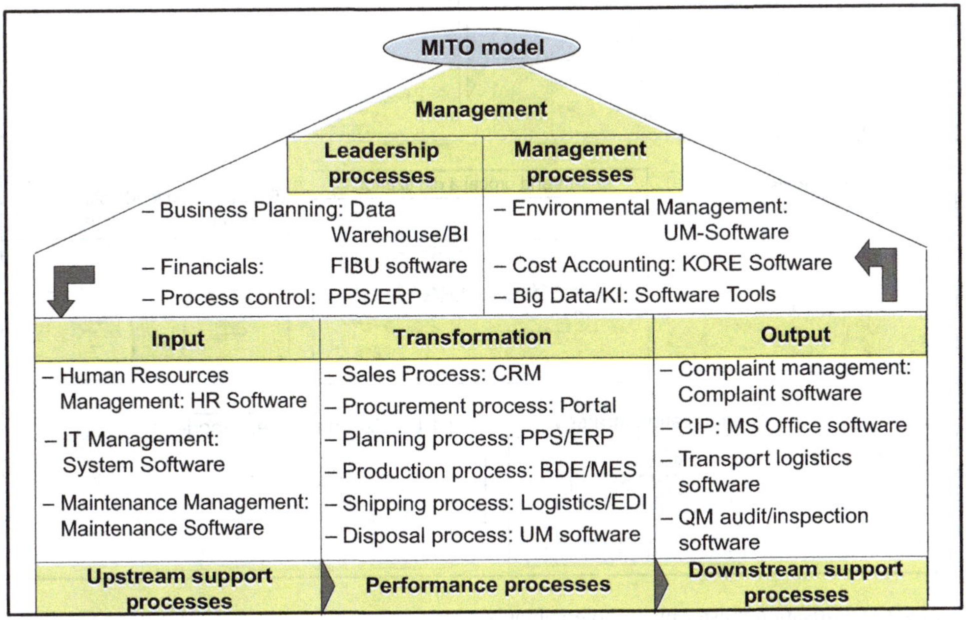

Fig. 5.2 MITO-related classical IT application mapping and data networking, e.g.

- No search and waiting times when providing information.
- Current comprehensive information status in real time.
- Error prevention due to complete data provision without data gaps.
- Guarantee of high data quality based on existing data consistency, i.e. freedom from contradictions in terms of content and form of the data stock.
- Company-specific knowledge storage with associative navigation.

5.2 Digitisation Master Plan Implementation Steps

In the following, the process model for the digital **business model transformation** with a requirements-based digitization implementation via a digitization master plan is explained. This master plan consists of the 6 steps listed in Fig. 5.3 and explained below:

- Step 1: Developing a digital business model with the associated digital value proposition.
- Step 2: Digital goal derivation and digital mission statement creation.
- Step 3: Digital business innovation analysis with digital strategy derivation.
- Step 4: Creation of a digital process model for the introduction of a process organization.

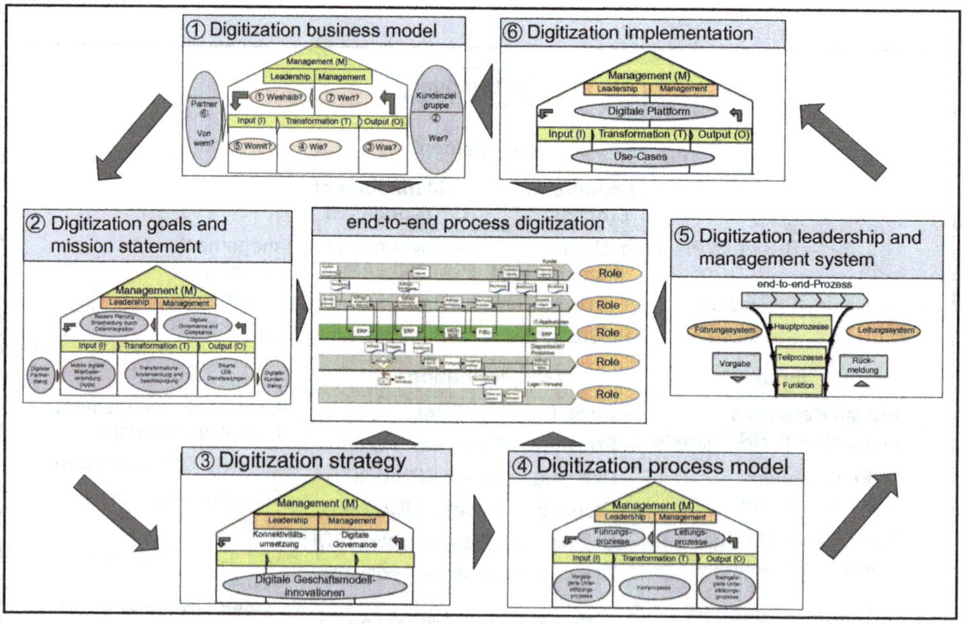

Fig. 5.3 Digitisation master plan implementation steps

- Step 5: Digital command and control system implementation.
- Step 6: Method-supported introduction of the digitization components via use case specifications.

The MITO model with its 5 model segments "Leadership, Input, Transformation, Output, Management" is also used for the uniform structuring of these 6 steps – as shown in Fig. 5.3.

The focus of the mapping is the digitization of the company-specific analyzed and documented business processes, starting from the end-to-end business processes in the role-based process mapping according to the globally valid BPMN 2.0 process visualization standard, corresponding to the hierarchical process level model across all process levels down to the workstation level, as described in detail in Chap. 3 "Process Organization Implementation".

5.3 MITO Model-Related Digital Target System

As also explained in detail above, the main task of management in this digital business model development, taking into account the digital transformation, is to create an organizational structure with which the company can achieve sustainable success with its stakeholders on the basis of digitized effective and efficient business processes. Within this process-oriented organizational system, managers must use target agreements with a full-implementation function to ensure that employees are motivated and willing to perform the tasks assigned to them in a quality-oriented and agile manner.

The overarching objectives structured in Sect. 2.10 in the MITO target system continue to apply in the digitization of **value chains**. They are implemented via the MITO leadership and management system and essentially relate to improving profitability together with increasing flexibility, transparency, quality and speed in order to respond to market demands in line with requirements. Managers are responsible for meeting these requirements. The company-specific targets now considered in more detail, differentiated according to formal, social, process-related, material and sustainability targets by management, are named from a holistic perspective in Fig. 5.4 within the individual MITO model segments.

The reference point for the structuring of the target system is again – as already explained in Chap. 4 – the MITO model with its five segments or organisational subsystems

- MITO leadership segment with the formal goals of.
- MITO input segment with the social objectives.
- MITO transformation segment with the process targets.
- MITO output segment with the objective of.
- MITO management segment with the compliance and sustainability goals.

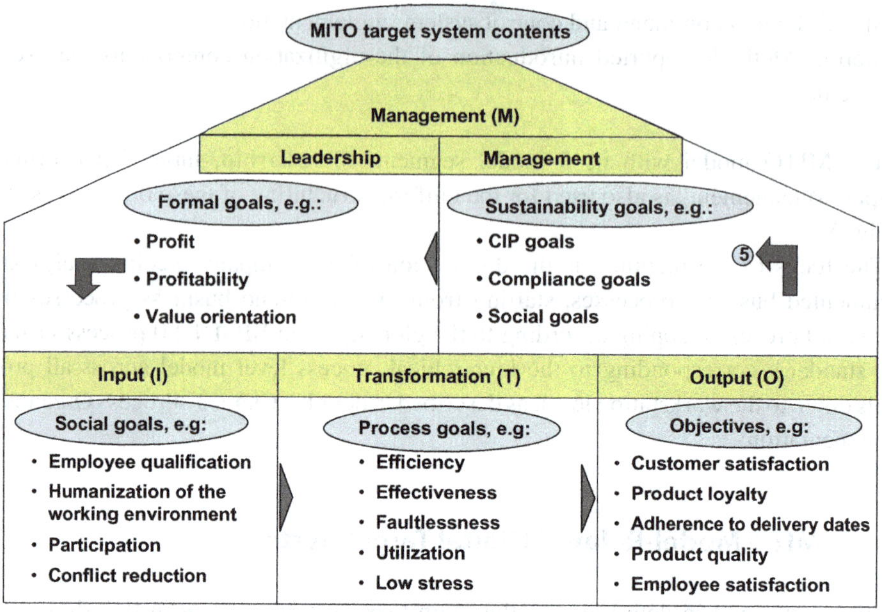

Fig. 5.4 Fulfilling corporate objectives as an organisational, management and leadership task

The organizational and cultural transformation explained in Chaps. 3 and 4 as a prerequisite for a transition from a conventional business model to a digital business model means that the existing target, management and leadership system will also be implemented digitally in the future. The overarching digitization goals to be achieved through the implementation of the digitization strategy are mentioned in Fig. 5.5. They are a means to an end for achieving the individual company goals listed in Fig. 5.4.

In brief, the process-oriented target system linked to customer needs and expectations is derived from the company-specific business model with its vision, mission, strategy and mission statement. This is often anchored in the form of an agenda. The digitalized management system with the provision of management tools for task planning and control supports the management in achieving these objectives. On the feedback side, the digitized management system is responsible for measuring the achievement of objectives, controlling and compliance. The **management and control system** form a functioning operational control loop across all process levels. Continuous target/actual comparisons at each process level result in permanent impulses for improvement.

The **digitalization procedure model** described below via the master plan offers managers assistance in mastering the future challenges in the world of work 4.0.

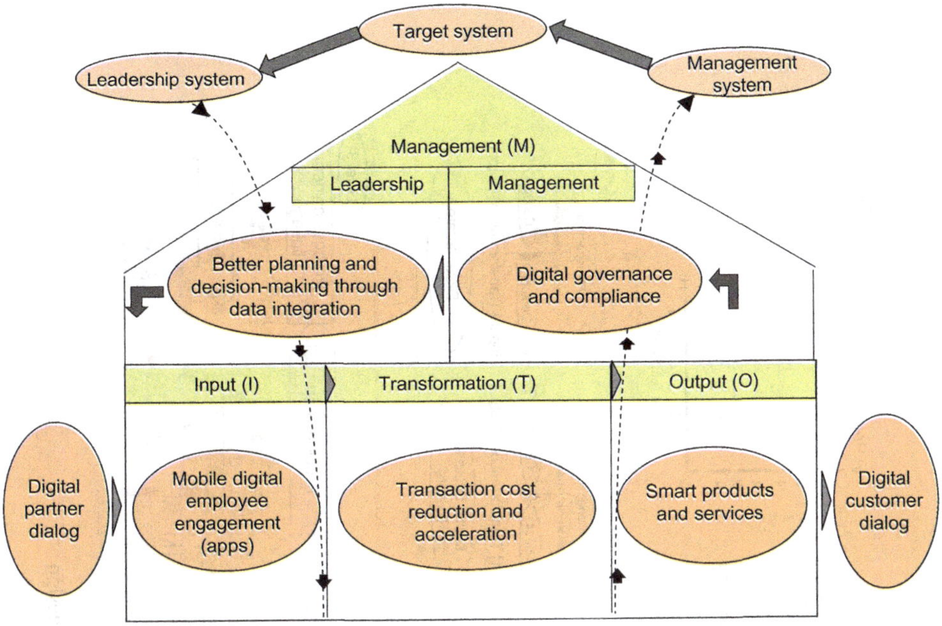

Fig. 5.5 MITO-related digitization strategy goals

5.4 Digital Master Plan Implementation in 3 Steps

The systematic implementation of the six steps contained in the digitalization master plan in Fig. 5.3 takes place via the process model shown in Fig. 5.6 in three levels. Level 1 is about the development and description of the digital business model in connection with the digital agenda, i.e. the description of the path of the digital transformation with objective, at the company with allocation of the necessary measures, resources and actors as well as the digital master plan specification. The result in level 1 is a clear allocation of the digitization topic areas or the digital business innovations that are to be introduced MITO business model-related.

These specifications are specified in level 2 with the development of the digital mission statement, the formulation of the digital policy, the specification of the digital objectives and the localisation of the digital success factors as the basis for the derivation of the digital strategy for achieving the targeted **digital value contributions**, as they were named in the agenda.

The further implementation, i.e. the digital transformation at the company according to the specifications of the digital agenda of the master plan for activating the digital value contributions is then carried out systematically using the process implementation models already described in detail in level 3.

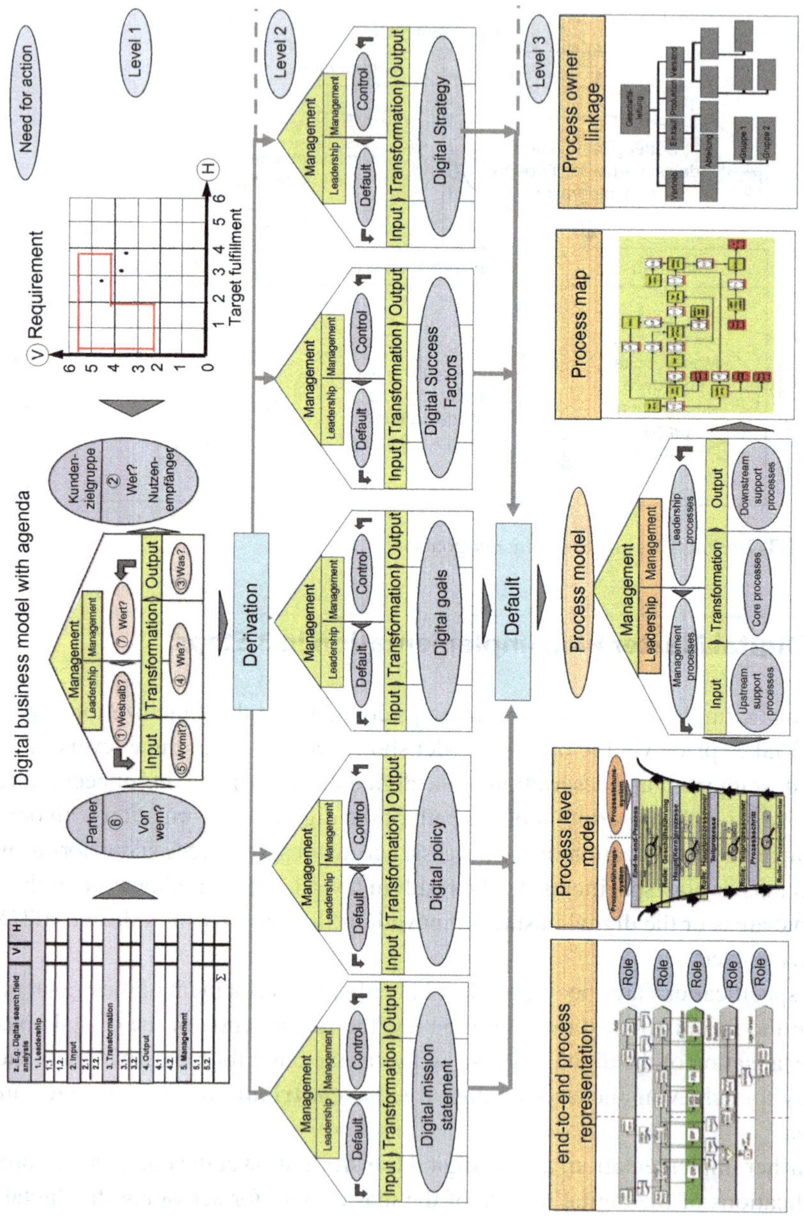

Fig. 5.6 Holistic MITO model-related digitization business model development and design

The starting point in level 3 is the role-based documentation of the end-to-end process with the factual/temporal/logical assignments of the individual work steps of the participants to each other and to the associated IT applications. This is done in increasing detail via the process level model, i.e. starting at the top level from the end-to-end process via the main process and subprocess down to the individual process functions. The processes are documented via the specific process model according to the MITO model structures. The interactions of the processes with each other and also the networking of the IT applications used in the process are created via the process map with the help of the BPM tool. If function-oriented organizational structures are still predominant in the company, a process organization chart can now also be created with assignment of the process owners for the individual processes in the process model.

5.5 Answering the Digital Business Model 7 W Core Questions

As explained in the previous Sect. 5.4, the digital business model development begins in level 1 with the answering of the 7 W-questions as a prerequisite for the selection of the digital business model innovations described below, followed by the selection and introduction of a digital business platform in line with the requirements.

To this end, once again as a reminder – as already described in Chap. 2 – is the MITO model structure together with the key customer and partner segment and the process level model. Reference point for the company-specific MITO business model development with the likewise method-based answering of the seven basic questions

Why, Who, What, How, With Whom, Value?

In the order of answering these questions shown in Fig. 5.7.

In this case, the 7 W-questions are always answered with regard to the integration of the **digital** transformation solution approaches, i.e. the digital business model innovations described in the following point 4.7.

On the basis of an implemented cloud-based digital **business platform**, the practical implementation of the digital objectives of a business model takes place systematically in the form of a control loop with all activities, as shown in the MITO model in the individual 5 MITO model segments in Fig. 5.8.

It begins in the management segment with the specification of the **digital master plan** and the digitalization strategy description contained therein together with the digital values that are formulated in the form of a mission statement and are to be applied in the digital transformation. Essentially, this involves an open culture of change without organizational or personnel barriers in the change process with close involvement of the employees.

In the MITO input segment, the method-based selection and provision of the required digital infrastructure takes place. The focus is on the selection of a cloud-based digital

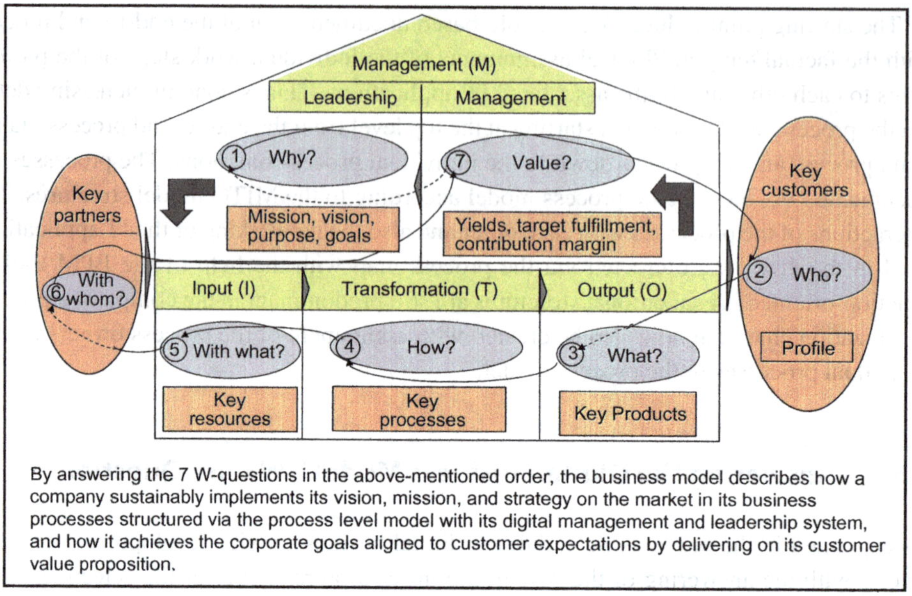

Fig. 5.7 MITO Business Model-7 W-Question Answer Order

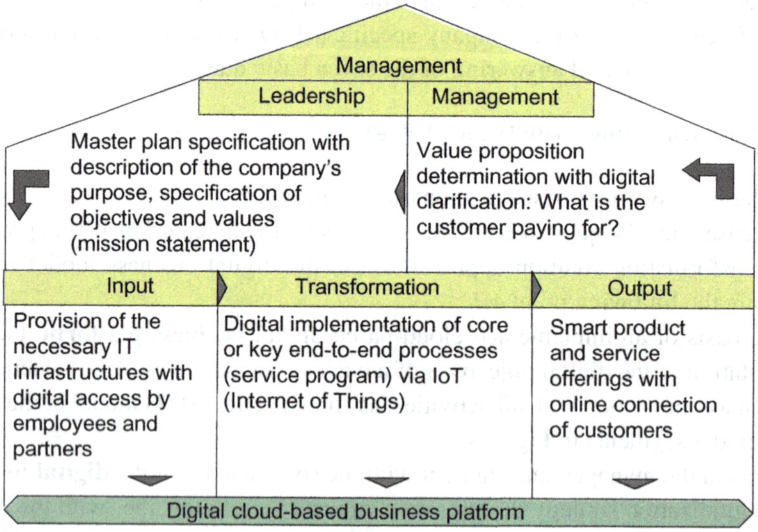

Fig. 5.8 MITO model-related digital business model implementation

business platform that provides employees, customers, and partners with mobile access to the integrated data assets so that they have all the information they need to perform their work in real time. In selecting the cloud-based digital business platform or platform provider, there are quite a number of MITO checklists to make a selection according to the requirements. These are, for example, the MITO-supported portal web services selection analysis or a platform provider evaluation matrix.

In the transformation segment, the digital implementation of the core and key processes then takes place after the implementation of the cloud-based digital platform. Here, due to the digital networking of the existing IT applications with a central master data management, the transaction costs are reduced due to the elimination of search, provision, connection, completion, coordination, monitoring and waiting times or costs and a fast application processing is guaranteed due to the elimination of media discontinuities. Due to the real-time data collection, there is a transparent overview of the status of the business transactions or the process execution.

In the output segment, the company's stakeholders can be provided with the smart products and services online via a **shop floor system** and also communicate directly with the responsible employees via the platform.

The final step in MITO management is a digital value model analysis. Here, it is examined whether the digital business model implementation has also brought the digital value contributions targeted in advance for all stakeholders within the individual model segments due to the digital business model innovations introduced there. Here, MITO analysis checklists are again applied together with the MITO method tool. Approaches for improvement are also localized via a multidimensional evaluation with graphical presentation of results in the portfolio or radar diagram.

5.6 MITO Model-Related Value Contributions of a Digital Business Platform

When introducing this cloud-based digital business platform, it is crucial to determine in advance the digital value contributions resulting from the digital business model innovations that make such a digital business platform interesting for the company.

This value contribution can be determined via a method-based **value contribution analysis** within the five MITO model segments. The digitization-relevant core statements are listed in Fig. 5.9. These core statements are specified using a predefined value contribution portfolio analysis with the MITO method tool.

Question 1 "Why does the platform add value to the company" can be answered clearly. Through a continuous data integration and connectivity of all IT applications available in the company with a central master data and document management, the quality of corporate planning and the increase in decision-making quality is significantly improved through the real-time data provision, and the risk of wrong decisions is greatly reduced.

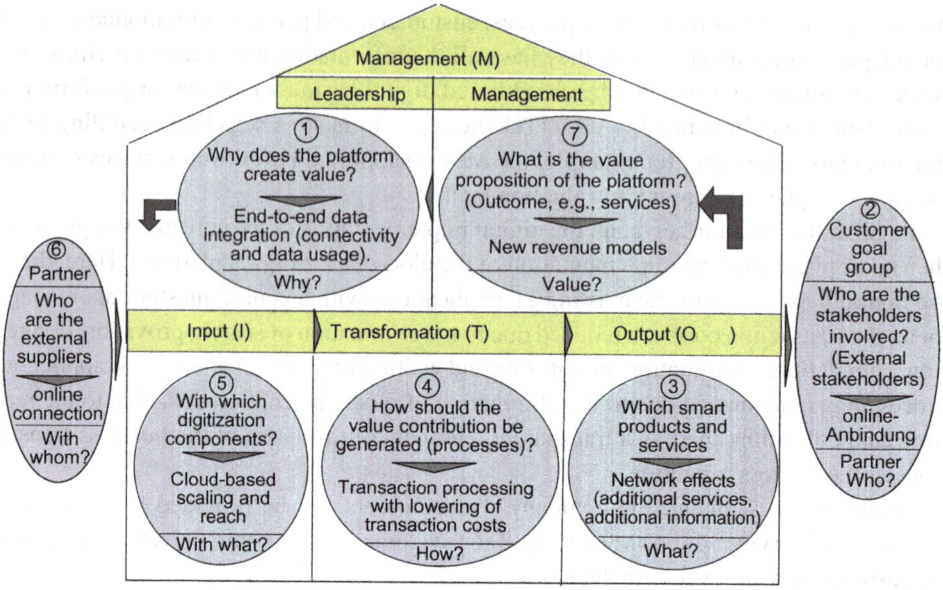

Fig. 5.9 MITO model-related value contributions of a digital business platform

For the fulfilment of customer expectations within the customer target groups "Who" in question 2, the digital business platform offers the possibility of a direct exchange of information online over the entire product lifetime of the purchased product or service with additional service offers or complementary products from partners. This data exchange also promotes networking among customers with the aim of exchanging experiences in product use. The result is a positive network effect.

The value contribution in the output segment in question 3 "What" refers to the smart products and services offered, which now enable diverse additional information when using the product or service. This also results in suggestions for new business models based on the product usage data provided by the customer as feedback.

The value contribution in relation to the basic question 4 "How" with the answer via the effective and efficient process execution in the transformation segment lies in the reduction of transaction costs in transaction processing. This is combined with higher process reliability and process quality. Real-time data acquisition during order execution generates a lot of production data, which enables predictive action via artificial intelligence and machine learning applications.

In the input segment, the value contribution with regard to question 5 essentially lies in the reduction of IT investment and structural costs through scalable cloud-based platform solutions that enable transparent cost/benefit analyses and, if required, also allow an expansion or a reduction of the IT infrastructure usage components without much effort.

With regard to the partners and suppliers of the company under consideration in question 6 "with whom", the value contribution lies, as already with the customers in question

2, in the direct connection, i.e. the online communication and the additional information that can be exchanged via the platform independent of time and place.

Overall, within the described MITO model segments, the MITO management segment finally results in the sum of all individual value contributions due to the digitization generated new revenue models as an answer to question 7 "What value contribution" with a significant contribution to the sustainable increase in success through the holistic digitization.

5.7 Business Model Innovation Mapping as a New Strategic Approach

In the digital MITO business model development approach presented here, the 7 MITO business model elements with the associated 7 W basic questions for systematic business model development – as already described in detail in Section 2 – are shown in Fig. 5.10. A large number of possible digital business model innovations are assigned to these 7 model elements as a solution approach for the MITO model-related strategy contents described in Sect. 2.15 and the starting points for successful process-oriented company development mentioned in Sect. 3.6. The contents of the individual business model innovations are then described in detail in Sect. 5.8.

In the basic question 1: **"Why?"** in the MITO leadership segment, innovations are mentioned for change management impulses. This is the leadership's responsibility to

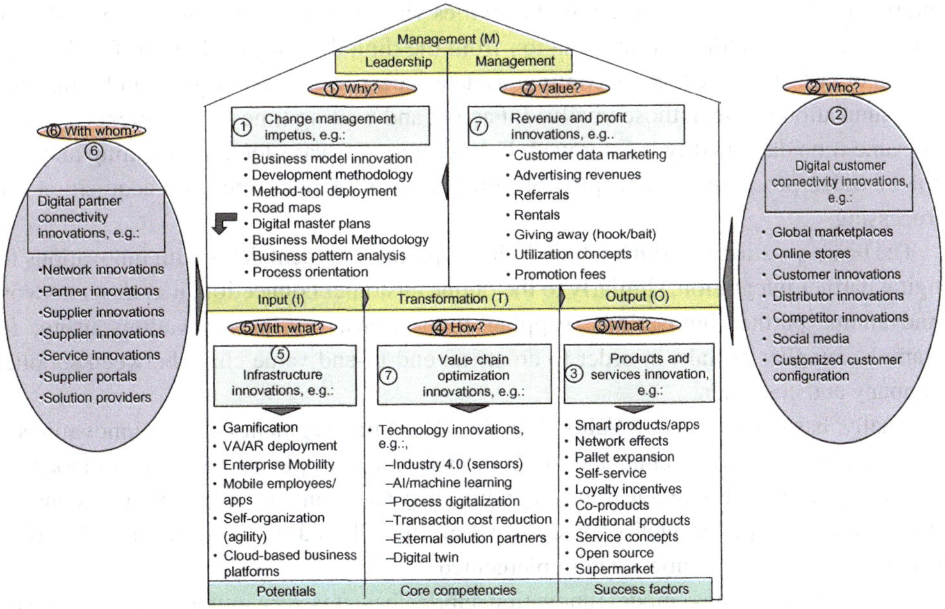

Fig. 5.10 MITO Business Model Innovation Stimuli

methodically identify digital business model innovations via roadmaps, master plans, business model methodologies, business pattern analyses, and other approaches.

In the customer segment for the basic question 2: **"Who?"** it is a matter of business model innovation impulses for digital customer connection. For example, via global marketplaces, online shops, customer innovation, sales partner innovation, but also digital-related competitor innovations as well as impulses from social media or via product configurations specified online by the customer.

Basic question 3: **"What?"** in the MITO output segment refers to business model innovations for smart, i.e. connectable, products and services that provide a great deal of data analysis for new revenue models during use by the customer. This is combined with loyalty incentives in connection with product range extensions.

With regard to basic question 4: **"How" in** the transformation segment, the focus is on innovations for digital value chain optimization, i.e. primarily on technology innovations in the area of Industry 4.0 or IoT, i.e. on networked plants, machines, objects via sensors and actuators, and on process digitalization with the aim of reducing transaction costs, also involving external solution partners. The acquisition of actual data in production in real time then enables the application of AI or machine learning technologies, which enable predictive action based on the knowledge gained from this.

Basic question 5: **"With what?"** in MITO input segment refers to innovations on IT infrastructure deployment via cloud, further also focusing on innovations related to employee skill development e.g. via gamification based on self-organization and self-management. Equipment for employees via enterprise mobility, employee mobile apps, VA/AR deployment enables real-time online connectivity. Every employee gets updated and timely information about required activities via smartphone and tablet. He or she can obtain even more additional information from the digital business platform for the completion of tasks because there is continuous data access, which also significantly improves communication between those involved. Factual and waiting times are shortened while at the same time data quality is improved. Furthermore, forward-looking planning and control of order processes is also possible on the basis of real-time data acquisition and processing.

The basic question 6: **"With whom?"** in the partner segment deals with innovations for digital partner integration, similarly to the online customer connection, it is about network innovations, partner innovations, supplier innovations, service innovations using, for example, supplier portals, in order to create an end-to-end value chain between supplier, company and customer.

Finally, basic question 7: **"Value?"** in the MITO line segment is about innovations in terms of new types of revenue and profit models, for example customer data marketing, advertising revenue, brokerage, rentals, giving away (hack and lure concept), usage instead of purchase concepts or auction models. All of this is based on the previously described business ideas that have now been implemented.

Among these business model innovation approaches, it is very important for a company to constantly question its own existing business model in order to find out where changes are necessary before new market participants or existing competitors initiate them. A differentiation of these digital business model innovations from the classic product and process innovations lies in the fact that at least three basic questions of the MITO business model are affected in the case of business model innovations. This also means that the business model is protected against imitations by competitors.

5.8 Basic Description of the Digitisation Components Within the MITO Business Model Elements

In the further implementation of the digitization strategy, it is important to select the most diverse **digitization components** that run within the business processes in individual MITO model segments of the MITO business model and to implement them via use case descriptions in order to then also establish the desired horizontal and vertical networking.

In the following, some essential digitization components are briefly explained with reference to the associated MITO model segment. It begins from the perspective of the higher-level digitization strategy definition with the basic descriptions of the basic IT architecture components in the MITO management segment.

5.8.1 Process Digitization Statements in the MITO Leadership Segment

5.8.1.1 Cloud Computing

The cloud is the building block of digitalization for new data-driven business models. In principle, cloud computing is about the dynamic provision of IT applications on demand and the corresponding IT resources via a network, usually the Internet.

According to the National Institute of Standards and Technology (NIST), cloud computing is when the following characteristics are met over the Internet:

1. IT services are accessible and available from different end devices.
2. IT resources such as computing power or storage space are automatically provided without any further interaction with the service provider.
3. Benefit capacities are automatically measured and optimized.
4. IT services are provided quickly and elastically, ideally also automatically.
5. IT services are multi-client capable, i.e. the provider's resources are available in a tool from which many users can draw.

By moving IT infrastructures to the cloud, also known as **outsourcing**, IT applications can be executed entirely via the Internet. Installations on local computers are therefore generally no longer necessary. Both the offer and the use of these cloud services are then carried out via technical interface protocols or even a web browser. The main advantage of cloud computing is that the required IT capacities are provided dynamically depending on the workload, i.e. they can be scaled as required.

Also according to a 2009 definition by the National Institute of Standards and Technology (NIST), **cloud computing** can basically be divided into the three service models:

1. **Infrastructure-as-a Service** (IAAS). The cloud offers access to computers, storage and other virtualized computer hardware resources. However, the user is responsible for the selection, setup, operation and functioning of the software at any time in his own data center. He can therefore individually design his own special virtual computer cloud solution, although the cloud offers him the typical components of a data center infrastructure, such as hardware, computer storage space or network resources virtually.
2. **Platform-as-a Service** (PaaS) Here, users develop their own software applications with the PaaS service or have them executed within a software environment already provided and operated by the respective as-a-service provider. The PaaS cloud provides access to runtime and programming environments for which dynamically adaptable, flexible computing and data capacities are provided.
3. **Software-as-a Service** (SaaS). Here, the user can access application programs and software collections via the cloud, each of which can be selected to be compatible with the respective existing infrastructure. This model is also known as software on demand. SaaS is understood as a subarea of cloud computing, since the requested IT applications are never directly available on the user's device.

In cloud computing, four relevant delivery models are considered to be established. These are:

1. The public cloud. Here, the respective cloud service provider offers IT infrastructures, whereby payment is based on the actual consumption or degree of use. In the public cloud, the platform remains the property of cloud service providers who offer services such as servers or storage space. In this case, all hardware, software and the infrastructure required for this is managed and operated by the respective cloud provider. Access to these services and the management of one's own account takes place via a web browser.
2. The private cloud is an in-house cloud solution. The required hardware is located within the own company or within the own organization. Access to abstracted IT infrastructures is provided. The private cloud can be physically located in the data center of this company. However, this is not a requirement. Many companies pay third-party providers for such services, which then host their private cloud. A private cloud is thus a cloud where the services and infrastructure run over a private network.
3. The hybrid cloud allows access to abstracted IT infrastructures from the private cloud and public cloud segments. This delivery model is explicitly tailored to the individual needs of users. The hybrid cloud extends the resources provided exclusively in an

in-house private cloud to the public cloud. If required, the hybrid cloud can flexibly scale the computing power, storage space or other services of the private cloud with services from the public cloud. The advantages of a hybrid cloud over a pure private or public cloud are fast and flexible response to changing requirements, fulfillment of security, data protection and compliance requirements, simple management and unification of the IT environment, further use of existing technologies, good scalability of services, optimization of business processes and acceleration of innovations.

4. The fourth delivery model is the community cloud. This model primarily addresses user groups that are usually distributed locally. In addition, there are delivery models that form hybrids of these four models. By far the most popular public cloud is the Amazon Web Services (AWS) Cloud as a public cloud service from the Amazon Cloud. AWS offers a wide range of cloud-based services, such as data processing, storage, databases, analytics networks, mobile devices, developer tools, management tools, Internet of Things. In addition, web and mobile applications of game development, data processing and data warehousing, as well as storage, archiving and many other solutions.

A multi-cloud enables the parallel use of different cloud services and platforms from multiple providers. From the user's point of view, it behaves like a single large cloud. Several cloud models, such as the private or public cloud, can be integrated in the multi-cloud.

5.8.1.2 On Premises

On-premises refers to a licensing and usage model for server-based computer programs. Here, the licensee, i.e. the company, purchases or rents the software and operates it under its own responsibility in its own computer center (on-premises). It is also possible for the licensee to operate the software on a rented server of a third-party computer center. In addition to the operating and acquisition costs for the software, maintenance fees must also be taken into account. On-premises solutions have the advantage of greater flexibility in the adaptation of the company's own processes to the software. Customer-specific requirements can therefore be better covered. However, this often involves considerable costs for ongoing software adaptation. The counterpart to on-premises is the cloud computing model, "Service as a Service". This involves purchasing the software as a service from an IT service provider. The provider is responsible for maintenance and operation. Whereas with on-premises all risks and burdens are transferred to the licensee, i.e. the company, through the purchase, with cloud computing the hardware, operation, line costs and maintenance are covered by the rental price. In the case of cloud services, if the IT service provider's server is located abroad, special data protection policy aspects must be taken into account. If the IT application is offered as software as a service, the data is also kept on the system of the IT service provider.

5.8.1.3 Internet

The largest computer network in the world is the **Internet**. It currently consists of several billion different computers, i.e. all size classes from the simple PC to the supercomputer, which are connected to each other on the Internet. The main common feature of these computers is that they communicate with each other using the same protocol "**TCP/IP**". The Internet originated from a military command and communication network "**ARPANET**" developed in 1969, which was intended to survive an enemy nuclear strike because the data in this network is not transported along fixed predictable and therefore destructible routes. For this reason, this network has no central control point. The decentralized network structure therefore makes it impossible to monitor this network. At the same time, it makes it difficult to find information because there is no central catalog. At any point in this network, it can be expanded at any time with new computers that can handle TCP/IP and thus with new information. Every user or institution that connects a computer to the Internet pays for the maintenance of the computer and the line itself. Complementary to the IT infrastructure, IT services are offered. These are cross-process and cross-procedural IT components with process-neutral components. The **World Wide Web (WWW)** is mentioned first because the Internet achieved the breakthrough to a mass communications network in 1992.

5.8.1.4 World Wide Web

The Internet made its breakthrough into a mass communications network in 1992, when it was given an easy-to-use graphical user interface, the **World Wide Web (WWW).** This enabled even computer novices to surf the net and retrieve information and documents. Every device connected to the Internet (e.g. server, laptop, IP camera, smartphone, tablet or printer) can be reached via a unique address (IPv6). Over time, IPv6 is expected to increasingly replace the IPv4 protocol that is mainly used today. Until then, every device (modem, router) that provides access to the Internet for one or more end devices receives a temporary or static **IP address** that is assigned by the **Internet service provider.** The end devices that share access to the Internet via such an access point or node thus appear to have the same address from the point of view of other Internet users. Within this access node, the individual devices are assigned an individual address by the router. The router also handles the distribution, or routing, of data from the Internet within its node. Large companies or data centers have a fixed IP address. For example, the search engine Google can be reached at the IP address 172.217.16.163.

The Provider provides the connection to the Internet for business and private customers. It maintains a permanent connection to the Internet and enables its customers to establish a temporary or permanent connection. Common access options to the Internet are narrowband connections via telephone or ISDN modem, broadband connections via DSL, fiber optic or cable modem as well as satellite and access via radio and mobile communications such as UMTS, HSDPA, LTE and 5G. The classic application software for accessing web content is called a web browser or "**browser**". There are a large number of different browsers from different manufacturers that enable the web content to be displayed on a variety of different end devices such as notebooks, smartphones, television sets or operator terminals. Here, the most used browsers in April 2020 according to Statista are Chrome with about 65% market share, Safari with about 8%, Firefox with about 7% and Microsoft Edge with about 5% market share. The browser software uses the Hyper Text Transfer Protocol (**HTTP**) protocol or the tap-proof Hypertext Transfer Protocol Secure (HTTPS) protocol. In today's age, however, the amount of data transferred via browsers is shifting more and more in favor of apps or programs, such as streaming software, video conferencing software or social media apps and online games, which connect to the Internet via a wide variety of end devices.

5.8.1.5 Hypertext

The WWW is a service of the Internet and is based on the principle of **hypertext**. Hypertext is a non-linear text and has neither beginning nor end. If the information offered anywhere on the Internet is not sufficient, one can jump from one cross-reference to another entry, from there again to a new cross-reference, and so on. In the WWW, these cross-references are called **hyperlinks** and the entries are called **web pages**. Hypertext allows the linking of text or image information by cross-references within documents, because **HTML** (Hyper Text Mark Language) is the description language for **hypertext documents.** It allows multimedia integration as another major Internet advantage. This is the simultaneous use of several types of information such as text, image, graphics, audio and video in one application. In this sense, **multimedia** can be defined as the software-controlled (digital) integrated generation, modification, presentation, storage and communication of information of several time-dependent and time-independent media. The click of a mouse on a link brings information stored in any place on earth to the screen of the display device. For this reason, the WWW is not subject to editorial control. The WWW information originates from all Internet participants. No guarantee can be given that this information is correct (Fig. 5.11).

5.8.1.6 Electronic Mail

Another important Internet service besides the WWW is **electronic mail**, usually called **e-mail.** This is an electronic mail service that was by far the most common Internet activity in the early days of the Internet. Letters can be sent electronically between Internet users in an uncomplicated way. The prerequisite for this is that both sides have an e-mail address. An e-mail usually reached the recipient within minutes, regardless of geographical location, and cost only a few telephone units to connect to the Internet provider. In modern times, the percentage of data traffic caused by emails is shrinking more and more due to the spread of services such as video on demand, music streaming or video conferencing, despite the increase in the number of mails sent worldwide every day. Modern broadband connections have also reduced transmission times to fractions of a second. In times of data flat rates, the file size no longer plays a major role, so that emails are sent with increasingly large file attachments.

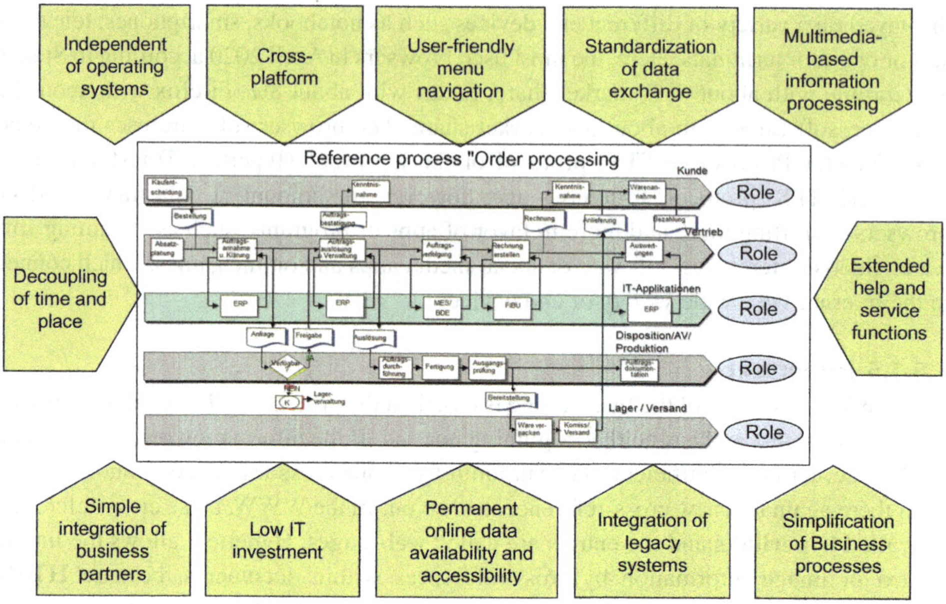

Fig. 5.11 Advantages of using the Internet

5.8.1.7 Intranet

An internal company network that is also based on the TCP/IP protocol and has interfaces to the Internet is the **intranet**. Here, the company-specific network structures are shielded from the Internet by "**firewalls**", i.e. software or hardware applications that prevent unauthorized persons from entering this network from the outside. Only the company's own members have access to this part of the Internet. In the case of the intranet, partner companies can be integrated and given partial access to the company's network content. However, due to the open structure of the Internet, there are risks regarding data security and data theft. At the moment of the connection of the own PC with the Internet not only the own access is possible but also the access from every other PC in the net to the own PC. A further risk is the danger of contamination by viruses which can get onto one's own PC via the Internet. The further spread of these viruses through data exchange within the local network represents a major threat. For this reason, all computers with access to the Internet should be equipped with current **virus check versions.**

5.8.1.8 Internet of Things (IoT)

The Internet application described above, characterized by mutual communication between humans and machines, received a significant innovation boost a few years ago with the creation of machine-to-machine communication = M2M. These machines can communicate directly and autonomously with each other due to the interface. This is also favoured by further development of transmission bandwidths for mobile data connections via the 5G standard. As a result of this and the comprehensive expansion of broadband transmission paths, it would now be possible for many objects such as machines, systems, components, transport containers, pallets, vehicles to be equipped with processors, sensors, transmitters and receivers that autonomously record and store data and exchange it with other devices. Objects networked via such digitalization components are also referred to as smart objects. These sensor and identification technologies are an important technical prerequisite for machine-to-machine communication, which is referred to as the Internet of Things (IOT). This includes Radio Frequency Identification (RFID) as an intelligent digitization technology that enables objects to identify and control themselves in near-field communication. In this way, people are supported in their activities and work execution and are largely freed from tedious routine tasks. With IOT, all objects have a unique identity and move in an intelligent environment. This automates many planning, control and monitoring tasks, especially in the area of industrial manufacturing. In this way, decentralized autonomous flexible processes can run in a self-organized factory (smart factory) in the future. Tools, workpieces, pallets, containers, measuring devices and systems will become intelligent autonomous factory objects through the integration of these sensor and identification technologies, which will independently take on a wide variety of organizational tasks and regulate them among themselves via the digital business platform.

5.8.1.9 IT Data Networks

Communication within the process levels and between the different organizational levels takes place via data networks. A data network is a spatially distributed connection system for the technical support of the exchange of information between communication partners. As Fig. 5.12 shows, there are different structuring aspects of networks, for example divided into open and closed networks according to the access options. Open networks are accessible to outsiders, i.e. external parties, while closed networks are only accessible to certain user groups. Furthermore, networks are divided into local area networks (LAN) and wide area networks (WAN) according to the distance between the end devices. This distinction is supplemented by Metropolitan Area Networks (MAN) and Global Area Networks (GAN).

A **Local Area Network** is a local network for the transmission of data between independent devices within the boundaries of a company. The goal is shared access to documents and data as well as shared use of cost-intensive resources, such as network printers and application programs.

Wide Area Networks are public networks that connect geographically distant, independent computers across company boundaries. The best-known WAN is the Internet, which is explained below.

Metropolitan area networks are limited to conurbations. They aim for a particularly high transmission volume.

Global Area Networks connect LAN and WAN networks with the help of satellite transmission or fiber optic cables. Further classification possibilities refer to the network operating systems used, the topology of the networks, the access organization and the transmission techniques.

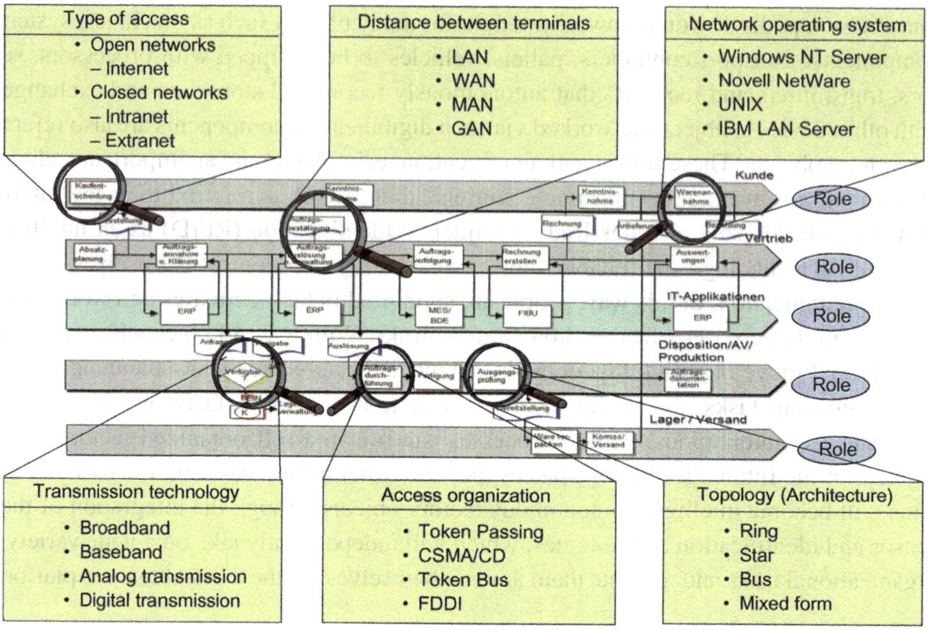

Fig. 5.12 Classification of networks

5.8.1.10 Transaction and Data-Oriented Business Platform

Connectivity is the data integration of all IT applications used in a company in a central data hub. This refers to the digital business platform that allows participants mobile access to applications and end devices at any time, regardless of location and time. The digital business platform is used to collect data from a wide variety of systems, process it and transmit it to other systems or evaluate it in real time.

With regard to the value contribution of a digital business platform, a distinction is made between transaction-oriented and data-oriented digital platforms. Transaction-oriented platforms stand for horizontal networking, data-oriented platforms for vertical networking. In the transaction-oriented digital platform, the focus is on the role as an intermediary between buyers and sellers. In other words, the platform acts as an electronic marketplace, bringing supply and demand together and thus enabling the realization of transactions.

The value proposition of horizontal networking via transaction-oriented business platforms is the bringing together of external suppliers and demanders in the horizontal value chain, as well as the support of transactions, e.g. payment processing, bookings, valuations or the provision of legal and regulatory frameworks in eBusiness.

In vertical networking with a data-oriented digital platform, the value proposition lies in internal data collection, use, networking and analysis in real time with the linking of hardware and software data and services across all process levels (vertical integration). This without certification by release procedures or search actions to the data-driven digital industrial platforms in the production areas belongs IoT. Here, the data is collected via sensors and mental objects.

The transaction-oriented and data-oriented digital platforms are becoming more interconnected, with the external stakeholders using more transaction-oriented digital platforms and the internal stakeholders in the production system using more data-oriented digital platforms. The digital platform provider or even operator must be neutral. It provides the technological infrastructure to the companies, defines standards and interfaces and determines the other platforms and solutions.

Digital platforms are characterized by their scalability and reach, i.e. they can react flexibly and at short notice to company-specific IT infrastructure adjustments, since computing capacity is no longer a limiting factor. Another value proposition of platforms is their transaction-cost-reducing effect, because data consistency reduces search and waiting times and the recipients of data do not have to digitize, archive or maintain them again. The value contribution of a digital platform lies in the network effect, scalability and reach (capacity expansion) as well as its transaction cost-reducing effect.

The digital business platform includes, for example, master data, document and interface management, compliance management, workflow and output management (automatic invoicing) and process-mining AI solutions.

5.8.2 Process Digitisation Core Statements in the MITO Input Segment

5.8.2.1 Enterprise Mobility, Work Place

Enterprise Mobility enables all participants in the company, i.e. managers and employees, to individually use mobile computer technologies by means of smartphones, tablet PCs and other devices in a business context, independent of space, time and location. In this way, Enterprise Mobility can give people greater scope for self-control in managing their work by providing all the necessary information in the form of intelligent and individualized assistance systems.

A digital business platform provides modern work environments (digital workplaces) for this purpose. Digital workplaces are central digital work platforms that make applications, information, tools and services available regardless of location. The most important role of digital workplaces is that they are accessible via smartphone or tablet, regardless of location or system. The focus is on the immediate and location-independent availability of information in the context of the process under consideration. Social collaboration enables the direct networking of project teams or experts from different departments across departments and locations on the basis of digital workplaces.

A workplace strategy makes it possible to provide your company with efficient workplace models tailored to the specific needs of predefined knowledge worker types. The goal of a digital workspace or workplace is to provide each process employee with exactly the team and tool they need to work efficiently in their process without having to configure special solutions.

A holistic workplace strategy comprises a flexible, efficiency-enhancing workplace model with a communication and data exchange that is independent of location, application, device and platform. The goal is to provide each employee with exactly the application and tools they need to work efficiently.

5.8.2.2 Smart Devices

With mobile **smart devices**, the right information can be made available at the right time and in the right place for the planning and control of company processes. Smart devices are electronic devices that are wirelessly mobile, networked and equipped with various sensors, e.g. geo-sensors, temperature cameras. These include smartphones, tablet PCs and data glasses.

The smart devices can be used in production, in logistics, in hospitals and with the built-in sensors they can support the control and monitoring of the order process, the material flow and patient care. The smart sensors collect and condense the information and deliver the results to the existing assistance systems.

The main advantage of smart devices is the easy collection, interpretation and transfer of status and environmental information from any location to a higher-level planning and control system, as well as direct access to the latest data and decisions from these systems.

5.8.2.3 eLearning Platform

Learning in the age of 4.0 currently focuses on learning videos and virtual seminars or webinars. Videos can be used to visually present processes and instructions, from scrincan movies that show how to operate software functions to tutorials on how to assemble a component. Virtual seminars with chat functions offer the possibility to teach participants at different locations simultaneously and interactively. Virtual reality and augmented reality play a major role in training via learning apps, industrial maintenance and the preventive maintenance of plant and machinery.

Employees can be trained in digitalization directly via terminals on the shop floor or at the machine. Here, the workers call up cloud-based mobile training modules that are stored in an **e-learning platform**. In this way, knowledge is imparted to employees in a targeted manner, independent of location and time.

5.8.2.4 Gamification

Gamification is increasingly being used as a digital business innovation to motivate employees in processes. The goal is to enable playful learning by transferring game-typical elements into the working world, which can also be used for performance evaluation and personnel deployment planning or in particular for team management. Gamification elements are, for example, progress indicators, where the user can clearly track his progress when completing a task. This also includes incentives, i.e. incentives that encourage the user to perform further actions. Prizes or awards can also reward the participant for his performance. Further characteristics of a gamification system are, for example, leaderboards, game levels and performance overviews, but also achieved scores and badges. The use of ranking lists can create a kind of competition between users, as they enable a comparison of one's own level of performance. In this case, the idea of competition can also promote performance.

Another element are quests. These are tasks that the user must complete in a given time. Often, the quest tasks build on each other, whereby the gain in competence is then reinforced. If these tasks have to be completed in a team, the ability to work in a team is also promoted. As the number of digital games on offer is increasing and many people also spend their free time playing video games, it makes sense to link these games to work processes via digital interfaces, thus enriching work performance with a gaming experience. However, the risk lies in the fact that gamification must also be dynamically developed further, because an unadapted gamification system becomes predictable for the player over a longer period of application and thus the gaming motivation decreases. Therefore, it makes sense to initiate a comprehensive company-specific change process with gamification in work systems, which promotes proactive change management.

5.8.2.5 Use Case Description

A use case is a definition of a use case. According to Wikipedia, a use case describes the interaction between user and system that is necessary to realize a technical goal of the user. The level of detail of use cases varies greatly. At a very high level, a use case only roughly describes what happens. However, a use case can also be refined down to the IT process level, so that the behavior of an application is described in detail. Use cases therefore describe what the environment or the user expects from the system. A distinction is made between business use cases and system use cases. In a system use case, the scope of the content is described by the system to be developed. In a business use case, the scope of the content is set by an organizational unit, such as a company or department. It makes sense and is also common practice to use business use cases to embed the system use cases in a common context and to describe further requirements. In the process-related use case description, the swimlane representation is used to link the business use case to the associated system use case in a factual, temporal and logical role-based manner. Here, the user is a person who is assigned a role within a process. He or she interacts with a system as an actor in order to achieve a certain goal in a defined sequence of actions. The name of the use case is usually derived from the intended goal of this action.

5.8.2.6 VR/AR Technologies

The term "Virtual Reality (VR)" describes a technology that enables the representation and perception of a real-time computer-generated, interactive virtual environment. The user is completely immersed in this artificial world.

The term “Augmented Reality (AR)” describes a computer-based augmentation of reality. Additional information on real objects is superimposed via data glasses. In principle, all human senses can be addressed. Most applications extend real perception with images, videos or by displaying additional visual information.

VR/AR data goggles enable training on the machines. The necessary apps can be downloaded for specific employees. This is also always in conjunction with further information, such as work safety instructions. High-tech data goggles are equipped with functions such as a camera, microphone, compass, WLAN and Bluetooth. They place a kind of computer screen over the wearer’s field of vision. The glasses are often controlled via verbal commands and motion sensors (gyrosensor).

AR can eliminate the need for conventional user manuals. Virtual tutorials and assistants will take over this task in the future with AR through superimposed suggestions, for example on machine settings, etc.

5.8.2.7 Wearables

The term **wearables** stands for the use of networked computer technologies that are worn on the body, for example through clothing or via fitness bracelets, smartwatches or data glasses. They use small chips and sensors to measure bodily functions such as blood pressure and pulse rate, but also environmental data relating to location, time and space. Fields of application can be found in the areas of “health, lifestyle, fitness” and ergonomic work design in the area of “production and logistics”.

Examples of wearables from the health sector are digital patches that are worn directly on the body. They measure posture, muscle activity, blood sugar levels, kidney function or pulse rate. Smart socks measure the weight, posture, movement behavior and other health data of the wearer and support them during training. Electronic shoes show the wearer which direction to walk when connected to a utility, such as Google maps. Wearables on people in need of care monitor them by measuring pulse rate, muscle activity, and sleep activity and sound an alarm when needed. For example, in relation to heart function or measuring blood glucose levels in diabetics.

When used in logistics or distribution centers, employees wear wearables to record the steps they take and the movements they make. This movement data can be evaluated by an AI tool. This software calculates how often employees bend over, what overhead work they perform and what distances they cover in order to use this database to design work processes more ergonomically. The aim is to reduce sick leave due to spinal and back complaints and to optimise work and movement processes in order to save time. In this anonymous analysis, walking routes, hand movements, execution times, etc. are recorded. The aim is to use this data to automatically sound the alarm if the processes are endangering the health of the worker.

5.8.3 Process Digitisation Core Statements in the MITO Transformation Process

5.8.3.1 MES

MES is about the case-by-case or regular transmission of product, production or machine data that is recorded or read out within the value creation process and analyzed. They allow conclusions to be drawn about environmental conditions, usage behavior, utilization, wear, quality and other aspects.

MES solutions have the direct connection to distributed process automation systems and thus enable the management, guidance, control and monitoring of production in real time. The connected systems, such as ERP/PPS, IoT, shop floor data collection, machine data collection, MDE and personnel data collection, AI and machine learning tools, also include other systems, e.g. maintenance and QM, which have a real-time impact on the manufacturing or production processes. MES is used for continuous controlling enforcement of an existing and valid ERP system planning under feedback from the process. In addition, MES offers the following functionalities, for example:

1. Management of production resources (resources with assignment to the products).
2. Ensure planned maintenance.
3. Collection of production and product data for statistical evaluation.
4. Interfaces e.g. to materials management, logistics, construction, personnel management as well as facility management and controlling.
5. Reporting for commercial order processing.
6. Provision of real-time data for performance, potential, compliance and CIP analyses.
7. Forwarding to reporting systems, which provide feedback to the application managers in real time, e.g. via dashboard evaluations, in order to react to deviations in an agile manner. This also results in CIP approaches. Compliance is also monitored.

The MES data recorded at the machines is visualized on the tablet or smartphone via a data analysis system, for example, and the results are made available via web browser. All values can then be exported to various file formats or printed out directly. For networking, digitization and automation in real time, MES software solutions are being developed by suppliers that collect machine data from each individual station at the customer's site in real time, process it visually and use it as the basis for controlling and optimizing production processes. Here, the productivity of each individual production machine is analyzed in real time and bottlenecks are pointed out preventively.

Based on the MES real-time data acquisition and evaluations, forward-looking specifications, such as Productive planning, Productive quality or Productive maintenance, result. With feedback to the ERP system, they enable the improvement of detailed planning, resource allocation, sequence planning or personnel deployment.

A digital MES production cockpit allows a precise overview of the machinery in real time. The current order status, the times of activity downtimes and their causes are recorded. Via integrated analysis functions, the monitoring module automatically generates activity reports with KPI key figures for each machine.

Cloud-based MES systems play a key role in the collection, analysis, graphical evaluation and provision of real-time information for other IT systems. They must be able to integrate a wide variety of controls, sensors or measurement technology on a cloud basis.

5.8.3.2 Digital Twin

A digital twin is the digital image of a real machine, production plant or a complete factory or product. A digital twin is a data provider that enables many evaluations. Sensors on the machine, plant or product continuously feed the digital twin with real production and machine data or product usage data. Ideally, the digital twin accompanies the physical product throughout its entire life cycle. In this way, comprehensive transparency is created within a production system. Production processes can be continuously analyzed and optimized. In the event of a product complaint, the cause of the defect can be identified and product use can be tracked. Furthermore, a **digital twin** can be used for predictive monitoring and predictive maintenance. In case of a virtual collision, the real production stops. Another application of digital twins are feasibility studies in the production development process for the virtual commissioning of plants in order to avoid downtimes of real plants. The same applies to quality control and assurance. The condition for the digital twin is that the production environment must be mapped in real time. Furthermore, a high-precision 3-dimensional CAD model forms the basis for the digital twin.

Digital twins synchronize the real process and machine components in real time, thereby enabling their monitoring. Process-integrated sensor technology in the context of IoT makes it possible to condense the sensor and production data of a production machine captured in real time in such a way that a virtual machine tool can be mapped in the form of a digital shadow. The captured data such as temperature, acceleration, deformation, vibration provide a complete picture of the machine tool. Methods from the field of machine learning can then be used to identify patterns and correlations, which enable process-oriented testing of the individual components of the machine tools and allow predictive statements to be made about the state of the machine and the manufacturing process.

The intelligent use of digital twin data takes place via Big Data, Smart Data or Data Mining. The first step is to interpret the collected data in terms of meaning in order to obtain the context, i.e. the knowledge of which sensor it is and which machine state the sensor detects. In further consensus, knowledge is generated from this information. For example, if it is known that a minimal unbalance has occurred in a machine at the axle, it can be predicted that the bearing will fail with a certain probability in a certain period of time if the load remains the same. Predictive maintenance can be derived from this.

5.8.3.3 3D Models

Adaptive 3D printer manufacturing allows fast and individualized production of products with small batch sizes. A digital twin enables the virtualization of manufacturing processes and thus creates many design advantages in continuous product development, test simulations or production planning, but also in the interaction with industrial robots. 3D visualization with virtual 3D models stored in the digital twin also plays a major role here. Machine operators receive production-relevant data from the digital twin, for example via augmented reality (AR). In this process, the current real environment is enriched with virtual information. This information is displayed on a tablet PC or via data glasses, for example.

Virtual reality (VR) offers the virtual mapping of real production environments into a closed virtual environment. The machine operator or employee then sees the information with his headset completely in a virtual environment. The virtual twin enables seamless monitoring of the process, machine and tool on the basis of the cyber-physical systems used on site, which make their production data available for data analysis in real time. The availability of the systems is increased, the service life is extended and the training times are significantly shortened.

When optimizing production processes, planners can meet virtually and further develop the 3D models together. In order to evaluate the work processes, it is no longer necessary to create elaborate real prototypes with VR. The work processes are tested virtually and the ergonomic framework conditions are evaluated directly. The same applies to individual product manufacturing in shipbuilding and aircraft construction. In a virtual environment, components are adapted and inserted as 3D models. Architects can also virtually visit the houses with their customers and make changes according to the customer's wishes.

With 3D printing in additive manufacturing, multiple elements of an assembly can be combined into a single component, reducing or eliminating assembly. By using 3D printing, a completely new design of the component becomes possible, e.g. a completely new design of cooling channels. However, common CAD files can also be used for 3D printing.

The possible applications of industrial 3 D model image processing are, for example, in robotics, presence checking and completeness checking, position detection, measurement, barcode and area code recognition, optical character recognition OCR, surface inspection. This in conjunction with the formation of object classes based on features.

5.8.3.4 RFID

RFID is a technology for transmitter/receiver systems for automatic and contactless identification and localization of objects and living beings by means of radio waves within the horizontal value chain. In principle, RFID technology can be described as a digitalized barcode, in which the information carriers are referred to as TAGS. RFID TAGS can be attached to almost any object, for example keys, goods, machine containers, process equipment, barrels or pallets, but also under the skin of living beings. The identification of the objects to be monitored by means of RFID chips is called tagging. A distinction is made between passive RFID tags (e.g. for product security in department stores) with a low communication distance and active RFID tags (e.g. for the identification of an object in a warehouse) with a high communication distance. Depending on the task, there are RFID tags that can only be written once but read as often as desired (WORM, write once, read many) or TAGS that can be written and read multiple times.

In logistics, intelligent containers (pallets) can be clearly identified via RFID transponders. The container can provide information about its position and contents at any time. This is used, for example, in the use of indoor and outdoor tracking and positioning systems. Here, the position and the stored identification data are read out by means of RFID receivers and transmitted via Bluetooth or WLAN to a container management or logistics software.

The intelligent networking of logistics or production objects requires equipment with microcontrollers, communication systems (chips), identifiers, sensors and actuators. The communication and interaction of these systems takes place via radio or wired networks. A barcode or RFID transponder are examples of identifiers. Actuators not only perform movement of components of the object, but also serve to transmit visual and acoustic information to people. The microcontroller represents the actual intelligence of the embedded system and analyzes the incoming data, determines the status of the object, prepares and executes decisions. The sensors provide the microcontrollers with the required information from the environment. They represent the senses of the artificial intelligence.

5.8.3.5 Business Intelligence (BI)

Business Intelligence (BI) is a term assigned in business informatics that describes procedures for the systematic analysis of one's own company. This includes the collection, evaluation and presentation of company data in electronic form. The aim is to gain insights from the data available in the company to support management decisions. The evaluation of this company data is carried out with the help of analytical concepts and specialized software. The English word "intelligence" refers to the knowledge gained from the collection and processing of acquired information (lat. understand).

In this way, Business Intelligence (BI) supports companies in decision-making, planning and control processes and provides valuable management information through structured data management.

The BI insights relate to business processes, customer and supplier relationships with aspects such as cost reduction, risk reduction or value creation improvement. The BI goal is to generate success-critical knowledge about growth potential and perspectives from inhomogeneous company, market and competitive data.

BI (business) analytics implementation can be divided into 3 phases.

1. Phase 1: Quantitative, qualitative, structured or unstructured key data collection.
2. The data acquisition takes place via the operative systems with the data warehouses based on them (data warehouse).

3. In phase 2, the data are correlated so that patterns and discontinuities become visible and can be compared with any hypotheses previously made, e.g. in the form of multi-dimensional analysis or data mining.
4. In phase 3, the findings are communicated within the company, i.e. knowledge management is integrated, in order to provide a basis for decisions on measures and actions.

The central challenge of BI solutions is the high effort required for the preparation of key figures and data. Processed data is often generated decentrally on different systems. The first task of a BI project is therefore to provide data from the existing applications – such as ERP systems – for analysis in a separate database – the data warehouse – in order to subsequently set up the reporting system for the necessary analytical evaluations. This can range from simple aggregations, such as sales figures for individual items over the last few days or months, to complicated trend analyses of customer behavior. Analysis methods include olap, data mining, text mining, web mining or case-based evaluation.

5.8.3.6 Smart Data

In a data warehouse, data is stored in a central database. This company-wide data storage enables the interactive analysis of all collected data in order to subsequently use the results of the analysis in the company for decision-making.

The term "smart data" refers to a process that describes how raw data is used to create new innovation through analysis (pattern recognition). In this process, the raw data is used to create models, which in turn can be used to analyze data. The starting point is large volumes of data such as big data.

With the raw data, the first thing that is required is an interpretation of this data in terms of meaning. Only in context, i.e. with the knowledge of which sensor or actuator is involved and in which machine condition the data was recorded, do the raw values acquire a meaning. In a machine condition analysis, a regular deviation of a measured value from average values means, for example, that there is a minimal unbalance on the axis of the machine. From this context, knowledge can be generated from this information, i.e. it is predicted when the bearing of the machine will fail with a certain probability in a certain period of time if the load remains constant. A defensive measure can be derived from this knowledge. The typical preparation of the analysis results can take place, for example, via dashboards, dynamically updated overviews with key figures and virtual measuring instruments, but can also be a data mining function, i.e. patterns in the data are searched for interactively.

5.8.3.7 Process Mining

Process mining is an electronic business data analysis based on real-time data that is intended to improve processes in the operational area of a company. The individual steps of the process stored in the IT systems are combined and thus the process is visualized in its entirety. It is important for the process mining application that the individual steps of a process are stored in an IT system in such a way that the coherence and chronology of the steps can be traced. This traceability is ensured by a process or flow protocol. In particular, this is supported by a workflow management system. The totality of the steps stored in the workflow management system finally results in a process that can be called up and constituted with process mining.

The fields of application are process harmonization across different organizational units and departments. The objectives are process optimization in terms of throughput times, process costs, process stability, and ensuring compliance requirements. Process mining can be used, for example, to analyze order processes in purchasing that are too long due to excessive release times of the departments. The best-known application of process mining is to reconstruct the processes contained in existing flow protocols from the data available, without first having information or models of existing processes. Another application of process mining is that a model about a process flow already exists. The existing data is now checked for conformity to the existing model on the basis of the model and the available process logs using process mining. Another example of process mining is the analysis of the order flow, i.e. it is recorded when an order is created, processed, changed, supplemented, or forwarded to another instance and by whom. This applies to individual orders as well as to all orders, so that it can be transparently recorded how the different employees in the company process the orders and in what time they do this. This data is compared with the target values from the documented BPM target processes. In this way, it is clearly recognizable at which process steps within the value chain disruptions have occurred and what effects they have had in the other departments.

5.8.3.8 Deep Learning

Deep learning is an implementation of machine learning with neural networks. These are based on structures in the human brain and are particularly well suited for implementing machine learning. They consist of thousands or even millions of densely interconnected artificial neurons. Each of these connections is assigned a weighting that determines how likely it is that information will be passed on this channel. The system can then adjust this weighting in the training phase depending on its purpose. This densely linked structure, which is divided into several layers – hence the name Deep learning – can be called the key to artificial intelligence. This involves deep learning with artificial neural networks (KNNs). They refer to algorithm algorithms that can learn from neurons using the replicated network structures. Values are input using input neurons. The KNN performs the calculations and determines the output values, i.e. the information runs through the network and flows out processed at the output neuron.

5.8.3.9 Artificial Intelligence (AI)

Basically, AI and learning systems are divided into deduction systems, knowledge-based systems, pattern analysis and pattern recognition systems, robotics systems, and systems that supported intelligent multimodal human-machine action.

AI systems as expert systems supported decision making by deriving recommended actions from historical data, for example, in insurance companies regarding claims settlement based on if-then rule trees of previous claims.

Artificial systems with pattern recognition methods. Here, AI solutions are able to recognize patterns in large amounts of data and derive repetitions, regularities or similarities, for example in speech and text recognition.

AI solutions related to the use of classification methods with the division of certain objects into classes, e.g. the automatic recognition and assignment of documents and emails to folders, files or company processes according to a certain algorithm.

AI systems that map neural networks are inspired by the structure of the human brain. The methods, also known as deep learning, are the basis for autonomous driving or machine translation, for example.

With AI based on MES data analysis, unplanned machine downtimes are seriously reduced by predictive maintenance measures. This is based on the application of machine learning algorithms. AI is also applied to the behavioral observation of users during equipment operation in order to detect and eliminate operating errors.

Machine learning tool providers receive the specific machine data from the customer and develop a simple automatic machine learning solution for it, by marking the deviations of the previously collected data.

An AI-based machine learning program autonomously evaluates the process data (e.g. image data, raw data such as temperatures, pressures, throughput times, etc.) on an ongoing basis and, using the unsupervised learning method, develops a data model that uses certain features (structures, geometric figures, color values) of the evaluated object to classify the component that has just been analyzed. Image data that classify the component as OK are then the orientation for image data that classify a component as faulty. Thus, the main task of machine learning is automated classification. This is found as a mapping function based on examples, or test data.

Automated facial recognition enables a significant acceleration of the check-in process for passengers on cruise ships as well as at the airport and is much more comfortable for the passengers or customers.

AI solutions in design processes leads to the fact that for the designers the artificial intelligence and machine learning tools the software recognizes which design steps the designer usually needs next. This is displayed to the designer.

Pattern analysis and pattern recognition is made possible by visual intelligence. Here, images or shapes are analyzed and recognized. Examples are handwriting recognition, person identification, facial recognition, fingerprint comparison, quality control, manufacturing automation in combination with robotics. Derived from this pattern analysis and recognition is pattern prediction. Such systems offer the advantage that, based on pattern recognition, they can also predict what the further development will look like, for example, in the healthcare sector of the course of a disease.

5.8.3.10 Machine Learning (ML)

In the future, operation and system monitoring will be carried out using machine learning (ML) functions, i.e. self-learning systems that recognize when deviations or anomalies from the normal state occur and report them in real time. In this way, production errors or increased tool wear on the machines, for example, are detected immediately. By comparing the automatically learned or trained models with the real-time data, anomalies are detected. Further functions that compare these with already known or similar patterns are used to derive a predictive need for action, i.e. by observing behavior in the past, predictive recommendations for action or predictions for the future are made.

For the machine learning solution, sensor data is collected in the production system from a machine or PLC, e.g. pressure, temperature, frequencies. Anomalies are detected and marked or labelled via a graphical data evaluation (pattern recognition). This corresponds to the training of the AI system and can be done by the machine itself or by a human. Using a simple software solution for machine learning, the machine automatically learns when anomalies occur and reports them to the responsible parties in real time during production operation.

Machine learning is therefore initially about identifying anomalies and deviations from the process data previously recorded on a specific machine for each process parameter in the graphical evaluation on the tablet or smartphone and highlighting these in order to train the machine's AI system. This allows the machine to automatically detect these anomalies the next time they occur and report them or fix them on its own. Further, machine learning is about deriving general rules from a large amount of test data with the then known input data that describes the system behavior, i.e. the function, that leads to a certain output. In case of deviations from this given rule, anomalies are detected leading to intervention. Mathematically, this is defined by calling the rule an approximation method.

The basic idea of machine learning is to learn from the experience gained during the execution of tasks how the task can be performed better in the future. For this purpose, decision rules are derived from the training data, with which the ML program adapts its future task execution to topics and calculation rules via feedback to the learned knowledge (hypotheses).

In supervised learning, an ML software program is first learned with the help of training data. The user evaluates the interpretation, for example the results, which the program produces on the basis of the training data. The input data, i.e. the training data, are combined with the desired interpretation, for example with the output variable (output) result to form rules. With the help of these rules, unknown input data can now be interpreted and results (output) predicted. The machine learning program has learned something new in the course of this supervised learning. After completion of the learning process, i.e. within the framework of the decision options trained with training data, it can now make autonomous output predictions based on previously unknown input data.

A simple mathematical method for model building in machine learning is regression. Regression creates a linear, or given non-linear, relationship between an input variable X and an output variable Y. This model is intended to predict previously unknown values. For example, the noise level of a running machine can be used to determine the probability that it will fail in the next hour due to wear of a component. The relationship can be represented as a linear function, i.e. with an independent input variable (noise level) and a dependent output variable (probability of failure). As a result, the regression generates a model with which the output variable (failure probability) can be predicted from the input variable (noise level).

The classification method is another important method of model building in machine learning. During the learning process, several input variables are considered and assigned to different classes. For example, when evaluating machine data, the temperature and the noise level can be recorded using sensors and divided into 2 classes. If both the operating temperature and the noise level are below a certain limit, the condition of a machine is classified as acceptable. If one or both of the input variables temperature or noise level exceeds this limit, the machine condition changes to faulty. During classification, several input variables are always evaluated in combination.

In unsupervised learning (machine learning via clustering), a previously known assignment or labeling of the input data is not required. The possible results are not known in advance. The learning software program can therefore not be trained, but must recognize certain patterns and structures in the actual data and interpret them autonomously. Applications for this are, for example, the analysis and prediction of customer behavior during online shopping, online translation software or product recommendation systems. Another application example from the production sector is quality assurance via image recognition systems. Here, a camera system records every manufactured component in the production line.

5.8.3.11 Industrial Robots

The goal of program development for **industrial robots** is to enable them to be controlled intuitively via simple commands or gestures without a great deal of programming effort and to learn complex processes independently from their human colleagues through imitation. In the predictive maintenance application of industrial robots, robot data is automatically recorded, analyzed and its remaining service life is predicted with a statistical uncertainty.

In the data acquisition of industrial robots, data on the wear condition of a machine, as well as the associated system properties, are recorded in order to map a clear relationship between and wear condition over time. Closure data is, for example, geometric wear data on bearings and gears or indirect wear variables related to the accuracy of axes and the backlash measurement of axes. The system parameters are, for example, mechanical vibration behavior, motor currents, acceleration of axes, temperature in the bearings, gears and motors.

5.8.4 Process Digitisation Core Statements in the MITO Output Segment

5.8.4.1 Smart Products and Services

The installation of sensors and actuators in technical products such as kitchen appliances, electrical tools, but also classic products that previously did not contain software components, such as taps, thermostats or running shoes, creates intelligent products in conjunction with intelligent services. Connectivity is established via these IT-enabled sensors, i.e. the linking with other IT components is made possible in order to be able to network with each other within the smart products in this way. This then also enables an evaluation of this usage and consumption data in the subsequent phase under the keyword "analytics" in order to offer a completely new digital service that relates to consumption habits, energy consumption, consumption costs, fault clearance, maintenance and many other service approaches during the product usage period. If these devices transmit their usage data to the manufacturer during use by the user, the manufacturer can also provide service information or fault information over the entire product life. This can also give rise to completely new service offerings.

Examples of smart products include intelligent elevator maintenance. In the future, elevator and escalator providers will rely on machine-to-machine (M2M) technologies for remote monitoring. The automatically triggered fault messages via mobile radio solutions enable a new maintenance service that reduces downtimes to a minimum.

Other smart products such as mattresses, clothing, shoes or fitness trackers measure personal blood pressure, heart rate, sleep log, body fat, step count acceleration in connection with smartphone apps. This can lead to performance-specific community building with exchange of experiences among each other.

5.8.4.2 Social Business/Shop Function

Social business is based on the new web-based communication channels with changed communication structures within social media, such as Xing, Facebook, Twitter, YouTube or LinkedIn. Here, companies can directly contact customers, business partners and other social groups via an Internet platform and directly address target groups or also carry out recommendation marketing. The advantages for companies are manifold. In addition to the simplified, rapid establishment of contact with the aim of improving customer loyalty and enhancing the company's image, it is also possible for companies to advertise cost-effectively and effectively. Furthermore, information from social networks can be evaluated very quickly in order to obtain information about new trends or consumer perceptions. Just as quickly, however, products, services, concepts or events can be presented on the net almost free of charge. Through quick customer feedback, questions or criticism can be reacted to in order to better understand or fulfill customer wishes.

Online marketing becomes possible through the online connection of the customers. In particular, very important experience can be gained by the product manufacturer about the wishes of the customer in order to develop individual or personalized products in this way.

In this way, high inventories with the inventory risks that there is no customer demand are also eliminated.

The shop function of the digital business platform provides customers with comprehensive online offers, e.g. for seminar service offers, individual consulting, course offers, hotel offers, flyer offers and other services, which can be accessed by customers on the move.

5.8.4.3 Telematics Solutions (Logistics)

According to Wikipedia, the term "telematics" is composed of the two terms "telecommunications and information technology". Telematics is the means of linking information from at least two information systems with the help of a telecommunications system as well as special data processing. The term was coined by Nora and Minc (1978) as part of their study of the computerization of society. Applications include: Telebanking, teleshopping, telelearning, televoting, telemedicine, teleworking.

Within the scope of telematics logistics solutions, vehicle fleets are controlled. However, the business platforms can also be used to create a logical link between drivers, vehicles and orders flexibly and across companies on the basis of order data. The collected data is evaluated and, as a result, suitable vehicles and drivers are suggested and scheduled for transport.

Another telematics application can run across all transport modes and platforms. Here, the software takes over the deployment planning of mobile resources and creates transparency about the respective status of orders as well as about the entire order situation currently to be processed, supported by dynamic smartphone apps via which mobile employees provide their feedback to the dispatcher. For example, drivers receive all current information about predecessors, follow-up trips, departure and arrival locations, and schedule changes via the app.

Through the use of fleet management systems, GPS data makes it possible to track exactly where a vehicle is, how fast it is travelling and which driver is currently using it and has refuelled it. On a central dashboard with the help of clearly designed interactive maps, diagrams, reports and graphically prepared analyses, driving behaviour is visualised, for example idle times, fuel consumption, distances travelled, vehicle and engine activities. In the case of fleet management systems that are directly connected to the vehicle's engine control unit, warnings and defects are reported in real time and. This serves to improve driving performance and road safety. Selectable parameters include average speeds and overruns, driving style, and idle times and number of stops. Reports and alerts can be activated directly, for example when speeding or when a maintenance appointment is due. Drivers also receive feedback if their driving style leads to increased fuel consumption, for example through frequent acceleration and braking, or the vehicle emits a warning tone as soon as the driver displays fuel-intensive driving behaviour. In this way, fuel consumption is recorded for each individual driver and can be optimized. The benefit is a significant improvement in driving behaviour, idle times per day and driver are reduced, fuel costs as well as maintenance costs are lowered.

In combination with existing traffic data, networked vehicles can plan their routes much better or react agilely in the event of disruptions. The German transport and logistics sector is one of the digital pioneers in German industry.

5.8.5 Process Digitisation Core Statements in the MITO Line Segment

5.8.5.1 Dashboard

A business intelligence dashboard (BI dashboard) is a tool for visualizing real-time data that displays the current status of a company's key performance indicators (KPIs). The **dashbord** brings together numbers, metrics and also rating systems such as traffic light or scale systems on one screen.

A BI dashport is an IT-based tool that provides a visual and easy-to-understand graphical representation of the insights gained with business intelligence. The dashport shows the current status of key KPI's and other relevant business metrics. They are brought together in the dashbort and visualized in the simplest possible presentation.

The aim of a dashboard is to present complex company data in a clear and concise manner, with a focus on key financial figures, in order to support planning, management and controlling tasks within the company. Dashports can contain strategic, tactical, dispositive and operative data. The type and arrangement of the individual screens of a BI dashport is similar to the displays and control elements of an aircraft cockpit.

5.8.5.2 Blockchain Technology

Blockchain is a decentralized transaction system in which all activities of all partners within a value chain are traceable and cannot be changed afterwards.

Blockchain technology ensures trustworthy transactions as well as their encryption and storage in the manner of a digital accounting system, in which all information about contracts, cash flows, transactions and much more is automatically documented. However, this is not done centrally on a single platform, but distributed across many network participants. Each node of the network, i.e. each computer of a network participant receives write or read access to the complete blockchain with all transactions and processes carried out to date and can store a complete copy of the chain on its hard drive. The so-called miners or stakers are the validators of the blockchain. Their task is to combine transactions of participants within the blockchain into blocks and to confirm them. After a certain amount of time, a block with a certain number of transactions is completed and entered into the blockchain. The first validator to enter this block receives a reward. At the same time, all other validators receive a kind of checksum of the newly generated block and must now confirm the result and thus the correct generation. The block is now added to all copies of the blockchain as the last valid one. If the validators detect discrepancies at any point in the transcations, this is announced directly within the validator network and measures are automatically taken to ensure the trustworthiness of the blockchain.

Another blockchain advantage is that the data cannot be changed afterwards. This has the advantage, for example, that you can track the origin of an item of clothing, check the cold chain of frozen food or accurately determine the mileage of a used car because the car's speedometer regularly reported its mileage.

Blockchain technology can significantly improve the transparency of the supply chain in the pharmaceutical industry, for example. The transport, distribution and storage of medical products must meet high standards. Validating inconsistencies, inabilities and deviations in real time and detecting them within the supply chain is difficult. Online sales in particular open the door to counterfeiting. Counterfeits cause immense economic damage as well as high health risks for patients. Traceability and transparency are among the most important foundations of logistics to verify authenticity. In the blockchain's ledger of accounts, the records of all network participants in the supply chain are updated and validated in real time. The customers and manufacturers can verify the authenticity of the products at any time. Blockchain technology creates a collaborative trustworthy environment, lowers costs, analyzes supply chains, expenses and shows savings opportunities, identifies erroneous data and enables communication and collaboration for all supplychain supply chain members.

5.8.5.3 Content Management System (CMS)

Content is understood here as all information in an organization that can be passed on to others, i.e. documents, texts, images, graphics, video or audio sequences. This is completely independent of whether it is in paper form, electronically or in any other way. For knowledge management, this content term plays an important role, as it includes all previously structured knowledge collections based on process analyses and document management or groupware systems. Content management assumes the following functions:

- Content creation (generation)
- Content management (organization and structure)
- Content provision (disposition)
- Content usage and processing options

A **content management system (CMS)** is an IT-based system for the organization, administration and execution of content management, often developed from database-oriented document management systems. Here, a further development to reaction systems took place. This is a database in which content is collected and stored on a topic-specific basis and made available to users, for example via the Internet in the form of websites. A reaction team is responsible for the suitable preparation of the information and deposit on the Internet, whereby the different documents, articles etc. are filed using keywords. The users or employees can actively search for information in this reaction system. An event-driven variant is also conceivable, i.e. users receive relevant documents when a certain event occurs. Furthermore, these reaction-relevant content management systems are often used to make information available to customers on the Internet.

In the meantime, a further development has taken place in the form that under the designation. In the meantime, a further development has taken place in the form of the term "enterprise content management system", in which not only information prepared on a website is made available to users, but all knowledge collections, i.e. the entire organisational information and knowledge base, are contained in such a content management system.

5.8.5.4 CMS Repository Content

A repository is a central archive for data, documents, objects and programs with their metadata in the form of a managed directory of digital objects. In addition to the actual data, the various versions, concepts and developments are also stored in the repository, which means that all stored software modules are saved with all their information. Data and documents stored in repositories can be accessed and modified by authorized authors and users. The combination of these models for building a content repository with combined search technologies is shown in Fig. 5.13.

The process-oriented structural and contextual knowledge determined with the help of a role-related process analysis in the swimlane representation provides the basic information for this. As shown, the context knowledge is about the creation of relationships, for example to the factually-logically, locally, spatially determined situation and action sequence with the associated role, problem, social, subject and purpose reference. The already developed and listed management instruments, regulatory frameworks and sets of rules – such as integrated management systems, including quality management, risk management, occupational health and safety management, environmental management as well as internal control systems that support compliance management. The ITIL set of rules for IT service management also supports this contextual knowledge. The structured use of methods in a company is described via holistic production systems (GPS). Human resource management has developed detailed job descriptions with neutral requirement profiles. The skills of those involved are stored in a structured manner via skills management. The IT applications used in the organization such as ERP/PPS systems, CRM (Customer Relationship Management) systems, HR (Human Resources) systems, groupware systems, databases and files, project management programs together with emails also contribute to the content knowledge.

The most important prerequisite for making this knowledge and the information behind it available in a targeted manner is a uniform filing structure with defined rules for selecting, combining, collecting, evaluating, ordering or preparing knowledge.

In this storage structure, content must be made available via metadata, such as content details, target groups or relationships to other documents for the networking of structured queries, interactions and collaborations. This metadata enables integrated search via different access paths such as full text search, associative navigation, interactive web services, taxonomies with thesauri and classification, pattern recognition, but also direct access to the visualized process chains within the product lifecycle. This linking of the Sycat process model with the meta reference data and methods is used to map the

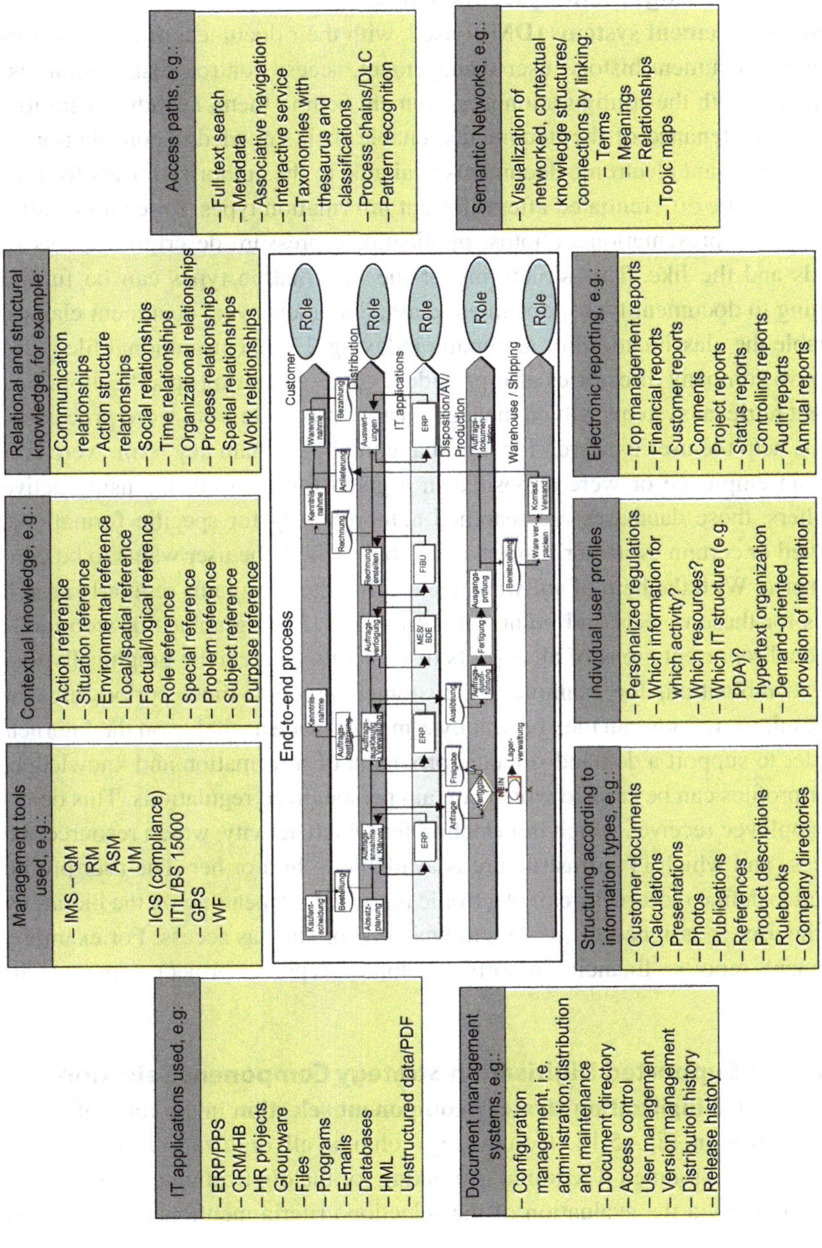

Fig. 5.13 Contents of an information repository with combined search categories (Research tools)

dependencies that are closely linked to the context and structure knowledge. These are, for example, social relationships, spatial relationships, communication relationships.

5.8.5.5 Document Management Systems (DMS)

The **document management systems (DMS)** used, with their document directories, version management, document history, user management, access control, distribution history, release history with the configuration management behind them, i.e. administration, distribution and maintenance of the documents, enable their knowledge contribution in order to make the relevant electronic documents available to the authorized users for processing. These are to be differentiated after different information types, for example after customer documents, presentations, photos, publications, pressure descriptions, sets of rules, standards and the like. This structuring of the information types can be further refined according to document types, document class, document type, document classes, in order to enable the classification for automatic indexing. Here, conventional file plans as comprehensive company directories also provide a good structuring specification. The use of document retrieval systems, which manage unstructured data from word processors or spreadsheets, help the user to search for files that contain a certain key term, were created by a certain employee or were deposited in a given time period. By using active information filters, these databases are searched autonomously for specific formations, locating specified or certain events or subject areas about which the user wants to be continuously informed. With the help of software agents, the filter programs regularly search the data stocks for these objects and point out the results. Using graphics or web tools, multi-dimensional representations of all aspects of company data can be graphically displayed in any combination, for example, by customer, product, time, period, area or account. The results or reports can then be sent by e-mail or made available on the Internet/intranet. In order to support a demand-oriented provision of information and knowledge, individual user profiles can be created which contain personalized regulations. This determines which employee receives which information for which activity, which resources he or she can access and which IT infrastructure is available to him or her. The user profile can also be used to define the structure of electronic reporting. Depending on the hierarchy and position, the user is assigned the reports to which he or she has access. For example, TOP management reports, financial reports, customer reports, project report comments, etc.

5.8.5.6 MITO Tool-Supported Digitisation Strategy Component Selection

A MITO tool-supported **digitization strategy component selection** in the form of a utility analysis is shown in Fig. 5.14. Column by column, all digitization components described above can be assigned if required. A ranking for the digitization components to be used is determined via the evaluation of the selection criteria mentioned with scores from 1 to 10.

Vertical and horizontal ABC grouping is also possible.

No.	Selection criteria, e.g.:	G	1	2	3	4	5	6	7	8	Σ Pkt.	%	Rank
			Digitization components, e.g.:										
			Mobile apps	Document management	AR/VR technology	CRM	ML/KI tools	Software development	Digital platform	Store system			
1	Strategic Target contribution	1	4	3	2	4	2	4	4	8	31	9.31	6
2	Customer benefit	1	3	4	4	4	2	5	3	4	29	8.71	8
3	Effort (cost)	1	2	5	3	3	4	6	2	5	30	9.01	7
4	Effort (time)	1	5	6	5	6	5	5	1	6	39	11.71	4
5	Feasibility	1	8	7	6	9	6	4	4	5	49	14.71	2
6	Personnel Resources	1	4	2	3	5	8	5	5	7	39	11.71	4
7	Qualification effort	1	6	4	5	7	9	4	6	8	49	14.71	2
8	Follow-up costs	1	8	8	7	9	10	8	8	9	67	20.12	1
Σ			40	39	35	47	46	41	33	52	333	100	
%			12.01	11.71	10.51	14.11	13.81	12.31	9.91	15.62			
Rank			5	6	7	2	3	4	8	1			

Fig. 5.14 MITO tool-supported digitization strategy component selection

5.9 Systematic Digitisation Strategy Derivation

With the knowledge of the digitization components described in the previous chapter as possible business model innovations within the 7 MITO business model elements, the right digitization strategy can now be selected. This is done with the knowledge that the questions already mentioned in the traditional business model derivation in Chap. 2 must be answered anew under the digitalization aspect. These questions are named within the individual MITO business model segments in Fig. 5.10.

The overriding objective in deriving a strategy for a company is to select the right market behaviour, competition and implementation strategies. This has already been discussed in detail in Sect. 2.12. These three interrelated strategy considerations are also included in the overall context of digital business model strategy derivation and are also included in the above-mentioned questions in the MITO business model.

It starts in the leadership segment with answering basic question 1 "What do we stand for?" Whereby a binding answer in relation to the overall strategy specification is only possible after the following basic questions have been answered (Fig. 5.15).

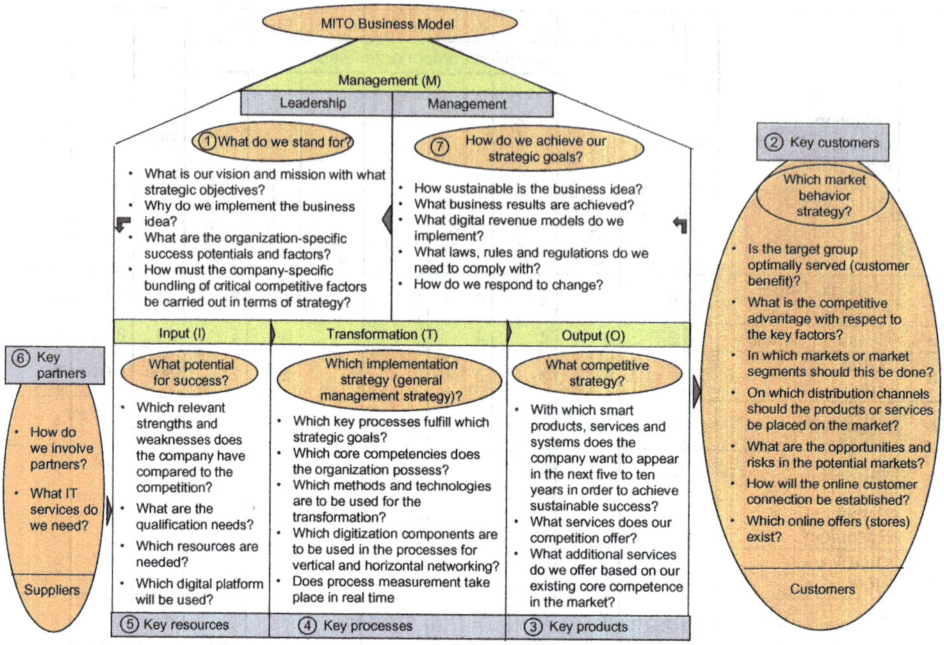

Fig. 5.15 MITO model-related questions for digitisation strategy derivation

The market behaviour strategies discussed in Sect. 2.12 are about the market behaviour of the company in relation to the activities of its competitors. Therefore, the answers to the market behaviour strategy questions are mapped to the customer or customer target group statements in basic question 2: "Who?" in the MITO business model description. The competitive strategy questions that build on this, discussed in Sect. 2.13, are mapped to Basic Question 3: "What?" in the MITO output segment and define the competitive behavior within the selected market behavior strategy. The operational implementation strategies for the market behavior strategy and competitive strategy – referred to here as the General Management Strategy (GMS) – are mapped to the MITO Transformation Segment when answering Basic Question 4: "How?". As already described in point 1.13, the individual general management strategies as management instruments with reference to the specified IMS standards ensure error-free and compliance-compliant competitive strategy implementation during process execution.

In the input segment, W-question 5 "With whom?" is about determining the potential for success, i.e. the strengths and the necessary skills of those involved in the process. The focus here is on the provision, in particular, of the IT service providers of the digital infrastructure and the qualification of the participants via digital media.

Upstream of the MITO input segment is the question of selecting the key partners for resource provision. After clarifying these questions up to this point, the overall strategy must now be formulated in the management segment with which the company and process goals are to be achieved. Finally, in the MITO leadership segment, it is a matter of demonstrating how the value contributions through the digital revenue models and the digitization goals are actually achieved through the implementation of these strategies.

For the implementation of the digitization strategy, you need a clear orientation through a digitization agenda, in which concrete goals, key measures and corresponding resources are named.

The core of the implementation of the digital strategy is the implementation of a **cloud-based digital business platform** as a horizontal and vertical networking and data hub for all IT applications, IT services and other digitalization components with all process participants, objects, products and processes within the five MITO model segments inside and outside the company, as described in point 4.11. The implementation of the digital strategy is based on the following principles: "The digitalization of the company is a process that is based on the digitalization of the company".

5.10 Digitisation Guideline Development

For the implementation of the digitization strategy derived on the basis of the targeted digital value propositions with the digitization benefits described in Sect. 5.16, a uniform understanding in top management of the need for the ability to change in conjunction with a digital corporate culture is a prerequisite. The joint elaboration in the development of a digitization mission statement between managers and employees should help to ensure that the benefits for all participants and also for the company from digitization are recognized and that the change process is jointly supported without barriers and resistance. This is achieved through an open corporate culture and the role model function of managers. The digitization principles formulated in the mission statement can be assigned to the individual MITO model segments, as shown in Fig. 5.16, and linked to each other in the form of a mission statement control loop. They complement the guiding principles on sustainable corporate culture formulated in Sect. 2.9.

For executives in the MITO management segment, digitization with the underlying data integration of all corporate data in a common data hub is an important prerequisite for improving the planning quality in corporate planning and thus also facilitating decision-making. Comprehensive data transparency in real time significantly reduces the decision-making risk.

During operational implementation, digitalization ensures comprehensive information provision and significantly facilitates communication for employees in the input segment. All those involved in the process can access all the data they need to complete the tasks in their process on a mobile basis, i.e. irrespective of location and time. They are supplied with additional information digitally via tablet or smartphone and can also query this themselves via the digital platform. This facilitates self-organisation and improves transparency in control.

In process execution itself in the transformation segment, the comprehensive provision of data enables process reliability and increases productivity and flexibility in process

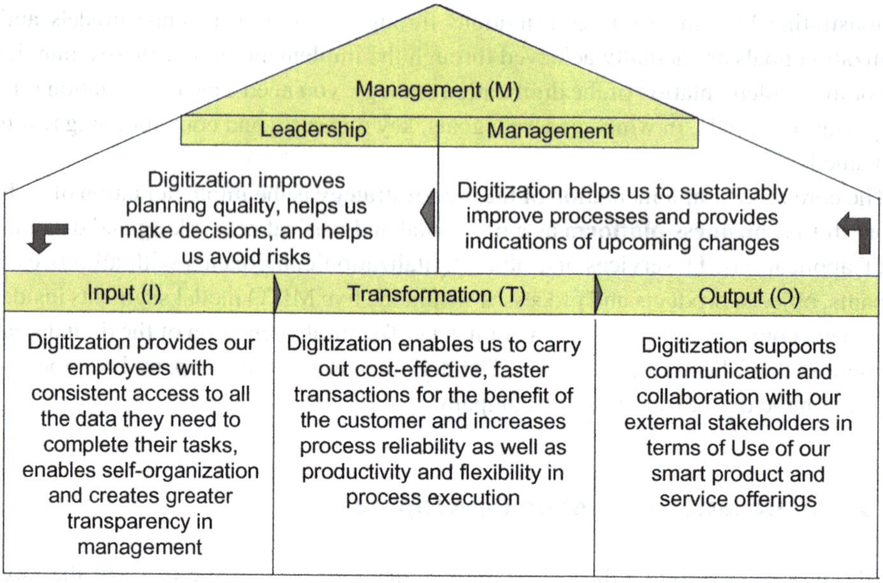

Fig. 5.16 Digitisation mission statement

execution through faster and more cost-effective transactions. In the output segment, the digitization objective formulated in the mission statement is that communication and coordination with internal and external stakeholders with regard to the provision or transfer of company-specific product and services leads to an intensive exchange of information, if possible over the entire product life cycle. The positive aspect of digitalization also comes into play in the MITO management segment. Here, digitalization is intended to support sustainable continuous process improvement and to enable forward-looking action on upcoming changes based on real-time evaluations. All statements together lead to a better understanding of the stakeholders in the organization and prevent blockades during implementation.

5.11 Digital Business Platform Enables Horizontal and Vertical Process Networking

A cloud-based business platform enables horizontal (external) and vertical (internal) digital process networking through data integration of all IT applications used in the company. With regard to the value contribution of a digital business platform, a distinction is made between transaction-oriented and data-oriented digital platforms. Transaction-oriented platforms stand for horizontal networking, while data-oriented platforms stand for vertical networking. In the case of transaction-oriented digital platforms, the focus is on connecting external stakeholders, i.e. customers, authorities, banks and others. The platform thus functions as an electronic marketplace, bringing together supply and demand and thus enabling the realization of transactions.

With the data-oriented digital platform, the value proposition lies in internal data collection, use, networking and analysis in real time with the linking of hardware and software data and services across all process levels (vertical integration), this without organizational barriers, e.g. through release or handover procedures. Access to the cloud-based business platform and thus to the digital data-based services is regulated via apps. These apps are also made available as new services via smartphone or tablet to the responsible process participants in the value creation process.

As already explained above, a digital business platform should enable the internal, i.e. vertical, networking of all applications and process participants as well as the smart objects in the company, but at the same time also enable the horizontal online connection of customers and suppliers in the horizontal value chain. The goal is therefore to achieve vertical and horizontal networking of all process participants, objects and activities or IT services that exist in the company.

Figure 5.17 shows the horizontal value chain with the main processes. Each main process is mapped schematically in the globally valid BPMN 2.0 process visualization standard in a role-based manner. The digital business platform offers customers and also partners, e.g. IT service providers, but also suppliers the possibility to communicate with the company online and mobile, i.e. independent of location and time.

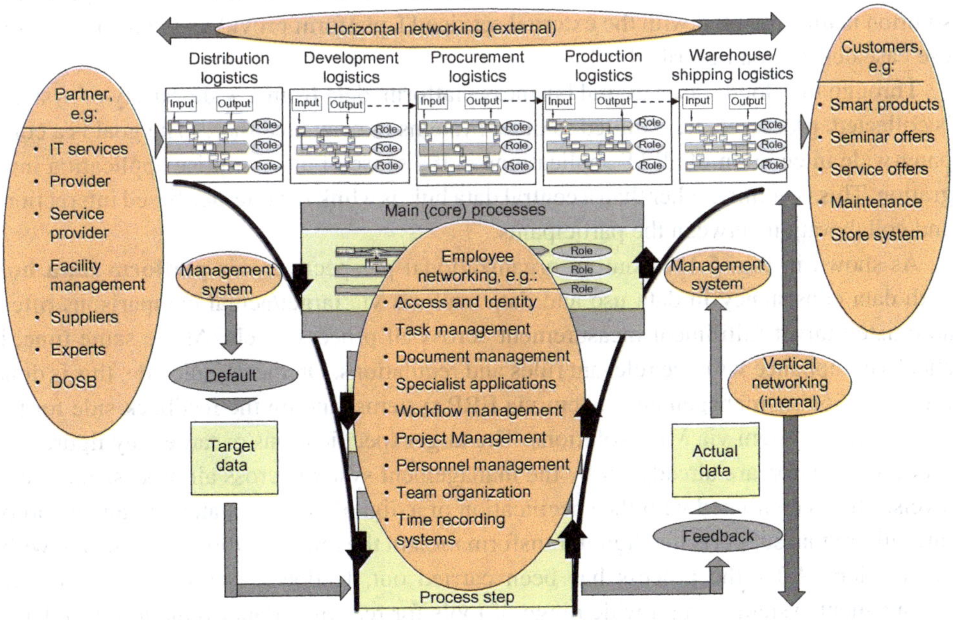

Fig. 5.17 Horizontal and vertical process networking

Furthermore, Fig. 5.17 shows the hierarchical process structure, starting from the end-to-end process via the main (core) process, sub-process down to the lowest level, i.e. the process step, as a specification for internal networking.

This includes internal IT-supported collaboration activities such as task management, specialist document management, specialist IT applications, workflow management, project management, collaboration management, team organisation, time recording software and other IT applications that are used in the vertical networking of the process participants within the company via the digital business platform networked with each other in the company-specific creation of products or services.

Employees can access all the information they need to carry out their work via the digital business platform. Of course, they also have access to the data from the horizontal value chain, i.e. the customer- or partner-related data they need. Order control and order tracking are carried out via individualized employee apps. This is always done using the operational control loop model, i.e. the target data is specified from the top down to the shop floor level. After the task has been carried out, the actual data collection with the target/actual comparison for the target fulfillment measurement follows bottom up from the lowest process step level to the highest end-to-end process level. In the event of deviations, those responsible for controlling provide the impetus for continuous improvement processes.

The implementation of these many different digitization components is initiated via the swimlane-related process analysis. The IT applications already used or to be used in the future are listed as separate roles in the respective business processes. The digitization solution is implemented with the external service IT platform providers via the role-based use case description described below.

Through the cloud-based digital business platform, data from a wide variety of systems is collected, processed, transmitted to other systems or evaluated there. The goal is a company-wide integration of all IT applications in the sense of an enterprise application integration. This is nothing other than a central data hub as a link for Internet-based interactions and collaboration between the participants.

As shown in Fig. 5.18, from an organizational perspective, this **platform data hub** with data consistency in data use and data analysis via target/actual comparisons offers automated target fulfillment measurement across all process levels. At the same time, it checks compliance with the relevant rules and regulations. On the default side, this is done for a functioning management system via ERP systems, and on the feedback side for the management system via MES solutions. The target specifications or target key figures for process execution are already set by the management system across all process hierarchy levels. This is combined with the specification of a digital mission statement and a corporate culture that supports the digital transformation in the minds of those responsible without barriers. After the process has been carried out, feedback is provided within the management system using a wide range of tools for real-time data evaluation in order to provide decision-making templates for risk governance, compliance, sustainability, CIP and forward-looking action. Here, collaborative intelligence is generated throughout

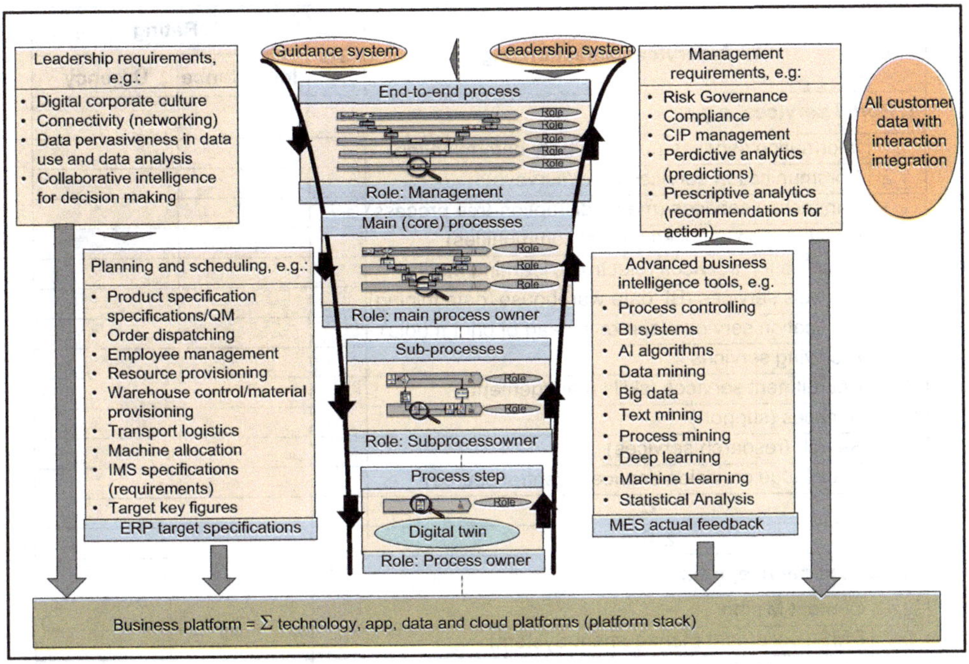

Fig. 5.18 Digital business platform as a link for Internet-based interactions in a user network

vertically as well as horizontally in all processes through communication among all stakeholders, leading to business excellence through real-time decision support. Figure 5.19 shows a MITO portfolio matrix for a portal web service analysis.

The evaluation result representation in the portfolio diagram shows which web services are required; these can then be subjected to the digitisation strategy component selection explained in Section 5.12.

5.12 Process-Oriented Implementation of the Digitisation Strategy

The challenge in the process-oriented implementation of the digitization strategy now consists of optimally networking the digitization components described in previous chapters across all process levels within the business processes, taking into account the strategy approaches mentioned in Sect. 2.15 and the process optimization concepts explained in Sect. 3.6. The process model for the company-specific implementation of a digitization strategy is shown in Fig. 5.20 with the **process subflows** shown there, which are now linked with each other in terms of information and the design activities required for this. The reference point for process networking is always the end-to-end process analyzed with the support of a BPM tool, which maps the horizontal value chain in a role-based

No.	Web services selection, e.g.:	GG	Rating	
			Importance	Urgency
1. Portal services, e.g.:				
1.1	Information services (responsibility determination)			
1.2	Communication services (chat/surveys)			
1.3	Transaction services (media disruption-free process)			
1.4	Collaboration services (virtual communities)			
1.5	Qualification services (electronic learning media)			
1.6	Analysis services (BI, data warehouse, data mining)			
1.7	Publication services (server instead of print media)			
1.8	Archiving services			
1.9	Recruitment services (skills management)			
1.10	Services (support)			
1.11	Search (research services)			
1.12	Knowledge provision services (central source)			
	C			
	$\sum$ C/n			
2. Content service, e.g.:				
2.1	Content Mining			
2.2	DMS (Document Management System)			
2.3	Archiving systems			
2.4	Groupware			
2.5	Workflow management systems			
2.6	Retrieval systems			
2.7	Community systems			
2.8	Editorial systems			
2.9	Interfaces			
2.10	Office applications			
	C			
	$\sum$ C/n			
3. Application services (specialized procedures), e.g..:				
3.1	ERP/PPS			
3.2	CRM			
3.3	CAD			
3.4	SCM			
3.5	PDM			
3.6	HR/Personal			
3.7	FIBU			
3.8	KORE			
3.9	Project Management			
3.10	Process Management			
	C			
	$\sum$ C/n			
Scale: 1 = low 6 = high		**Total**		

Fig. 5.19 MITO Portal Web Service Analysis

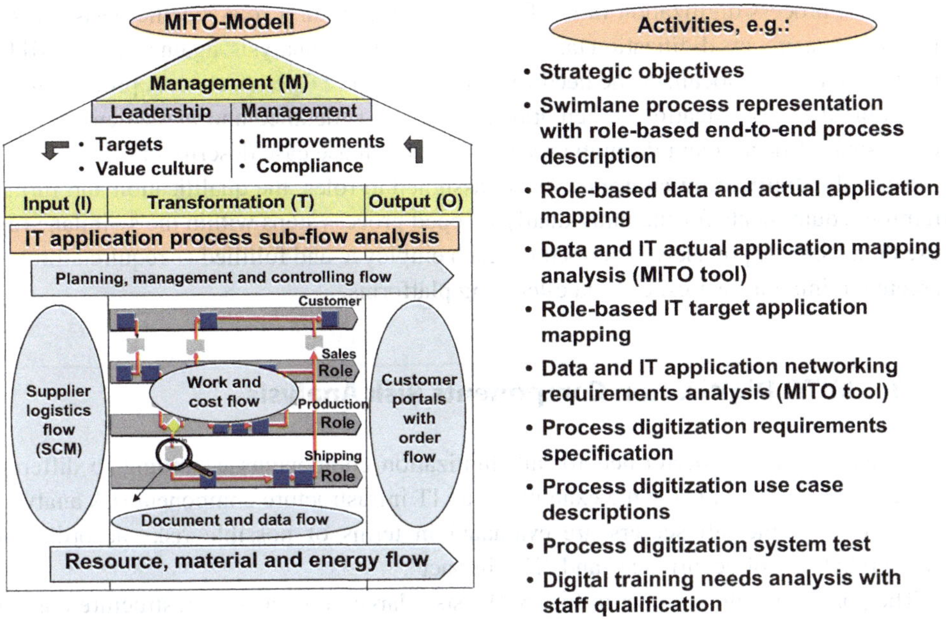

Fig. 5.20 Process-oriented digitization strategy implementation

manner. This value chain must be oriented to the customer's requirements and be designed with few interfaces. The end-to-end process from the receipt of the customer's order to the processing in the company to the delivery of the product or service to the customer should then run within the individual core processes in the company without errors or waste.

The process subflows, which were previously considered separately and which, from a historical point of view, were each supported by stand-alone IT applications, are networked with each other within the framework of the digitalization strategy via the new information technologies such as cloud computing, big data, Industry 4.0 or social business. In this case, this means that the planning, management and controlling flow is interconnected with the work and cost flow, with the document and data flow, with the resource, material and energy flow, with the supplier-related logistics flow and the customer-related order flow via a new digitization platform to be implemented.

The process-related order structure for all these subflows is the swimlane representation. The process activities are related factually-temporally-logically between the roles involved. This organizational order structure specification is then the starting point for process digitization with the MITO segment-related digitization targets. As part of the as-is analysis, all existing as-is IT applications that currently support this end-to-end process, also from a separate, i.e. process sub-view, are analyzed and documented. Subsequently, the MITO method tool can be used to determine the extent to which the existing actual applications already communicate with each other by means of a data and actual application networking analysis. In the next step, the target IT applications that are to support process digitization in the future are selected on a role-specific basis. This is followed by a process digitization target-actual networking analysis, again using the MITO method tool, which localizes the need for action from an IT perspective. A process digitization platform specification is then drawn up, which is detailed and implemented by the responsible IT department through process digitization use case descriptions.

Since the **digitization components** are assigned to roles, the qualification and further training requirements for the individually mapped process steps within the swimlane representation can be precisely described for each employee and fulfilled as required through targeted training measures, e.g. via e-learning platforms.

5.13 MITO Digitisation Components Risk Analysis

Risk analysis can be performed for all digitization components according to different aspects. This is shown using the example of an IT infrastructure component risk analysis. Here, for example, all servers are evaluated in terms of possible risks according to "V = probability of occurrence" and "H = impact".

The portfolio matrix shown in Fig. 5.21 lists a large number of infrastructure components without claiming to be complete. The risk types are assigned in columns and can be added to immediately. An assessment has been carried out for the risk type "Internal Stakeholders". The assessment results are shown in Fig. 5.22.

5.14 MITO-Supported: IT Application Linkage Needs Analysis

As already explained, **interoperability** and connectivity are the decisive prerequisites for successful process digitization. Interoperability is the ability of different IT systems or IT applications to work together by adhering to common standards, e.g. data formats and protocols (data integration). Connectivity is the networking of people, objects, production systems, processes and products by connecting them to a digital infrastructure, for example via the Internet with cloud-based IT services. Interoperability and connectivity play a key role as a prerequisite for effective use of cloud services, i.e. exchanging and evaluating information in many application areas such as e Government, e Heaths, e Logistics or e Business.

In order to obtain an overview of which roles and IT applications are to be networked with each other during process digitization, a wide variety of organizational and IT networking analyses can be performed with the MITO method tool. On the one hand, the organizational roles with the process participants and the individual process steps are mapped in the factual-time-logical sequence of the order processing. The template for this is provided by the process documented in the swimlane representation. Furthermore, the applications used in the process with the individual application steps are also directly assigned to the organizational process steps in a role-related manner. Using this

No.	Criteria	Risk types									
		Risks from internal stakeholders		Risks from external stakeholders		Risks due to theft		Risks from IT-specific manipulation		Risks through malware	
		V	H	V	H	V	H	V	H	V	H
2 IT infrastructure components											
2.1	Application server	2	1								
2.2	Web server	2	1								
2.3	Database server	2	1								
2.4	File server	2	1								
2.5	FAX server	2	2								
2.6	Software distribution server	2	1								
2.7	PC	1	1								
2.8	Terminal	2	2								
2.9	Monitor	1	1								
2.10	Mainframes	2	2								
2.11	Mini computers	1	1								
2.12	WAN network	3	3								
2.13	LAN network	1	6								
2.14	MAN network	1,5	5								
2.15	Network infrastructure	5	3								
2.16	Security components	5	5								
2.17	Building infrastructure	6	1								
2.18	Web service	1	3								
2.19	Browser	3	1								
2.20	PDF reader	5	1								
C		**49.5**	**42**								
Â C/n		**2.48**	**2.1**								
Scale: 1 = low 6 = high		**49**	**42**								
		2.48	**2.1**								

Fig. 5.21 MITO-IT components- Cluster 2: IT infrastructure components

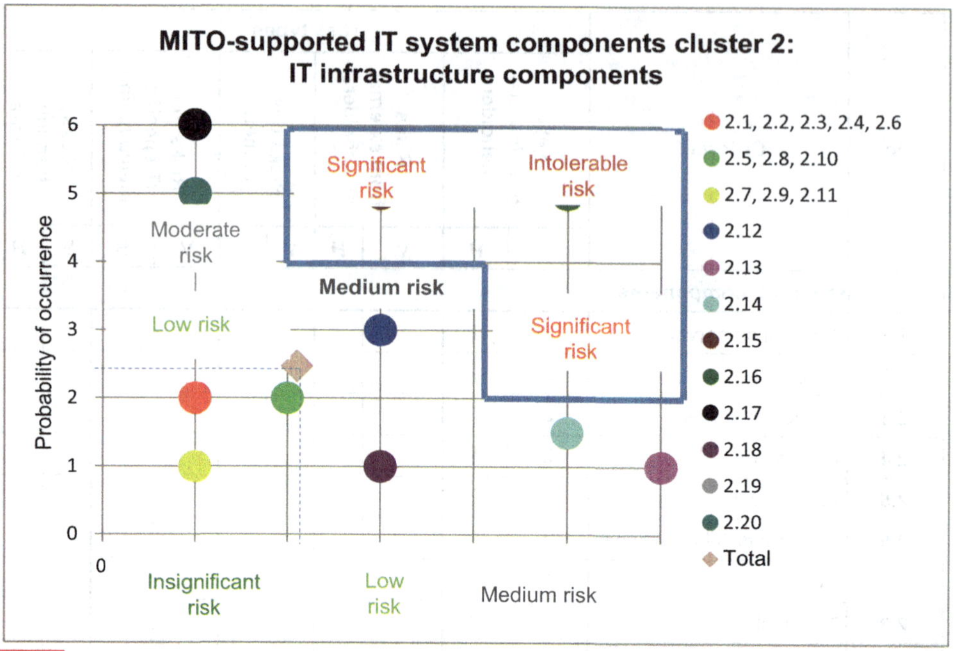

2.1	Application server
2.2	Web server
2.3	Database server
2.4	File server
2.6	Software distribution server
2.5	FAX server
2.8	Terminal
2.10	Mainframes
2.7	PC
2.9	Monitor
2.11	Mini computer
2.12	WAN network
2.13	LAN network
2.14	MAN network
2.15	Network infrastructure
2.16	Security components
2.17	Building infrastructure
2.18	Web service
2.19	Browser
2.20	PDF reader

Fig. 5.22 Individual criteria portfolio diagram: MITO-IT components- Cluster 2: IT infrastructure components

representation, the interfaces can be mapped graphically using portfolio and assignment matrices. Here, the actual state can be represented once, as well as the target state. As Fig. 5.23 shows, 6 different networking portfolio assignment and relation matrices are depicted there, which represent different networking aspects.

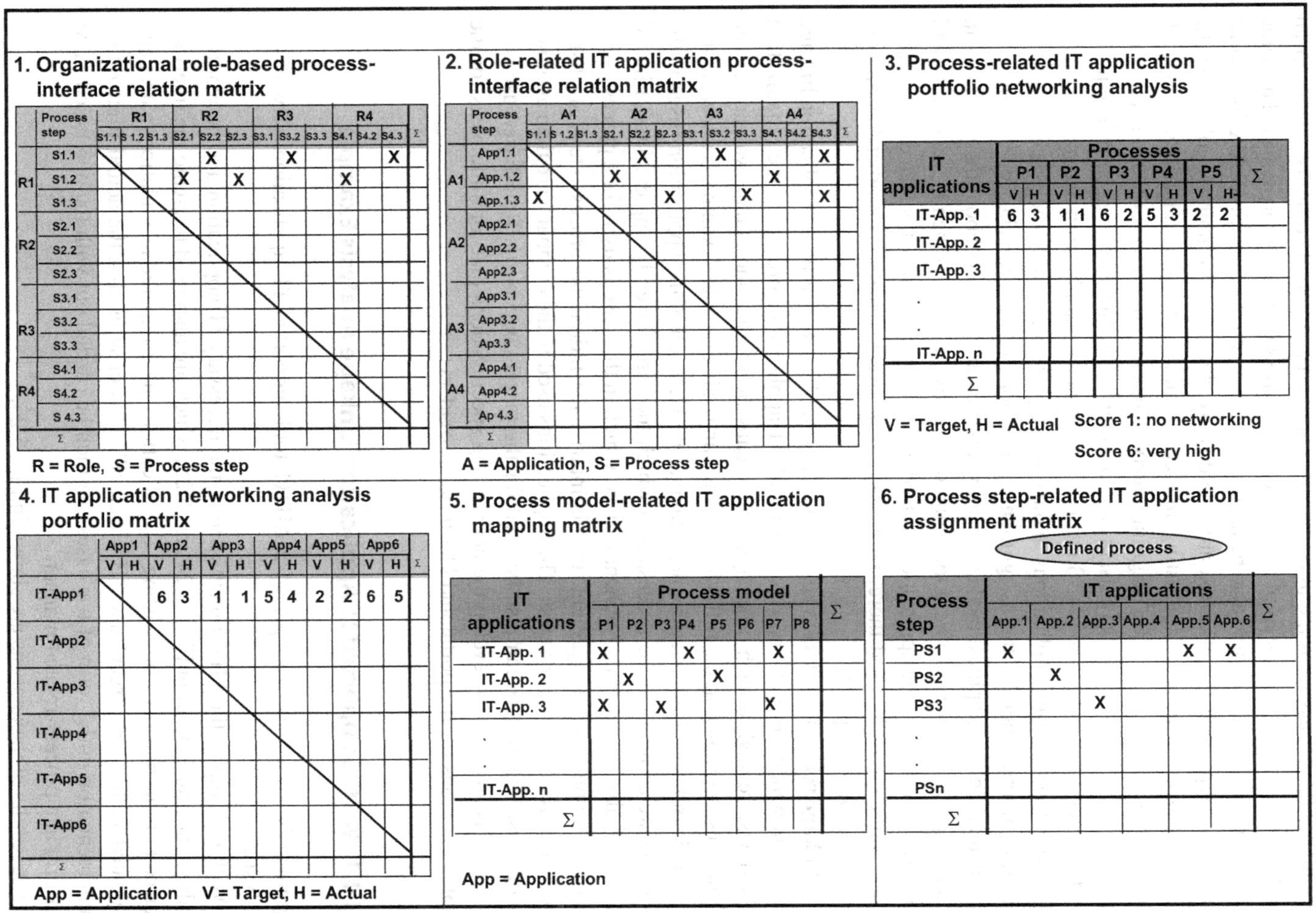

Fig. 5.23 MITO tool-supported IT networking analyses for process digitization

First, an organizational role-based **interface relation matrix** is shown in the upper left. The individual process steps are assigned to each role in rows and columns. Wherever an interface exists per process step, it is marked with a cross in the relation matrix. The same type of representation can now also be used for the individual applications. The individual transaction steps per IT application are also displayed row and column by column in the relation matrix. Here, too, an existing interconnection of these applications with each other is marked in this portfolio diagram matrix. This analysis can refer to the actual state and to the target state. In this way, users can document where networking action is required.

MITO networking example no. 3 is a process-related IT application networking analysis in which the existing applications in the company are assigned to the processes line by line in columns, whereby the assignment in the portfolio matrix via "V = target" and "H = actual" in the graphical evaluation provides a clear statement about the processes in which IT applications are to be implemented. Line by line, it can then be seen across all processes where the same application is used. Column by column, it is stated per process which applications are used there. How they are networked with each other has already been shown in example 2.

A **linkage relation matrix** is also shown in example 4. This is an IT application linkage analysis in which, column and row by row, all IT applications present in the organization are likewise related to each other again by means of a target and actual evaluation. The evaluations are shown in the following linkage analysis example. Example 5 shows a process model related IT application mapping matrix. Here, all of the applications used in the company are assigned to the processes in which they are currently implemented. Finally, Example 6 also shows an assignment matrix, which in this case is used for a process-step-related IT application assignment. In this matrix, the individual process steps are listed row by row for a selected process. The applications used in the company are then assigned in columns. This matrix can also be used for the target conception. Role-based use case descriptions are used to develop the networking specifications that form the basis for the implementations for the portal and IT service providers.

5.14.1 MITO-Supported IT Application Linkage Analysis Example

Figure 5.24 shows an example of a MITO tool-supported IT application networking analysis.

With the help of the MITO method tool, the necessary IT application and networking analyses are carried out in Figs. 5.24 and 5.25, which are also used to create the interface matrix. For this purpose, the existing IT applications are compared in a relation matrix and evaluated with "V = target" and "H = actual". This ensures that the actual digitization implementation in the form of use cases can then be carried out with the purchased PLM platform in a process-related manner.

The results of the analysis are shown in Fig. 5.25.

No.		GG	IT-Applications																			
			PLM		PPS/ERP		Specialized		FIBU		ECM system		MES		CPS		Cloud Computing		Enterprise Mobility		Big Data	
			V	H	V	H	V	H	V	H	V	H	V	H	V	H	V	H	V	H	V	H
1.IT-Applications																						
1.1	PLM				5	1	3	1	4	1	3	2	5	2	3	3	5	2	3	3	3	1
1.2	PPS/ERP		5	2			4	1	4	1	4	2	4	1	4	3	4	3	4	3	3	2
1.3	Specialized		3	3	4	2			4	1	4	2	2	1	4	2	4	3	4	4	5	2
1.4	FIBU		4	3	3	3	6	2			5	3	3	2	5	2	5	2	5	1	3	3
1.5	ECM system		6	2	5	3	3	2	4	1			4	2	5	2	4	3	5	1	6	2
1.5	MES		3	2	5	3	4	3	4	1	3	2			4	2	3	1	4	2	6	2
1.7	CPS		5	4	4	4	4	3	4	1	3	1	4	3			3	2	3	2	5	1
1.8	Cloud Computing		5	1	3	1	5	3	4	1	4	2	5	2	3	2			3	2	4	1
1.9	Enterprise Mobility		4	1	6	2	2	3	4	1	5	2	5	1	3	2	4	1			5	2
1.10	Big Data		6	2	3	1	4	1	4	1	4	3	4	2	5	1	4	4	4	4		
C			41	20	38	20	35	18	36	9	35	21	36	16	36	19	36	21	41	20	28	20
ΣC/n			4.5 6	2.2	4.2	2,2	3.9	2.0	4.0	1.0	3.9	2.3	4.0	1.8	4.0	2.1	4.0	2.3	4.5 6	2.2	4.2	2.2
Scale: 1 = no linkage 2 = organizational link 3 = Integration through tools 4 = File transfer 5 = Shared database 6 = Program integration		Rank	1	4	3	4	8	7	4	10	8	2	4	8	4	6	4	2	8	1	2	8

Fig. 5.24 MITO®-supported – IT application linkage needs analysis

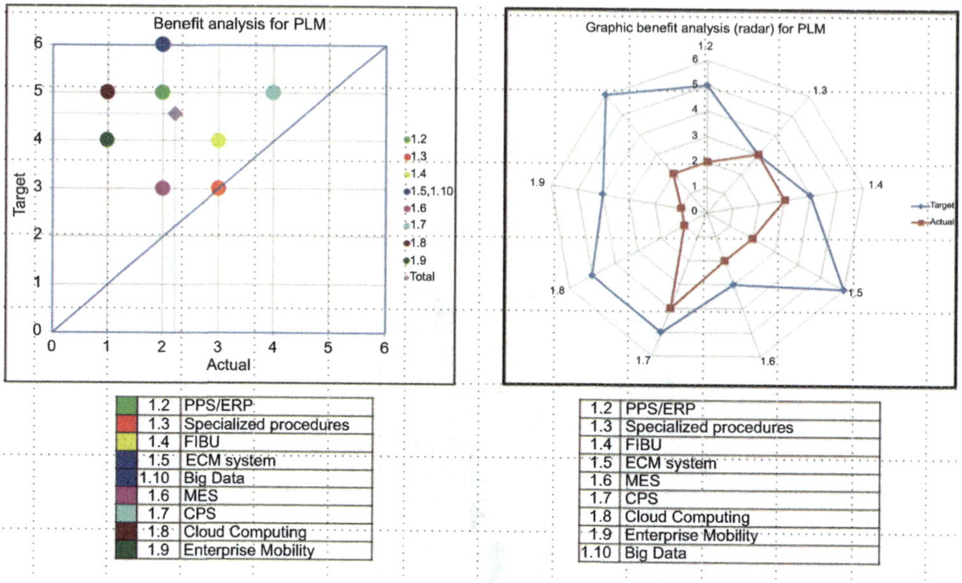

Fig. 5.25 Graphical representation of the results of the linkage requirements analysis for PLM

5.15 Role-Based Use Case Description

The implementation of the digitization strategy specified in the digitization master plan at the operational, i.e. process level, takes place via the role-based use case description. Here, the business processes, IT infrastructures, applications and smart objects are factually and temporally logically assigned to the organizational roles in which they are used. This is done at the process step level and is thus an unambiguous assignment of the respective transactions to the work step executed in the process. In this way – as also shown in Fig. 5.26 – the organizational business application description is linked to the IT-related process description. The process participants, i.e., the business departments as well as the IT departments, use this role-based use case application description as a basis for the implementation of process digitization, e.g., by IT service providers.

Figure 5.26 shows the contents of a role (swimlane)-related use case description. The reference point is the models shown. This is the company-specific process model in the MITO model representation with the management and leadership processes in the management segment, the upstream support processes in the input segment, the core processes in the transformation segment and the downstream support processes in the output segment with feedback to the leadership processes in the MITO leadership segment. Thus, the high-level content structure for integrated management systems is also mapped in chapters. The process documentation also results in the link connectors of the processes among each other, which are then represented in the form of a process map. This process map

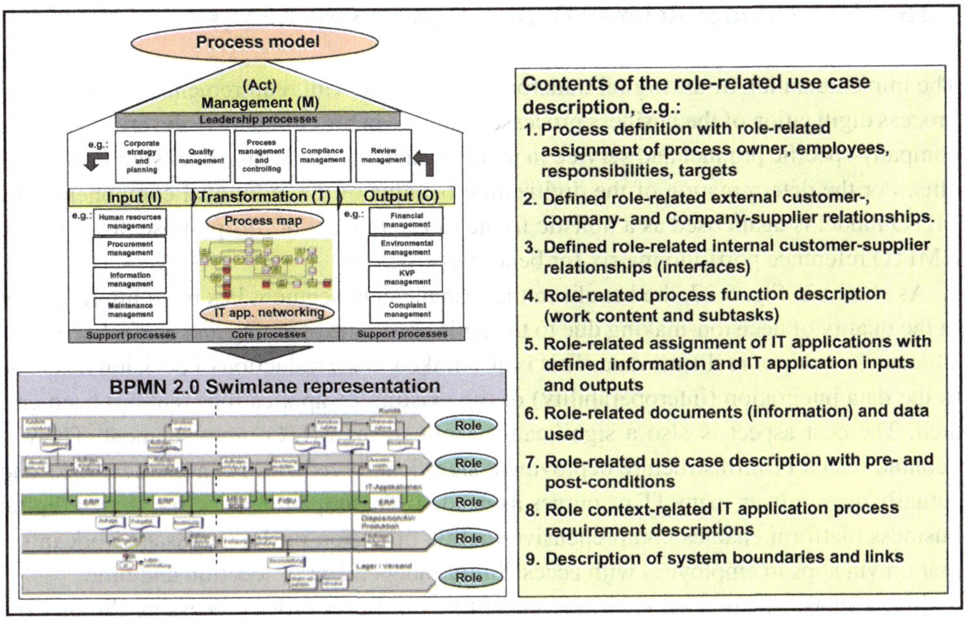

Fig. 5.26 Contents of the role (swimlane)-related use case description

shows the interactions of the processes with each other and, from an IT perspective, can also depict the networking of the IT applications used in the processes in the same form.

Based on the BPMN 2.0 swimlane process representation, which is also shown, the role-related assignment of process owners, employees, responsibilities and targets is then made. Further, a defined role-based external customer-company-supplier relationship is created. This also applies in the same way to the internal customer-supplier relationship shown in the swimlane representation with the existing internal process interface descriptions. The work contents and subtasks are then named for each process function within a role or for each process step. For these work contents and subtasks, the description of the assigned defined IT application input and output is then also made in the respective application role. This applies in the same way to the role-related assignment of the documents and data used. This is followed by the use case description with the required content scope of the system to be developed or used, always with assignment to the graphical process mapping. In addition, specific IT application process requirement descriptions and the description of the system boundaries can also be included. Furthermore, the links to other IT applications are also explained in an interface-related manner. This is based on the previously created MITO method-tool-supported IT application networking analyses. In summary, this information provides the platform and IT service provider with the specifications for process digitization in line with requirements.

5.16 MITO Model-Related Digitisation Benefit Analysis

The implementation of the digital transformation in line with requirements, especially the process digitization of the business processes running in the company in the creation of the company-specific product and service in many organizational areas offers significant benefits. For the determination of the digitization benefits of the individual components, the MITO model is again used as a holistic frame of reference. For this purpose, there is also a MITO reference portfolio matrix for benefit assessment.

As shown in Fig. 5.27, the benefit in the management segment lies in an improvement in the quality of decision-making due to the agile corporate planning and control now possible on the basis of real-time data. This is also linked to the reduction of decision risks due to the data integration (interoperability) of the existing IT applications that has been created. The cost aspect is also a significant benefit in the MITO input segment. The on-demand scaled IT infrastructure deployment significantly reduces IT investment risks and actually uses only as many IT resources as needed. The implemented cloud-based digital business platform enables comprehensive mobile provision of the necessary work information via apps to employees with accessibility independent of location and time.

In the transformation segment, the benefit lies in faster order processing through the integration of workflows and coordination processes within digital process execution. This is combined with a lower use of resources through the avoidance of overcapacities and the creation of buffers. At the same time, process quality also increases due to real-time data

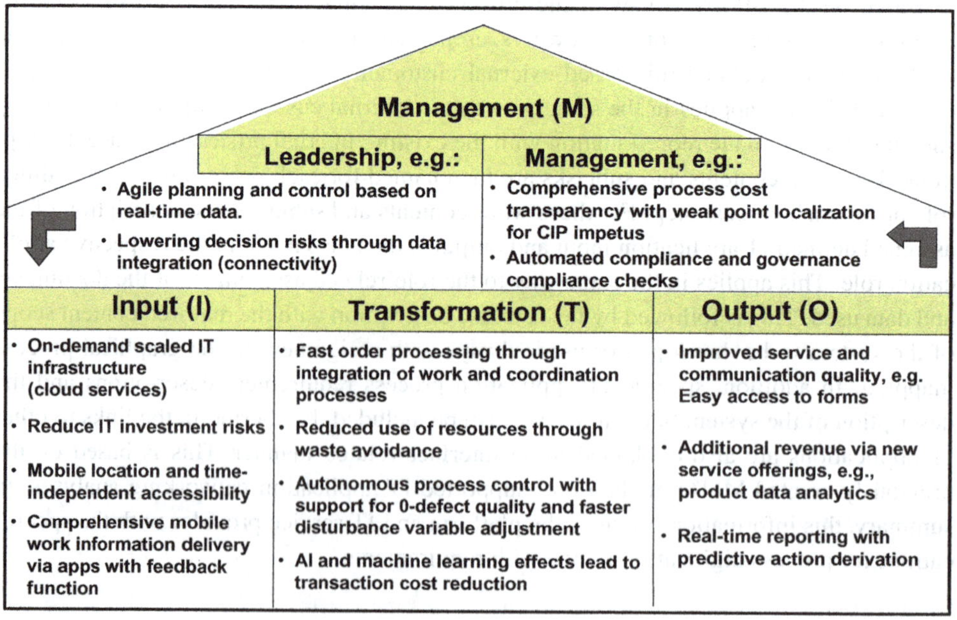

Fig. 5.27 MITO model-related digitization benefits

acquisition on site. This is supported by zero-defect quality with faster disturbance variable adjustment. The real-time data can also be used in conjunction with AI and machine learning tools to detect anomalies in the process and impending changes and respond to them by acting proactively.

In the output segment, the focus is on the customer. They receive improved service and communication quality because they are also connected online to the digital business platform. Additional revenues can arise for the company through new service offers based on product data feedback from the customer during the usage phase. Here, too, real-time analyses can be used to localize demand trends with forward-looking action derivation.

In the line segment, comprehensive process cost transparency is also created due to real-time data collection and display. The previously common overhead cost calculations are replaced by direct cost recording on site and result in a much more accurate cost picture in the creation of products and services. The real-time data collected also provides information on compliance with sustainability, compliance and good governance requirements. In the event of deviations, CIP triggers can then arise again. The digitization cycle starts all over again.

5.17 MITO Tool-Based Implementation Assessment of the Process Digitisation Master Plan

In order to check whether a holistic implementation of the digitalization master plan has taken place successfully or also to analyze which activities are necessary for this digital master plan implementation in advance, a digital transformation checklist was developed in which a whole number of questions are stored in the logical order of the activities to be completed (approximately 100 questions). The structure of this MITO portfolio digitalization checklist is based on the 5 MITO model segments in order to control the activities in the sense of the cybernetic control loop model. The individual digitization master plan steps are also given in this order. It starts in the MITO leadership segment with the assessment of the digital agenda and digital business model development activities. From this, the digital mission statement and the digital strategy blueprint are derived. The MITO input segment is about selecting the right digital platform and IT services provider, digital infrastructure provision for all workplaces with access for all process participants and real-time reporting. In this context, targeted digitalization training is to be provided for all participants.

In the transformation segment, the focus is on the actual creation of products or services via digital process execution. Here, there is a large number of IoT components and IT applications, such as robotics software, machine learning, digital twins, ERP, MES, BDE, PLM or CRM applications, which are used networked with each other in the production system or on the shop floor level.

In the output segment, the focus is on the customer with online customer communication. The goal is to accompany the customer throughout the entire product usage period and to generate new service or product offerings from the user data obtained during product or service usage. The aim is to achieve a positive network effect in order to further improve customer benefits, for example through the exchange of experiences between a community of users. The management segment is concerned with checking whether the digitization strategy has been successfully applied in the company. This is determined via digital value contribution, sustainability and compliance audits.

As is known, the evaluation with the MITO method tool is always 2-dimensional, whereby the evaluation dimensions V and H can be freely selected by the user. In this case, there is evaluation variant 1 with V = requirement and "H = implementation" as well as evaluation variant 2 with "V = relevance" and "H = degree of fulfilment".

From the graphical presentation of results in the portfolio diagram, it becomes clear for each individual question whether there is a need for action. However, it is also possible to display the results graphically in the form of a radar chart, from which it is also immediately apparent where there are still gaps in the implementation by comparing target/actual key figures. The evaluation in the evaluation dimensions of V and H in the grades from 1 to 6 is also to be defined by the user himself. As an example, the scaling with the scores from 1 to 6 for the evaluation dimension "V = Relevance" and for the evaluation dimension "H = Implementation or Degree of Fulfilment" is shown in Fig. 5.28. Once the need for action has been localized, the MITO tool can again be used to derive method-based goal/action trees with the associated to-do lists in order to ensure that the deficits identified are worked through in a targeted manner. The final step is a 2-dimensional evaluation, also carried out with the MITO method tool, for example with the evaluation dimensions "V = Effectiveness" and "H = Efficiency".

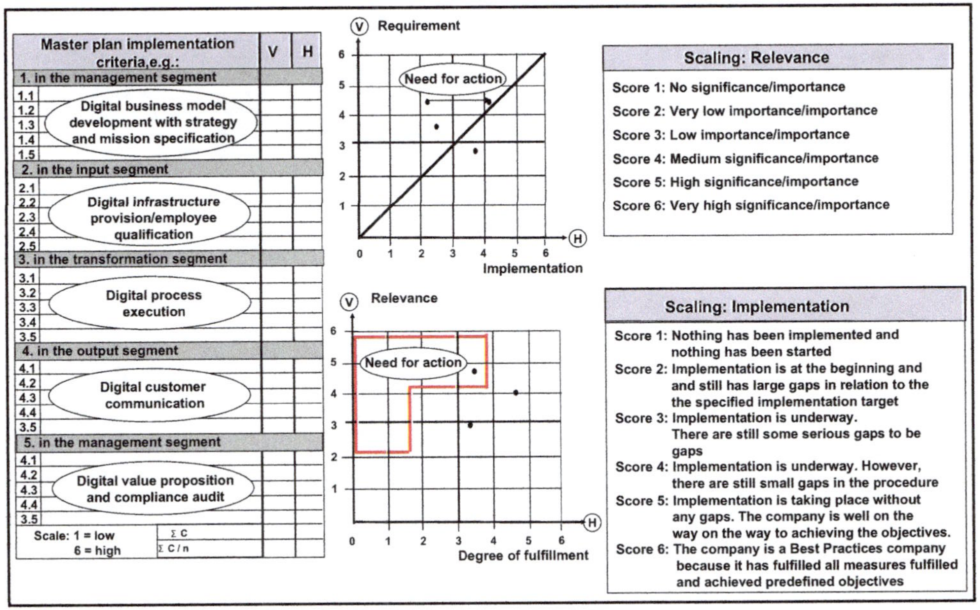

Fig. 5.28 MITO-based implementation assessment of the process digitisation master plan

Method-Based Good Governance Implementation 6

Abstract

After the implementation of the organizational transformation in Chap. 3, the cultural transformation in Chap. 4 and the digital transformation in Chap. 5, the change management process responsible for this should be concluded with an implementation assessment of the now newly created digital business model in this chapter.

As an example, the MITO tool-supported audit, evaluation and maturity level implementation of some management system verifications frequently required in practice is explained below.

6.1 Systematic Process Governance Evaluation

Process governance is understood to be a control and regulation system for a process organization in order to fulfill all process requirements, in particular the compliance requirements in the creation of the product and service. The achievement of the process goals set by management and the decision-making process should also be improved by process governance.

The structure of the process-related control and regulation system necessary for this and explained in detail in Chap. 4 and the digital support and implementation described in Chap. 5 via the IT applications implemented on the input and output side, such as ERP, MES systems and other IT applications, is carried out via the detailed description of the process order structures with the associated rules for process control (input), process transformation and process controlling (feedback/output).

H. F. Binner, *Holistic Business Model Transformation*,
https://doi.org/10.1007/978-3-658-37367-2_6

The basis for a systematic **good governance evaluation** is thus the process governance structures described in Chaps. 2 and 3. They consist of the following models and will be briefly explained once again:

1. MITO business model
2. MITO process model
3. MITO process map
4. Role-based process visualization according to the worldwide valid BPMN 2.0 process visualization standard (swimlane model)
5. Process level model
6. MITO-IT application networking model

The starting point for the process governance development with the control and rule specification is the description of the company-specific digital business model, which has already been discussed in detail.

As also already described in detail, the conception of the management and leadership system as a control and regulation instrument for the creation of the principles and rules builds on this. Fig. 6.1 shows the overall context. The leadership system is topdown softfact-related responsible for the definition and achievement of the objectives.

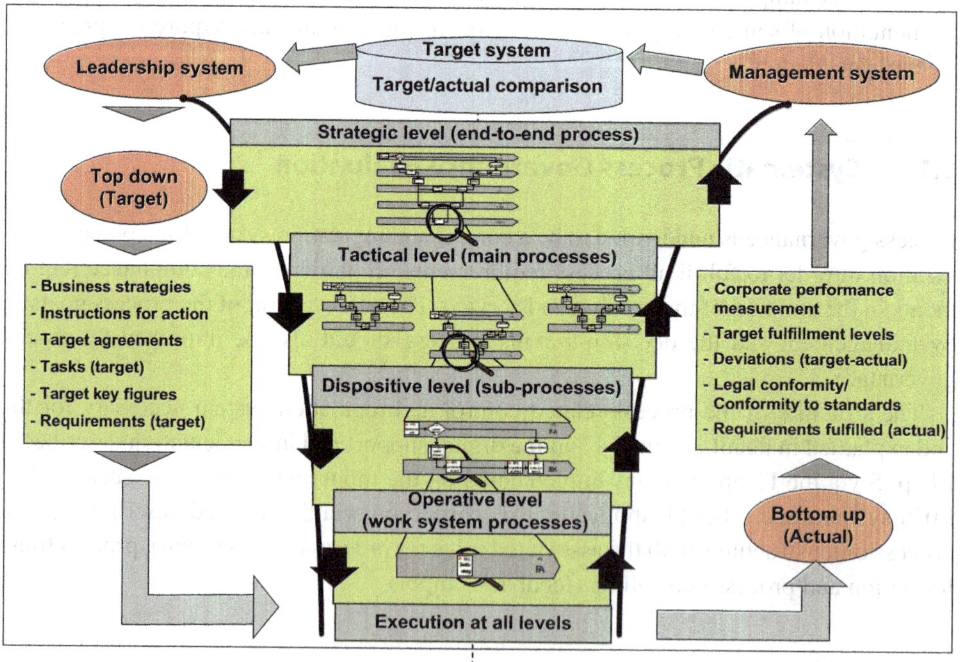

Fig. 6.1 Process governance control and regulation system

After the process execution within the shown process levels, the **actual data acquisition** takes place within the framework of the hardfacts-related management system in order to check whether the requirements are fulfilled, whether the standard and legal conformity are complied with and to what extent deviations determined during the target-actual comparison are to be eliminated by corrective measures. From a management perspective, the company's performance is measured, for example in connection with a **customer satisfaction survey**. The establishment of a process governance-related control and regulation system is intended to comprehensively and consistently implement the governance principles with respect to

1. Accountability
2. Responcability: Responsibility
3. Transparency: Openness and transparency of structures and processes
4. Fairness, respect, loyalty and reliability

Be fulfilled. This is also always in conjunction with compliance with **data governance**. This is the company's internal policy for handling data, i.e. the regulation of tasks, roles, access rights and responsibilities around the information processes.

The superordinate **risk governance** discussed below is also based on this process governance control and rule system. Based on the company-specific business model, the objective of risk governance is to review the business transactions from a compliance perspective with regard to potential hazards and risks that could jeopardize stakeholder benefits and thus also the success of the business. The reviews result in risk management geared to the various target groups, as explained in the following chapter. Topics include sustainability (CSR), occupational health and safety, health management, anti-corruption, violations of the law, complaints, etc.

6.2 Systematic Risk Governance Assessment

In many integrated management system standards, such as compliance, environmental, sustainability or quality management, performance of the risk analyses is required. In Fig. 6.2, the MITO business model also lists the risk types that are to be localized within the MITO model segments shown in relation to the 7 W basic questions assigned there. The following distinction is made here.

For the strategic level with the management leadership segment, risk governance should ensure proactive control of all corporate risks related to its target groups, i.e. in relation to the owners, banks, cooperation partners, customers, suppliers, the public, employees. This is a penetration of the company with a stakeholder-oriented risk management from a strategic point of view.

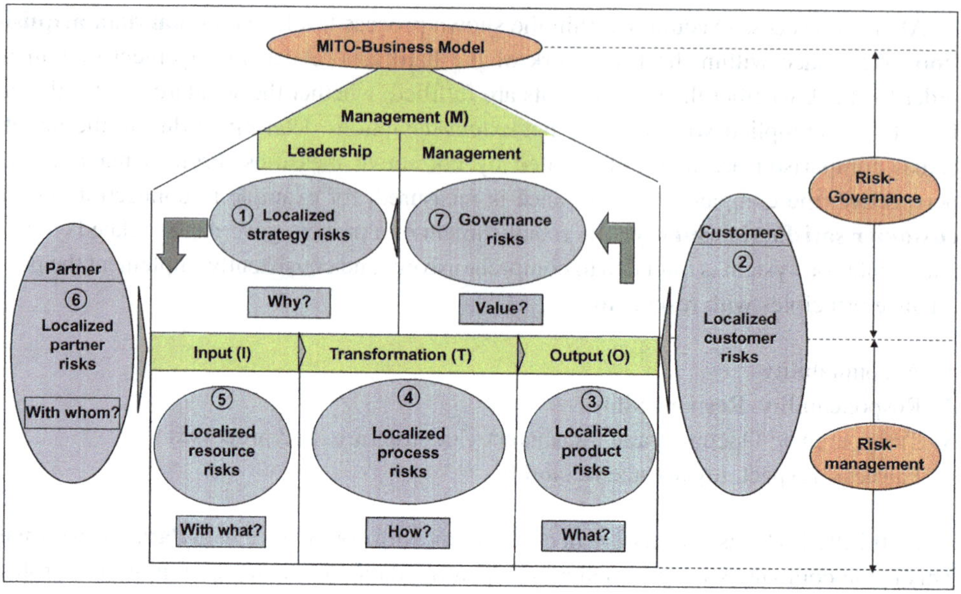

Fig. 6.2 Risk-proof MITO business model answering the "7 W-Questions"

Classic risk management, on the other hand, relates to the execution of business processes at the operational level, i.e. in day-to-day business. Here, the focus is on resource risks in the input segment, process risks in the transformation segment, and product and service risks in the output segment. They must be systematically identified and reduced by appropriate measures if the risk materializes. With regard to the partners also assigned on the input side and the customers assigned on the output side, both distinctions apply on the one hand from a strategic point of view, i.e. with regard to the implementation or achievement of the company's long-term strategic goals, but also in day-to-day operational business in the production of products or services, for example due to delivery bottlenecks or machine failures.

Due to the different objectives in process-oriented organizational development and design within the five MITO model segments, there are very many different types of risks strategically as well as operationally that challenge the intended business and process objectives such as customer, employee, financial, safety, health, occupational health, cost and process objectives, etc. Therefore, it is very important to apply a uniform systematic approach to ensure a consistent approach to risk analysis and assessment from a holistic perspective to many different tasks in each MITO segment. Via the MITO method tool with a digitalized spectrum of methods, users can carry out these risk analyses from very different perspectives in a method-based manner.

The use of the MITO method tool is explained below using the example of a 3-step compliance **risk analysis**. The risk analysis required by the ISO 19600-2014 standard "Compliance Management System Guidelines" is intended to ensure that cross-process identification, implementation and compliance with legal requirements, regulations, rules and laws is demonstrated with current updates or improvements to the compliance management system (CMS). With the MITO-Method-Tool such a risk analysis can be carried out system-supported. The required evidence, for example for certification, is then available in digital form. Fig. 6.3 shows a three-stage MITO-supported compliance risk analysis, diagnosis and therapy.

It begins in stage 1 with the specification of a portfolio matrix in which all laws, regulations, rules, guidelines are listed line by line. Column by column, the possible types of risks that can jeopardize compliance with these laws and regulations are now mentioned. The two-dimensional analysis with the MITO method tool with the evaluation "V = risk relevance" and "H = degree of risk" then shows in the BV1 result display in the portfolio diagram which compliance with laws and regulations is most at risk. These are located in the graphical result display in the upper right portfolio diagram. The hazard category is determined by the grade assignment shown, from grade 1 in the lower left portfolio diagram to grade 6. All the laws and regulations in the upper right-hand field of action, which therefore have a high hazard category due to the scores 5 and 6 in the portfolio diagram, are then also transferred to a portfolio matrix in stage 2 and an assessment is carried out for the risks now assigned in columns according to "V = probability of occurrence" and "H = impact" (BV2). The

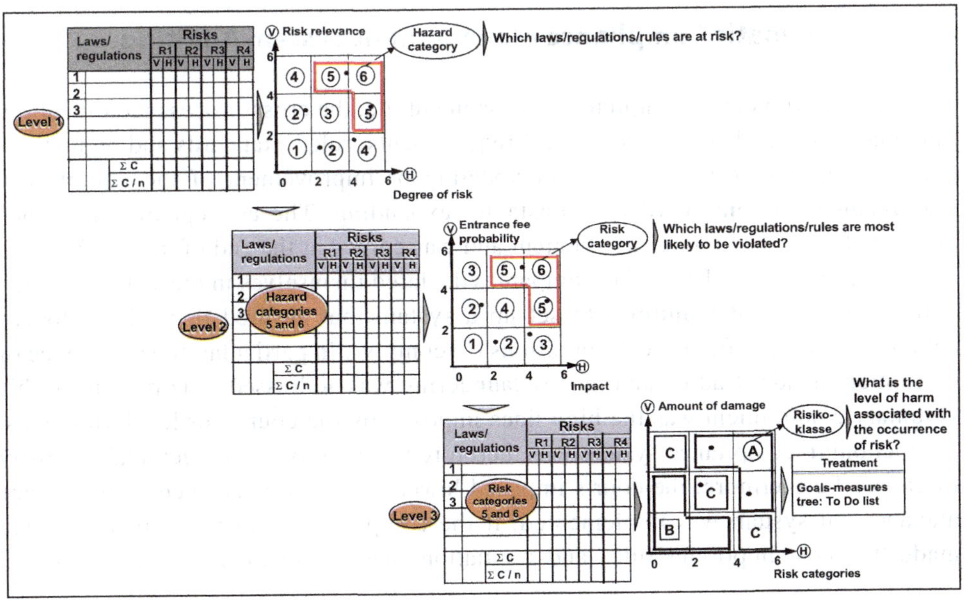

Fig. 6.3 MITO tool-supported 3-step compliance risk analysis, diagnosis and therapy

graphical result, again in the portfolio diagram, now shows the risk category for the individual laws, regulations and rules mentioned line by line, as in BV1, with the grade assignment from 1 to 6. Also in the upper right corner of the portfolio diagram are those laws that are most likely to be violated and that have the most serious impact. The laws and regulations located there are now evaluated once again in the 3rd stage with regard to the possible amount of damage and risk category, in order to obtain a statement as to what damage will occur for the company if the risk materializes. Here, too, in the portfolio matrix in stage 3, the laws are again assigned line-by-line and the risk types column-by-column. In the graphical presentation of results, three risk classes can now be formed in the portfolio diagram with A = severe, B = medium, C = slight. For risk class A, a goal/measure tree derivation now takes place in the MITO tool therapy phase in order to generate a to-do list and initiate the necessary measures to reduce the localized risks. A risk measure catalogue is available for the selection of measures.

The user can configure the portfolio matrices used for the **compliance risk analysis** himself; for example, a MITO relevance portfolio matrix could also be used as a starting point to identify the processes in which the risks can occur at all. In a further step, these processes would then be assigned the laws and regulations that apply there, in order to then carry out the 3-stage risk analysis described above in a similar way on an individual process basis. The MITIO analysis, diagnosis and assessment results for the required CMS verification are automatically available in digital form for easy forwarding and further processing.

6.3 Systematic Compliance Management System Auditing

The topic or problem of compliance management, i.e. the cross-process identification, implementation and adherence to legal requirements, rules, standards and regulations with regular monitoring and current updating or improvement of the **compliance management system (CMS)** is constantly expanding. The concept of compliance originated in the economic environment and was coined at the end of the 1980s in the financial sector in the USA. The companies declared themselves in the sense of a self-obligation (**Code of Conduct**) to set up a system that ensured that all employees adhered to the legal framework conditions (to comply). In particular, the abundance of corruption, insider trading and money laundering was addressed. The reason for this voluntary commitment was the high fines imposed by the courts for legal violations. A functioning compliance system was therefore the solution to protect against costly litigation. Furthermore, the courts imposed lower penalties when such a compliance management system was implemented, if the companies could prove that they had made the most important rules and regulations accessible to their employees and monitored their compliance. This compliance management idea initially spread to internationally operating corporations in the energy, pharmaceutical and chemical industries, whose markets are strictly regulated and who needed a system to manage the complexity of constantly changing global regulations. Here too, the aim was to identify the risks in these areas as early as possible before expensive legal proceedings arose.

In recent years, compliance management has become increasingly important in corporate and organizational development due to blatant violations of laws and regulations, especially by internationally active companies. Quite a number of DAX companies have set up a dedicated compliance board position for this purpose. Their task is to ensure compliance with laws and guidelines, but also with voluntary codes in companies.

The purpose of compliance management (CM) as an overarching management guidance tool is to ensure that all process flows in the company operate in a legally effective manner. The area of conflict in the implementation of the compliance management system (CMS) on the basis of the integrated management system framework (IMS) explained below is shown in Fig. 6.4.

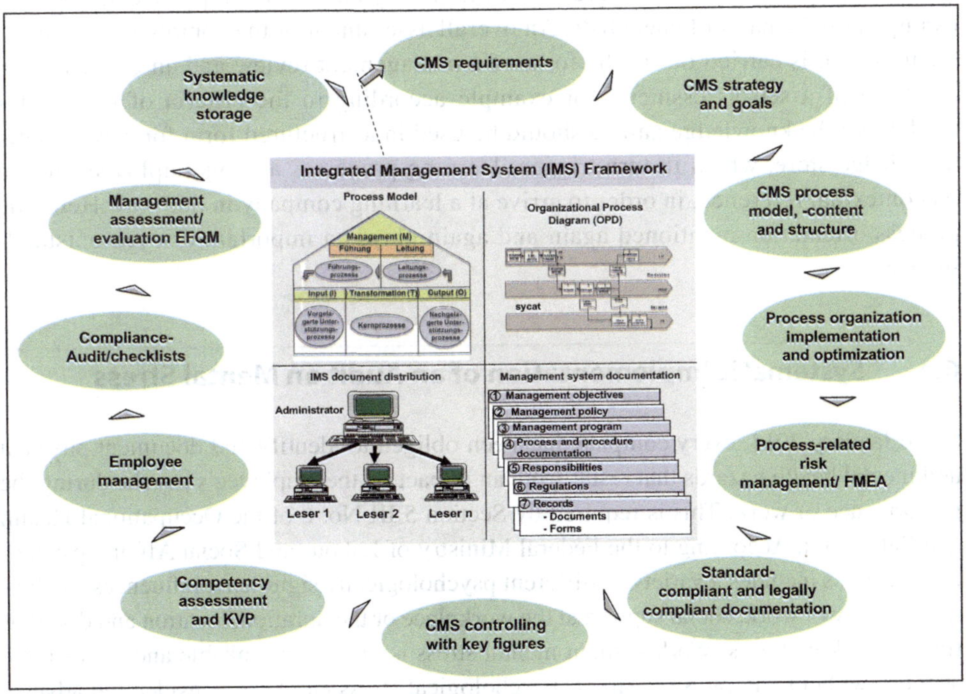

Fig. 6.4 Tension between process-based and knowledge-based compliance management (CM)

CM strategies and objectives are derived from the CMS requirements, but these are always integrated into the overall strategy and corporate policy. The compliance management processes must be identified within the company-specific process model with management, leadership and support processes. These compliance management processes ensure that all processes named in the defined process model can be carried out in a compliance-compliant manner.

The process-related risk management described in the previous point is necessary in order to identify and eliminate compliance-relevant risks. At the same time, importance is attached to a detailed documentation of the compliance management system that conforms to standards and is legally compliant. Part of every management system is the development of controlling indicators – in this case to check the CMS strategies and objectives as well as to measure the fulfilment of objectives. For this purpose, the employees within the processes must be provided with the necessary competencies so that they are able to independently carry out continuous process improvements and rule monitoring. In this context, it is important to have an employee management that motivates the employees to achieve the goals.

The individual requirements that a compliance management system must meet can be reviewed in terms of their degree of fulfillment by means of compliance audits – for example, on the basis of checklists. An overall assessment of the compliance management system is carried out in the form of a management review and an evaluation in the form of a self-assessment, for example according to the criteria of the EFQM model. All the knowledge gained should be used in a structured form for a systematic knowledge store, which in turn triggers learning processes among employees due to its contextual reference, in order to arrive at a learning company in this way. Here, the process orientation mentioned again and again plays an important or even outstanding role.

6.4 Systematic Implementation of an Audit on Mental Stress

Since January 2014, every company has been obliged to identify and document physical and mental health hazards that result from an impact on the employee's psyche during the performance of work. This is required by Section 5 III No. 6 of the Occupational Health and Safety Act. According to the Federal Ministry of Labour and Social Affairs, psychological stress includes a variety of different psychologically significant influences, such as the intensity of work, social support at the workplace or the duration, location and distribution of working hours. Work without mental stress is just as unthinkable and undesirable as work without any physical stress. Psychological stress can have considerable adverse effects on health during the performance of work. For this reason, they must also be taken into account in risk assessment in accordance with the Occupational Health and Safety

Act. In the following, a MITO method-tool-supported risk assessment of mental stress in connection with an analysis of objectives and measures is explained in six steps. These six steps are based on the German occupational health and safety strategy drawn up jointly by the GWA Psyche work programme of the Federal Ministry of Labour and Social Affairs, together with the associated recommendations for implementing the risk assessment of mental stress. They are also based on the action steps for the design of safe and healthy work systems specified by the Association of the Metal and Electrical Industry of North Rhine-Westphalia (Verband der Metall- und Elektro-Industrie NRW).

It should be emphasised at this point that mental stress is conceptually independent of the individual and only the resulting stresses and their consequences are dependent on the individual. Therefore, only person-independent design measures can help to optimise the stress, which are applied to the concrete working conditions and not to the persons. Using standardised checklists for recording mental stress risks with the MITO method tool, appropriate indications can be derived from the result evaluations.

The procedure described below for MITO tool-based hazard analysis and assessment involves the following 6 steps:

1. Work system delimitation and description
2. Process structure analysis with work system assignment
3. Employee-related mental stress analysis
4. Hazard type, consequence, cause analysis (hazard network)
5. Risk prioritization analysis
6. Development of alternative solutions (objectives-measures tree) with to-do list

In these individual six steps for assessing the risks of mental stress factors, different methods stored in the MITO method tool are used. Fig. 6.5 shows the methods and procedures used in the MITO tool-supported mental stress analysis within the six steps.

Step 1 "Delimitation and description of the work system" involves delimiting the area of investigation, in this case the selection of the work system for which the mental stress analysis and assessment is to be carried out. The individual work system should not be considered in isolation, but rather role-based in the associated business process, in order to reduce mental stress in the measures from a holistic design perspective.

For the localization of the work system in step 1 of the hazard analysis, the MITO process model is applied once.

A further delimitation can be made using the four levels of the process hierarchy of the process level model shown.

This work system delimitation is specified in step 2 with a systematic business process analysis, modelling and documentation in order to create a clear reference to the activities and areas in which these mental stresses arise or can occur. The process mapping is role-based according to the globally valid BPMN 2.0 process visualization standard in the Swimlane representation. Here, all process or work steps are graphically represented in their factual temporal logical linkage with all other roles (participants). This process

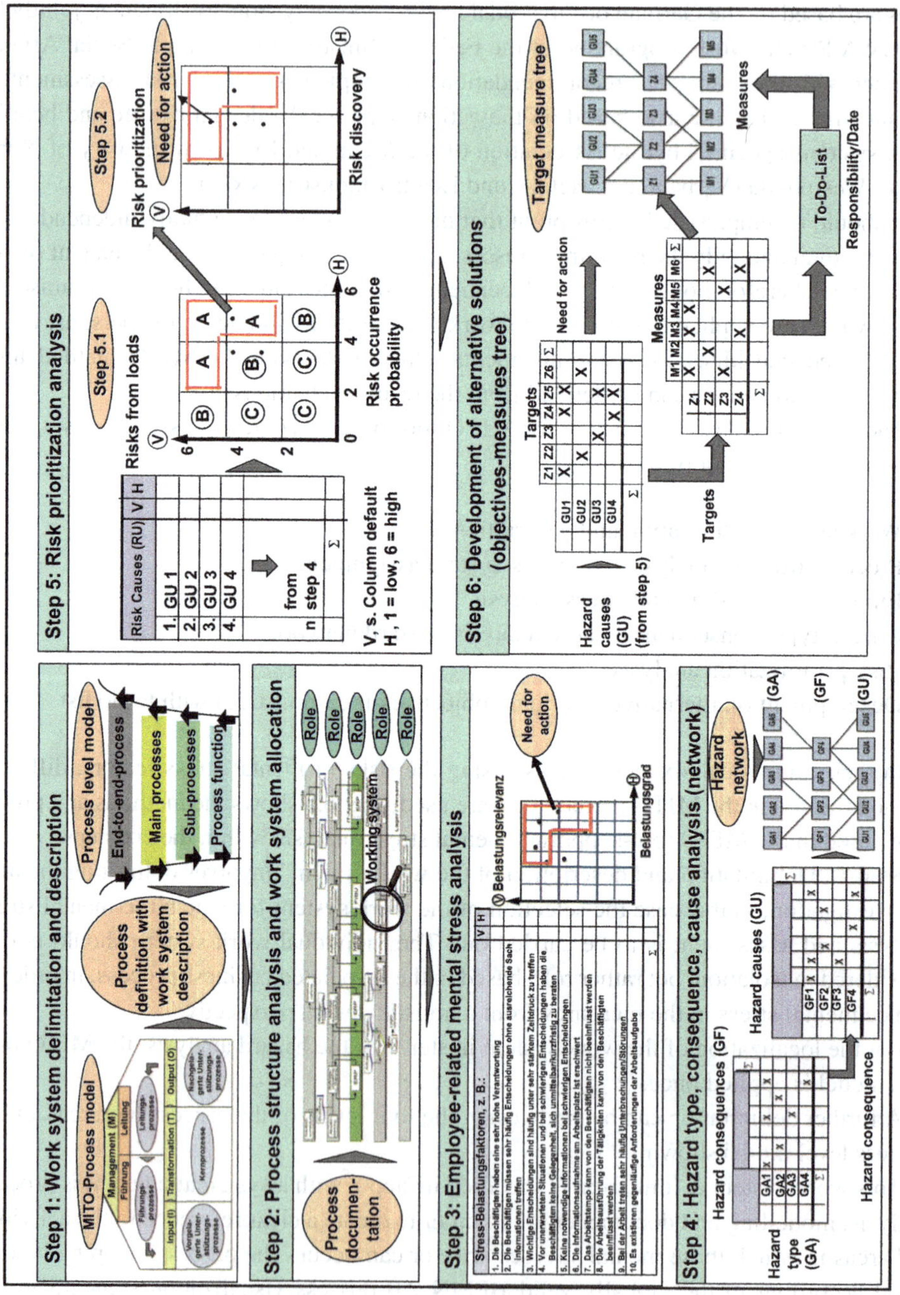

Fig. 6.5 MITO tool-supported workplace-related risk assessment

analysis – often related to the creation of the end-to-end business process – is then also the basis for many other process-oriented optimization and design activities, such as the introduction of Integrated Management Systems (IMS) or the process-related work tasks and requirements analyses mentioned in step 2. These analyses are carried out multi-dimensionally with the MITO method tool. Portfolio reference checklists are already available here to support the user. He is thus able to perform the problem analysis with the help of the tool according to different evaluation variants (BV) with the associated evaluation dimensions, such as evaluation variant (BV) 1: "V = requirement", "H = implementation" or BV 2: "V = effort", "H = benefit" or BV3: "V = importance", "H = urgency" and many other evaluation variants.

The employee-related mental stress factor hazard analysis in step 3 refers to the role-based process structure documented in step 2 with the work system described there. With the support of prepared MITO portfolio matrices, a hazard analysis is now carried out for each work system, e.g. with the assessment dimensions "V = hazard relevance" and "H = **degree of hazard**" by mental stress factors.

Hazard relevance assesses the risk that a hazard (exposure) may occur when performing an activity (task). The grading scale is:

Grade 1: There is no risk of danger when carrying out the activity.
Grade 2: There is a low risk of danger when carrying out the activity.
Grade 3: There is a medium risk of danger when carrying out the activity.
Grade 4: There is a higher risk of danger when carrying out the activity.
Grade 5: There is a serious risk of danger when carrying out the activity.
Grade 6: There is a very high risk of danger when carrying out the activity.

In the case of the degree of risk, the grades are scaled from grade 1 to grade 6 per individual question.

In the MITO Hazard Reference Checklists, a large number of hazard sources within a work system are clustered by:

- Work content/work task/information offered
- Organisation of work
- Working environment
- Workflow
- Social relations
- Work equipment
- Workplace and information design

The presentation of the results in the portfolio diagram shows graphically the need for action, i.e. in which sources of risk which types of risk can lead to mental stress.

After the **hazard identification** of possible mental stress factors in step 3, a hazard prioritization analysis follows in step 4, also supported by the MITO method tool and based on the FMEA method. This involves determining possible hazards per work system or process step with the identification of possible hazard causes and the visualization of hazard relationships, i.e. of hazard consequence, hazard type and hazard cause. This can then be mapped graphically in a hazard network. Based on the determination of possible hazard types – again with the support of MITO portfolio checklists – the hazard sequence and hazard cause are then determined via an assignment matrix cascade formation. For the assignment of hazard consequences to the hazard type and hazard causes, there are prepared hazard consequence and hazard cause catalogs in the MITO method tool that facilitate the selection for the user.

After the assignment in the assignment matrices, the hazard network – also referred to as the consequential cause tree – can be graphically depicted with software support in relation to mental stress. It shows the relationships between which hazard types and which hazard consequences and hazard causes can occur in a network.

In step 5, the localized hazard causes from step 4 are subjected to a risk analysis and risk prioritization. The purpose of this **risk analysis** is to locate potential hazard risks by evaluating the significance, occurrence, and detection or recognition of psychological stress factors, followed by the assignment of avoidance and detection measures in Step 6. Avoidance measures are intended to facilitate optimal process planning in order to minimize the possibility of hazards occurring. Detection measures are intended to locate existing hazard causes or hazard types either automatically or manually before the hazard actually occurs.

The risk analysis carried out with the MITO method tool to localise and prioritise the risks of mental stress factors with the assessment of the extent of damage, probability of occurrence and probability of detection is carried out in step 5 in two analysis sub-steps. The starting point for this is the hazard consequences, hazard types and hazard causes determined in step 4. In step 5.1, the risk assessment focuses on the possible extent of damage and probability of occurrence of the risk due to the localised mental stress factors. As shown in Fig. 6.6, a total of 6 assessment levels are defined for the extent of damage and the probability of occurrence as well as for recognition.

The **risk assessment** in step 5.2 refers to the identification of the hazard cause and/or hazard type that has occurred depending on the risk priority determined in step 5.1, which is divided into 3 ABC classes. This risk priority (RP) replaces the risk priority number RPN from the classical FMEA analysis.

The starting point is therefore – as also shown in Fig. 6.5 in step 5.1 – a portfolio matrix. It is now evaluated with the aid of the MITO method tool according to the evaluation dimensions: "V = risk damage extent" and "H = risk probability of occurrence" with the specified scales of 1–6. The portfolio result diagram now shows the hazard priority on the basis of the associated ABC classification. A risks have the highest hazard priority. Further risk analyses must therefore be carried out here in order to identify these hazards. This is done in step 5.2, where the initial portfolio matrix is also evaluated again, now according to the "V = hazard priority" and "H = hazard recognition" determined in step 5.1. With score 6, hazard detection is hardly possible and with score 5, hazard detection is

Scaling

Ongoing no.	Psychological stress factors, e.g.:
1. Extent of damage of mental stress	
Grade 1	No impairment
Grade 2	Very slight impairment, e.g. fatigue
Grade 3	Low impairment, e.g. sometimes headaches
Grade 4	Moderate impairment, e.g. frequent headaches
Grade 5	High impairment, e.g. weakened immune system
Grade 6	Very high impairment, e.g. heart attack
2. Probability of occurrence	
Grade 1	Unlikely
Grade 2	Very low
Grade 3	Low, occurrence very rare
Grade 4	Moderate, occasional occurrence
Grade 5	High, frequent occurrence
Grade 6	Very high, very frequent occurrence
3. Recognition and evaluation of the hazard	
Grade 1	Always reaction possible
Grade 2	Almost always reaction possible
Grade 3	Frequent reaction possible
Grade 4	Reaction possible under certain conditions
Grade 5	Hardly to little reaction possible
Grade 6	Not possible at all (situation comes suddenly)

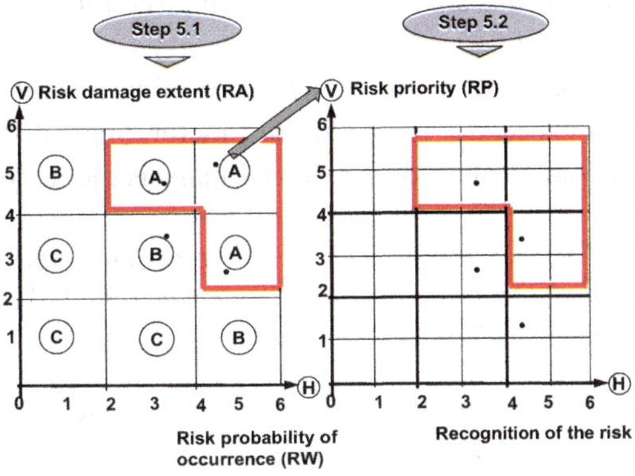

Fig. 6.6 Scaling of scores for risk assessment for the individual stress factors in step 5

very unlikely. Here, too, it can be seen in the presentation of results in the portfolio diagram for step 5.2 that the greatest need for action to eliminate the possible hazard exists in the upper right segments.

This is followed in step 6 by the development of alternative solutions. This is again MITO tool-supported by the derivation of a goals/measures tree with the graphical representation of the measures derivation, similar to the hazard network representation in step 4. As shown, the need for action for risk elimination localized in step 5.2 is linked in the first assignment matrix on the top level with the goals that are to be achieved when the hazard is eliminated, column by column. Again, there is a risk objectives catalogue in the MITO method tool for this purpose, which can be freely configured by the user. After assigning the risk objectives from this objectives catalogue in the assignment matrix on the first level, the assignment matrix on the second level is activated. Here, the previously assigned column-wise objectives in this assignment matrix one level lower are now arranged row by row and the measures required to achieve these objectives are listed column by column.

These measures for the elimination of hazards caused by mental stress factors are also stored in a risk/measure catalogue and can be transferred there to the objectives/measure allocation matrix. In this risk/measure catalogue, the measures are further differentiated according to avoidance and detection measures. For each goal, a to-do list is then created with the assigned measures for hazard elimination with responsibility and deadline. Furthermore, this action requirement goals/measures tree is graphically depicted. The final step is an evaluation of the implementation of the measures, also in the MITO method tool.

Here an evaluation according to efficiency and effectiveness takes place again 2-dimensionally via a portfolio matrix evaluation. Since the entire implementation of all 6 steps is carried out with the support of the MITO method tool, the hazard and risk assessment results are available in digitalised form and can also be used again and again in modified form.

The described implementation of the hazard and risk assessment with the MITO method tool especially for the hazard factor "mental stress" enables the users a simple, fast and safe application of the hazard analysis methodology in 6 steps. Thus, the requirement:

> *The organisation shall develop procedures to assess the hazards arising from work, operations, processes and installations and the risks arising from those hazards, if any, from a health and safety perspective.*

Fully met. The MITO method tool as a method construction kit provides effective support in this regard.

6.5 Systematic Risk Analysis Audit

Very similar to the procedure of a mental stress audit described above is the implementation of a systematic **hazard analysis audit**. The Occupational Health and Safety Act requires the design of safe and healthy work systems. According to § 5 of the Occupational Health and Safety Act, the employer has a fundamental duty to assess working conditions. According to § 6 of the Occupational Health and Safety Act, the results of the assessment, derived measures and their effectiveness must be documented if the company size exceeds 10 employees.

An essential core of a functioning **occupational health and safety management system** is therefore, in accordance with § 5, the continuous performance of stress and hazard assessments for determining the need for action in the area of occupational health and safety as an impetus for the initiation of measures in accordance with § 6. For the performance of stress and hazard assessments, the MITO method tool provides a large number of digitalized elementary analysis, diagnosis and assessment methods in linked form. This makes it very easy for the user to systematically assess each individual process step or each work system with regard to the exposure and hazard situation.

The purpose of hazard analysis is to avoid potential hazards in the workplace from the outset through a systematic assessment, rather than discovering and correcting them after the fact. Prior to the implementation phase of a hazard-prone process or work system, this hazard analysis is carried out to locate potential risks and subsequently analyse the cause and consequences of such hazards and finally document avoidance and detection measures for risk and hazard reduction.

The procedure described below for the MITO tool-supported risk analysis and assessment is based on the action steps for the design of safe and health-related work systems specified by the Association of the Metal and Electrical Industry of North Rhine-Westphalia. This involves the following 6 steps:

1. Work system delimitation and description
2. Process structure analysis with work system assignment
3. Work system hazard analysis
4. Hazard type, consequence, cause analysis (hazard network)
5. Hazard prioritization analysis
6. Development of alternative solutions (objectives-measures tree) with to-do list

Different methods stored in the MITO method tool are used in the individual six hazard identification steps. Fig. 6.7 shows these six steps with the methods and procedures used in the MITO tool-supported hazard analysis.

Step 1 “Delimitation and description of the work system” involves delimiting the area of investigation, in this case the selection of the work system for which the risk analysis and assessment is to be carried out. The individual work system should not be considered in isolation, but rather role-based in the associated business process, in order to reduce the hazards in the measures from a holistic design perspective.

For the localization of the work system in step 1 of the hazard analysis, the MITO process model is applied once. Here, according to the high level structure of the integrated management systems (IMS), the processes are divided into the five MITO model segments:

1. Management processes in the MITO management segment
2. Upstream support processes in the MITO input segment
3. Core processes in the MITO transformation segment
4. Downstream support processes in the MITO output segment and
5. Controlling and CIP processes in the MITO management segment

A further delimitation can be made using the four levels of the process level model shown. Furthermore, this step 1 also includes detailed descriptions of the framework data for performing the analysis using a predefined checklist.

In step 2 “Process structure analysis and work system assignment”, a process analysis and description takes place according to the globally valid BPMN 2.0 process visualization standard in the role-related swimlane representation. Here, all process steps or work systems with the associated roles are mapped chronologically, factually and logically in the Swimlane representation. If there is no process documentation, for example from the quality management system manual, this process documentation must first be created in the swimlane representation.

All norms, rules and design views can then be unambiguously assigned to and described in context, i.e. factually-logically-temporally to this process and the work systems.

The work system hazard analysis in step 3 refers to the role-based process structure documented in step 2 with the work system located there. With the support of prepared

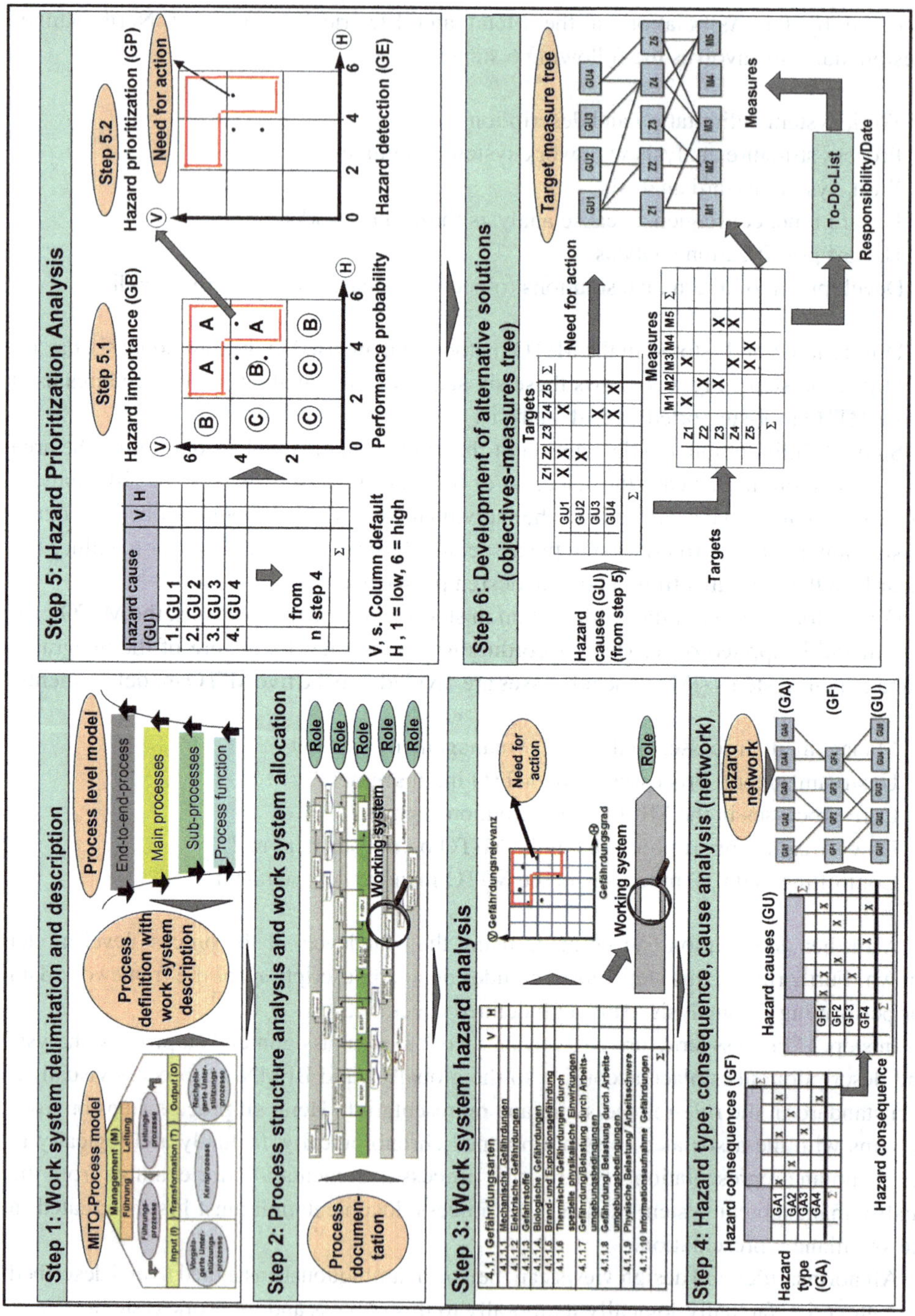

Fig. 6.7 MITO tool-supported workplace-related risk assessment

MITO hazard type portfolio matrices, a hazard analysis is now performed for each work system, e.g. with the assessment dimensions "V = hazard relevance" and "H = degree of hazard". In the case of hazard relevance, the risk is assessed that a hazard ((exposure)) can occur during the execution of an activity (task). For the degree of hazard, a separate scaling from 1 to 6 is specified for each hazard source or cluster.

Grade 1: There is no risk of danger when carrying out the activity.
Grade 2: There is a low risk of danger when carrying out the activity.
Grade 3: There is a medium risk of danger when carrying out the activity.
Grade 4: There is a higher risk of danger when carrying out the activity.
Grade 5: There is a serious risk of danger when carrying out the activity.
Grade 6: There is a very high risk of danger when carrying out the activity.

In these MITO hazard reference checklists, a large number of hazard sources within a work system are clustered by:

- Work content/work task/information offered
- Organisation of work
- Working environment
- Workflow
- Social relationship
- Work equipment
- Workplace and information design

The graphical representation of the results in the portfolio diagram shows graphically the need for action, i.e. which sources of danger pose risks for which types of danger.

This is followed in step 4 by a hazard prioritization analysis, also supported by the MITO method tool and based on the FMEA method. This involves determining possible hazards per work system or process step with the identification of possible hazard causes and the visualization of hazard relationships, i.e. hazard sequence, hazard type and hazard cause. This can then be mapped graphically in a hazard network. Based on the determination of possible hazard types, again with the support of MITO portfolio checklists, the hazard sequence and hazard cause are then determined using an assignment matrix cascade. For the assignment of hazard consequences to the hazard type and hazard cause, there are prepared hazard consequence and hazard cause catalogs in the MITO method tool. To create the hazard cause catalog, it makes sense to perform a hazard cause analysis with the MITO method tool beforehand. Here, typical hazard causes are clustered in the MITO portfolio matrix, for example according to Ishikawa's classic 4 M's methods, i.e. analysed in terms of hazard causes for people, machines, materials and the environment.

After the cascaded assignment of hazard types, consequences and causes in the assignment matrices, the hazard network – also referred to as the consequence-cause tree – can be graphically mapped with software support in step 6. It shows the relationships between which hazard types and which hazard consequences and hazard causes can occur in a network.

In step 5, the localized hazard causes from step 4 are subjected to risk analysis and risk prioritization. The purpose of this risk analysis is to identify potential hazard risks by evaluating significance, occurrence and detection, followed by the assignment of avoidance and detection measures. Avoidance measures are intended to facilitate optimal process planning to minimize the possibility of hazards occurring. Detection measures are intended to locate existing hazard causes or hazard types either automatically or manually before the hazard actually occurs.

The risk analysis carried out with the MITO method tool to localise and prioritise the hazard risks is carried out in step 5 in two analysis sub-steps. The starting point for this is the hazard consequences, hazard types and hazard causes determined in step 4. In step 5.1 the risk assessment focuses on the significance of the hazard causes. A total of 6 assessment levels are defined here for the significance of the hazard consequences. The evaluation of the occurrence of risks stands for the hazard cause. Here, too, a default of 6 occurrence levels is defined.

The risk assessment in step 5.2 refers to the discovery of the hazard cause and/or hazard type that has occurred depending on the hazard priority determined in step 5.1, which is divided into 3 ABC risk classes. This hazard priority (RP), replaces the risk priority number RPN from the classic FMEA analysis.

The starting point is therefore – as also shown in Fig. 6.7 in step 5.1 – a hazard cause or hazard type portfolio matrix. It is now classified using the MITO method tool according to the assessment dimensions: V = significance of the hazard and H = probability of occurrence of the hazard with the given scales of 1–6. The portfolio result diagram now shows the hazard priority with classification into the given ABC priority classification. A-hazards have the highest hazard priority. Further risk analyses must therefore be carried out here in order to detect this hazard. This is done in step 5.2, where the initial portfolio matrix is also evaluated again, now according to the V = hazard priority and H = hazard discovery determined in step 5.1. With a score of 6, hazard detection is hardly possible and with a score of 5, hazard detection is very unlikely. Here, too, it can be seen in the presentation of results in the portfolio diagram for step 5.2 that the greatest need for action to eliminate the possible hazard exists in the upper right segments.

This is followed in step 6 by the development of alternative solutions. This is again MITO tool-supported by the derivation of a goal/measure tree for hazard elimination with the graphical representation of the measure derivation. Similar to the hazard network representation in step 4. As shown in Fig. 1, the need for action for risk elimination localized in step 5.2 is linked in the first assignment matrix on the top level with the goals to be achieved when the hazard is eliminated, column by column. Again, there is a hazard-goal catalog in the MITO method tool for this purpose, which can be freely configured by the user. After assigning the hazard objectives from this objective catalog in the assignment matrix on the first level, the assignment matrix on the second level is activated. Here, the previously assigned column-wise objectives are now arranged row by row in this assignment matrix one level lower and the measures required to achieve these objectives are listed column by column.

These measures for hazard elimination are also stored in a hazard measure catalogue and can be transferred there to the objectives/measure allocation matrix. In this hazard-measure catalogue, the measures are further differentiated according to avoidance and detection measures. For each goal, a to-do list is then created with the assigned measures for hazard elimination with responsibility and deadline. Furthermore, this action requirement goals/measures tree is mapped graphically.

The final step is an evaluation of the implementation of the measures, also in the MITO method tool. Here, an evaluation according to efficiency and effectiveness also takes place in 2 dimensions via a portfolio matrix evaluation. Since the entire implementation of all 6 steps is carried out with the support of the MITO method tool, the risk assessment results are available in digitalised form and can also be used again and again in modified form.

In this case, too, the described performance of the risk assessment with the MITO method tool enables users to apply the risk analysis methodology simply, quickly and safely in 6 steps. As described in Sect. 6.4, a risk assessment is also carried out in the same way with the associated reference portfolio matrices specifically for the risk factor "mental stress". The MITO method tool as a method construction kit provides effective support in this respect.

Another essential advantage of the described approach is that the MITO method tool with the methods contained in it can always be used in the same way to carry out very many other 2-dimensional analyses on a wide variety of problems, for example compliance, stress, CIP, FMEA, competence analyses and many more.

6.6 Systematic Sustainability Management Audit

More and more large – often globally active – companies are increasingly demanding that their suppliers act sustainably in the sense of DIN EN ISO 26000 and also provide evidence of this through prequalification. This proof of the assumption of social *responsibility* or *Corporate Social Responsibility* (CSR) in social, economic, ecological and societal fields is provided through prequalification. This prequalification is the prerequisite for the supplier to be allowed to submit offers to the company at all.

Prequalification is generally understood to mean the provision of evidence for specified requirements in the form of a suitability test. This is an upstream, contract-independent, pre-competitive suitability test of the service providers (suppliers) to fulfill the correspondingly prescribed qualification requirements. CSR prequalification is about providing evidence of social responsibility. The requirements or recommendations are contained in the sustainability standard DIN EN ISO 26000. The DIN ISO 26000 standard offers detailed "Principles of Social Responsibility", each with "Measures and Expectations", as well as detailed "Recommendations for Action for the Organization-wide Integration of Social Responsibility", in English "Corporate Social Responsibility (CSR)".

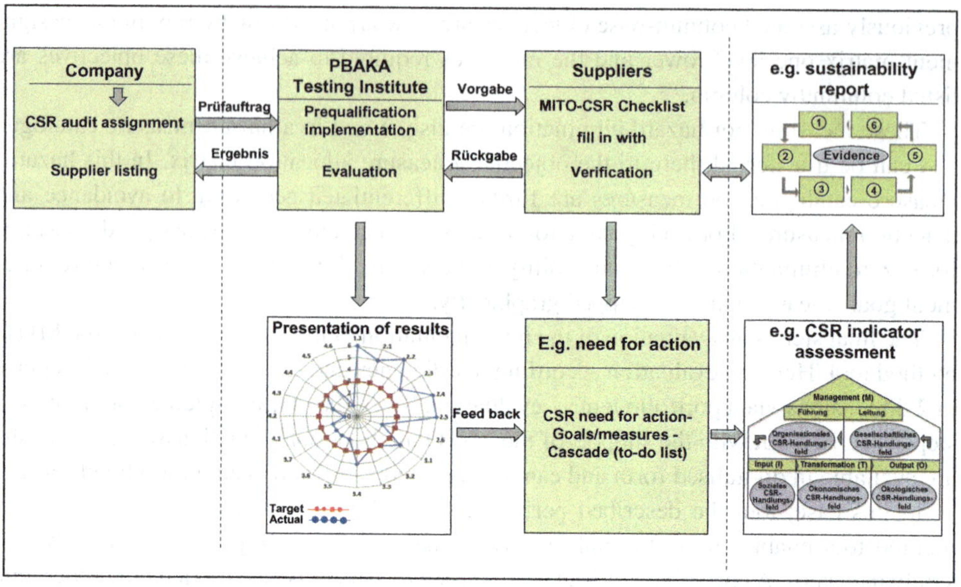

Fig. 6.8 MITO model-related CSR prequalification procedure model

As a rule, however, the prequalification is not carried out by the company that requires this evidence; instead, suitable certification, audit or testing institutes are commissioned to carry out this prequalification for them. With the MITO-related CSR prequalification procedure model shown in Fig. 6.8, this prequalification can be carried out at the suppliers and the result then communicated to the client. If the prequalification is successful, these companies are then included in the client's supplier list.

The starting point is a MITO-CSR pre-qualification checklist, which is to be completed by suppliers with the relevant evidence. The suppliers themselves, who have undergone this prequalification check, receive a detailed evaluation per question as a result, which is displayed graphically in the form of a radar diagram. From this, the need for action in the case of identified deficits can be derived, also with the support of the MITO tool, and the appropriate goals and measures can be assigned, which are necessary in order to demonstrably fulfil the CSR requirement or stakeholder expectation contained in the question.

The method-based procedure for CSR prequalification based on the performance of a CSR core topic audit with the support of the MITO method tool is explained below. Fig. 6.9 shows the individua l analysis and assessment steps for each core topic, which are based on Chap. 7 of DIN ISO 26000. These are

1. Core theme evaluation	In Chapter 6
2. Field of action evaluation	In Chapter 6.4.x
3. Evaluation of recommendations for action (measures)	In Chapter 6.4.2.x
4. Evaluation of key figures	In Chapter 6.4.2.2

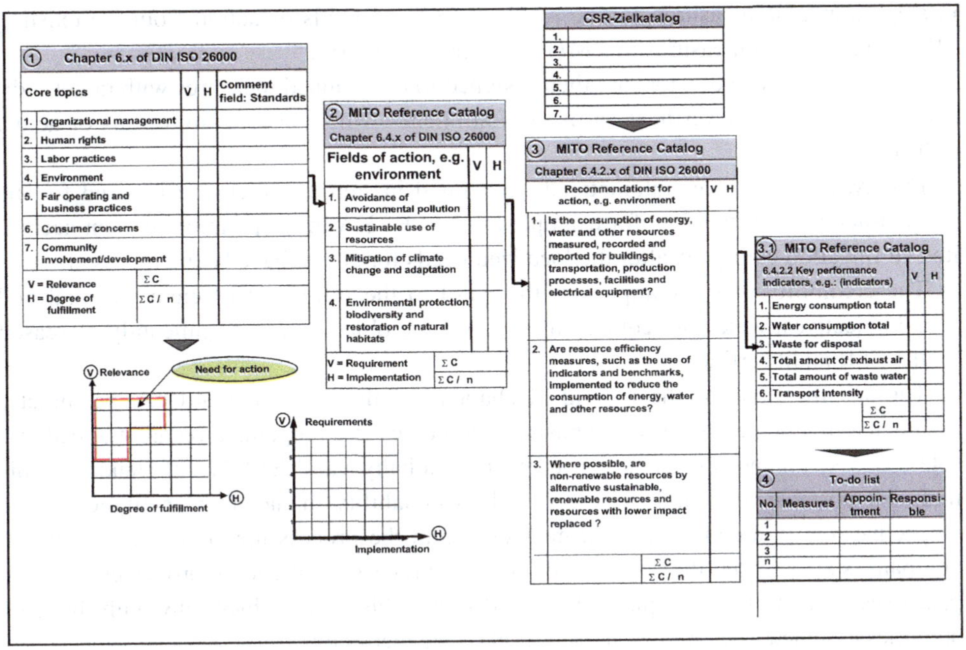

Fig. 6.9 MITO-supported CSR analysis structure according to DIN ISO 26000

The starting point in step 1 for the systematic identification of the need for action are the core issues listed in the sustainability standard in Chap. 7. These are

6.2. Organisational management
6.3. Human rights
6.4. Labour practices
6.5. Environment
6.6. Fair operating and business practices
6.7. Consumer concerns
6.8. Community involvement and development

The individual fields of action for each of these individual core topics are also listed in Chap. 7. Corresponding measures and expectations are assigned to these fields of action, which are also stored in a MITO measures portfolio matrix. In the first step, the stakeholder groups or stakeholders localized from the analysis in Chap. 6 from the Norm ISO 26000 can then be assigned to these core topics in order to subsequently determine via "V = Relevance", "H = Degree of Fulfilment" for which stakeholder which core topic requirements are to be fulfilled.

In step 2 of the procedure, a field of action analysis is now carried out for each stakeholder in the relevant core topic identified in step 1, again according to relevance and degree of fulfilment. The result of step 2 is then a clear statement of which fields of action in which core topics are to be considered further for the various stakeholders. Furthermore, in step 3, specific measures can be assigned to these fields of action from the existing MITO catalogue of measures in a MITO assignment matrix.

In step 3.1, CSR indicators are then assigned to the planned measures with target indicators for subsequent verification of the fulfilment of the measures by means of actual indicators.

Finally, a to-do list is automatically generated in step 4, which can be used for the prequalification certification, for example by the PBAKA in cooperation with an accredited certification company, after the localized needs for action have been processed.

The credibility of the company with regard to the fulfilment of environmental and social objectives, which are equivalent to economic objectives, is significantly increased by the CSR audit certificate.

The specifications of the individual chapters of the CSR standard can be directly assigned to the process steps if the business processes in an organization are mapped in a role-based swimlane representation using the globally valid BPMN 2.0 standard. This makes it possible to assign the individual sustainability management activities to the respective role in a context-related manner within the process hierarchy existing in the company, starting from the company end-to-end process via the main processes and subprocesses down to the workplace. Fig. 6.10 shows this process hierarchy with the CSR activities assigned as examples at each level of the hierarchy.

Using the magnifying glass function in this representation, the CSR requirements specified in the chapters of DIN ISO 26000 are precisely assigned to the individual process steps in the process level under consideration in a factual, temporal and logical manner. In addition, it is then explained, for example in a sustainability report, how these CSR requirements are fulfilled in the company under consideration on a process-related basis. This procedure refers to all processes that take place in a company. At the same time, this Swimlane process representation is always also the reference point for users to make continuous sustainability improvements in the individual roles.

6.7 Systematic Business Model Maturity Assessments

For the fulfillment assessment of the corporate, risk and process governance requirements to be met by management and process owners in the implementation of the digital business model, the MITO method tool provides a comprehensive set of analysis and evaluation tools. The MITO model-supported integrated audit, evaluation and maturity assessment of organizations, processes, projects, programs and much more is a holistic approach to procedure, method and result assessment, which can be most easily explained and implemented by means of a consistent frame work with all the evaluation assessment criteria mentioned therein, which build on each other.

The evaluation framework used here is structured cluster-related by the MITO model with the 5 segments "management, input, transformation, output as well as the customer and supplier segments". Fig. 6.11 shows the evaluation criteria within the segments.

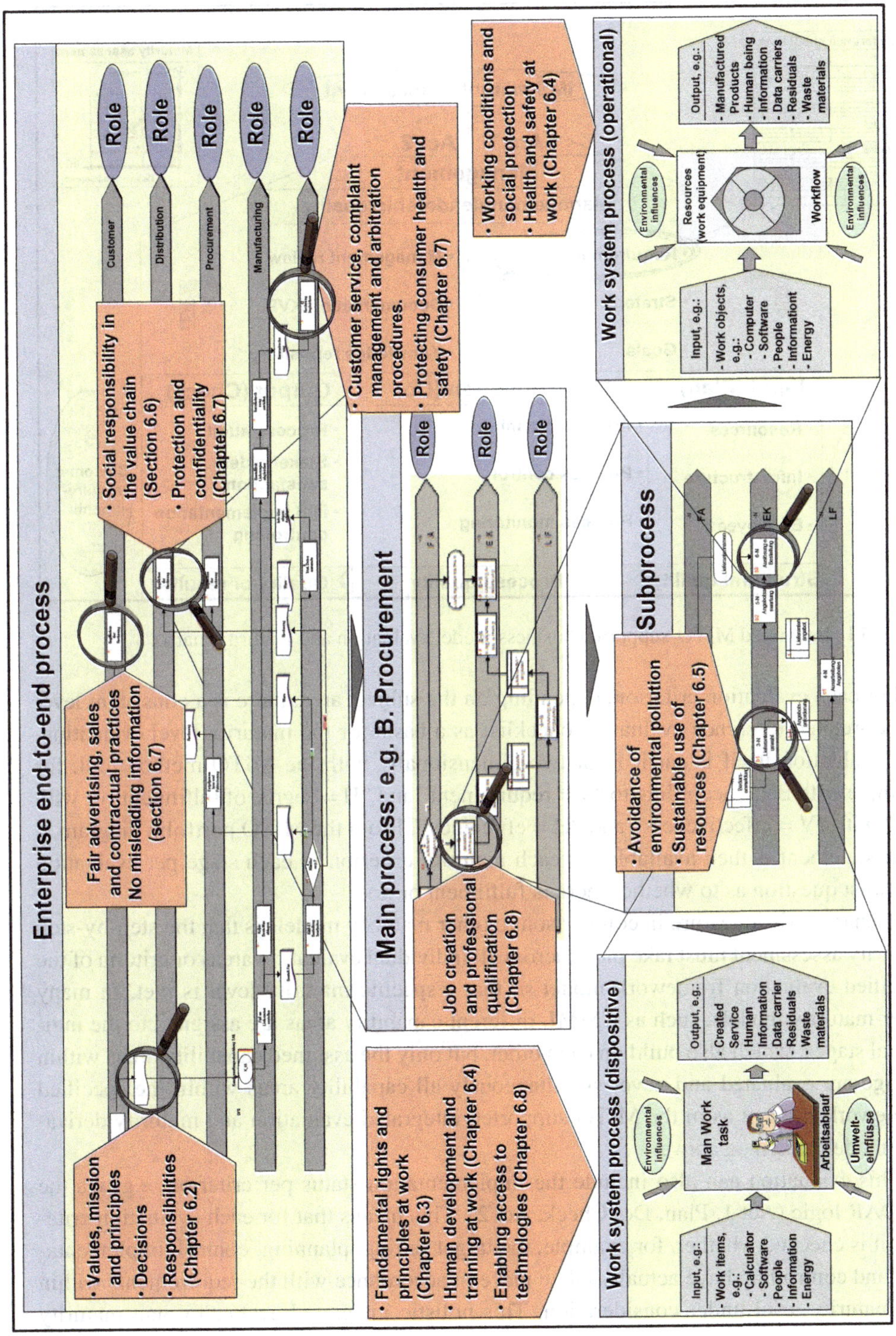

Fig. 6.10 Process-oriented sustainability management activities according to DIN ISO 26000

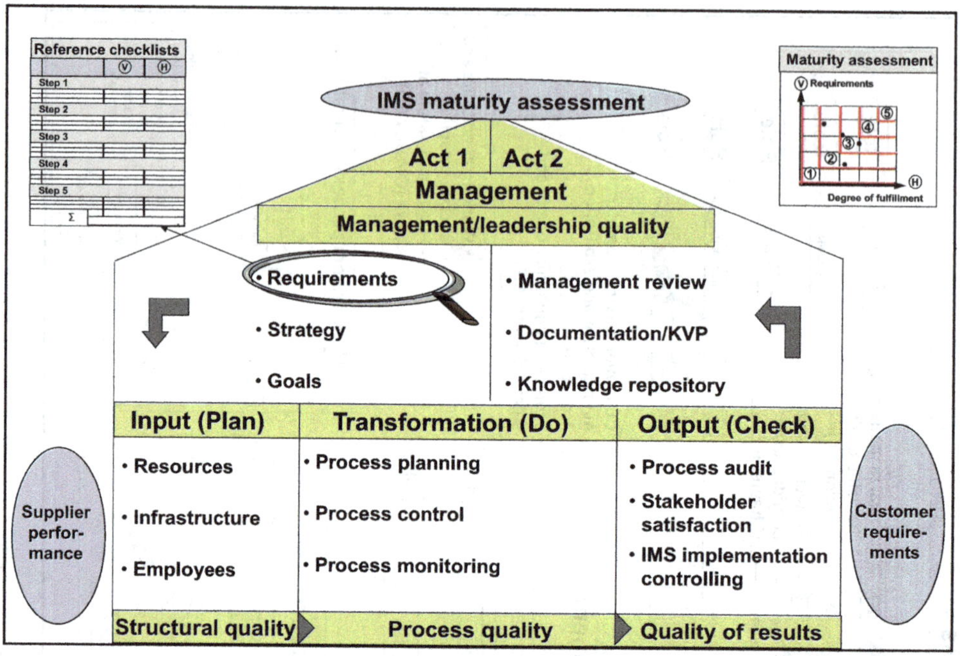

Fig. 6.11 Integrated MITO-supported business model evaluation and maturity matrix

For each evaluation criterion, depending on the subject area, there is a consistent level model-related reference evaluation checklist as a basis for the maturity level evaluation. The evaluation itself is carried out two-dimensionally with the MITO method tool, for example with BV1: according to "V = requirement" and "H = degree of fulfilment" or with BV2 with "V = effectiveness" and "H = efficiency". From the MITO portfolio diagram, a clear statement is then available for each maturity criterion in each stage per evaluation checklist question as to whether there is fulfilment or not.

A characteristic feature in comparison to other maturity models is that the step-by-step maturity assessment must take place across all individual evaluation areas or criteria of the specified evaluation framework model so that a specific maturity level is met. In many other maturity models, such as CMMI, different capability areas are assigned to the individual stages, which also build on each other, but only the assigned capability areas within a stage are evaluated and never simultaneously all capability areas within the specified framework concept as in the MITO-supported integrated evaluation and maturity derivation model described above.

This evaluation can also include the implementation status per criterion, e.g. via the RADAR logic (Act 1, Plan, Do, Check, Act 2). This means that for each evaluation criterion it is checked whether, for example, the target setting, planning, control, implementation and controlling have actually taken place in accordance with the requirements within the maturity level under consideration. This holistic integrated evaluation and maturity assessment is shown with all individual steps using the example of a business model implementation assessment in Fig. 6.12.

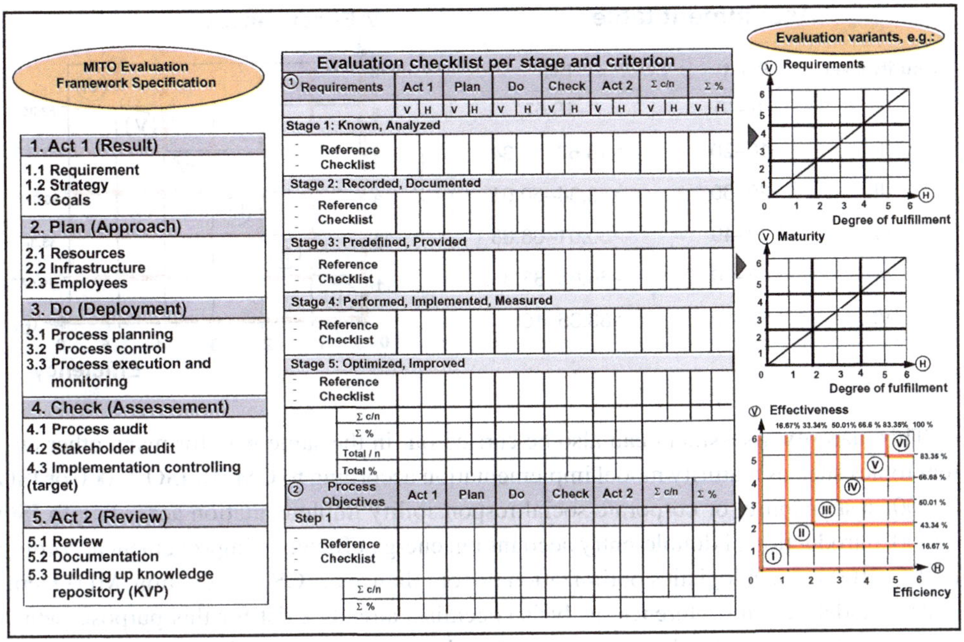

Fig. 6.12 Integrated evaluation and maturity assessment with implementation status assessment

The 5 maturity levels for the above 15 evaluation criteria are defined here as follows:

Level 1 Known, Analyzed
Level 2 Recorded, Documented, Defined
Level 3 Predefined, Provided
Level 4 Performed, Implemented, Measured
Level 5 Optimized, Improved

For each of the 15 evaluation criteria shown, the implementation status in the respective maturity level is shown graphically in the portfolio diagram for each evaluation question.

Another, i.e. separate, form of evaluation and maturity assessment is also possible. In this case, no continuous level evaluation checklists are used, but all requirements are specified per evaluation criterion in the form of a single checklist and these are then evaluated absolutely (number of points) or relatively (%) with regard to the degree of fulfilment. The maturity level assignment itself then takes place using a previously defined assignment table (as shown) according to the absolute or relative evaluation results.

Assignment table

Maturity level	Points	[%]
I	0–10	0–16.67
II	>10–20	>16.67–43.34
III	>20–30	>43.34–50.01
IV	>30–40	>50.01–66.68
V	>40–50	>66.68–83.35
VI	>50–60	>83.35–100

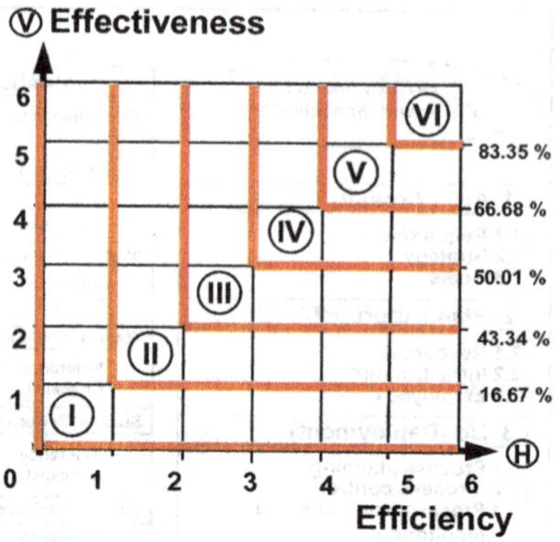

This maturity assessment can also be carried out in the same way for many other current topics such as maturity model implementation according to CMMI, ISO 20000 or ISO 27000, sustainability or corporate social responsibility implementation according to ISO 26000, introduction of double-entry accounting, energy efficiency improvement according to ISO 51000, green logistics optimization or compliance or ICS introduction. MITO templates, guidelines and reference analysis checklists already exist for this purpose, which allow a detailed and compliance-compliant evaluation, auditing and maturity assessment. Localized and documented deviations are systematically eliminated in a cascade as explained above.

Summary

7

Abstract

The necessary change management process described in the introduction as the common thread in this book for the holistic digital business model transformation began in Chap. 2 with the description of the currently existing, i.e. current business model via the answering of the 7 W basic questions with

1. Why? 2. Who? 3. What? 4. How? 5. With what? 6. With whom? 7. Value?

The MITO model segments:

Leadership, Input, Transformation, Output, Direction.

And the downstream customer and upstream partner segments. The change management process was continued in Chap. 3 with the organizational transformation, i.e. the systematic introduction of a process organization via a company-specific process model, also in the MITO model structures.

The processes analyzed, modeled and documented in this process then formed the basis for the cultural transformation in Chap. 4 with the implementation of an integrated management and leadership system via the hierarchical process level model. The balance between soft facts (leadership) and hard facts (management) ensures that the scope for action assigned to employees can be used by them independently with a high level of motivation and qualification on an equal footing with their superiors. This set the stage for the continuation of this change management process in Chap. 5 for a successful digital transformation. This is implemented on the basis of a digital master plan with a large number of digital business innovations to be selected in advance, which were also assigned to the MITO model segments.

H. F. Binner, *Holistic Business Model Transformation*,
https://doi.org/10.1007/978-3-658-37367-2_7

The conclusion of this change management process in Chap. 6 was the method-based review of whether all the requirements of good and meaningful corporate governance (purpose and good or process governance) had been fulfilled and also whether all other requirements from different integrated management system design views or the measures required for them had been successfully implemented.

Figure 7.1 shows a summary of the 10 main steps within this change management process with a focus on systematic process digitization. The four models used within these 10 steps are also shown. First, the MITO model as a control loop-oriented reference and regulatory framework for process-oriented organizational development and design. Secondly, the process level model, which, starting from the end-to-end process on the top level of consideration, represents the company-specific value chain in connection with suppliers and customers with dissection into the lower process levels. This end-to-end process is broken down into the main processes at the level below, the main processes in turn into the sub-processes, and the sub-processes at the lowest level into the individual process step.

The management system to be developed is based on this structure from the top down, and the process management system with feedback to the target system is based on the feedback from the bottom up to the top level.

The swimlane model shows the role-based process mapping in the factual-temporal-logical processing of the individual work steps of the participants among each other according to the worldwide valid BPMN 2.0 process visualization standard.

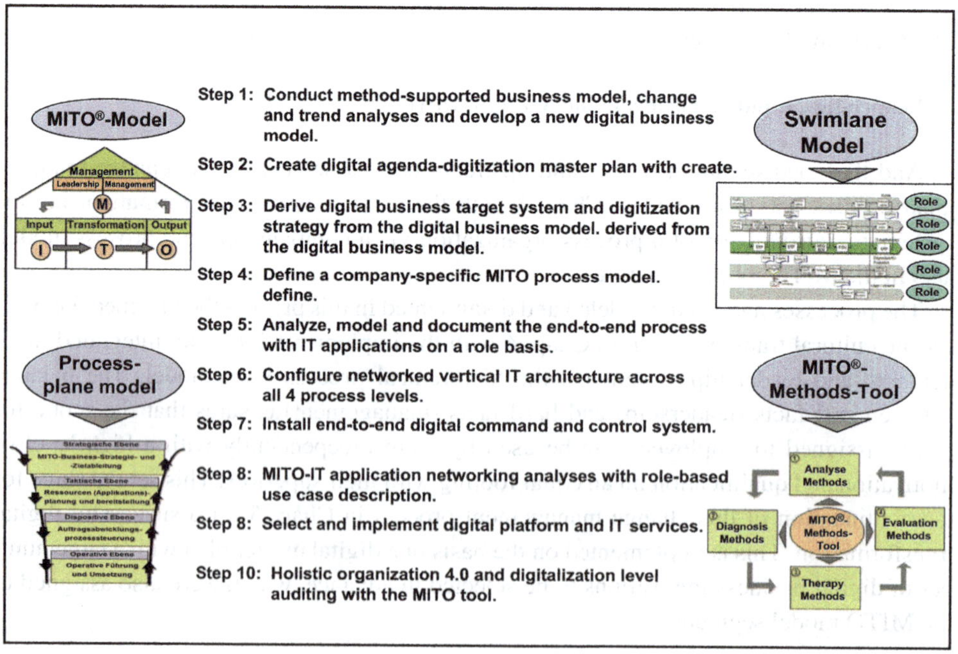

Fig. 7.1 Systematic process digitization in 10 steps

Finally, the superordinate procedure model "analysis, diagnosis, therapy, evaluation" with employment many practice examples explained MITO method tool.

The implementation of the change management process described here with the MITO method tool in 5 chapters can be considered in much more detail. Separate key topics can be formed for each of the 7 basic questions within the business model structures under the main heading "Organization 4.0". In Fig. 7.2, the associated 4.0 design focal points are named.

Each of these individual 4.0 design views in the associated MITO segment can be considered one level deeper in the implementation according to the classical management functions

Design, plan, execute, control, improve.

Be optimized as a control loop with the following contents.

1. From a leadership perspective 4.0, the detailed specifications for successful corporate development with goals, visions and missions are to be developed in accordance with the company's purpose (Why?).
2. From a Human Resources Management 4.0 perspective, the required human resources with the corresponding qualification in the MITO input segment are to be described and provided in a role-related manner (With what?).

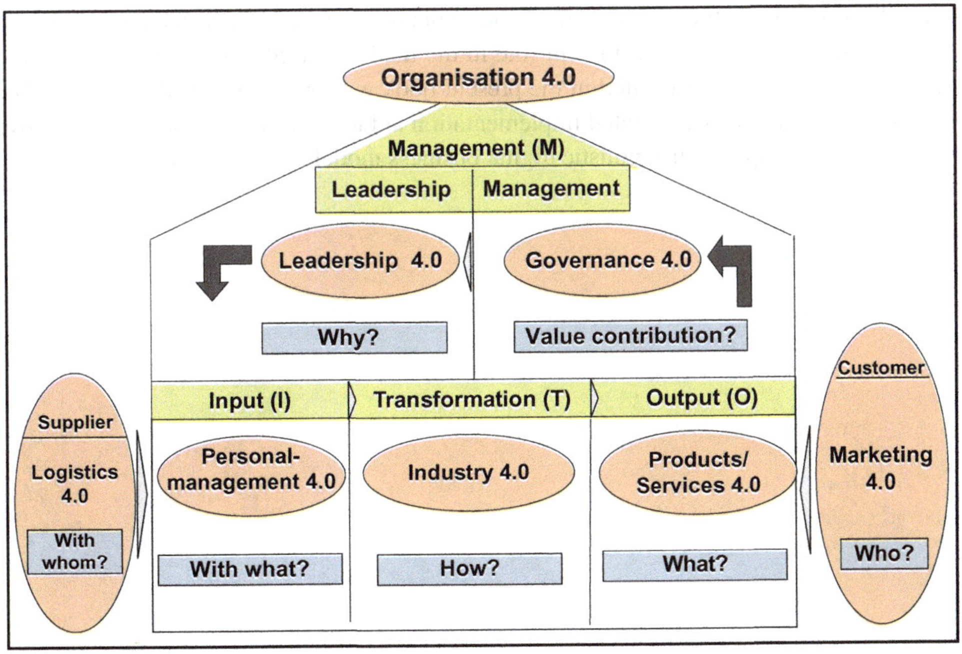

Fig. 7.2 Holistic business model transformation "Organization 4.0"

3. To this end, the right suppliers and partners must be systematically selected from a Logistics 4.0 perspective (With whom?).
4. The core processes in the value chain must be further optimized and digitized from an Industry 4.0 perspective in the transformation segment.
5. The results of smart products and service creation 4.0 (What?) are to be offered and marketed online to the customer in the output segment.
6. The smart offers with additional services should fully deliver the customer value proposition to the customer target group (who?) over the product lifetime.
7. Governance and Compliance 4.0 in the management segment must be reviewed and further improved. If necessary, initiate CIP measures. (What value contribution?).

The common object of knowledge for each of these 4.0 design views is always the company-specific end-to-end process in the role-based BPMN 2.0 process visualization schema with the process hierarchy mapped in the process level model. Whereby the process owner is responsible for the selection of the level of detail, i.e. to determine whether he wants to realize the respective design topic on the end-to-end process, main process, sub-process or even at the process function on site. Due to the factual-temporal-logical description of the process flow with the roles involved, there is a high degree of transparency, which also reveals the interaction between the design view.

Using these four described models, i.e. MITO Business Model, Process Level Model, BPMN Swimlane Model and MITO Tool Procedure Model, the entire Organization 4.0 design tasks can now be processed and documented systematically and interlinked by the control loops within the framework of the explained digital transformation. Here, the MITO method tool plays a prominent role in the method-based implementation of these tasks. This is variously deposited in the present book with many practical examples. The reader thus has a practice-oriented implementation aid to achieve sustainable competitive success in his company via a holistic digital business model transformation approach.

References

Abolhassan, Ferri (Hrsg.): Was treibt die Digitalisierung? Warum an der Cloud kein Weg vorbeiführt. Springer Fachmedien, Wiesbaden 2016.

Aengenheyster, Sandra; Dörr, Kim Miriam (Hrsg.): Praxishandbuch IT-Kommunikation. Verlag Springer Gabler. Springer-Verlag GmbH Deutschland, ein Teil von Springer Nature 2019.

Adams, Marilee: QT – Question Thinking. Die Kunst, die richtigen Fragen zu stellen. Dtv Verlagsgesellschaft, München 2017. ISBN: 978-3-423-26154-8.

Agiplan; Fraunhofer IML; ZENIT 2015: Studie „Erschließen der Potenziale der Anwendung von ‚Industrie 4.0' im Mittelstand", Mülheim an der Ruhr, http://www.bmwi.de/BMWi/Redaktion/PDF/Publikationen/Studien/erschliessen-der-potenziale-der-anwendung-von-industrie-4-0-immittelstand, property=pdf,bereich=bmwi2012, sprache=de,rwb=true.pdf.

Akao, Y.: Quality Function Deployment. Wie die Japaner Kundenwünsche in Qualitätsprodukte umsetzen. Verlag Moderne Industrie, Landsberg/Lech 1992.

Al-Ani, Ayad; Gattermeyer, Wolfgang (Hrsg.): Change-Management und Unternehmenserfolg – Grundlagen – Methoden – Praxisbeispiele. 2., aktualisierte und erw. Aufl., Gabler-Verlag, Wiesbaden, 2001.

Allweyer, Thomas: Geschäftsprozessmanagement, W3L-Verlag, Herdecke/Bochum, 2005.

Antoni, C.: Gruppen- und Teamarbeit, in: Bullinger, H.J./Warnecke, H.J./Westkämpfer, E. (Hrsg.). Neue Organisationsformen im Unternehmen, 3. Neu bearb. Aufl. Berlin 2009, S. 213–223.

Antoni, C.: Gruppen- und Teamarbeit, in: Bullinger, H.J./Warnecke, H.J./Westkämper, E.(Hrsg.) Neue Organisationsformen im Unternehmen, 2. Aufl., Berlin 2003, S. 410–420.

Appelfeller, Wieland; Feldmann Carsten: Die digitale Transformation des Unternehmens: Systematischer Leitfaden mit zehn Elementen zur Strukturierung und Reifegradmessung, Verlag Springer/Gabler, Wiesbasden 2017.

ArbStättV: Verordnung über Arbeitsstätten vom 25.03.1975, Bundesgesetzblatt, Teil I, S. 729–742.

Atiker, Ömer: In einem Jahr digital: Das Praxishandbuch für die digitale Transformation Ihres Unternehmens. Wiley VCH Verlag, Weinheim 2017. ISBN: 978-3527509072.

Atkinson, J.W.: Motivational Determinants of Risk-Taking Behavior. In: Atkinson, J.W., u. a.: A Theory of Achievement Motivation, New York 1966.

Aulinger, Andreas: Roadmap Organisation: Ein Wegweiser für Studierende und Führungskräfte. IOM-Edition Band 2. Herausgegeben von Andreas Aulinger und Markus Heudorf. Steinbeis-Edition, Stuttgart, 1. Auflage 2017. ISBN: 978-3-95663-093-4.

Aupperle, G.; Burr, G.: Der Leitstand: Werkzeuge für dezentrale Organisationsformen. In: PPS Management, 2. Jg. (1997), Industrie Management special, S. P40–P45.

H. F. Binner, *Holistic Business Model Transformation*,
https://doi.org/10.1007/978-3-658-37367-2

Aversa, Paolo; Haefliger, Stefan; Rossi, Alessandro; Baden-Fuller, Charles: From Business Model to Business Modelling: Modularity and Manipulation, in: Baden-Fuller, C.; Mangematin, Vincent (Hrsg.) Business Models and Modelling, Emerald Group Publishing Limited, Bingley 2015.

Ayad Al-Ani/Gettermeyer: Change Management und Unternehmenserfolg. Gabler Verlag. ISBN-13:9783409215015. 04/2001.

Backhaus K./Schneider, H. (2007): Strategisches Marketing, Stuttgart.

Bamberger, I./Worana, T. (2004): Strategische Unternehmensführung, München.

Bardmann, Theodor M.; Groth, Torsten (Hrsg): Organisation, Management und Beratung. Wiesbaden 2001.

Bauernhansl, Thomas 2014: Die Vierte Industrielle Revolution – Der Weg in ein wertschaffendes Produktionsparadigma, in: Bauernhansl, Thomas; ten Hompel, Michael; Vogel-Heuser, Birgit (Hrsg.): Industrie 4.0 in Produktion, Automatisierung und Logistik, Wiesbaden, S. 5–35.

Baumgarten, H.; Risse J.: Logistikbasiertes Management des Produktentstehungsprozesses. In: Hossner R. „Jahrbuch der Logistik" 2001, Düsseldorf 2001, S. 150–156.

Baumol, William J.: Business Behavior, Value and Growth. New York 1967.

BDA Band 3: Zuverlässigkeitssicherung bei Automobilherstellern und Lieferanten – Verfahren und Beispiele, Verband der Automobilindustrie e.V. (VDA), Frankfurt, o.J.

Becker, H./Langosch, I.: Produktivität und Menschlichkeit. Organisationsentwicklung und ihre Anwendung in der Praxis, 5. Aufl. Stuttgart 2002.

Becker, Jörg; Kugeler, Martin; Rosemann, Michael (Hrsg.): Prozessmanagement – ein Leitfaden zur prozessorientierten Organisationsgestaltung. 3., vollst. neu bearb. und erw. Aufl., Berlin u. a., Springer-Verlag, 2002 (627 S.). ISBN 3-540-41325-1.

Becker, L.: Management des Unternehmenswandels am Beispiel der Bayer AG – von der Stammhaus- zur Holdingstruktur, Unterlagen zum Vortrag am 18.5.2006 an der Justus-Liebig-Universität Gießen.

Beierle, Christoph; Kern-Isberner, Gabriele: Methoden wissensbasierter Systeme. Grundlagen, Algorithmen, Anwendungen. 3. Aufl., Wiesbaden 2006.

Bellmann, Vivian K.; Meyer, Gerrit: Prozess- und kompetenzorientierte Methodenauswahl, in: Zeitschrift für wirtschaftlichen Fabrikbetrieb, Hanser Verlag, Februar 2016.

Berger, Roland (2014): Industry 4.0, The new industrial revolution, How Europe will succeed, München, http://www.rolandberger.com/media/pdf/Roland_Berger_TAB_Industry_4_0_20140403.pdf.

Berghaus, Sabine; Back, Andrea (2016): Wie packen Unternehmen die digitale Transformation an? Ratgeber und Fallstudien zur Strategiearbeit für das digitale Zeitalter (Teil 2). Studien-Publikation 2016. T-Systems Multimedia Solutions GmbH (Hrsg.).

Berghaus, Sabine; Back, Andrea (2016): Rollen, Prozesse und Führung in der digitalen Transformation. Ratgeber und Fallstudien zur Strategiearbeit für das digitale Zeitalter. Studien-Publikation 2016.

Bergmann, R./Garrecht, M. (2008): Organisation und Projektmanagement, Heildelberg.

Besanko, D./Dranove, D./Shanley, M./Schaefer, S. (2007): The Economics of Strategy, 4. Aufl., New York.

Best, E./Weth, M.: Geschäftsprozesse optimieren: Der Praxisleitfaden für erfolgreiche Reorganisation, Wiesbaden 2003.

Biehal, Franz; Karner, Günter (Hrsg.): Gratwanderung Change-Management – richtige oder falsche Schritte im Large-System-Change. Neuwied/Kriftel (Taunus). Luchterhand-Verlag, 2000.

Binner, Hartmut F.: SYCAT-Software Tools für die Produktionslogistik. In: Deutsches IEJahrbuch 1991. REFA-Verband für Arbeitsstudien und Betriebsorganisation e.V. Beitrag Nr. 5.

Binner, Hartmut F.: Anforderungsgerechte Datenermittlung für Fertigungssteuerungssysteme. Betriebstechnische Reihe RKW REFA. Beuth Verlag Berlin Köln, 1987.

Binner, Hartmut F.: Integrierter Leitstand-Einsatz in PPS- und BDE-Systemen. Online 92, Kolloquiumsband (Herausgeber), o.O., o.J., 130 Seiten.

Binner, Hartmut F.: Prozesskostencontrolling erfasst Lean-Production-Nutzen. In: CIM-Management 4/93.

Binner, Hartmut F.: Steuerungsgesichtspunkte zur Flexibilitätssteigerung VDI-Z, Zeitschrift für integrierte Produktionstechnik. Spezial: Steuerungen, Oktober 1990, S. 24–34.

Binner, Hartmut F.: Umfassende Unternehmensqualität. Ein Leitfaden zum Qualitätsmanagement. Springer-Verlag, Berlin Heidelberg 1996. 253 Seiten. ISBN 3-540-58995-3.

Binner, Hartmut F.: Integriertes Organisations- und Prozessmanagement. REFAFachbuchreihe Unternehmensentwicklung, 3. Auflage, Carl Hanser Verlag, München 1997 536 Seiten. ISBN 3-446-19174-7.

Binner, Hartmut F.: Organisations- und Unternehmensmanagement. Reihe: Organisationsmanagement und Fertigungsautomatisierung (Bd. 1). Carl Hanser Verlag, München 1998. 256 Seiten. ISBN 3-446-19375-8.

Binner, Hartmut F.: Prozessorientierte Arbeitsvorbereitung. Reihe: Organisationsmanagement und Fertigungsautomatisierung (Bd. 2)., 2. verbesserte Auflage. Carl Hanser Verlag, München Wien 2003. 372 Seiten u. 214 Bilder. ISBN 3-446-22363-0.

Binner, Hartmut F.: Prozessorientierte TQM-Umsetzung. Reihe: Organisationsmanagement und Fertigungsautomatisierung (Bd. 3). 2. (verbesserte und aktualisierte) Auflage. Carl Hanser Verlag, München Wien 2002. 364 Seiten. ISBN 3-446-21852-1.

Binner, Hartmut F.: Strategie des General-Management. Ausweg aus der Krise. Springer-Verlag 1993. 400 Seiten. ISBN 3-540-57021-7.

Binner, Hartmut F.: Unternehmensübergreifendes Logistikmanagement. Reihe: Organisationsmanagement und Fertigungsautomatisierung. Carl Hanser Verlag, München Wien 2001/2002. 306 Seiten u. 196 Bilder. ISBN 3-446-21675-8.

Binner, Harmut F.: Handbuch der prozessorientierten Arbeitsorganisation. (UT: Methoden und Werkzeuge zur Umsetzung). REFA-Fachbuchreihe „Unternehmensentwicklung". 3. Auflage. Carl Hanser Verlag, München Wien 2008. Copyright REFA Bundesverband e. V. Darmstadt. REFA-Bestell-Nr. 280052. 1036 Seiten. ISBN 978-3-446-41627-7.

Binner, Hartmut F.: Managementleitfaden „Auf dem Weg zur Spitzenleistung", 1. Auflage, Carl Hanser-Verlag, München Wien, Nov. 2005, 267 Seiten. ISBN 3-446-40481-3.

Binner, Hartmut F.: MITO-Methoden-Tool – Die neue Qualität der Ganzheitlichen Prozessoptimierung ZWF 1-2/2012. Carl Hanser-Verlag, München Wien.

Binner, Hartmut F.: Business Analyst und Business Process Professional, die neuen Organisatorenprofile in prozessorientierten Organisationen. zfo 2011/12.

Binner, Hartmut F.: Pragmatisches Wissensmanagement – Systematische Steigerung des intellektuellen Kapitals. REFA-Fachbuchreihe „Unternehmensentwicklung". 1. Auflage. Carl Hanser Verlag, München Wien 2007. 896 Seiten. ISBN 978-3-446-41377-1.

Binner, Hartmut F.: Methoden-Baukasten für ganzheitliches Prozessmanagement. Systematische Problemlösungen zur Organisationsentwicklung und -gestaltung. 1. Auflage 2015, 246 Seiten, broschiert, Springer Gabler Verlag, Berlin u. a. ISBN 978-3-658-08408-0.

Binner, Hartmut F./Schnägelberger, S.: Prozessmanagement-Tools: Große Marktübersicht über den BPM-Markt, in: zfo 02/2011 (80. Jg.), S. 121–124.

Bitkom e.V.: In 10 Schritten digital: Ein Praxisleitfaden für Mittelständler, #kmudigital. Berlin 2017.

Bitkom Research (Hrsg.): DIGITAL ENGINEERING, Agile Produktentwicklung in der deutschen Industrie. Eine Studie von Bitkom Research im Auftrag von Autodesk. Berlin, 2017.

Blom, Frank; Harlander, Norbert A.: Logistik-Management. Der Aufbau ganzheitlicher Logistikketten in Theorie und Praxis (Band 22 der Reihe „Die Betriebswirtschaft – Studium +

Praxis“). expert verlag Renningen-Malmsheim, ISBN 3-8169-1715-1 und Linde Verlag Wien, 2000. ISBN 3-85122-890-1.

Blonski, Harald/Stausberg, Michael: Prozessmanagement in Pflegeorganisationen. Grundlagen – Erfahrungen – Perspektiven. Verlag Schlütersche GmbH & Co., Hannover, 2003.

Bodo Wiegand, Philip Franck: Lean Administration – Die Analyse. So werden Geschäftsprozesse transparent. Workbook, Lean Management Institut 2004, ISBN 978-3-9809521-0-1.

Bogle, John C.: Reflections an CEO Compensation. In: Academy of Management Perspectives. 22. Jg. 2008, Nr. 2, S. 21–25.

Bokranz, R.: Personalbedarfsplanung, in: Gaugler, E. et al. (Hrsg.): Handwörterbuch des Personalwesens, Stuttgart 2004, Sp. 1380–1394.

Borell, Nicki: Das Industrie 4.0-Arbeitsbuch: Sind Digitalisierung, Industrie 4.0 und Disruption unterschiedliche Dinge? Verlag tredition, Hamburg 2016.

Borg, I.: Mitarbeiterbefragungen – kompakt, Göttingen 2002.

Braunmiller, Ulrich; Ziegahn, Karl-Friedrich: BMBF-Projekt – Vision Logistik, Teilprojekt Umsetzung ökologischer und kreislaufwirtschaftlicher Anforderungen in die Modellierung logistischer Systeme, Endbericht Verb.-Nr.: 00002322, Förderkennz.: 02PF3008/7.

Brehm, Carsten R.: Organisatorische Flexibilität der Unternehmung. Bausteine eines erfolgreichen Wandels. Wiesbaden 2003.

Bruhn, Manfred; Hadwich, Karsten (Hrsg.): Dienstleistungen 4.0: Konzepte – Methoden – Instrumente. Band 1: Forum Dienstleistungsmanagement. Band 2: Geschäftsmodelle – Wertschöpfung – Transformation. Verlag Springer Gabler, Berlin Heidelberg 2017. ISBN Band 1: 978-3658175498. ISBN Band 2: 978-3658175511.

Brunner, Franz J.: Japanische Erfolgskonzepte, 3. Überarbeitete Auflage, Carl Hanser Verlag, München 2014.

Buchholz, Ulrike; Schach, Annika; von der Haar, Victoria: Werte und Metaphern in der Unternehmenskommunikation. Sensemaking, Mindset, Sprache. Verlag Springer VS. Springer Fachmedien Wiesbaden GmbH, ein Teil von Springer Nature 2019.

Bühner, Rolf (2004): Betriebswirtschaftliche Organisationslehre. 10. Aufl., München und Wien.

Bundesministerium für Wirtschaft und Energie (BMWi) (Hrsg.) 2015: Memorandum der Plattform Industrie 4.0, Berlin, https://www.bmwi.de/BMWi/Redaktion/PDF/M-O/memorandung-industrie-4-0,property=pdf,bereich=bmwi2012,sprache=de,rwb=true.pdf.

Bundesministerium für Wirtschaft und Energie 2017: Den digitalen Wandel gestalten. BMWI. Online verfügbar unter https://bmwi.de/Redaktion/DE/Dossier/digitalisierung.html.

Bundesministerium für Wirtschaft und Energie (BMWi) 2014: Monitoring Report Digitale Wirtschaft 2014, Berlin, http://www.bmwi.de/BMWi/Redaktion/PDF/Publikationen/monitoring-report-digitale-wirtschaft-2014-langfassung,property=pdf,bereich=bmwi2012,sprache=de,rwb=true.pdf.

Bungrad, W.: Mitarbeiterbefragungen, in: Jöns, I,/Bungrad, W. (Hrsg.): Feedbackinstrumente im Unternehmen: Grundlagen, Gestaltungshinweise, Erfahrungsberichte. Wiesbaden 2005, S. 162–175.

Champlin, Brett: ‘Business Process Management Professionals’, BPM Strategies, October 2006.

Connected Industry (Hrsg): Industrie 4.0 & Digitalisierung. Data Leader Guide 2017. Compete and Lead in the Digital World. Beuth Verlag, Berlin, 2017.

Cornelius, Siewerin: Das A und O der Telearbeit: Information, Kommunikation und Kooperation. Niedersächsisches Innenministerium 04/2001.

Corsten, Hans; Gössinger, Ralf; Schneider, Herfried: Grundlagen des Innovationsmanagements, Vahlen Verlag, München 2006.

Cox D.; Hoover J.: Führungsqualität in Krisenzeiten, Carl Hanser Verlag, München, 1995.

Dalluege, C.-Andreas: IQM – Integriertes Qualitätsmanagement in der Aus- und Weiterbildung: Selbstbewertung für EFQM, DIN EN ISO 9001 und andere QM-Systeme. Bertelsmann Verlag. Bielefeld 2008.

Demont, A., Paulus-Rohmer, D.: Industrie 4.0-Geschäftsmodelle systematisch entwickeln. In: Schalmo, D. et al.: Digitale Transformation von Geschäftsmodellen, Wiesbaden 2017.

DIN 31051: Instandhaltung, Begriffe und Maßnahmen, Beuth Verlag, Berlin, o.J.

DIN 55350, Teil 11: Begriffe der Qualitätssicherung und Statistik, Grundbegriffe der Qualitätssicherung. Berlin, Mai 2008.

DIN ISO 10012-1: Forderung an die Darlegung der Qualitätssicherung von Prüfmitteln; Teil 1: Management von Prüfmitteln. Nov. 2003, DIN Deutsches Institut für Normung e.V., Berlin.

DIN ISO 19011: (Deutsche Norm) – Leitfaden f. Audits von QM- und/oder Umweltmanagementsystemen, März 2003. DIN e. V., Berlin. Beuth-Verlag GmbH, 10772 Berlin.

DIN EN ISO 9004:1: Qualitätsmanagement und Elemente eines Qualitätssicherungssystems – Leitfaden für Qualitätsverbesserung. Nov. 2003, DIN Deutsches Institut für Normung e.V., Berlin.

Dombrowski, Uwe: Arbeitswissenschaft in Deutschland. Industrial Engineering 3/2012, http://www.refa.de.

Doppler, Klaus; Lauterburg, Christoph: Change Management – Den Unternehmenswandel gestalten. 9. Aufl., Frankfurt am Main/New York. Campus-Verlag, 2000.

Doppler, K./Fuhrmann, H/Lebbe/Waschke, B./Voig, B.: Unternehmenswandel gegen Widerstände: Chance Management mit den Menschen. Frankfurt/New York, o.J.

Doppler, Klaus; Lauterburg, Christoph: Change Management – Den Unternehmenswandel gestalten. 9. Aufl., Frankfurt am Main/New York. Campus-Verlag, 2000.

Doppler, K./Lauterburg, Ch. (2008): Change Management. Den Unternehmenswandel gestalten. 12. Auflage, Frankfurt und New York.

Dorschel, Joachim (Hrsg.): Praxishandbuch Big Data. Wirtschaft – Recht – Technik. Springer Gabler Fachmedien GmbH. Wiesbaden 2015. ISBN-13: 978-3-658-07288-9.

Dostal, Werner; Kupka, Peter (Hrsg.): Globalisierung, veränderte Arbeitsorganisation und Berufswandel. BeitrAB 240. Bundesanstalt für Arbeit. Nürnberg, 2001. ISSN 0173-6574.

Ebert, Bernd: Prozessoptimierung bei Industrie 4.0 durch Risikoanalysen Gefährdungen erkennen und minimieren. Verlag Springer-Verlag, Belin Heidelberg 2018.

Ecker, Frieder, Kohstall Thomas, Marggraf Michael (Hrsg.): Arbeitsschutz besser managen. Organis. u. Integr. von Sicherheit u. Gesundheitsschutz im Unternehmen (Lose BlattLiteratur Sammlg.). Aktueller Stand: 6. Akt./Erg.-Lieferung April 2000. TÜV Verlag GmbH Köln, 2000, ISBN 3-8249-0584-1.

Eder, Martin: Digitale Evolution: Wie die digitalisierte Ökonomie unser Leben, Arbeiten und Miteinander verändern wird. Springer Fachmedien Wiesbaden GmbH 2017. ISBN: 978-3-658-16284-9.

Ehrmann, T. (2006): Strategische Planung, Heildelberg.

Ehrmann, Harald: Kompakt-Training „Balanced Scorecard" (Serie: Kompakt-Training Praktische Betriebswirtschaft (Hrsg.) K. Olfert). 3., aktualis. und erweiterte Auflage. Friedrich Kiehl-Verlag, Ludwigshafen 2003. ISBN 3-470-51763-0.

Emrich, Ch.: Erfolgsfaktoren des Business Reengineering-Managements – Theoretische Ableitung und empirische Messung. Dissertation Inivers. Hamburg 2004. *EN ISO 19011 (Europäische Norm) – Deutsche Fassung*: Leitfaden f. Audits von QM und/oder Umweltmanagementsystemen (ISO 19011:2002), Okt. 2002. Europ. Komitee f. Normung, Management-Zentrum, Brüssel.

Erdmann, Jörg: Integriertes Prozessmanagement. Ein multidimensionaler Ansatz für das Management von Prozessen in Unternehmen. Verlag: Books on Demand GmbH, 2000.

Erlach, K.: Wertstromdesing: Der Weg zu schlanken Fabrik, Berlin/Heidelberg/New York, o.J.

Erner, Michael (Hrsg.): Management 4.0-Unternehmensführung im digitaler Zeitalter. Springer-Verlag GmbH Deutschland, ein Teil von Springer Nature 2019.

Falkenreck, Christine: Digitalisierungsprojekte erfolgreich planen und steuern. Kunden und Mitarbeiter für die digitale Transformation begeistern. Springer Fachmedien Wiesbaden GmbH, ein Teil von Springer Nature, Wiesbaden 2019.

Feddern, Uwe; Knppertz, Thilo; Dr. Krings, Kai; BPM&O GmbH Whitepaper. Köln, Dezember 2017.

Feddern, Uwe; Knppertz, Thilo; BPM&O GmbH: (Digitale) Strategie prozessorientiert umsetzen. Wie sich mit prozessorientierten Methoden die Unternehmensstrategie schneller, effektiver und nachhaltiger umsetzen lässt. BPM&O White Paper. Köln, Dezember 2017.

Fischer, Franz; Scheibeler, Alexander A. W.: Handbuch Prozessmanagement – Effizienzsteigerung mit ISO 9001+9004; 1000 Beispiele aus der Praxis. Carl Hanser Verlag, München Wien 2003. 680 Seiten. ISBN 3-446-21925-0.

Fischer, Joachim; Hluchy, Ralf (Hrsg.): Prozessteams als eigenständige Akteure im Unternehmen. Physika-Verlag. Heidelberg, 2001. ISBN 3-7908-1354-0.

Fischermanns, Guido; Liebelt, Wolfgang: Grundlagen der Prozessorganisation, 5. Aufl., Gießen. Schmidt-Verlag, 2000.

Fischermanns, Guido: Praxishandbuch Prozessmanagement, Gießen, Verlag Dr. Götz Schmidt, 2009.

Fleischmann, Albert, Oppl, Stesfan; Schmidt, Werner; Stary, Christian: Ganzheitliche Digitalisierung von Prozessen Perspektivenwechsel – Design Hinging – Wertegeleitete Interaktion. Verlag Springer Vieweg. Wiesbaden 2018.

Foegen, Malte: Der Ultimative Scrum Guide 2.0, wibas, Darmstadt 2014.

Föll-Laubengeiger, Christoph: Arbeitsorganisation und integrative Materialwirtschaft, o.J.

Forschungsunion Wirtschaft und Wissenschaft; acatech 2013: Umsetzungsempfehlungen für das Zukunftsprojekt Industrie 4.0, Abschlussbericht des Arbeitskreises Industrie 4.0., Frankfurt am Main, https://www.bmbf.de/files/Umsetzungsempfehlungen_Industrie4_0.pdf.

Franken, Rolf: Grundlagen einer handlungsorientierten Organisationstheorie, o.J.

Fraunhofer IAO 2013: Produktionsarbeit der Zukunft – Industrie 4.0, Stuttgart, http://www.produktionsarbeit.de/content/dam/produktionsarbeit/de/documents/Fraunhofer-IAO-Studie_Produktionsarbeit_der_ZukunftIndustrie_4_0.pdf.

Fraunhofer IPA: Strukturstudie 2014: „Industrie 4.0 für Baden-Württemberg", Studie im Auftrag des Ministeriums für Finanzen und Wirtschaft Baden Württemberg, https://mfw.baden-wuerttemberg.de/fileadmin/redaktion/m-mfw/intern/Dateien/Downloads/Industrie_und_Innovation/IPA_Strukturstudie_Industrie_4.0_BW.pdf.

Frese, Erich; Theuvsen, Ludwig: Organisationsmanagement: Wissensbasen und Erscheinungsformen. In: Organisationsmanagement: Neuorientierung der Organisationsarbeit, hrsg. von Erich Frese, Stuttgart 2000, S. 7–40.

Freund, Jakob; Götzer, Klaus: Vom Geschäftsprozess zum Workflow. München, Carl Hanser Verlag, 2008.

Freund, Jakob; Rücker, Bernd: Praxishandbuch BPMN 2.0, 3. Auflage, Carl Hanser Verlag, München 2012.

Friedrichs, G./Groebler, G./Kyaw von F.: Dramaturgie einer Reorganisation, in: Personalführung. 11/2009.

Frost, Jetta/Osterloh, Margit: Prozessmanagement als Kernkompetenz. Wie Sie Business Reengineering strategisch nutzen können. Gabler-Verlag, Wiesbaden, 2003.

Frost, Jetta/Osterloh, Margit: Prozessmanagement als Kernkompetenz. Wie Sie Business Reengineering strategisch nutzen können. Gabler-Verlag, Wiesbaden, 2003.

Füermann, Timo; Dammasch, Carsten: Prozessmanagement – Anleitung zur Steigerung der Wertschöpfung. 2. vollständig überarbeitete Auflage. Carl Hanser Verlag, München Wien 2002. 128 Seiten. ISBN 3-446-21916-1.

Gadatsch, A.: Grundkurz Geschäftsprozess-Management, 4. Aufl. Wiesbaden 2005.

Gadatsch, Andreas: Management von Geschäftsprozessen. Methoden und Werkzeuge für die IT-Praxis: Eine Einführung für Studenten und Praktiker. Braunschweig, Wiesbaden, 2001.

Gadatsch, Andreas: Grundkurs Geschäftsprozess-Management, Wiesbaden, Vieweg Verlag, 2003.

Gaitanides, Michael: Prozessorganisation. 2. Aufl., München 2007.

Gassmann, Oliver; Frankerberger, Karolin; Csik, Michaela: Geschäftsmodelle entwickeln. 55 innovative Konzepte mit dem St. Galler Business Model Navigator, 2. Überarbeitete Auflage, 398 Seiten, Carl Hanser Verlag München, 2017.

Gattermeyer, W./Al-Ani, A.: Entwicklung und Umsetzung von Chance Management-Programmen, in: Gattermeyer, W./Al-Ani, A.(Hrsg): Chance Management und Unternehmenserfolg: Grundlagen – Methoden – Praxisbeispiele, 2., aktualisierte und erweiterte Aufl., Wiesbaden 2001, S. 13–43.

Gatzki, C./Gatzki, Y. (2006): Economic Value Added. Steigerung des Unternehmenswertes mittels Werttreiberbaum und Maßnahmenkatalog, in: Controller Magazin, Herf 5, S. 418–426.

Gebert, Diether: Führung und Innovation. Stuttgart 2002.

Geitner U.W.: Betriebsinformatik für Produktionsbetriebe, 2. überarb. Auflage. REFA-Fachbuchreihe Betriebsinformatik. Carl Hanser Verlag München, 6 Teilbände, darunter besonders wichtig: Georgi, Dominik: Wirtschaftlichkeit des Qualitätsmanagements, o.J.

Gerstbach, Ingrid: Design Thinking im Unternehmen: Ein Workbook für die Einführung von Design Thinking (Dein Business). Gabal Verlag, Offenbach 2016.

Gierhake, Olaf: Integriertes Geschäftsprozessmanagement. Effektive Organisationsgestaltung mit Workflow-, Workgroup- und Dokumentenmanagement-Systemen. Vieweg Verlag. Braunschweig/ Wiesbaden 2000. ISBN 3-528-25665-6.

Gladen, Werner: Performance Measurement: Controlling mit Kennzahlen, Springer Gabler Verlag, Wiesbaden 2014.

Glauner, Friedrich: Zukunftsfähige Geschäftsmodelle und Werte – Strategieentwicklung und Unternehmensführung in disruptiven Märkten. Verlag Springer Gabler, Berlin Heidelberg 2017. ISBN: 9783662492420.

Gloger, Boris: Scrum. Produkte zuverlässig und schnell entwickeln. 3. Auflage, Hanser Verlag, München 2011.

Gomez, P./Fasnacht, D./Wasserer, C./Waldispühl, R.: Komplexe IT-Projekte ganzheitlich führen. Ein Praxiserprobtes Vorgehen, Berlin u. a. 2002.

Göpfert, Ingrid: Logistik. Führungskonzeption (Gegenstand, Aufgaben und Instrumente des Logistikmanagements und -controllings). Aus der Reihe: Vahlens Handbücher der Wirtschafts- und Sozialwissenschaften. Verlag Franz Vahlen München, 2000, ISBN 3 8006 2564 4.

Graebig, Klaus: Fallbeispiele ISO 9001 – Erfahrungen aus der Auditpraxis bei der Anwendung der DIN EN ISO 9001/9002/9003 und des DQS-Auditprotokolls. DQS-Schrift 02-01, Beuth-Verlag, Berlin 1998.

Greiling, Michael: Pfade durch das klinische Prozessmanagement. Methodik und aktuelle Diskussionen. Kohlhammer-Verlag. Stuttgart, Berlin, Köln, 2003.

Grünig, Rudolf; Kühn, Richard: Methodik der strategischen Planung. Ein prozessorientierter Ansatz für Strategieprojekte. Praxishilfen für Unternehmungen Band 5Verlag Paul Haupt. Bern, Stuttgart, Wien, 2000. ISBN 3-258-06137-8.

Grünig, R./Kühn, R. (2002): Methoden der strategischen Planung, 2. Aufl., Bern.

Günther, Hans-Otto: Produktion und Logistik. Springer-Verlag Berlin Heidelberg New York, 2000.

Günther, H.-O. und Tempelmeier, H. (2016): Produktion und Logistik – Supply Chain and Operations Management. 12. Aufl., Norderstedt: Books on Demand.

Günthner, Ralf, Dollinger, Daniela: Hirn 1.0 trifft Technologie 4.0. Der Mensch und seine kreativen Potentiale im Fokus. Springer Fachmedien Wiesbaden GmbH, ein Teil von Springer Nature 2019.

Habermann, Frank: Management von Geschäftsprozesswissen. IT-basierte Systeme und Architektur. Schriften zur EDV-orientierten Betriebswirtschaft (Hrsg.: Prof. Scheer). Diss. Deutscher Universitätsverlag. Wiesbaden, 2001. ISBN 3-8244-9065-X.

Habermas, J. (1981)*:* Theorie des kommunikativen Handelns, Bd. I, Frankfurt a. M. Universitätsverlag. Wiesbaden, 2001. ISBN 3-8244-9065-X.

Hahn, Dietger; Hugenberg, Harald: PuK. Wertorientierte Controllingkonzepte, 6. Aufl., Wiesbaden 2001.

Haselbauer, Daniela (ayway media) (Hrsg.): Handbuch Digitalisierung – die vernetzte Gesellschaft. Nikolaus BASTIAN Druck und Verlag GmbH. Vettelschoß 1. Auflage 2018.

Hauschildt, Jürgen; Salomo, Sören: Innovationsmanagement. 5. Aufl., München 2011.

Helbig, Ralf: Prozessorientierte Unternehmensführung. Eine Konzeption mit Konsequenzen für Unternehmen und Branchen dargestellt an Beispielen aus Dienstleistung und Handel. Physika-Verlag. Heidelberg, 2003.

Helfrich, Christian: Praktisches Prozess-Management, Vom PPS-System zum Supply Chain Management. 2., verbesserte Auflage. Carl Hanser Verlag, München Wien, 2002. ISBN 3-446-22049-6.

Hesse, Dr. R.: „Simultaneous Engineering, Produktentstehungsprozess mit System", Workshopergebnisse der GfA-Herbstkonferenz: Gestaltung betrieblicher Veränderungsprozesse, Bremen 2000.

Hessenberger, Manfred; Krcal, Hans-Christian: Innovative Logistik-Versorgungsstrategien, Standortkonzepte, Steuerungselemente, Betriebswirtschaftlicher Verlag Dr. Th. Gabler GmbH, Wiesbaden, o.J. ISBN 3-409-18958-0.

Hinrichsen, Sven; Jungkind, Wilfried; Könneker, Martin: Industrial Engineering – Begriff, Methodenauswahl und Lehrkonzept. Betriebspraxis und Arbeitsforschung, Ausgabe 221/2014, S. 28–35.

Hirschsteiner, Günter: WK-Praxishandbuch Strategische Management-Konzepte und Techniken für Materialwirtschaft und Logistik, o.J.

Hoffert, Svenia; Thonet, Claudia: Der agile Kulturwandel. 33 Lösungen für Veränderungen in Organisationen. Verlag Springer Gabler. Springer Fachmedien Wiesbaden GmbH, ein Teil von Springer Nature 2019.

Hofmann, Johann: Die digitale Fabrik. Auf dem Weg zur digitalen Produktion – Industrie 4.0. Beuth Innovation/VDE-Verlag, Berlin 2016.

Hofmann, Josephine (Hrsg.): Arbeit 4.0 – Digitalisierung, IT und Arbeit. IT als Treiber der digitalen Transformation. Verlag: Springer Fachmedien Wiesbaden 2018. Print ISBN: 978-3-658-21358-9. Electronic ISBN: 978-3-658-21359-6.

Homburg, C. (2000): Quantitative Betriebswirtschaftslehre, 3. Aufl., Wiesbaden.

Horváth, P.: Controlling, 10. Aufl., München 2006.

Horváth, Peter; Gleich, Ronald (Hrsg.): Neugestaltung der Unternehmungsplanung. Innovative Konzepte und erforderliche Praxislösungen. Stuttgart 2003.

Horváth & Partner (Hrsg): Prozessmanagement umsetzen. Schäffer-Poeschel Verlag, Stuttgart 2005.

Hungenberg, H. (2006): Strategisches Management in Unternehmen, Ziele – Prozesse – Verfahren, 4. Aufl., Wiesbaden.

Huber, Walter: Industrie 4.0 kompakt – Wie Technologien unsere Wirtschaft und unsere Unternehmen verändern. Springer Vieweg Verlag, Wiesbaden 2018. ISBN: 978-3-658-20799-1.

Hungenberg, H.: Strategisches Management in Unternehmen, 3. Aufl., Wiesbaden 2004.

Hungenberg, H./Wulf, T. (2011): Grundlagen der Unternehmensführung, 4. Aufl., Heidelberg.

Ifaa: http://www.arbeitswissenschaft.net/Ergonomische-Arbeitsplatzgestaltung.632.0.html, o.J.

Industrie 4.0-Readiness, im Auftrag der IMPULS-Stiftung des VDMA, Frankfurt, http://www.impuls-stiftung.de/studien;jsessionid=D371AF8942274C06B67E99721D269ED4, o.J.

Ingenics; Fraunhofer IAO 2014: Industrie 4.0 – Eine Revolution der Arbeitsgestaltung, Wie Automatisierung und Digitalisierung unsere Produktion verändern werden, Ulm, S. 19. Institut der deutschen Wirtschaft Consult (IW Consult); FIR 2015.

Ishikawa, Kaoru: What is Total Quality Control? The Japanese Way, Prentice Hall, Eagle Wood Cliffs, N.Y. 1985.

ISO/TS 16949:2002,: Qualitätsmanagementsysteme – Besondere Anforderungen bei Anwendung von ISO 9001:2000 für die Serien- und Ersatzteilproduktion in der Automobilindustrie.1 Ausgabe, 2002. VDA-QMC, Frankfurt.

Jeffrey K. Liker: Der Toyota Weg – 14 Managementprinzipien des weltweit erfolgreichsten Automobilkonzerns, 2006.

Its OWL Clustermanagement GmbH: Auf dem Weg zu Industrie 4.0: Digitale Transformation im Mittelstand. Paderborn 2019.

Jung, Berndt: Prozessmanagement in der Praxis. Vorgehensweisen, Methoden, Erfahrungen. TÜV-Verlag, Köln 2002. ISBN 3-8249-0690-2.

Jung, Hans H.; Kraft, Patricia (Hrsg.): Digital vernetzt. Transformation der Wertschöpfung. Szenarien, Optionen und Erfolgsmodelle für smarte Geschäftsmodelle, Produkte und Services. Carl Hanser Verlag, München Wien 2017.

J.; Kugeler, M.; Rosemann, M. (Hrsg.): Prozessmanagement. 3., vollst. neu bearb. und erw. Aufl., Berlin u. a., Springer-Verlag, 2002, S. 263–281. ISBN 3-540-41325-1.

Kaplan, R.S./Norton, D.P.: Die strategiefokussierte Organisation: Führen mit der Balanced Scorecard, Stuttgart 2001.

Keese, Chritoph: Silicon Germany – Wie wir die digitale Transformation schaffen. Albrecht Knaus Verlag, München 2016.

Keiser, Alfred; Ebers, Mark: (Hrsg.): Organisationstheorien. 6. Aufl., Stuttgart-Berlin-Köln 2006.

Kirsch, W. (1997): Strategisches Management – die geplante Evolution von Unternehmen, Herrsching.

Klimmer, M.: Divisionale Organisation, in: Pepels, W. (Hrsg.): Organisationsgestaltung in markorientierten Unternehmen, S. 61–82, Heidelberg 2001.

Knapp, Jake; Zeratsky, John; Kowitz, Braden: Sprint: Wie man in nur fünf Tagen neue Ideen testet und Probleme löst. Redline Verlag, München 2016. ISBN: 978-3-86881-638-9.

Knuppertz, T./Ahlrichs, F.: Prozesscontrolling: Prozessorientierte Unternehmenssteuerung durch modernes Controlling, Freiburg 8.

Koch, R.: Das 80/20-Prinzip: Mehr Erfolg mit weniger Aufwand, 2. Aufl., Franktfurt/New York 2004.

Kraus, G./Becker-Kolle, Ch./Fischer, T.: Handbuch Change Management, Berlin 2004.

*Krause, Diana Eva (Hrsg.):*Personalauswahl: Die wichtigsten diagnostischen Verfahren für das Human Resources Management, Springer Gabler Verlag, Wiesbaden 2017.

Kreutzer, Ralf T.: Neugebauer, Tim; Pattloch, Annete: Digital Business Leadership. Digitale Transformaiton-Geschäftsmodell-Innovation – agile Organisation – Change-Management. Verlag Springer Gabler, Beline Heidelberg 2017.

Krüger, W. (2006): Excellence in Change – Wege zur strategischen Erneuerung, 3. Aufl., Wiesbaden.

Kugeler, M.; Vieting, M.: Gestaltung einer prozessorientiert(er)en Aufbauorganisation. In: Becker, J.; Kugeler, M.; Rosemann, M. (Hrsg.): Prozessmanagement. 3., vollst. neu bearb. und erw. Aufl., Berlin u. a., Springer-Verlag, 2002, S. 187–232. ISBN 3-540-41325-1.

Lambardt-Mitschke, U.; Weber, J.; Radermacher, V.: EDV-gestützte Modellierung von Geschäftsprozessen. In: Walther, J. (Hrsg.): Zertifiziert und was dann? Unternehmensqualität ganzheitlich steigern. Frankfurt am Main, 2000.

Lamm, Stefan: Systematische Digitalisierungsgradermittlung für den Mittelstand. Vortrag CeBIT 2017.

Landesarbeitsamt Baden-Würtemberg: Qualität in der beruflichen Bildung, o.J.

Lang, Michael; Bartel, Daniel; Scherber, Stefan (Hrsg.): Agiles Management – innovative Methoden und best practices. 1. Auflage. Symposion publ., Düsseldorf 2015, ISBN 978-3-86329-639-1.

Lean Enterprise Institute (Hg.): Lean Lexicon, 3rd edition, Lean Enterprise Institute, ISBN 0-9667843-6-7, o.J.

Lehnen, Marc: Wettbewerbsstrategie und regionale Reichweite. Internationalisierung mittelständischer Maschinenbauunternehmungen. Wiesbaden 2002.

Leibold, Marius; Voelpel, Sven C.: Digital Rebirth. Wie sich intelligente Unternehmen neu erfinden. Publicis Pixelpark, Wiley VCH Verlag. Erlangen 2018.

Lewrick Michael: Design-Hinging: Radikale Innovationen in einer digitalisierten Welt. C.H. Beck, München 2018. ISBN: 978-340-672060-4.

Liebermann, Barbara: Digital ist egal: Mensch bleibt Mensch – Führung entscheidet. Gabal Verlag, Offenbach 2017. ISBN: 978-3-86936-750-7.

Lindner, Dominic: KMU im digitalen Wandel. Ergebnisse empirischer Studien zu Arbeit, Führung und Organisation. Springer Fachmedien Wiesbaden GmbH, ein Teil von Springer Nature, Wiesbaden 2019.

Logistik 2000plus: Herausforderungen, Trends, Konzepte/6. Magdeburger Logistik-Tagung, Magdeburg, 16./17. Nov. 2000. LOGISCH GmbH, 2000.

Luczak Holger; Wiendahl H.-P.; Weber Jürgen (Hrsg.): Logistik-Benchmarking (Praxisleitfaden mit LogiBEST). Springer-Verlag Berlin Heidelberg New York, 2001. ISBN 3-540-67499-3.

Luczak, H.; Eversheim, W; Stich, V. (Hrsg.): Betriebs- und Arbeitsorganisation im Wandel der Zeit. TÜV-Verlag Rheinland/Berlin-Brandenburg, 2000.

Lucks, Kai: Praxishandbuch Industrie 4.0: Branchen Unternehmen M&A Schäfter-Poeschel Verlag, Stuttgart 2017. ISBN: 978-379103851-3.

Maak, T./Ulrich, P. (2007): Integre Unternehmensführung. Ethisches Orientierungswissen für die Wirtschaftspraxis, Stuttgart.

Macharzina, K./Wolf, J. (2010): Unternehmensführung, 7. Aufl., Wiesbaden.

Madison, Daniel J.: Process Mapping, Process Improvement and Process Management. Patton Press, 2005.

Matthias, Klimmer: Unternehmensorganisation, NWB Verlag GmbH &Co. (1. Auflage 2012). ISBN 973-3-482-54973-1.

Matzler, Kurt; Bailom, Franz; von den Eichen; Stephan Friedrich; Anschober, Markus: Digital Disruption: Wie Sie Ihr Unternehmen auf das digitale Zeitalter vorbereiten. Verlag Franz Valen, München 2016. ISBN: 978-3800653782.

Meffert, Jürgen; Meffert, Heribert: Eins oder Null: Wie Sie Ihr Unternehmen mit Digital@Scale in die digitale Zukunft führen. Econ (Ullstein). Berlin April 2017. ISBN-13: 978-3430202398.

Mengedoht, F. W.: Erfahrungsgeleitetes Qualitäts- und Prozessmanagement in kleinen und mittleren Unternehmen, o.J.

Meiswinkel, Roland: Der ganzheitliche Weg zu Industrie 4.0 – Internet der Dinge – Digitale Transformation. Aufbruch in die 4. Industrielle Revolution. VDI-Vortrag in Hannover, 2017.

Meyer, Jens-Uwe: Digitale Disruption. Die nächste Stufe der Innovation. Business Village GmbH. Göttingen 2016. ISBN-13: 978-3-86980-345-6.

Miebach, Bernhard: Organisationstheorie: Problemstellung – Modelle – Entwicklung. Wiesbaden 2007.

Mielke, C.: Geschäftsprozesse. UML-Modellierung und Anwendungs-Generierung. Heidelberg, Berlin, 2002.

Mintzberg, Henry: The Structuring of Organizations. A Synthesis of the Research. Englewood Chiffs, NJ 1979.

Müller, B. (2007): Porters Konzept generischer Wettbewerbsstrategien, Präzisierung und empirische Überprüfung. Dissertationsschrift, Universität Bern. Wiesbaden.

Müllerleile, Thomas: Prozessakzeptanz. Theoretische und empirische Untersuchung der Akzeptanz und Ablehnung betrieblicher Prozesse. Verlag Springer Gabler. Springer Fachmedien Wiesbaden GmbH, ein Teil von Springer Nature 2019.

Müller-Stewens, G./Lechner, C. (2005): Strategisches Management – Wie strategische Initiativen zum Wandel führen, 3. Aufl., Stuttgart.

Negri, Christoph (Hrsg.): Führen in der Arbeitswelt 4.0 Springer Verlag GmbH Deutschland, ein Teil von Springer Nature, Berlin 2019.

Neumann, S.; Probst, C.; Wernsmann, C.: Kontinuierliches Prozessmanagement. In: Becker, o.J.

Niess, P./Spandau, A.: Industrielle Organisation – vom tayloristischen zum virtuellen Unternehmen, München 2005.

N.N.: Praktische Wege zu Industrie 4.0. Die Hindernisse digitaler Transformation und wie Hersteller sie überwinden können. Neue Studie von Siemens Financial Services, Frühjahr 2018.

Nowotny, Valentin: Agile Unternehmen: nur was sich bewegt, kann sich verbessern: fokussiert, schnell, flexibel. 1. Auflage. BusinessVillage, Göttingen 2016, ISBN 978-3-86980-330-2.

Obermaier, Robert (Hrsg.): Industrie 4.0 als unternehmerische Gestaltungsaufgabe: Betriebswirtschaftliche, technische und rechtliche Herausforderungen. Verlag Springer Gabler, Berlin Heidelberg 2017. ISBN: 978-3658165260.

Olfert, Klaus (Hrsg.): Kompakt-Training Praktische Betriebswirtschaft Managementkompetenzen, Kiehl Verlag, Herne 2015.

Osterloh, Margit; Frost, Jetta: Prozessmanagement als Kernkompetenz – Wie Sie Business Reengineering strategisch nutzen können. Gabler-Verlag, Wiesbaden, 2006.

Osterwalder, Alexander; Pigneur, Yves: Business Model Generation: Ein Handbuch für Visionäre, Spielveränderer und Herausforderer. Campus Verlag, Frankfurt, New York 2011.

Peters, Ralf; Nauroth, Markus: Process-Minning. Geschäftsprozesse: smart, schnell und einfach. Verlag Springer Gabler. Springer Fachmedien Wiesbaden GmbH, ein Teil von Springer Nature 2019.

Pfeifer, T.; Siegler, S: Ganzheitliche Qualitätsregelung von Entwicklungsprozessen im Simultaneous Engineering, Heidelberg 2004, S. 1–15.

Philipp, Mathias: Proaktive Prüfung von Geschäftsprozessen. Reihe Revision und Controlling. Ottokar Schreiber Verlag, Hamburg 2000. ISBN 3-930291-13-4.

Pichler, Roman: Scrum – Agiles Projektmanagement erfolgreich einsetzen. d.punkt Verlag, Heidelberg 2009.

Pickering, A.: Cybernetics and the Mangle: Ashby, Beer and Pask. In: Social Studies of Science, Vol. 32, 2002, S. 413–437.

Picot, A./Reichwald, R./Wigand, R.: Die grenzenlose Unternehmung, 4., überarbeitete und erweiterte Aufl., Wiesbaden 2001.

Piontek, J.: Kennzahlen und Kennzahlensysteme in der Logistik, 2002.

Plattform Industrie 4.0, 2015: Umsetzungsstrategie Industrie 4.0, Ergebnisbericht der Plattform Industrie 4.0.

Pollety, Wolfgang; Blaeser-Benfer, Andreas (Hg.): Digitalisierung. Betriebliche Handlungsfelder der Unternehmensentwicklung. RKW Kompetenzzentrum. Frankfurter Allgemeine Buch. Frankfurt am Main 2017. ISBN: 978-3956011634.

Porter, M.: Wettbewerbsvorteile: Spitzenleistungen erreichen und behaupten, 6. Aufl., Frankfurt 2000.

Prockl, Günter; Krieger, Winfried; Pflaum, Alexander; Niehues, Ekkehard; Wilhelm, Mirko; Kille, Christian: Unternehmensübergreifende Optimierung von logistischen Prozessketten in der mittelständischen Konsumgüterwirtschaft unter Integration logistischen Dienstleister. Verlag: Books on Demand GmbH, 2002.

Rademacher, Ingo: Digitalisierung selbst denken: Eine Anleitung, mit der die Transformation gelingt. Business Village GmbH, Göttingen, 2017.

Ramsauer, Christian; Kayser, Detlef; Schmitz, Christoph: Erfolgsfaktor Agilität: Chancen für Unternehmen in einem volatilen Marktumfeld. 1. Auflage. Wiley-VCH, Weinheim, o.J. ISBN 978-3-527-50901-0.

REFA Bundesverband e. V.: Ausgewählte Methoden zur prozessorientierten Arbeitsorganisation. In der Reihe: REFA-Modulkonzept für Kooperationen in der Aus- und Weiterbildung. (REFA-Sonderdruck Methodenteil 2002). Verlag des REFA-Bundesverbandes e. V., Darmstadt, 1. Auflage, 2002. REFA-Bestell-Nr. 198213.

Rehbehn, R./Yurdakul, Z. B.: Mit Six Sigma zu Business Excellence: Strategien, Methoden, Praxisbeispiele, 2. Aufl., Erlangen 2005.

Reinhart, Gunther (Hrsg.): Handbuch Industrie 4.0: Geschäftsmodelle, Prozesse, Technik, Carl Hanser Verlag, München, 2017.

Reinnarth, Jörg; Schuster, Claus; Möllendorf, Jan, Lutz, Andre: Chefsache Digitalisierung 4.0, Springer Gabler Verlag, Berlin Heidelberg 2018. ISBN: 978-3-658-20967-4.

Rickert, D.: Multi-Projektmanagement in der industriellen Forschung und Entwicklung. Wiesbaden 1995.

Riemensperger, Frank; Falk Svenja: Titelverteidiger – Wie die deutsche Industrie ihre Spitzenposition auch im digitalen Zeitalter sichert. Redline Verlag, München 2019.

Rogers, David L.: Digitale Transformation – Das Playbook. Wie Sie Ihr Unternehmen erfolgreich in das digitale Zeitalter führen und die digitale Disruption meistern. Mitp Verlags GmbH & Co. KG. Frechen 2017. ISBN: 978-3-95845-573-3.

Rohm, A. *(Hrsg.):* Change-Tools: erfahrene Prozessberater präsentieren wirksame Workshop-Interventionen, 3. Aufl., Bonn 2008.

Rosemann, M.: Vorbereitung der Prozessmodellierung. In: Becker, J.; Kugeler, M.; Rosemann, M. (Hrsg.): Prozessmanagement. 3., vollst. neu bearb. und erw. Aufl., Berlin u. a., Springer-Verlag, 2002, S. 45–90. ISBN 3-540-41325-1.

Rosenkranz, Friedrich: Geschäftsprozesse. Modell- und computergestützte Planung. Springer-Verlag. Berlin Heidelberg, 2002. ISBN 3-540-43434-8.

Rosenstiel, Lv.: Grundlagen der Organisationspsychologie, 5. Aufl., Stuttgart 2003.

Rothlauf, Jürgen: Total Quality Management in Theorie und Praxis. Zum ganzheitlichen Unternehmensverständnis. 3. Aufl., München 2010.

Rummler-Brache Group: Business Process Management in U.S. Firms today. A study commissioned by Rummler-Brache Group. March 2004.

Sackmann, S.: Unternehmenskultur: Analysieren – Entwickeln – Verändern. Neuwied 2002.

Schäfer-Kunz, Jan; Tewald, Claudia: Make-or-Buy-Entscheidungen in der Logistik, DUV Deutscher Universitäts Verlag, Reihe DUV Wirtschaftswissenschaft, ISBN 3-8244-0392-7, o.J.

Schaible, B.: Unternehmenskultur als Rahmen für die Umsetzung. In: Lean Production, Institut für angewandte Arbeitswissenschaften e.V. Köln, o.J.

Schat, Hans-Dieter: Ältere Fachkräfte beschäftigen, BC Publications. Auflage 2011. ISBN 978-3-941717-08-04.

Scheer, A.W.; Ferri Abolhassan, Wolfram Jost, Mathias Kirchmer (Editors): Business Process Automation. Springer-Verlag, 2004.

Scheer, A.W.: Unternehmung 4.0 – Vom disruptiven Geschäftsmodell zur Automatisierung der Geschäftsprozesse. AWSi Publishing. Saarbrücken, 2018.

Schell, Otto; Meiswinkel Roland: Speed of Innovation: Human Kapital or Human Threat. Ist der Mensch der Motor der Innovation oder ihr größter Hemmschuh? The Diplomatic Council Otto Schell Institute for Digital Transformation (DCOS Institute – The Global Think Tank). Den Haag und Hannover, 2017.

Scherber, Stefan; Coldewey, Jens; Lang, Michael (Hrsg.): Agile Führung: vom agilen Projekt zum agilen Unternehmen. 1. Aufl. Symposion Publ., Düsseldorf 2015, ISBN 978-3-86329-674-2.

Scherber, Stefan; Bergmann, Thomas; Lang, Michael (Hrsg.): Erfolgsfaktoren wirklich agiler Unternehmen – Erfahrungsberichte aus der Praxis. 1. Auflage. Symposion Publ., Düsseldorf 2015, ISBN 978-3-86329-672-8.

Scherm, E./Pietsch (2007): Organisation – Theorie, Gestaltung, Wandel. München und Wien.

Schircks, Arnulf D.; Drenth, Randy; Schneider, Roland: Strategie für Industrie 4.0 – Praxiswissen für Mensch und Organisation in der digitalen Transformation. Springer Gabler Verlag, Berlin Heidelberg 2017.

Schmalzl, Bernhard/Schröder, Jakob: Managementkonzepte im Wettstreit. Total Quality Management versus Business Process Reengineering, o.J.

Schmelzer, H.; Sesselmann, W.: Geschäftsprozessmanagement in der Praxis. Kunden zufrieden stellen – Produktivität steigern – Wert erhöhen. 3., vollst. überarb. Auflage. München, Wien, 2003. 430 Seiten. ISBN 3-446-22298-7.

Schmidt, G.: Methode und Techniken der Organisation, 13. Aufl., Gießen 2003.

Schmidt, B. Ch.: Integration von Arbeitsplanung und Fertigungssteuerung mit Netzarbeitsplänen, Fortschrittsberichte VDI, Reihe 20, VDI-Verlag, Düsseldorf 1996.

Schmidt, Günter: Prozessmanagement. Modelle und Methoden. Springer-Verlag. Berlin Heidelberg, 2002.

333Schnaitmann, Hermann: Prozessorientierte Unternehmensführung. Schriften zur Unternehmensplanung. Band 59. Peter Lang Verlag. Frankfurt a.M., 2000. ISBN 3-631-36843-7.

Schneider, Johannes; Klein, Thomas M.: Wilfinger, Sandra; Blaschke, Michael: Wir haben mit Sicherheit vielleicht ein Orga-Problem. Der Contrast-Organisationscheck zum Verstehen von Unternehmensorganisationen. THE POWER OF INSIGHT, contrast Management – Consulting, http://www.contrast-consulting.com/fileadmin/user_upload/press_file/POI_3_Orga-Check.pdf, 2014.

Schober, Holger: Prozessorganisation: Theoretische Grundlagen und Gestaltungsoptionen. Deut. Universitäts-VLG, 2002.

Scholz-Reiter, B.: Höhns, H.: König, F.: Müller, D. H.; Gsell, H. (2003): Kollaboratives Änderungsmanagement-Bedeutung des technischen Änderungsmanagements im Rahmen des Collaborative Engineering, in: Industrie Management 19, 5, 2003, S. 45–49.

Schönsleben, Paul: Integrales Logistikmanagement (Planung und Steuerung von umfassenden Geschäftsprozessen). 2., überarb. und erweit. Aufl., Springer Verlag Berlin Heidelberg New York, 2000, ISBN 3-540-66844-6.

Schramm, Helmut: Umsetzung der integrierten Produktionslogistik, o.J.

Schreyögg, Georg, Sydow, Jörg: Strategische Prozesse und Pfade. Managementforschung 13. Gabler-Verlag, Wiesbaden, 2003.

Schreyögg, G./Koch, J. (2010): Grundlagen des Managements, 2. Aufl., Wiesbaden.

Schreyögg, Georg: Organisation. Grundlagen moderner Organisationsgestaltung. 5. Aufl., Wiesbaden 2008.

Schreyögg, Georg; Sydown, Jörg (Hrsg.): Strategische Prozesse und Pfade. Wiesbaden 2003.

Schröder, Ernst F.: Modernes Unternehmens-Controlling. 8. Aufl., Ludwigshaufen 2003.

Schubert, Petra; Wölfl, e Ralf; Dettling, Walter: E-Business-Integration – Fallstudien zur Optimierung elektronischer Geschäftsprozesse. Auflage. Carl Hanser Verlag, München Wien 2003. 287 Seiten. ISBN 3-446-22462-9.

Schuh, Günther; Anderl, Rainer; Gausemeier, Jürgen; ten Hompel, Michael; Wahlster, Wolfgang (Hrsg.): Industrie 4.0 Maturity Index: Die digitale Transformation von Unternehmen gestalten (acatech-Studie). Verlag Herbert Utz, München 2017.

Schulte, H.: Strategische Standortplanung – Auswirkungen der Standortwahl auf die Unternehmensorganisation, in: Bullinger, H.J./Warnecke, H.J./Westkämper, E. (Hrsg.) Neue Organisationsformen im Unternehmen, 3. neu bearb. Aufl., Berlin 2009, S. 333–337.

Schulte-Zurhausen, M.: Organisation, 5. Überarb. Und erw. Aufl., München 2010.

Schwab Klaus: Die Zukunft der Vierten Industriellen Revolution. Wie wir den digitalen Wandel gemeinsam gestalten. Deutsche Verlags-Anstalt, München 2019.

Schwarz, Horst; Nicolai, Christiana: Arbeitsplatzbeschreibungen. 13. Aufl., Freiburg i. Br. 1995.

Seeck, Stephan: Erfolgsfaktor Logistik: Klassische Fehler Erkennen und vermeiden. Wiesbaden 2010.

Seibert, S.: Technisches Management: Innovationsmanagement, Projektmanagement, Quallitätsmanagement, Stuttgart/Leipzig 2006.

Simon, Hermann (Hrsg.): Das große Handbuch der Strategiekonzepte – Ideen, die die Businesswelt verändert haben. Frankfurt am Main, New York. Campus-Verlag, 2000.

Smith, A.(1776/2005): Reichtum der Nationen, Nachdruck 2005, Paderborn.

Smith, Howard and Peter Fingar: Business Process Management: The Third Wave. Meghan-Kiffer Press, 2003.

Smith, A.: An Inquiry into the Nature and Causes of the Wealth of Nations, 1776 (dt.: Untersuchung über Wesen und Ursachen des Reichtums der Völker, Stuttgart 2005).

Spanyi, Andrew: More for Less: The Power of Process Management. Meghan Kiffer Press, 2006.

Specht, Philip: Die 50 wichtigsten Themen der Digitalisierung. Künstliche Intelligenz, Blockchain, Bitcoin, Virtual Reality und vieles mehr verständlich erklärt. Redline Verlag, München 2018.

Spitzer, Manfred: Cyberkrank! Wie das digitalisierte Leben unsere Gesundheit ruiniert. Droemer Verlag, München 2017. ISBN: 978-3-426-30104-3.

Springer, R. (2004): Wettbewerbsfähigkeit duch Innovationen – Erfolgreiches Management organisatorischer Veränderungen, Berlin u. a.

Staud, J.: Geschäftsprozessanalyse. Ereignisgesteuerte Prozessketten und objektorientierte Geschäftsprozessmodellierung für Betriebswirtschaftliche Standardsoftware. 2. Auflage. Berlin, Heidelberg, New York, 2001.

Steinbach, W.: Anforderungen und Auswahlkriterien bei CAQ-Systemen. QZ 32 (1987) 2, S. 90–94.

Stöger, Roman: Prozessmanagement: Qualität, Produktivität, Konkurrenzfähigkeit, 3. Auflage, Schäffer-Poeschel Verlag, Stuttgart 2011.

Strohhecker, Jürgen; Gerberich, Claus W.: Geschäftsprozesse optimieren. RKW-Verlag Eschborn, 2002 (RKW-Nr. 1426). ISBN 3-89644-173-6.

Tata Consltancy Services (TCS) und Bitkom Research (Hrsg.): Digitalisierung – Deutschland endlich auf dem Sprung? Die Trendstudie von Tata Consultancy Services (TCS) und Bitkom Research. Frankfurt/Main und Berlin, 2017.

Tavanli, Serkan; Erwerle, Bülent Jens: Veränderungsprojekte erfolgreich umsetzen. Ihr Kompass zur Unternehmens- und Prozessoptimierung in KMU's. Verlag Springer Gabler. Springer-Verlag GmbH Deutschland, ein Teil von Springer Nature 2019.

Thienel, A.: Professionelles Qualitätsmanagement in Dienstleistungsunternehmen, o.J.

Thom, Norbert; Wenger, Andreas P.: Die effiziente Organisation. Bewertung und Auswahl von Organisationsformen. Glattbrugg 2002.

Thom, Norbert; Wenger, Andreas P.: Die optimale Organisationsform. Grundlagen und Handlungsanleitung. Wiesbaden 2010.

Töpfer, Armin (Hrsg.): Handbuch Kundenmanagement. Anforderungen, Prozesse, Zufriedenheit, Bindung und Wert von Kunden. 3. Aufl., Berlin-Heidelberg 2008.

Trappmann, Markt; Hummell, Hans J.; Sodeur, Wolfgang: Strukturanalyse sozialer Netzwerke. Konzepte, Modelle, Methoden. Wiesbaden 2005.

Ulich, E.: Arbeitsgestaltung. In: Schuler, H./Sonntag, K.H. (Hrsg.): Handbuch der Arbeits- und Organisationspsychologie, Göttingen 2007, S. 165–174.

Utikal, Hannes: Organisation industrieller Geschäftsbeziehungen. Strategie, Struktur, Effizienz. Wiesbaden 2001.

Uwe, Dombrowski: Arbeitswissenschaft in Deutschland. Industrial Engineering 3/2012, http://www.refa.de.

Vahrenkamp, Richard; Vogt Monika; Eley Michael: Logistikmanagement. 4., verb. Aufl., R. Oldenbourg Wissenschaftsverlag GmbH München Wien, 2000, ISBN 3-486-25317-4.

Vahs, D.: Organisation: Einführung in die Organisationtheorie und -praxis, 5., überarbeitete Aufl., Stuttgart 2005.

Van Alphen, Christian; Bärtle, Doris (Projektleitung) u. a: Studie Digitale Transformation 2018. Hemmnisse, Fortschritte, Perspektiven. Trendreport. Etventure GmbH. Berlin, 2018.

Vahs, D.: Organisation: Ein Lehr – und Managementbuch, 7., überarbeitete Aufl., Stuttgart 2009.

Vahs, D. (2012): Organisation, Einführung in die Organisationstheorie und -praxis, 8. Aufl., Stuttgart.

VDA Band 1: Nachweisführung – Leitfaden zur Dokumentation und Archivierung von Qualitätsforderungen und Qualitätsaufzeichnungen, Verband der Automobilindustrie e.V. (VDA) Frankfurt, o.J.

VDA Band 4: Sicherung der Qualität vor Serieneinsatz – Teil 1: Partnerschaftliche Zusammenarbeit, Abläufe, Methoden, Verband der Automobilindustrie e.V. (VDA), 1. Aufl. 2003, Frankfurt.

VDA Band 4: Sicherung der Qualität vor Serieneinsatz – Teil 2: System-FMEA, Verband der Automobilindustrie e.V. (VDA), 1. Aufl. 2003, Frankfurt.

VDA Band 4: Sicherung der Qualität vor Serieneinsatz – Teil 3: Projektplanung, Verband der Automobilindustrie e.V. (VDA), 1. Aufl. 2003, Frankfurt.

VDA Band 6: Grundlagen: Qualitätsaudit, allgemeine Grundlagen – Teil 2: QM-Systemaudit, Dienstleistung, Verband der Automobilindustrie e.V. (VDA), Frankfurt, o.J.

VDA Band 6: Grundlagen: Qualitätsaudit, allgemeine Grundlagen Teil 3: Prozessaudit, Verband der Automobilindustrie e.V. (VDA), Frankfurt o.J.

VDA Band 6: Grundlagen: Qualitätsaudit, allgemeine Grundlagen – Teil 4: QM-Systemaudit, Produktionsmittel, Verband der Automobilindustrie e.V. (VDA), Frankfurt o.J.

VDA Band 6: Grundlagen: Qualitätsaudit, allgemeine Grundlagen – Teil 5: Produktaudit, Verband der Automobilindustrie e.V. (VDA), Frankfurt o.J.

VDA Band 6: Grundlagen: Qualitätsaudit, allgemeine Grundlagen – Teil 6: Produktaudit, Dienstleistung, Verband der Automobilindustrie e.V. (VDA), Frankfurt o.J.

VDA Band 7: Grundlagen zum Austausch von Qualitätsdaten – Abwicklung von Qualitätsdaten-Nachrichten, Verband der Automobilindustrie e.V. (VDA), Frankfurt, o.J.

VDA Band 8: Leitfaden zur Qualitätssicherung bei Anhänger-Aufbauten- und Containerherstellern, Verband der Automobilindustrie e.V. (VDA), Frankfurt, o.J.

VDA Band 9: Qualitätssicherung – Emissionen und Verbrauch, Verband der Automobilindustrie e.V. (VDA), Frankfurt, o.J.

VDMA (Hrsg.): Leitfaden Industrie 4.0. Orientierungshilfe zur Einführung in den Mittelstand. Frankfurt/Main, 2017.

VDI-Richtlinie Nr. 2266, Bl. 3: Messung der Staubkonzentration am Arbeitsplatz; Messung der Teilchenzahl; Messen unter Benutzung von Membranfiltern, 4 S., o.J.

Vogel-Heuser, Birgit; Bauernhansl; Thomas; ten Hompel (Hrsg.): Handbuch Industrie 4.0 Bd. 1 Produktion. Springer Verlag GmbH. Deutschland. 2017.

Vogel-Heuser, Birgit; Bauernhansl; Thomas; ten Hompel (Hrsg.): Handbuch Industrie 4.0 Bd. 2 Automatisierung. Springer Verlag GmbH. Deutschland. 2017.

Vogel-Heuser, Birgit; Bauernhansl; Thomas; ten Hompel (Hrsg.): Handbuch Industrie 4.0 Bd. 3 Logistik. Springer Verlag GmbH. Deutschland. 2017.

Vogel-Heuser, Birgit; Bauernhansl; Thomas; ten Hompel (Hrsg.): Handbuch Industrie 4.0 Bd. 4 Allgemeine Grundlagen. Springer Verlag GmbH. Deutschland. 2017.

Volkens, Bettina; Anderson, Kai: Digital human: Der Mensch im Mittelpunkt der Digitalisierung. Campus Verlag, Frankfurt/New York 2017.

Von Mutius, Bernhard: Disruptive Thinking. Das Denken, das der Zukunft gewachsen ist. Gabal Verlag, Offenbach 2017. ISBN: 978-3-86936-790-3.

Vossen, Gottfried; Becker, Jörg (Hrsg.): Geschäftsprozessmodellierung und Workflowmanagement – Modelle, Methoden, Werkzeuge. Bonn et al.: Thomson, 1996.

Wagner, Helmut: Qualität – Herausforderung und Chance. Der sichere Weg zum QM-Handbuch nach DIN EN ISO 9000-9004. 2., völlig neubearbeitete Auflage. Expert-Verlag, Renningen Malmsheim 1995.

Wagner, K.W.(Hrsg.): PQM – Prozessorientiertes Qualitätsmanagement: Leitfaden zur Umsetzung der ISO 9001:2000, 2., vollständig überarbeitete Aufl., München/Wien 2003.

Wahren, Heinz-Kurt E.: Change Management – Veränderungsprozesse gestalten. Eschborn. RKW-Verlag, 2000.

Walgenbach, Peter: Neoinstitutionalistische Ansätze in der Organisationstheorie In: Organisationstheorien, hrsg. von Alfred Kieser und Markt Ebers, 6. Aufl., Stuttgart 2006, S. 353–401.

Weihermann, Astrid E., Dipl.-Kff.: Auswirkungen von Global Sourcing auf die industriebetriebliche Logistik – Arbeitsbericht Nr. 46, Universität Leipzig – Wirtschaftswissenschaftliche Fakultät, o.J.

Weise, Horst: Aufbruch in ein neues Zeitalter (Wirtschaft u. Gesellschaft im Netz der Logistik). FAZ, Verlagsbereich Buch, Frankfurt/Main 2000, ISBN 3-933180-52-X.

Welge, M.K./Al-Laham, A. (2008): Strategisches Management, 5. Aufl., Wiesbaden.

Welge, Martin K.; Al-Laham, Andreas: Strategisches Management. Grundlagen, Prozess, Implementierung. 4. Aufl., Wiesbaden 2003.

Wiendahl, H.-P.: Projekt: Logistische Gestaltung und Steuerung produktionsnetzfähiger Unternehmen, Arbeitsfeld 4: Optimierung und Betrieb von Logistiksystemen, Schlussbericht zum BMBF-Verbund-projekt – VISION LOGISTIK – Logistik wandelbarer Produktionsnetze zur Auflösung ökonomisch-ökologischer Zielkonflikte, o.J.

Wiggers, Peter, Kok, Henk, De Boer-de Wit, Maritha: IT Performance Management, Butterworth-Heinemann, Amsterdam 2004.

Wildemann, H. (2002): Leitfaden Änderungsmanagement zur Einführung eines effizienten Managements technischer Änderungen, 10. Auflage, München 2002.

Wilhelm, Rudolf: Prozessorganisation. Managementwissen für Studium und Praxis. Oldenbourg-Verlag, München Wien, 2003. ISBN 3-486-27412-0.

Wirtz, B. (2003): Mergers & Acquisitions Management. Strategie und Organisation von Unternehmenszusammenschlüssen, Wiesbaden.

Wittig, Hans-Jürgen: Prozessmanagement. Qualitätsmanagement nach ISO 9001:2000. Umweltmanagement nach ISO 14001:1996. EFQM-Modell für Excellence. Schlembach Fachverlag, 2002.

Wittpahl, Volker (Herausgeber): Digitalisierung (Bildung/Technik, Bildung/Innovation). Springer Vieweg Verlag. Braunschweig, Wiesbaden, 2017.

Wolf, J. (2011): Organisation, Management, Unternehmensführung – Theorien, Praxisbeispiele und Kritik, 4. Aufl., Wiesbaden.

Zollondz, Hans-Dieter: Grundlagen Qualitätsmanagement. Einführung in Geschichte, Begriffe, Systeme und Konzepte. 2. Aufl., München 2006.

Zöller, Sascha: Ja zur Digitalisierung! Mit der richtigen Einstellung die Zukunftsfähigkeit des Unternehmens sichern. Springer Fachmedien Wiesbaden GmbH, ein Teil von Springer Nature, 2019.

Zur Muehlen; Michael: Workflow-based Process Controlling. Foundation, Design and Application of workflow-driven Process Information Systems. Logos, Berlin 2004.

9783658373665